D0848084

Jews in the Center

Jews in the Center

Conservative Synagogues and Their Members

EDITED BY JACK WERTHEIMER

RUTGERS UNIVERSITY PRESS
New Brunswick, New Jersey, and London

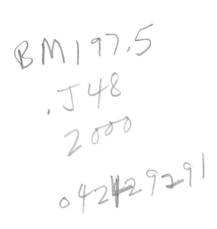
Research for this project was funded by The Pew Charitable Trusts.
Publication of this book has been made possible in part by a grant from
the Mandell L. and Madeleine H. Berman Foundation.

Library of Congress Cataloging-in-Publication Data

Jews in the center : conservative congregations and their members / edited by
    Jack Wertheimer.
        p.   cm.
    Includes bibliographical references and index.
    ISBN 0-8135-2821-6 (alk. paper)
    1. Conservative Judaism—United States.   2. Judaism—20th century.
    3. Jews—United States—Social life and customs.   I. Wertheimer, Jack.
    BM197.5. J48 2000
    296.8'342'0973—dc21   99-045701

British Cataloging-in-Publication data for this book is available from the British Library

Manufactured in the United States of America

Contents

List of Figures

List of Tables

Acknowledgments

THIS BOOK represents the culmination of an ambitious project to examine Conservative synagogues and their members. Research for this project was made possible by a generous grant from The Pew Charitable Trusts. I am grateful to Rebecca W. Rimel, the president of the Trusts, and grants officers in its Religion Division for their support of this project.

In addition, the book has been made possible through the generosity of the Mandell L. Berman and Madeleine H. Berman foundation. The Bermans have a long history of sponsoring research on the current condition of the American Jewish community.

The ongoing support and encouragement of Professor Ismar Schorsch, chancellor of the Jewish Theological Seminary of America (JTS), have sustained the project from its inception. His determination to scrutinize synagogues unflinchingly in order to strengthen Jewish religious life has been critical to the success of this project. Other members of the seminary's administration have shared their expertise to help with the complex logistics of this project.

The research team benefited during the planning process from the wisdom of an academic advisory board consisting of the following individuals: Aryeh Davidson (JTS), Carl Dudley (Hartford Seminary), Bethamie Horowitz, Neil Gillman (JTS), Charles Liebman (Bar Ilan University), Moshe Shokeid (Tel Aviv University), Allan Silver (Columbia University), David Roozen (Hartford Seminary), Chaim Waxman (Rutgers University), and Barbara Wheeler and Mark Wilhelm (Auburn Seminary). Leaders of the rabbinic and congregational arms of the Conservative movement provided much helpful support and guidance. The team is grateful to Rabbi Joel Meyers, executive vice president, and Rabbi Alan Silverstein and Rabbi David Lieber, former presidents of the Rabbinical Assembly, for their assistance and advice. At the United Synagogue, Rabbi Jerome Epstein, executive vice president, and his staff provided vital information and helpful suggestions. We also appreciate the support of Alan Ades, former president of the United Synagogue.

Staff members of the Ratner Center for the Study of Conservative Judaism at JTS handled a variety of logistical tasks that facilitated our work greatly. Dr. Ariela Keysar managed the technical work of this project with meticulous attention to detail and great diligence. Her work on the actual process of interviewing and mailing questionnaires, as well as her efforts to compile the data, proved invaluable. Early in the project, Tim Hanssen was the key administrative assistant; he was ably succeeded by Paul Radensky.

In addition, I wish to thank the staff of Rutgers University Press, including David Myers and Brigitte Goldstein, for their devoted efforts. Our copyeditor, Eric Schramm of Columbus, Ohio, also deserves much thanks for his diligent and conscientious job of preparing the final manuscript for publication.

As editor and compiler of this volume, I thank the members of the research team for investing so much of themselves to ensure the high quality of our work. The specific research projects undertaken by team members are detailed in the chapters of this book. It needs to be added, however, that we met often for days at a time over a two-year period in order to learn from each other, critique each other's work, and find the means to integrate our findings. I am deeply appreciative of the investment each member of this project has made.

Jack Wertheimer

Jews in the Center

Introduction

JACK WERTHEIMER

THE AMERICAN SYNAGOGUE attracts more members and affords greater opportunities for participation than any other voluntary institution established by Jews in the United States. This has remained true even in the closing decades of the twentieth century, when rates of Jewish affiliation have declined. According to the National Jewish Population Survey of 1990, 41 percent of entirely Jewish households claimed current membership in a synagogue.[1] Since many Jews hold synagogue membership for only a limited period, it is estimated that as many as four out of five American Jews affiliate with a synagogue at some point in their lifetime. Large numbers of American Jews also attend religious services: 59 percent of adults who identified themselves as Jewish by religion claimed to have attended synagogue on the high holidays, as did 12 percent of Jewish adults who professed to be secular Jews. No other type of institution in the American Jewish community approaches such high rates of membership and participation.

The continuing popularity of the synagogue should not come as a surprise given its historical centrality in Jewish communal life. For over two millennia, the synagogue has served in different permutations as a house of prayer, study, and assembly wherever Jews have settled. Synagogues, moreover, have been given a major boost in the United States, where congregationalism is one of the defining features of religious life: "For most people in the United States, congregations are the heart of individual and collective religious history," write the editors of a major guide to congregational life. "Any[one] . . . who is curious about how ordinary people experience their religion would do well to begin his or her exploration in the gathered communities that have formed a bedrock of American religion."[2]

Jews in the Center takes up this challenge by examining the largest movement of synagogue-affiliated Jews in the United States: members of Conservative congregations. Situated at the center of the Jewish religious spectrum and occupying an ideological middleground between more liberal Reform temples and more traditional Orthodox shuls, houses of worship of Conservative Judaism attract the plurality of American synagogue members: nearly half (47 percent) of all households that affiliate with a synagogue belong to a Conservative congregation, as compared to 36 percent that join Reform temples, 11 percent Orthodox synagogues, and 6 percent other types of Jewish congregations.[3]

The Jews who join Conservative synagogues and sit in their pews come with a wide range of life experiences. Some grew up in Conservative synagogues, but many others come from other types of congregations or none at all. Almost all were raised as Jews, but some converted from other religions. A relatively small percentage have a life history of engagement with synagogues; but for most members involvement with a congregation intensifies or wanes due to a variety of life-cycle events and personal circumstances.

The fluid and complex nature of participation in synagogue life is evident in the biographies of individuals we will encounter in the coming pages:[4]

One of the most active torah readers at a Midwestern congregation is a physician in his forties who when growing up had attended a Conservative synagogue mainly on the major holidays: "My wife and I became more observant when the kids were growing up. . . . We started getting involved in the nursery school and that was an entry place where we started saying, 'What are we doing; what do we want to do as far as practice?' We did a lot of things one at a time. I think we're fairly observant [now], keeping kosher in the home and observing holidays. . . . It was a gradual process, and we kind of would try things. . . . We added things over the years. . . . We do lots and we like it and our kids are pretty comfortable with it."

Another member of a Midwestern congregation, a woman with grown children, describes shifting from participation in fund-raising activities to intensive study as her primary mode of involvement with the synagogue: "I have found enormous satisfaction in my Judaism from getting back in touch with our texts. . . . Everything comes with different stages in life. . . . My husband is in a different place than I am. . . . No one goes in lockstep in their trip through life. I feel happy to come to services by myself. When he feels like coming to services, he comes with me."

A businessman in his sixties, who served as president of his east coast Conservative synagogue, was reared in a Reform temple. After journeying to Israel and experimenting with different synagogues, he began to study with the rabbi of a Conservative congregation. In time, he no longer could consider himself a Reform Jew. Instead he regarded himself in the mainstream: "I think the majority of Jews are Conservative Jews; I think the majority of Jews have lived somewhere in the middle, whatever they've said to themselves. They weren't hasids way out here with their *shtreimels* and they weren't the super-liberals who weren't doing anything. They were somewhere, finding themselves in the middle." For him, "Conservative Judaism tries to move the tradition forward; it's not frozen. It wrestles with tradition, and I like that wrestling."

Another member of the same congregation grew up as a traditional Jew in Iran. While pursuing an advanced degree in the United States, he found his way to the local Hillel house and was exposed to Conservative religious services. When he settled in a suburb of New York, he joined a Conservative congregation and enrolled his children in the local Solomon Schechter day school (also Conservative). He approvingly characterizes his fellow Conservative congregants as "challenging a lot of things. Every day we are questioning, and questioning these things is difficult and good."

Still another member of the same congregation describes his synagogue and Conservative Judaism as "holding firmly with an open hand." He observed that "most of the people in this congregation do not feel that they're bad Jews or bad Conservative Jews if they're not doing everything. . . . There's a sense in which this is their place, and these are their friends. You flow in and flow out."

These brief biographical sketches raise questions about the religious lives of synagogue members that beg for clarification: How do these Jews reconcile themselves to a form of Judaism that affirms its commitment to norms of religious behavior, even as they quite self-consciously "pick and choose" rituals they will observe? How do they negotiate the tensions between "tradition and change" that characterize their movement? And what roles do synagogues play in the resolution of these tensions? On another plane entirely, these vignettes prompt some reflection on the relationship between class, educational attainments, and religious participation. What circumstances attract highly educated, generally upper-middle-class individuals to join synagogues? Why do they invest significant sums of money and time in these institutions?[5] And why do some participate regularly in religious services and educational programs, whereas others attend only sporadically? Put in utilitarian terms, why do some families pay considerable membership dues to institutions they barely frequent? And why do some members and their families find sufficient meaning in congregational life to set aside time for regular participation, whereas others participate hardly at all? These vignettes also prompt questions about the nature of the "gathered communities" these Jews have created: Do they differ from Conservative synagogues of the past? Do they require any new types of commitments and skills? Which aspects of synagogue life are most compelling to contemporary Jews and which are least appealing? How do young people fit into congregational life and how are they socialized to take their place in the Jewish community?

This is a propitious time to address such questions. For one thing, the American Jewish community is preoccupied with its own "continuity," its ability to imbue the coming generation with a strong commitment to Jewishness, as well as transmit the skills and knowledge necessary to live as Jews. There is a growing recognition that synagogues are critical in this process of religious formation and indeed the construction of a Jewish identity. Synagogues provide a Jewish education for the majority of young people and they are the setting for the rites of passage, especially of the bar and bat mitzvah, for the preponderant majority of young Jews. If we wish to gauge the future direction of American Jewish life, we would do well to take the measure of congregations.

The great strides taken by the entire field of congregational studies in the past decade provide another important impetus for examining members of synagogues. Historians, sociologists, and ethnographers have joined in an effort to chart the contours of congregational life out of conviction that congregations "create local cultures out of the accumulation of pasts that Americans bring into their places of worship."[6] Congregations, thus, embody and in turn shape the surrounding society and culture. As neighborhood institutions maintained through voluntary membership, synagogues necessarily reflect the lives of their members. Not surprisingly, the dynamic changes in the American Jewish community are on display within congregational life: accelerating geographic mobility, spiraling rates of intermarriage, shifting denominational allegiances, conversion into and out of Judaism, and the ebb and flow of Jews moving toward greater engagement with their religion, combined with the simultaneous departure of many more from any serious involvement. The synagogue serves as a mirror of all these patterns and therefore provides direct access to the preoccupations of "ordinary" Jews.

The present moment offers an unusual opportunity to reassess the Conservative synagogue in particular. Not since the trail-blazing research of Marshall Sklare conducted nearly fifty years ago has there been a comprehensive study of the largest synagogue movement of American Jews.[7] When Sklare wrote, the Conservative movement was entering its period of most explosive growth. There were years in the 1950s in which over 150 new congregations were founded. These synagogues were riding a wave of massive demographic and social transformation: the return of soldiers; the explosive growth of suburbia; the post-war economic boom; the turn to religion as an expression of middle-class respectability; and the Americanization of massive numbers of second-generation Jews, children of the mass migration from Eastern Europe. In the intervening half century, third and fourth generation Jews have assumed leadership of Conservative synagogues, steering their congregations in new directions. Even the casual observer cannot fail to notice the new roles assumed by women and the shift in style and tone that characterize the contemporary Conservative synagogue. This volume takes the measure of these and other transformations in order to delineate the contours of late twentieth century Conservative synagogues.

Jews in the Center is the culmination of an unusual collaboration between academic scholars, religious and lay leaders, and members of congregations, including young people. The Ratner Center for the Study of Conservative Judaism at the Jewish Theological Seminary embarked on a plan in 1994 to study the contemporary Conservative synagogue. Armed with a generous grant from The Pew Charitable Trusts, I, as director of the Ratner Center, recruited a team of sociologists to work in concert on the project. After intensive consultation with the rabbinic and congregational leadership of the Conservative movement, we were able to enlist support from hundreds of rabbis and synagogue presidents who brought us into contact with members of congregations.[8] All told, some six thousand individuals of all ages served as informants to this project by completing questionnaires, participating in interviews, and joining focus groups.

Team members engaged in a multipronged effort to assess the current Conservative synagogue. Their analysis is based on the following:[9]

1. The National Jewish Population Survey of 1990 that was prepared under the auspices of the Council of Jewish Federations was reanalyzed by Sidney and Alice Goldstein in order to develop a profile of the entire population of Jews in the United States who identify themselves as Conservative Jews.
2. In order to gather detailed information on the practices and programs of Conservative synagogues, Ariela Keysar and I conducted a congregational survey. Approximately half of the affiliates of the United Synagogue of Conservative Judaism, the umbrella organization of Conservative synagogues, participated in this survey (378 synagogues out of some 760 affiliates of the United Synagogue). The rabbis of those congregations completed a detailed questionnaire through mail and telephone interviews.
3. A membership survey was conducted by Steven M. Cohen and Paul Ritterband to elicit information about the characteristics and Jewish commitments of synagogue members. Over 1,700 questionnaires were completed by members of twenty-seven randomly selected congregations in the United States and Canada.
4. A survey of recent Bar and Bat Mitzvah celebrants was conducted by Barry A. Kosmin in order to learn about the Jewish identity and experiences of young people. Nearly 1,500 youngsters from all over North America who celebrated their bar or bat mitzvah during the Hebrew calendar year 5755 (1994–95), along with one parent of each celebrant, completed telephone interviews.

5. To complement quantitative data gathered through survey research, two separate ethnographic studies were conducted by Samuel C. Heilman and Riv-Ellen Prell. The former studied two congregations in the Northeast and the latter observed two congregations in the Midwest.

Over the course of two years, the team met regularly in order to coordinate the various pieces of research and inform each other's thinking. The interplay between quantitative and qualitative research, between statistical and ethnographic perspectives, proved especially illuminating and complementary. At every stage, our thinking was also informed by the wider understanding brought to the project by Nancy T. Ammerman, a leading sociologist of American religion with a speciality in congregational studies. She was enormously helpful in situating the specific case of the Conservative synagogue within the wider landscape. The goal throughout was a coherent and unified study rather than a series of loosely connected projects.

Jews in the Center presents our findings for the first time in a comprehensive fashion.[10] It opens with Steven M. Cohen's sustained assessment of the current vitality of the Conservative movement based upon the survey of members. Cohen's diagnosis is generally positive: he notes that the movement attracts a narrower band of Jews, but those who do affiliate are well-educated, committed, and more engaged than was previously the case. Sidney and Alice Goldstein reach a different conclusion. They examine larger patterns of denominational switching and compare current synagogue members with all self-identified Conservative Jews. At bottom, the differences between the Goldsteins and Cohen revolve around their contrasting assessments of self-identified Conservative Jews who are not members of synagogues: the former regard such Jews as integral to the Conservative movement, whereas the latter suspects that most form an entirely different population. Samuel Heilman's article caps the book's first section by introducing flesh and blood individuals. His ethnographic study permits synagogue members to speak in their own voices: they explain what has brought them to join congregations and how synagogue life fits into their Jewish identifications. He then situates members in their congregations by examining dramatic episodes in synagogue life.

The second section of the book examines how synagogue members function as a congregation—the interplay between the individual and the group. Paul Ritterband's opening essay in Part 2 analyzes participation in public worship, a central feature of Conservative synagogue life. His essay underscores the critical role played by families in nurturing religious individuals and the environmental circumstances that erode synagogue participation. Barry A. Kosmin then introduces the coming generation. His analysis of recent bar and bat mitzvah celebrants provides a unique perspective: American congregations invest heavily in young people, but it is in Kosmin's essay that we meet the generation in all its complexity. We learn much in this chapter about generational continuity and fissure. Rounding out this section is Riv-Ellen Prell's ethnographic portrait of two congregations. Prell is particularly intrigued by the disparate cultures of neighboring Conservative synagogues. Her essay pays particular attention to the role synagogue functionaries play in the shaping of those cultures and especially weighs the impact of rabbis.

In her concluding essay, Nancy T. Ammerman places the entire study into the larger context of American religion at the close of the twentieth century. Ammerman regards Conservative Judaism as a case study of how modern, well-educated Americans negotiate between religion and secularity. Rather than view these two as dichotomous, she argues, we would do well to understand that many Americans, including Conservative Jews, create a religious identity through a process of negotiation. Their flexibility, she contends, is not a symptom of capitulation to the secular, but rather a viable middle ground.

It should be apparent even from this cursory overview that members of the team are not of the same mind in their assessment of the current health of the Conservative synagogue or a prognosis for its future. Our goal, rather, was to present a variety of points of view regarding a religious phenomenon that often attracts little attention, namely, the religious lives of those in the middle. Most writing on religion in America focuses either on those who succumb to secularization or those who retreat into exotic but self-isolating communities in order to maintain a strong engagement with traditional religion. This volume, by contrast, highlights a religious population firmly in the center. Little wonder that such a population should elicit different characterizations.

Still, a number of common themes run through this volume, particularly as they are emblematic of today's Conservative synagogue:

> *The widespread adoption of egalitarian practices:* Perhaps the most dramatic and visible change in Conservative synagogues during the past quarter century has been the introduction of egalitarian practices in virtually every aspect of congregational life. Women have assumed new leadership roles on congregational boards and have served as presidents in 79 percent of Conservative synagogues. Women also are employed as rabbis, cantors, ritual directors, and administrators of educational programs. And they also share responsibility with men in approximately four out of five congregations for leading the religious service by reading torah, chanting the haftarah, delivering sermons, leading study sessions, and serving as prayer leaders. Bat mitzvah celebrants generally are treated no differently than their male counterparts. The process of change did not always occur smoothly, but the preponderant majority of Conservative congregations has adopted a range of egalitarian practices.[11] Virtually every critical aspect of synagogue life—worship,

religious leadership, voluntarism, governance, and institutional culture—has been reshaped as women have assumed new roles.

The coming of age of baby-boomers: Most Conservative synagogues are now guided by a new generation of leaders who differ considerably from their parents' generation. For one thing, baby boomers tend to have higher levels of educational attainment and post-graduate degrees. Unlike the generation that sustained congregations at mid-century, the boomers tend to be in the professions rather than own their own businesses, an occupational shift with important implications for the fiscal well-being of synagogues. The shift in generation has also reshaped relations between synagogue professionals and their lay leaders: as a result of their educational and occupational experiences, younger leaders tend to be less deferential to rabbis, cantors, and educators; they also expect to play a different role in shaping congregational policies.

New Jewish sensibilities: Members of Conservative synagogues today also come with different Jewish experiences than their elders. Younger synagogue members tend to have been exposed to a broad range of Jewish educational experiences—formal education, Jewish summer camping, youth movements, Judaica study on college campuses, and visits to Israel. They also were shaped by the cultural expectations that emerged in the 1960s: a preference for spontaneity, informality, and participation. All of these circumstances have created a very different Jewish sensibility than that prevalent at mid-century.

The turn from ethnicity to religion: It was widely assumed at mid-century that the Conservative synagogue functioned as an "ethnic church." In the words of Marshall Sklare, "We can assume that Conservatism resulted in part from the feeling that the Orthodox synagogue was inadequate to meet the demands of the environment, that ethnic solidarity would have to be perpetuated chiefly under religious auspices and that consequently a new type of institution was required."[12] A half century later, there is much evidence of "religious seeking" within American society generally, a trend that we have encountered as well in Conservative synagogues.

Jews in the Center examines how this turn to religion expresses itself in the lives of individuals in the center rather than on the extremes. Focusing on a well-educated, financially secure population, it sheds light on those who have taken the conscious step of joining a congregation for the purposes of worship, study, and social interaction. Their experience of synagogue life has much to teach about the future of Jewish life in the United States and the fluid nature of religious commitment in contemporary America.

Notes

1. Barry A. Kosmin et al., *Highlights of the CJF National Jewish Population Survey* (New York: Council of Jewish Federations, 1991), tables 27 and 28. The 41 percent figure represents membership at the instant when the survey was taken; the higher estimates refer to patterns of affiliation over the course of the lifetime of American Jews.

2. Nancy T. Ammerman, Jackson W. Carrol, Carl S. Dudley, and William McKinney, eds., *Studying Congregations* (Nashville, Tenn.: Abingdon, 1998), 7.

3. Synagogues have received relatively scant attention as compared with other Jewish institutions. The major works on Reform synagogues are Frida Furman, *Beyond Yiddishkeit: The Construction of American Jewish Identity* (Albany: State University of New York Press, 1987); Mark L. Winer et al., eds., *Leaders of Reform Judaism: A Study of Jewish Identity, Religious Practices and Beliefs, and Marriage Patterns* (New York: Union of American Hebrew Congregations, 1987), and Leonard Fein et al., eds., *Reform Is a Verb: Notes on Reform and Reforming Jews* (New York: Union of American Hebrew Congregations, 1972). On Orthodox synagogues, see Samuel Heilman and Steven M. Cohen, *Cosmopolitans and Parochials: Modern Orthodox Jews in America* (Chicago: University of Chicago Press, 1989), and Samuel Heilman, *Synagogue Life: A Study in Symbolic Interaction* (Chicago: University of Chicago Press, 1973). The major study of Conservative congregational life at mid-century is Marshall Sklare, *Conservative Judaism: An American Religious Movement* (Glencoe, Ill.: Free Press, 1955). For an insightful journalistic account of life in a Conservative congregation, see Paul Wilkes, *And They Shall Be My People: An American Rabbi and His Congregation* (New York: Atlantic Monthly Press, 1994). On Havurot, see Riv-Ellen Prell, *Prayer and Community: The Havurah in American Judaism* (Detroit: Wayne State University Press, 1989), and Lenore E. Weissler, "Making Judaism Meaningful: Ambivalence and Tradition in a Havurah Community," Ph.D. diss., University of Pennsylvania, 1982. I have edited a volume of historical essays entitled *The American Synagogue: A Sanctuary Transformed* (New York: Cambridge University Press, 1987; reprint, Hanover, N.H.: University Press of New England, 1995). In addition, quite a number of congregations have chronicled their own histories in anniversary volumes. Several recent studies of educational programs in congregations serve to illuminate broader facets of synagogue life. See, for example, Isa Aron, Sara Lee, and Seymour Rossel, eds., *A Congregation of Learners: Transforming the Synagogue into a Learning Community* (New York: Union of American Hebrew Congregations, 1995); Joseph Riemer, *Succeeding at Jewish Education: How One Synagogue Made It Work* (Philadelphia: Jewish Publication Society, 1997); and David L. Schoem, *Ethnic Survival in America: An Ethnography of a Jewish Afternoon School* (Atlanta: Scholars Press, 1989).

4. These biographies are drawn from the extended ethnographic studies of Riv-Ellen Prell and Samuel C. Heilman that appear later in this volume.

5. Unlike most churches, which subsist on offerings, tithes, and pledges, virtually all synagogues in the United States levy mandatory membership dues, in many cases exceeding $1000 annually. It is therefore instructive to learn why people choose to make such payments especially if they do not attend regularly. On the financing of churches, see Dean R. Hoge, Charles Zech, Patrick McNamara, and Michael J. Donahue, *Money Matters: Personal Giving in American Churches* (Louisville: Westminster/John Knox, 1996), 98–99.

6. James P. Wind and James W. Lewis, *American Congregations: Portraits of Twelve Religious Communities*, vol. 1 (Chicago: University of Chicago Press, 1994), 1.

7. Sklare's *Conservative Judaism: An American Religious Movement* was based on research conducted in the late 1940s. Charles S. Liebman and Saul Shapiro issued two reports on a survey they conducted of Conservative synagogue members in 1979, but these were never published.

8. The names of many academics, rabbis, and communal leaders who helped inform our thinking appear in the acknowledgments.
9. A more detailed discussion of the study design appears as an appendix to this volume.
10. Three interim reports have appeared thus far, all published by the Jewish Theological Seminary. In October 1996, a synthesis of major findings appeared, entitled *Conservative Synagogues and Their Members: Highlights of the North American Survey of 1995–96*; one year later, a second pamphlet was issued to illuminate specific themes: *Jewish Identity and Religious Commitment: Conservative Synagogues and Their Members*. Both were edited by the present author. The third publication is a book-length study by Sidney and Alice Goldstein, *Conservative Jewry in the United States: A Sociodemographic Profile*.
11. Findings about "The Triumph of Egalitarianism" in Conservative synagogues are based upon the congregational survey conducted by Jack Wertheimer and Ariela Keysar. These findings are reported in Wertheimer, *Conservative Synagogues and Their Members*, 14–18, 44.
12. Sklare, *Conservative Judaism*, 40.

Part I   The Members

Assessing the Vitality of Conservative Judaism in North America

Chapter 1

STEVEN M. COHEN

Evidence from a Survey of Synagogue Members

Studying Conservative Judaism: Its Significance for American Jewry

For many years, pessimism and disappointment have characterized the feelings of many Conservative Jewish leaders toward their own movement. In 1948, in the midst of considerable expansion of Conservative synagogues, and on the brink of the biggest building boom of American Conservative congregations, Rabbi Morris Adler, speaking to the United Synagogue convention, offered the following assessment:

> Multitudes of our people are untouched, uninformed, uncovenanted.
> They have not enough Judaism to live it, nor enough interest to reject
> it. They go on in routine indifference. Only now and then does some
> climactic circumstance briefly touch them and evoke a fitful response.
> Their personal lives are uninfluenced by the fact of their Jewishness. . . .
> There are others just equally inert, but on the side of Judaism. You find
> them crowding the membership rolls of our numerous organizations,
> synagogues and Zionist districts. . . . On the surface they are affiliated,
> but theirs is a frigid and uninspired affiliation. . . . Unimpassioned
> themselves, they communicate but little to their children. Theirs is a
> creed without a color, a faith without a fire. (Adler 1958: 280)

During much of the middle twentieth century, some of even the highest-ranking figures in the Conservative movement saw it as a necessary but unfortunate compromise with modern reality, an imitation of traditional Judaism amidst difficult circumstances. Louis Finkelstein, the renowned president and later chancellor of the Jewish Theological Seminary from 1940 to 1972, is reported to have called his own movement "a gimmick to get Jews back to real Judaism." (His personal problems with Conservatism were apparent in his practice of arriving at Conservative synagogues "*up-gedavent*"—having already said his morning prayers—so as to circumvent the necessity of formally worshiping in congregations whose liturgical practices he must have regarded as religiously defective.)

The downbeat views of Conservative Judaism echo in the words of another intellectual closely attached to the movement. In his classic work on Conservative Judaism, sociologist Marshall Sklare had the following to say about "The Next Conservative Generation":

> The present-day Conservative elite . . . is no longer so confident that its formula will be attractive to the younger generation. There are two aspects to this crisis of confidence. One is the problem of Jewish continuity, the problem of whether the battle against assimilation can be won. . . . In addition . . . Conservatism in recent years has lost its older confidence of being in possession of a formula that can win the support of younger Jews. . . . Rather than having an assured constituency as before, Conservatism finds itself placed under the uncomfortable necessity of winning adherents to its cause, and having to do so without the undergirding of cultural compulsions. . . . The reason for Conservative pessimism resides in the disjunction between its cultural system and that of younger Conservative Jews. (Sklare 1972: 277, 278–279)

Today, the mood within major sectors of the contemporary Conservative movement remains cautious at best, chastened by the anxiety attached to the future of American Jewry at large. That anxiety has been fueled by reports of high and growing rates of intermarriage that emerged from the first analyses of the 1990 National Jewish Population Study (Kosmin et al. 1991). The publication of the preliminary findings marked something of a turning point in the self-perceptions of American Jewry. Communal leaders repeatedly expressed considerable anxiety over the prospects for the very "continuity" of the Jewish group in the United States. If intermarriage rates remain high, and if mixed married families remain distant from Jewish practice and affiliation, prospects for American Jews seem bleak indeed. Even if, as some have argued, the intermarriage rates are, in fact, not quite as high as the early analysts concluded (see Cohen 1994, as well as Kosmin et al. 1991 and Cohen 1995b), the rather downbeat projections are only softened, but not at all reversed. A high and growing intermarriage rate translates, it would seem, into both fewer Jews and less of what might be called Jewish activity ritual practice, institutional support, informal ties, and so forth.

Many believe the Conservative Jewish subsegment of North American Jewry is hardly immune from these tendencies. Accordingly, if declines in numbers and in levels of Jewish activity (ritual practice, formal affiliation, informal ties) will characterize the Jewish population generally, then we would expect similar trends among Conservative Jewry in particular.

It is in this context that we turn to a close examination of Conservative Judaism in the United States and Canada toward the end of the twentieth century. This context is important not only because it generates pessimistic expectations regarding the vitality of Conservative Jewry. It is also important in that it lends an added significance to this investigation. Against the background of rising intermarriage and its threat to American Jewish continuity, the prospects for Conservative Judaism and Conservative Jewry become critical not only in its own right (which would be reason enough to examine the issues), but also critical for the future of American Jewry in general.

The pivotal position of Conservative Jewry is apparent when we consider simultaneously two very different groups: the Orthodox and the intermarried. Most observers would agree that Orthodoxy has reasonably succeeded in establishing itself in the face of the challenges of modernity. The number of Orthodox Jews and their proportion in the population increases as one moves from middle-aged to younger adult Jews to children. The norms of Orthodoxy have shifted in a traditionalist, more demanding direction, and younger Orthodox Jews often comply with the more stringent norms of Orthodoxy (Liebman 1979; Heilman and Cohen 1989; Soloveitchik 1994). Moreover, retention rates have increased: that is, the percentage of children of Orthodox parents who remain Orthodox in their adulthood has climbed decade by decade. If the American Jewish future is troubled, then from the point of view of sheer continuity, Orthodoxy is the least troubled (however, for a pessimistic assessment of Orthodoxy, see Heilman 1996).

In terms of sheer involvement in ritual practice, organizational affiliation, and informal ties to other Jews, the intermarried are situated at the other extreme from the Orthodox. Study after study has documented the low levels with which the intermarried undertake Jewish ritual observance, affiliate with Jewish institutions, and raise their children as Jews if only in name, let alone as practicing Jews (see, for example, Medding et al. 1992).

Between these two poles—the intermarried being more numerous than the Orthodox—lies what may be called the crucial middle of American Jewish identity, populated heavily by affiliated Conservative and Reform Jews. Sometimes referred to as the "moderately affiliated" (Cohen 1985), these Jews and their offspring, it can be argued, will determine the contours of American Jewry in the twenty-first century. Figure 1.1 displays the number of Jews by denomination and synagogue affiliation, using the data from the 1990 National Jewish Population Survey (Kosmin et al. 1991).

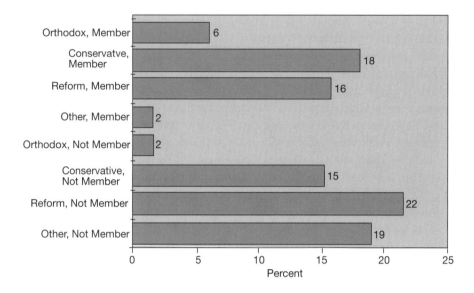

Figure 1.1. American Jewry by Denomination and Synagogue Membership

The population is divided into four denominational groups: Orthodox, Conservative, Reform, and Other (including Reconstructionists and a large number
of non-denominationally identified Jews). These, in turn, are divided into synagogue members and nonmembers. The more traditional the denomination, the
more likely one is to report synagogue membership. In other words, of the self-
identified Orthodox, the vast majority claimed synagogue membership; of the
so-called Conservative Jews, a slim majority did so; among the self-declared Reform, a clear majority did not belong to a temple. All told, Orthodox synagogue
members constitute about 6 percent of the U.S. Jewish population, as compared
with about 18 percent for Conservative synagogue members, 16 percent for Reform members, and 2 percent for "other" members.

Figure 1.2 reports the average level on a total Jewish activity index for each
of these groupings (again using data from the 1990 National Jewish Population
Study). The index simply takes twenty items from the survey covering rituals,
affiliation, friendship, and so forth, and computes a total ranging from zero for
those who reported none of these to one hundred for those who reported all.[1]

Two trends are clearly apparent. First, all synagogue members are far more
active than nonmembers. Even members who are not denominationally affiliated outscore Orthodox Jews who are not members (46 versus 37 on the index).
The second outstanding trend is that the level of activity among synagogue members, as well as among nonmembers, follows a denominational gradient from Orthodoxy to Conservative to Reform to "Other."

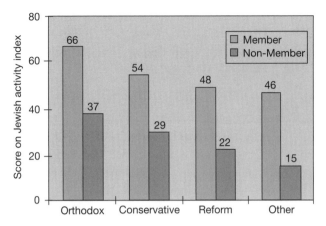

Figure 1.2. Jewish Activity by Denomination and Synagogue Membership

Clearly, Conservative synagogue members occupy a crucial and a central position on the "Jewish identity map" of American (and by extension North American) Jewry. Their number is three times that of Orthodox members; they slightly outnumber Reform synagogue members; and they constitute over two-fifths of all synagogue-affiliated Jews. Beyond their numerical strength, they are critical for another reason: their levels of Jewish involvement. Conservative synagogue members, as a group, are second in Jewish involvement only to their Orthodox counterparts (whom they clearly trail), and are more active than Reform temple members (whom they clearly lead).

All of this argues for their crucial importance for the future of American Judaism. Should Conservative Jews shrink numerically, or should their Jewish involvement decline precipitously, the most active American Jews would consist almost entirely of Orthodox synagogue members (now only 6 percent of all U.S. Jews). Hence, anything said about the strength, health, vitality, and prospects of synagogue-affiliated Conservative Jewry also can be said with modification for North American Jewry as a whole. A declining Conservative Jewry means a declining North American Jewry; a healthy Conservative Jewry virtually guarantees Jewish continuity in North America. The problem for us now is to define more precisely such terms as "strength," "health," and "vitality."

Defining "Vitality"

Undoubtedly, the meaning of the term "vitality" (or "health" or "strength") as applied to the Conservative Jewish movement in the United States can be the subject of a lengthy philosophic discourse. In this matter, this study's horizons are limited by the available data. This essay primarily analyzes survey data of members of North American Conservative synagogue members (although it also looks briefly at survey data of all U.S. Jews). As such, we are limited to quantitative indicators that are tied to the characteristics of individual Jews. In particular, we examine the following issues:

1. *Membership Size and Growth*: How many Jews are affiliated with Conservative synagogues? What has been the direction of change in the proportions affiliating, both as a fraction of the entire Jewish population and as a fraction of synagogue members in particular? Based upon the age contours of Conservative members, is membership likely to change dramatically in character or number in the coming years?

2. *Differentiation from Orthodoxy and Reform*: To what extent is Conservatism differentiated from Orthodoxy and Reform? The question takes on significance in light of the concerns of some Conservative leaders that Orthodoxy and Reform represent competition from the ideological right and left, respectively. Orthodoxy may draw off some of Conservatism's more traditional members, even as the Reform movement may encroach upon the Conservative constituency from the left. A Conservative movement that is more differentiated from its denominational counterparts figures to experience fewer losses to either side, although at the same time it may also pick up fewer erstwhile members of the Orthodox or Reform movements.

   Observers have noted that more observant Conservative Jews are restrained from transferring over to the Orthodox in large part because of their (and the movement's) commitment to egalitarian treatment of women in Judaism, a feature almost unavailable in Orthodox synagogues. On the other side of the spectrum, owing to Reform's recent embrace of traditionalism, Reform leaders have argued that the two constituencies greatly overlap, and that many Conservative Jews ought to feel equally comfortable in Reform temples.

   Accordingly, we would want to examine those issues or practices that distinguish the movements and assess the extent to which Conservative Jews are indeed different from their counterparts to the ideological left and right. To what extent is the Conservative constituency really more observant than the Reform constituency? To what extent are Conservative Jews, particularly the most observant, committed to egalitarianism?

3. *Ritual Observance and Synagogue Involvement*: The extent to which Conservative congregants practice key rituals and are active is at the core of the question of vitality. Beyond the question of current levels of such activities, we are interested in their direction of change. Accordingly, to provide some indication of likely future trends in terms of the Judaic "quality" of

Conservative congregants, we may compare younger with older Conservative Jews in terms of ritual practice and synagogue participation. In addition, we may compare current congregants with their parents (based on retrospective reports) to ascertain trends in ritual observance over generations, asking: to what extent are today's Conservative congregants more or less observant than their parents, and in what ways?

4. *Jewish Education*: Aside from asking whether they can read a siddur, the data we collected provide no direct evidence on how much congregants actually know about Judaism. We did, however, collect quite a large amount of information about the formal and informal Jewish educational experiences of Conservative synagogue members. To what extent, and in what ways, are younger congregants more or less learned than the older members whom they will inevitably replace with the passing of the years?

5. *Denominational Identity and Attachment*: To what extent have Conservative Jews developed a sense of attachment to their denomination as distinctive from Orthodoxy and Reform? The rise in Conservative denominational identity is, in fact, a relatively recent phenomenon, which some historians date to some years following the emergence of movement consciousness among Orthodox and Reform Jews. When the overwhelming majority of synagogue-affiliated Jews were Conservative Jews, as they were in the 1940s and 1950s, it made little sense for them to think of themselves as a distinct movement within American Judaism. For many intents and purposes, they were American Judaism. To what extent have Conservative Jews indeed developed a strong attachment to their own movement, accompanied by a rejection of Orthodoxy and Reform? Is that attachment, such as it may be, likely to deepen and widen with the maturation of currently younger Conservative Jewish adults?

Taking these criteria together, they amount to an operational definition of a vital Conservative movement. Such a movement is one which is substantial in size and growing larger, maintains strong differentiation from competing denominations, and is characterized by high and mounting rates of ritual observance, synagogue involvement, Jewish education, and ideological affirmation.

Beyond these criteria, one other issue is worthy of mention and examination. To forecast our findings a bit, we will see that rising rates of Jewish education and rising levels of intermarriage exert significant influence on the vitality of Conservative Judaism. Not surprisingly, their impacts are very different from one another. We need to examine the relative strength of these two contrary tendencies, as well as their interaction, to refine our understanding of the vitality of the movement or, more precisely, its prospects. In bald terms, to what extent has expanded Jewish educational participation by younger Conservative Jews offset the clearly deleterious and growing impact of intermarriage? A healthy movement, then, is also one that can contend with the major forces affecting its character, which, in this case, include most prominently Jewish education and intermarriage.

A Survey of North American Conservative Synagogue Members

To address these complex questions, this essay relies upon a random sample social survey, with both advantages and limitations for the purposes of this study. In 1995, the Ratner Center for the Study of Conservative Judaism surveyed 1,617 members of 27 Conservative congregations in the United States and Canada. It addressed concerns pertinent to the study of Conservative Jews, their identity, and their relationship to their congregations. The study is the most comprehensive survey of Conservative congregants in North America to date.

To what extent is the Ratner Center sample representative of affiliated Conservative Jews? Comparisons of items found in both the Ratner and the 1990 National Jewish Population Survey, (Kosmin et al. 1991; Goldstein 1992; Goldstein and Goldstein 1996) facilitate the identification of possible sample biases in the Ratner survey (see table 1.1). With respect to most Jewish identity characteristics, the Ratner Center survey is reasonably representative and unbiased. However, it departs from representativeness with respect to three issues.

First, the Ratner sample underrepresents Conservative congregants in certain major metropolitan areas. Within the United States, the New York region is represented by just one congregation (out of the twenty-two sampled across the country). In Canada, the random sampling procedures managed to pick all five congregations outside Toronto and Montreal, Canada's two largest Jewish population centers. The reasons for these departures from randomness are straightforward: we selected synagogues controlling for size and country, obtaining the appropriate balance between the United States and Canada, as well as among congregations that are small, medium, and large in size (under 400 units, 400–799 units, and 800 or more family units). However, we did not impose any further sampling constraints, and felt obligated to live with the luck of the draw.

Second, the sample overrepresents socially upscale congregants, that is, those with higher levels of education and income. We believe this feature derives from our primary reliance on a mail-back survey, rather than prohibitively costly telephone interviews (although, of the 1,617 respondents, 200 were, in the end, interviewed by telephone). Numerous methodological investigations have demonstrated that more highly educated individuals tend to return written survey instruments at a higher rate than others.

Finally, the sample underrepresents congregants under the age of thirty-five.

Table 1.1

Comparison of NJPS with Ratner Center Survey on Selected Variables

	(respondents who belong to Conservative synagogues)	
	NJPS	RATNER CENTER
Age		
65+	36	29
55–64	13	15
45–54	16	27
35–44	21	25
Less than 35	14	4
Sex		
Men	47	45
Women	53	55
Generation		
First (immigrant)	11	10
Second (child of immigrant(s)	47	40
Third (parents American-born)	34	41
Fourth (3–4 grandparents native)	9	9
Men's education		
Graduate school	30	57
BA	34	24
Less	36	20
Women's education		
Graduate school	19	40
BA	29	28
Less	52	32
Denomination raised (Jews only)		
Orthodox	34	26
Conservative	56	57
Reform	7	11
Other	3	6
Jewish education (main form)		
Day school	14	6
Part-time (2+ times a week)	48	49
Sunday	17	17
None or tutor only	21	28
Fasts Yom Kippur	87	79
Lights Sabbath Candles	35	56
Kosher Dishes	27	31
Spouse Jewish	92	95
Been to Israel		
Never	50	37
Once	27	28
Twice or more, or born there	23	36

We cannot be sure of the reasons for this bias. Perhaps the particular congregations we sampled have relatively few members who are so young. Perhaps younger members were underrepresented on the congregational lists that were, of necessity, about a year out of date by the time we processed them. Perhaps younger adults are busier or less interested in completing ten-page questionnaires, be it on their Conservative Jewish identity or on other matters.

Membership Size and Growth

Concerns about the numerical stability of the Conservative movement date back at least twenty years, if not more. Writing in 1979, Liebman and Shapiro concluded: "The Conservative movement of the 1970s resembled Orthodoxy of fifty years ago: an appearance of numerical strength but the absence of a strong infrastructure. Conservative Judaism as the mass movement of American Jews might be a peculiarly second generation American Jewish phenomenon" (1979: 1, 22, cited in Wertheimer 1987: 133). More recently, Wertheimer was equivocal about whether the movement has indeed attracted "sufficient numbers of third- and fourth-generation Jews" to replace the aging (and dying) members of their parents' generation. On the one hand, he writes, "There is evidence that Conservative congregations are gradually attracting younger people." On the other, the signs of rejuvenation of some congregations, he opines, "cannot entirely forestall the numerical decline of Conservative synagogues during the last decades of the twentieth century" (Wertheimer 1993: 134).

These concerns can be reduced to some very straightforward questions: How many Conservative Jews are there in the population? Do they seem poised for growth or decline? How do they compare to the Reform movement, the other major denominational choice of North American Jews? The answers to these critical questions are contained in the findings in the NJPS portrayed in figure 1.3.

We learn that, whatever the future may hold, the number of Conservative Jews affiliated with a congregation still exceeds their Reform counterparts. A total of 907,000 Jewish individuals are in families affiliated with Conservative synagogues as opposed to 834,000 affiliated with Reform temples. Of course, the sheer distribution by denomination offers only a static portrait of this phenomenon. For a sense of trends, of changes in denominational affiliation over time, we may turn to distributions by age.

Among the synagogue affiliated, the rate of Conservative affiliation has eroded fairly steadily over the years, dropping from 51 percent of those 65 and over, to 47 percent of those 55–64, 44 percent of those 45–54, and 38 percent of those 35–44. (This inference presumes that static age distributions in 1990 are a reflection of a dynamic process of affiliation choices over the previous 30–40 years.) The Conservative market share is somewhat higher among the 18–34 year olds (42 percent) and a little lower among those under 18 (37 percent). Clearly, the Conservative age distribution is "top-heavy" with a large number of congregants 65 and older (almost twice as many as in Reform temples). This datum suggests that as a result of anticipated mortality or migration to retirement areas, the movement may expect significant losses in dues-paying mem-

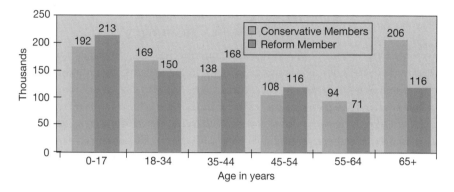

Figure 1.3. Conservative and Reform Jews by Age

bers in the next decade or so. Of course, some individual synagogues will grow significantly; but across the continent, the large number of Conservative elderly will translate into shrinkage in total North American levels of affiliation with Conservative synagogues, barring unforeseen countervailing tendencies.

These remarks notwithstanding, below age 65, the age pattern shows something of a reversal. Between the ages of 35 and 64, the Conservative movement is "bottom-heavy" with many more younger adults than relatively older adults. Of those 55–64 (born during the low-birthrate years of 1926–35), only 94,000 are Conservative synagogue members, as opposed to 138,000 members 35–44 years old (born during the postwar baby boom decade of 1946–55).

These patterns suggest two parallel trends in the near-term future for the Conservative movement: (1) a decline in absolute numbers of members, coupled with (2) a more youthful character to its membership, or, more precisely, a sharp decline in elderly members. From the vantage point of numbers of members alone, then, the Conservative movement cannot be seen as particularly "vital" or "healthy." But sheer membership size alone is not the only criterion of health; North American Orthodoxy must be regarded as a very successful movement despite its small size (among synagogue-affiliated Jews, roughly a third of the Conservative or Reform memberships). The claim for the success of Orthodoxy is based on such issues as commitment, piety, knowledge, education, cohesiveness, and other such qualitative matters. How the Conservative movement is performing and how it will perform in these areas is the concern of the remainder of this study.

Differentiation from Reform:
A More Observant Constituency

To what extent and in what ways are Conservative Jews different from their counterparts in other denominations, that is, congregants in Orthodox synagogues and Reform temples? The next section explores the extent and nature of commitment to egalitarianism, a vital issue that sets off the Conservative from the Orthodox movement. The present section examines the extent to which Conservative synagogues appeal to families who are ritually more committed than those found in Reform temples. Evidence of considerable overlap in terms of ritual practice would point to a future of greater competition with Reform. Evidence of differentiation would suggest that the Conservative movement has less to fear from an exodus to the Reform left, but also less to hope for by way of appealing to a more observant subgroup within Reform temples. (To be sure, the contours of observance are not the only factors that affect the extent to which the Reform-Conservative boundary is porous or sealed tight.)

The findings reported in table 1.2 and figure 1.4 derive from the 1990 NJPS.[2] They refer to synagogue members only, excluding those who say they identify with a particular denomination, but have not joined a temple or synagogue.[3] The data point to some areas of overlap, where members of all three movements—the Orthodox data are provided for comparison purposes—are almost equally active. For other measures, we find a clear (and anticipated) gradient where Orthodox Jews are more active than the Conservative, and both are more active than Reform congregants. Sometimes, the true break is between the highly active Orthodox and Conservative members versus the less active Reform group; and in others the Orthodox are sharply differentiated from the much less active Conservative and Reform congregants.

Clearly practices vary in terms of the frequency with which they are observed. Practices can be divided into "easy," "moderate," and "hard" categories, in line with a descending order of frequency, from most to least frequently observed. The denominationally related patterns generally align with the popularity of the practices. The "easy" practices (attending a Passover seder of any sort, lighting Hanukkah candles, having at least some close friends who are Jewish, and some indicators of Jewish organizational affiliation) are performed by members of all three major denominations with roughly equally high frequencies. The "hard" practices (fasting on the Fast of Esther) sharply differentiate the Orthodox from the other two denominations. And the "moderate" practices (e.g., Shabbat candle lighting, kashrut, indicators of intensive organizational involvement, having mostly Jewish friends, High Holiday attendance, never having Christmas trees, celebrating Israel Independence Day) are those where we find an orderly denominational gradient, with rates among the Orthodox lead-

Table 1.2
Selected Jewish Identity Measures by Denomination

	(Synagogue Members Only)		
	ORTHODOX	CONSERVATIVE	REFORM
Has a Passover Seder	88	92	91
Lights Hanukkah candles	89	94	90
Attends High Holiday services	91	91	82
Does not have a Christmas tree	94	92	81
Fasts on Yom Kippur	92	87	70
Celebrates Purim	61	48	53
Lights candles on Friday night	71	38	28
Celebrates Yom Ha-Atzmaut	37	38	31
Buys kosher meat only	76	29	10
Has two sets of dishes	73	28	10
Is Shomer Shabbat	60	15	12
Observes the Fast of Esther	46	3	1
Donates at least $100 to a Jewish charity	68	51	53
Belongs to a Jewish organization	52	52	49
Reads a Jewish newspaper	48	47	43
Has been to Israel	59	48	28
Donates at least $100 to the UJA yearly	28	27	35
Does volunteer work for a Jewish organization	33	27	22
Belongs to two Jewish organizations	38	29	27
Donates at least $500 to a Jewish charity yearly	43	22	19
Lives in a Jewish neighborhood	90	80	75
Some close friends are Jewish	92	92	89
Most friends are Jewish	79	64	48

SOURCE: NJPS

ing those among the Conservative members who in turn surpass their Reform counterparts.

In terms of ritual observance,[4] Conservative Jews are clearly unlike Reform Jews. In ten of the twenty-three items in table 1.2, the Conservative congregants' rates exceed those of the Reform congregants by five percentage points or more. The former lead the latter on all but three of the measures, and differ considerably on just under half the measures. These data are consistent with the classic observation that Conservative Jews are situated somewhere between Reform and Orthodox Jews. However, they lend no support to the impression that Conservative and Reform Jews hardly differ at all. In fact, using the very crude tools of

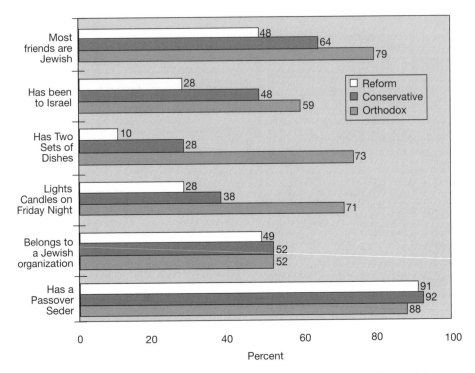

Figure 1.4. Selected Jewish Identity by Denomination (Synagogue Members Only)

comparison here, it may be said that, on the whole, across several measures of Jewish involvement, *Conservative Jews are almost as different from Reform Jews as they are from their Orthodox counterparts.*

Given these implicit cultural boundaries between the denominations, they suggest that many (though certainly not all) Conservative Jews would find Reform congregations unappealing owing to their relatively lower levels of observance. The same may be said for Orthodox Jews with respect to most Conservative congregations. To be sure, these data present only a very limited and narrow portrait of the cultural variations that set off one denomination from another. But even with this limitation, they do establish that Conservatism is, for better or worse, distinctive both from Reform to its ideological left, and, as we shall see in even greater depth in the next section, from Orthodoxy to its right.

Differentiation from Orthodoxy: The "Women's Issue"

Over the years, and particularly during the first half of the twentieth century, little distinguished many Conservative congregations from many nominally Orthodox congregations. As opposed to Reform temples of the time, both sorts of congregations prayed in Hebrew, uttering almost the same words, using essentially the same melodies; male congregants wore kippot and tallitot; rabbis affirmed the centrality of Shabbat, kashrut, and halakha; and congregants surreptitiously violated rabbinic teachings, even as they rhetorically affirmed their sacred validity. Conservative scholars enjoyed a measure of respect from some Orthodox counterparts, and the Jewish Theological Seminary trained a significant number of students from Orthodox homes. In fact, in most respects, Conservatism could be seen as a modernized version of Orthodoxy, where differences were, in some eyes, arguably more aesthetic than fundamental.

With all this said, one critical difference separated most Conservative from most Orthodox synagogues, as early as the 1920s (Sarna 1987: 380). Conservative synagogues allowed for mixed seating, in contravention of the traditional separation of men and women in worship, with women often relegated to a peripheral section of the sanctuary. In the early 1980s, the gulf between Orthodoxy and Conservatism around the treatment of women widened even further as the Conservative movement accepted women for rabbinical training and for cantorial school. In the period leading up to that decision, many congregations had begun counting women in the minyan and permitted them to assume major liturgical roles that traditionally had been reserved for men.

Certainly by the 1980s, the largely egalitarian stance of the Conservative movement served to mark a clear boundary with the Orthodox. In the past, most differences between the two could be chalked up to Conservative concessions to the demands of modernity. In contrast, the egalitarian stance constituted the first major distinction with Orthodoxy where Conservative leaders could point to a clear difference of principle, rather than a surrender to the pressures of a religiously lax constituency.

Although we have no survey data on the position of Orthodox Jews regarding the participation of women in religious leadership and liturgical roles, we can be sure that Orthodoxy almost universally retains traditional prohibitions against women functioning in such a fashion, even as a few institutions struggle to expand women's roles in Orthodoxy. In contrast, Conservative leaders have proudly claimed that the treatment of women constitutes a distinctive difference between their movement and Orthodoxy.

Liebman and Shapiro (1979) were more equivocal over whether the innovations in the treatment of women were so healthy for the movement. Their study of Conservative congregants found that the most traditional and the most active congregants were among the staunchest opponents of egalitarianism. Has the situation changed since then? Widespread support of egalitarianism among Conservative congregants may help distinguish the movement from Orthodoxy;

but if more observant congregants are unhappy with egalitarianism, then the movement may also be paying a price in the diminished enthusiasm of its potentially most committed members.

The two key questions to be examined, then, are (1) What is the extent of support for egalitarian treatment of men and women, and (2) To what extent is that support confined to the more liberal sectors of the movement?

With regard to "Jewish religious services," an overwhelming majority of respondents (85 percent) agreed that "women should have the same rights as men." We also asked about the more controversial issue of women serving as rabbis. Here, as many as 71 percent would not object to having a woman as a rabbi of their congregation, while just 15 percent would object (14 percent were unsure).

Clearly, the congregants widely support the move to egalitarian treatment of women in Conservative Judaism. But who exactly are the supporters or opponents of this tendency? Are the more traditional less supportive, as Liebman and Shapiro found almost two decades ago? Does the support come more from younger people or from women?

To examine these questions, we constructed an index of egalitarianism out of the two questionnaire items noted above. An "egalitarian" was defined as someone who agreed with equal treatment of men and women and had no objections to a woman serving as a rabbi in his or her congregation. "Traditionalists" were defined as those who provided neither egalitarian answer (we assumed that those who answered unsure, in this pro-egalitarian social context, were in fact indicating traditionalist sentiments).

Women are only slightly more egalitarian-minded than men (71 percent of the women versus 63 percent of the men qualified as egalitarian). Perhaps surprisingly, women's participation in Conservative congregations is not an issue that sharply divides male from female congregants. We also find scarcely any relationship with age. From age 35 and older, attitudes on women's participation are uniformly and overwhelmingly favorable, ranging from a split between egalitarians and traditionalists of 72 percent to 13 percent among those 35–44, and 63 percent to 14 percent of those 65 and over. However, those below age 35 take a somewhat less one-sided position, where just 53 percent are egalitarian versus 19 percent who are traditionalist. Although the egalitarians still outnumber the traditionalists by a wide margin, the balance between the two groups is nowhere as lopsided as that among those 35 and over. These results testify to the unusual nature of the few congregants under 35, who, unlike almost all their age-peers, have officially joined Conservative congregations.

Finally, the original results found by Liebman and Shapiro (1979) are repeated almost two decades later, as more observant and more active members are less enthusiastic about women's participation than their less involved counterparts. With respect to an index of ritual practice, those least active report

Table 1.3
Attitudes Toward Women's Participation by Ritual Observance

	Ritual Observance			
	VERY LOW	LOW	MODERATE	HIGH
Egalitarian	72	71	62	55
Mixed	19	19	22	19
Traditionalist	9	10	16	26
Total	100	100	100	100

egalitarian attitudes somewhat more often than the most ritually active (72 percent versus 55 percent). Smaller differences, although in the same direction, characterize infrequent versus frequent attenders at synagogue services. Clearly, the more observant and the more active are somewhat more reserved about the distinctive Conservative position regarding women's participation, although it must be emphasized that majorities of even the most observant group of Conservative congregants still favor egalitarian positions.

In any event, the broad endorsement of egalitarianism does help set the Conservative movement apart from Orthodoxy, even if those whose practices mark them as closer to Orthodoxy may share some sympathies with Orthodoxy's more traditional stance.

A "Mapping" of Jewish Activity in the Home and Synagogue

Jews may partake of a variety of activities at home and in the synagogue that, to varying extents, express their piety, communal involvement, and cultural proficiency. They may practice rituals, attend services, perform a number of liturgical functions available to lay people, socialize with fellow congregants, partake of a variety of synagogue activities, assume congregational leadership, and make charitable financial contributions. Given that not everybody is equally active, and not everybody is active in the various areas to the same relative extent, the question arises as to the extent to which active congregants are "specialists" or "generalists." Specialists are those who choose to be especially active in only one or two areas, to the exclusion of all else. Generalists are those who essentially are equally active in all possible areas of Jewish involvement, at home and in the synagogue. Before examining the extent to which Conservative congregants conform to movement norms by participating in Jewish life at home and in the synagogue—a topic to which we shall turn shortly—we would do well to examine how the alternative dimensions of Jewish activity are related.

The Ratner Center survey asked respondents about a very large number and a diverse collection of practices, activities, and affiliations. The empirical clustering of certain items is evidence of an underlying factor or dimension. Thus, to illustrate, the analysis demonstrated that Yom Kippur fasting, having kosher dishes, lighting Shabbat candles, and building a Sukkah are more related to one another than they are to the two dozen or so other activities about which the respondents were questioned. This pattern suggests that these items stand for some larger concept, such as "ritual observance" (the choice of what to call such a cluster is a judgment call). Thus, the relationships among the numerous diverse activities included in the questionnaire are themselves of some intrinsic interest in that they help define the major dimensions of Jewish activity in the Conservative home and synagogue. In point of fact, the analysis isolated seven key dimensions of Jewish activity, each of which embraces one or more activities, as follows:

1. *Ritual Observance*: fasting on Yom Kippur, kosher dishes, Shabbat candle lighting, and building a Sukkah.
2. *Synagogue Attendance*: a single item that moderately correlated with a large number of items from other dimensions.
3. *Liturgical Activity*: chanting the haftarah, chanting from the torah, leading the service, and giving a *d'var torah*.[5]
4. *Informal Associations*: attendance at congregants' life-cycle celebrations, having friends in the congregation, having Shabbat dinner with congregants.
5. *Synagogue Activities*: participation at lectures, classes, social action programs, family programs, men's club, sisterhood, social activities, and family Shabbat services.
6. *Leadership Activities*: serving on the board; attending board and committee meetings.
7. *Charitable Donations*: Contributing financially to the synagogue, and to other Jewish causes.

As table 1.4 reports, all dimensions but charitable donations are moderately to substantially correlated with one another. That is, one sort of activity leads to another: the more ritually active attend services more often; the frequent worshipers more often undertake liturgical activities (obviously, one can hardly give a *d'var torah* unless one attends services); all these activities are also related to having informal ties to other congregants (the ritually observant invite each other to their homes for dinner; those who regularly attend services make friends with other congregants; and so forth); those who participate in a variety of synagogue activities come to serve in leadership capacities in the congregation; and so on. Sociologists call this phenomenon "the more, the more." The rabbis had a more elegant formulation: "mitzvah goreret mitzvah," or performing one commandment brings (literally, drags) another.

Table 1.4
Correlations Among Jewish Identity Scales

	Rituals	Attends Services	Liturgy	Informal Ties	Synagogue Activities	Leader	Donor	Total Index[a]
Home Rituals	1.00	0.41	0.25	0.34	0.31	0.19	0.15	0.62
Attends Services		1.00	0.35	0.46	0.45	0.33	0.12	0.74
Liturgy			1.00	0.31	0.24	0.23	0.12	0.58
Informal Ties				1.00	0.55	0.36	0.21	0.74
Synagogue Activities					1.00	0.49	0.08	0.75
Leadership						1.00	0.13	0.64
Donor							1.00	0.19
Total Index								1.00

a The total index comprises the first six scales. Since the "donor" scale bore much weaker relationships with the other six indices, it was excluded from the Total Index.

Although six of the dimensions were correlated with each other, they all bore only weak relationships with making charitable donations.[6] Apparently, this is the one area in which we can speak of specialists: those who are the most financially generous are not necessarily the most active or connected with the congregation; and those who are the most active in a variety of ways have only a slightly greater tendency than others to donate to the congregation and other Jewish causes.

For some observers, the finding that synagogue leadership activity is corre-lated with ritual practice and liturgical activities may strike them as somewhat counterintuitive. While it may make perfect sense that the ritually active at-tend services more, a widely held image of Conservative synagogue board mem-bers argues in the other direction. According to this image, board members are recruited or drawn to service for reasons connected with their recognized lead-ership capacities that entail higher (secular) education, higher social status, and greater wealth. If so, then one would not expect board members to be especially active in terms of ritual practice at home, attendance at services, and possibly other matters. How do, in fact, the congregations' board members (past and present)[7] differ from others?

Board members are indeed far more active in all areas of Jewish home and congregational life than those who have never served on the board (see figure 1.5). The differences are generally so large that twice as many board members are highly active in a given area than others. Ritual observance is the least dra-matic difference, where 19 percent of board members are highly observant as compared with 13 percent for others. The results here not only demonstrate the higher levels of activity in all areas by board members; they also strengthen the point made earlier about the relationships between conceptually distinct dimen-sions of Jewish activity. Those who score high in one area tend to score higher

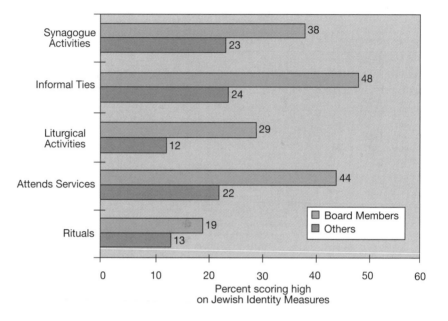

Figure 1.5. Jewish Identity Measures for Board Members and Others

in other areas, even if the areas are seemingly as remote as serving as a board member and practicing rituals.

The extent to which the six dimensions of Jewish activity are correlated suggests that it is analytically and conceptually reasonable to construct a single measure of Jewish activity at home and in the synagogue based upon the six dimensions with moderate intercorrelations. For each of the dimensions, the analysis focuses on the percent below the percent scoring high in any given dimension, an arbitrary cut-off point generally representing the most active sixth to third of the respondents. To examine overall involvement in Jewish activities, the analysis uses a summary index that combines all six intercorrelated indices of Jewish activity. This summary measure refers to the percent who scored high on at least three of the six dimensions.

Age-Related Differences in Jewish Activity

The best available evidence we have with which to forecast the near-term trends in the Conservative movement is found in the differences between younger and older adults. The logic here is that, inevitably, younger adults come to replace older cohorts. As a result, the entire population will come to more closely resemble today's younger adults, and depart from the characteristics of the older generation. Indeed, the logic of cohort replacement has special relevance here. The expectation that North American Jews are experiencing increasing assimilation (whatever that might mean), and that, by extension, the Conservative movement is experiencing similar tendencies, carries with it the idea that cohort replacement is the main engine of change. That is, assimilation is thought to affect younger adults, with higher rates of intermarriage, than older adults. Over time, as the younger adults age, their lower levels of Jewish involvement ought to bring about overall declines in the aggregate level of Jewish involvement in the entire population including the Conservative movement—or so proponents of the assimilation perspective would argue.

Of course, there is nothing at all foolproof with this reasoning. The unfolding of events over time can produce changes in the entire population that are distinct from cohort replacement. For example, the increased interest in Israel after 1967 and the more recent decline in the 1990s of political activity as an expression of Jewish engagement are phenomena that affected all Jews, and not primarily younger or older Jews. These important and profound changes transpired by ways other than cohort replacement.

Still, other problems complicate the use of age-related variations as a predictor of future trends. In particular, interpreting differences between older and younger adults is not entirely straightforward. Individuals of different ages may differ not merely because some were born to a different time than the others; rather, life-cycle factors (in this case, the presence of school-age children) may explain age-related variations. In other words, younger people may be more (or less) active not because they are intrinsically different than older people and can be expected to maintain their levels of activity as they age. Rather, they may be more or less involved because of their particular stage in life. The very youngest adults may be uninvolved because many are starting careers or families, or because they have recently arrived in their communities. Other relatively young adults may be active in part because of the presence of school-age or bar mitzvah-age children at home. And, to be fair, these are only some of the most outstanding reasons to be cautious about predicting the future on the basis of the distinctive characteristics of the younger adults. All this is to say that old-young comparisons from data collected at one point in time offer clues as to future trends, but the clues are far from clear or decisive.

With these cautionary notes in mind, we can proceed to examine the Jewish identity patterns of Conservative congregants. How do younger congregants differ from their older counterparts with respect to Jewish activity in the home and the synagogue?

Table 1.5 presents levels of Jewish activity for the six dimensions and for the summary measure described above for the five age groups, ranging from those under 35 to those 65 and over. Several findings are noteworthy and all merit

Table 1.5
Jewish Identity Indices (Percent "Highly Involved") by Age

	65+	55–64	45–54	34–44	LT35
Rituals	12	10	14	23	15
Attends Services	36	18	27	31	15
Liturgical Activities	17	15	18	19	13
Informal Ties	33	23	31	35	23
Synagogue Activities	32	21	22	34	15
Leadership	15	14	21	24	8
"Elite" (High on 3+ of the above)	29	17	27	30	15

explanation. First, the youngest congregants (those under 35) are, on most measures, among the least active in congregational activity. Aside from the small number of cases that represent this group (N = 53, or 3.3 percent of the total sample), several considerations argue against taking any results presented here for the under-35 cohort with a great degree of seriousness. These young people especially lag in the areas of synagogue attendance and serving in leadership capacities in the synagogue, and they lag the least with respect to ritual observance and liturgical leadership. The youngest congregants consist of a large number of singles, married couples without children, and couples with pre-school children. They are a highly select group, representing only a small fraction of their age-cohort, something of an "advance guard" who will undoubtedly be joined in Conservative congregations by their age-peers when they build their families.

As for now, the sharp contrast between their very low congregational involvement and their nearly average ritual activity suggests that young adults, who have only recently joined their congregations, need time to fully integrate into them. Possible explanations for this phenomenon also include the recency of their affiliation with a congregation, as well as the pressures of career-building and parenting very young children. Their levels of ritual practice and liturgical activity do suggest, however, that this group may be both capable and interested in taking on more congregational activity once they are thoroughly acclimated to their new congregations.

Those over 65 represent quite a different pattern, but one that also reflects their life circumstance. When compared with those slightly their junior (those ages 55–64), the oldest members differ little with respect to home ritual practice, liturgical activity, and leadership activity. However, they are far more likely to attend services, maintain friendships within the congregation, and attend all manner of synagogue activities. Upon reflection, the reasons behind these variations become apparent. Those over 65 are more often retired or semi-retired and

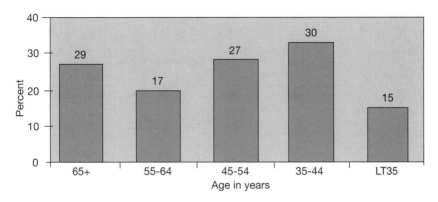

Figure 1.6. Jewish Identity (Percent High on 3 or More of 6 Measures of Jewish Iden-tity) by Age

have the time and the interest to socialize (be it through prayer, friendship, or synagogue programs) with other congregants. Life-cycle factors, it appears, heavily tilt participation in the congregation toward the upper end of the age spectrum.

The thirty-year age range (from 35 to 64) constitutes the critical testing ground for any theories about cohort-based changes in Jewish identity (see figure 1.6). Within this age spectrum, special life-cycle circumstances are less preva-lent. Unlike the youngest congregants, those 35–64 are not particularly excep-tional for having joined a synagogue; the vast majority of Conservative Jews their age have done so. Unlike the oldest congregants, they do not enjoy the free time occasioned by retirement.

In this critical age range, a rather remarkable pattern may be noted. On every measure, for every comparison (between those 35–44 and 45–54, as well as between 45–54 and 55–64) younger people are more Jewishly active than older people. The results are uniform across all measures and all age comparisons. In sum: *Within the 35–64 year old age range, in all respects, younger congregants are more Jewishly active in home and synagogue than are older congregants.*

Do these patterns point to cohort differences, those that can be expected to last over the years and bring with them more active, more committed congregants? Or do they reflect family life-cycle effects such that the higher levels of activity of the younger members of this age range will dissipate once their children mature and leave home?

Activity levels rise through the early stages of family-building, peaking among married couples with teenage children at home. With the departure of children (producing "empty nest" homes), Jewish activity plummets. In light of the concentration of teen-agers among homes headed by parents 35–44 and 45–54, one wonders whether the age-related patterns reported above are really

Table 1.6

Measures of Jewish Identity among Selected Age Groups and Stage of Family Life Cycle

Family Life Cycle:	Parents of Teenagers		Empty Nest	
AGE (YEARS)	35–44	45–54	45–54	55–65
Rituals	22	16	13	9
Attends Services	30	35	23	16
Liturgical Activities	19	19	15	15
Informal Ties	43	41	26	21
Synagogue Activities	35	27	18	19
Leadership	31	30	18	11

attributable to family configurations. In other words, do relatively younger adults participate more in Jewish life in the home and synagogue primarily because they are impelled to do so by virtue of being active Jewish parents, with school-age children and teen-agers at home?

To address this question, table 1.6 presents Jewish activity levels for two pairs of age groups with the same family configurations, respectively. We may compare parents of teen-agers 35–44 with those 45–54, and we may compare empty nest couples of ages 45–54 with those 55–64. In so doing, we examine differences between age groups while holding constant their family status.

The differences between age groups are small, certainly smaller than when we failed to control for family life cycle. Yet the younger age groups do retain an edge over their comparable older counterparts. Among parents of teenage children, those age 35–44 generally outscore those age 45–54; in empty nest households (married couples, no youngsters present), those 45–54 outscore those 55–64 on almost all measures of Jewish involvement. In other words, family life cycle does account for a substantial portion of the age-related differences in Jewish activity. That said, the age-linked differences remain after controlling for family life cycle and are, indeed, genuine: *younger Conservative Jewish adults are indeed more Jewishly active than their older counterparts, even when taking family life stage and the presence of children into account.*

Perhaps these differences can be explained in terms of upbringing. Perhaps younger Conservative congregants are more active in the home and synagogue today because their parents were more active when the respondents were children. Figure 1.7 presents levels of parental ritual observance (as reported by the respondents) against the respondents' own levels, using indices of ritual observance incorporating identical practices. These indices represent the average proportion (percent) who perform five selected practices (fasting on Yom Kippur, lighting Shabbat candles, kosher dishes at home, eating only kosher meat, and building a sukkah).

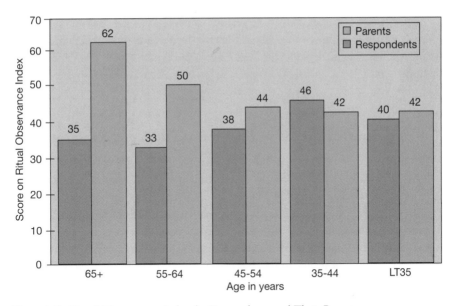

Figure 1.7. Ritual Observances Index for Respondents and Their Parents

Several trends emerge quite clearly. As we have seen before in other ways, for those between 35 and 64, younger respondents are more observant than older respondents. At the same time, younger respondents *do not* report more observant parents. Quite the contrary is the case. Parental observance levels are *lower* among younger respondents and, correspondingly, *higher* among older respondents. As a result, in terms of ritual observance, older respondents fall far short of their parents' levels, and younger respondents tend to equal or surpass those of their respective parents. For example, respondents 65 and older report having experienced a large drop (from a 62 percent level for their parents to 35 percent among themselves). In contrast, those age 35–44 report a slight rise (from 42 percent for their parents to 46 percent for themselves).

The history of Jews' adaptation to modernity has been marked by consistent intergenerational declines in ritual practice (Cohen 1983, 1988). Conservative Jews age 45 and older behave in a manner consistent with this generalization, just as their own levels of observance trail those levels they report for their parents when the respondents themselves were children. However, those between the ages of 35 and 44 are reversing this pattern, as they surpass their parents in the frequency of ritual practice.

The higher level of Jewish activity on the part of younger Conservative congregants is not entirely happenstance. This pattern does not, as we have seen, derive from increased levels of parental religiosity. The opposite is the case: *younger Conservative congregants are more ritually active than older congregants despite having been raised by less observant parents.* If parents are not to be credited with driving this move toward higher levels of activity, then the answer may lie elsewhere, specifically in the age-related patterns of Jewish education and socialization, and in the selection process occasioned by higher rates of intermarriage.

Age-Related Trends in Jewish Education and Socialization

The increases in observance and other Jewish activities are not the only significant differences in Jewish identity associated with age. In point of fact, the Jewish educational background and socialization of Conservative congregants have been changing even more dramatically than have the patterns of observance, affiliation, and synagogue involvement.

Most fundamental has been the change in the denominational background, as revealed in questions about the way in which the respondents were reared (see figure 1.8). As we move from older to younger congregants, the denominational patterns of their childhood shift dramatically from Orthodoxy to Conservatism. Among those over 65, significantly more were raised by Orthodox than by Conservative parents; of those between 45 and 54, those with Conservative origins outnumber those reared by Orthodox parents by more than three to one. Of those under 45, few come from Orthodox backgrounds, as roughly two-thirds of all congregants were raised in Conservative homes.

Among Conservative congregants, the growth in Conservative upbringing, and the commensurate decline in Orthodox roots, are but two signs of increasing denominationalism, characteristic of North American Jewish life generally. As compared with, for example, thirty years ago, denominational boundaries are less permeable; accordingly, the denominational loci for socializing and education are more numerous and widespread (more movement camps, youth groups, Israel trips, and so on). Retention rates for Orthodox families (the percent of adults who were raised Orthodox and who stay Orthodox) have increased dramatically over the years (Heilman and Cohen 1989). The results here point in the same direction for the Conservative movement.

The shift in the denominational background of Conservative congregants has clear consequences, as we shall soon see. Over the years, the Conservative movement has experienced a clear shift in its self-image, one visible in the pronouncements of its leaders, and perhaps a little less obvious among the membership. Once the Conservative movement saw itself as a less demanding, more Americanized version of Orthodoxy; in fact, many of its rabbis were Orthodox in mentality and had come to Conservatism after giving up hope of finding satisfying employment in the Orthodox community. However, over the decades, Conservative rabbis, educators, lay leaders, and laity saw their movement as pro-

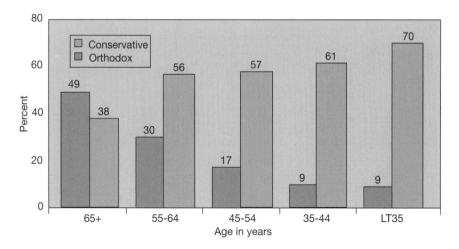

Figure 1.8. Conservative Synagogue Members Raised as Conservative or as Orthodox

viding a legitimate alternative to Orthodoxy, and not merely a toned-down imitation of the "real thing." The shift in denominational background from "fallen Orthodox" to "Conservative from birth" noted above probably helped provoke and resulted from the shifting denominational stance of Conservative leaders.

Not only has the denominational background of Conservative congregants been changing. So too has the intensity of their Jewish education and the extent to which they are exposed to specifically Conservative instruments of Jewish education. Figure 1.9 portrays utilization of several forms of Jewish education taking place during adolescence. It clearly indicates that younger congregants more widely participated in Camp Ramah, Israel travel (presumably, often under Conservative auspices), and USY (the Conservative youth group). Whereas of those age 45 and over, no more than 3 percent ever attended a Ramah Camp (the first opened in 1947), of those 35–44, fully 9 percent had been to Ramah, and among those who have apparently joined synagogues relatively early in their lives (those under 35), twice as many (18 percent) are Ramah alumni.

We asked respondents whether they had traveled to Israel before the age of 22. Illustrative of these results are the vast differences in Israel travel as a youth for two groups just twenty years apart in age. Of those 55–64, just 5 percent had been to Israel as youngsters; of those 35–44, the figure climbs tenfold to 49 percent.

Complementing these changes in Israel travel and Ramah participation are equally dramatic changes in USY participation. The levels rise from 4 percent of those 65 and over, to 17 percent of those 55–64, to twice as many (34 percent) of those 35–44, and a majority (54 percent) of the youngest (and earliest-joining) congregants under the age of 35.

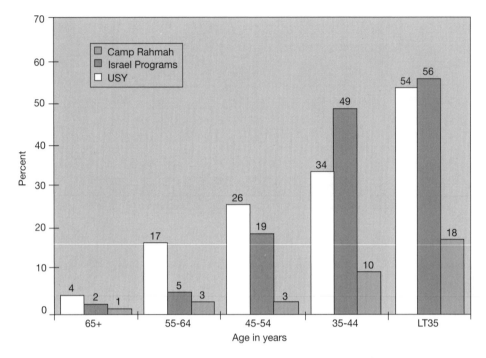

Figure 1.9. Participation in USY, Israel Programs, and Camp Ramah

These results reflect two parallel tendencies: increased opportunity and increased consumption. That is, over the years, these various forms of Jewish education have become more widely available and affordable for Conservative families. At the same time, such families have become increasingly predisposed to make use of these educational instrumentalities.

Similar patterns may be observed with respect to Jewish educational and socialization opportunities during the undergraduate years (figure 1.10). Participation in Hillel activities on college campuses was more than twice as high among those 35–64 years old as among those 65 and over, in part because many of the oldest congregants never attended university. A more steady rise, from decade to decade, can be seen with respect to participation in Jewish studies classes. One comparison is particularly noteworthy. Of those 55–64, about 90 percent of whom attended university (usually in the 1950s), just 10 percent recall having taken a course in Jewish studies of any sort. A mere twenty years later, this figure more than triples. As many as 31 percent of those 35–44 took a university course of some sort in Judaica, reflecting in part greater interest in these matters, as well as the greater accessibility of such courses (Ritterband and Wechsler 1994).

When taken together, these results point to a Conservative laity that is in-

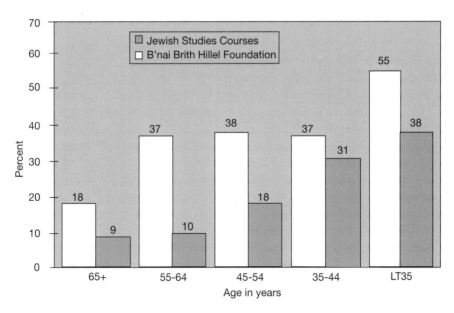

Figure 1.10. College-Age Jewish Activities by Age

creasingly learned in Jewish matters, and increasingly exposed to Conservative upbringing, education, and socialization. We cannot be sure of all the consequences of these patterns. We do know that younger congregants are more active in all sorts of home and synagogue activities. We suspect that they are more skilled and knowledgeable in Judaic matters. And we shall find that younger Conservative Jews also depart from the older age cohorts in a variety of ways that bear upon their understanding of themselves as Jews and as adherents of Conservative Judaism.

An Emerging Conservative Affirmation

For many years, Orthodoxy and Reform seemed more denominationally conscious than Conservatism. One reason is that the former two movements were both small minorities within American Jewry. Conservative Jews made up a very large majority of Jews affiliated with synagogues and, as such, Conservative Judaism could conceive of itself as American Judaism and not just a movement thereof. Secondly, Orthodoxy and Reform, each in their own way, represent the ideological extremes on the modernity-tradition continuum, while Conservatism sits squarely in the middle. Those in the extremes are more likely to develop a partisan consciousness than are centrists. Another reason for the more advanced movement consciousness in Orthodox and Reform circles may be connected with the ideologies of the movements. Both Orthodoxy and Reform have a history of Jewish separatism. Both, in their not-too-distant pasts, have discerned a need to separate themselves from the larger Jewish community. Conservative rabbis, in contrast, starting with Solomon Schechter at the turn of the century, emphasized "Catholic Israel" (Clal Yisrael or the unity of the Jewish people) as a central tenet of Conservative Jewish philosophy. The commitment to the wider Jewish community on the part of Conservative Jewish leaders is seen in their striking prominence in Federation and UJA circles; among the laity, it is evident in a greater emphasis on Jewish community and unity than among Reform or Orthodox rank-and-file (Cohen 1991).

However, several factors over the last few decades have worked to promote a stronger sense of denominational distinctiveness, allegiance, and ideological *affirmation* among Conservative Jews. One has been the growing sense of partisanship among Orthodox and Reform Jews. The Orthodox have seen themselves as increasingly self-sufficient and the non-Orthodox as increasingly deficient in terms of learning, piety, and commitment. As a result, the Orthodox have become more sectarian in their approach, more fundamentalist in their belief, and more rigorous in their practice. At the same time, the Reform movement has experienced significant numerical growth, while adopting a more traditional approach to liturgy and customs, and a more modernist stance toward matters of personal status (such as intermarriage, patrilineal status, and homosexuality; Wertheimer 1993). The result here, too, is a new denominational stridency, though of a different form from Orthodoxy.

In addition, the educational institutions associated with Conservatism that grew appreciably during the middle of the twentieth century have by now had a chance to exert a long-term impact upon the accumulated tens of thousands of alumni who have passed through them. United Synagogue Youth, Camp Ramah, and Conservative synagogues (which are, after all, educational institutions) have now had several decades in which to work their changes on the currently mature generation of Conservative adults. In addition, the other expanded opportunities for Jewish education which may not be directly associated with the Conservative movement may work to fortify a denominational identity that was more explicitly forged at an earlier time by Conservative educational instruments.

If this view of an emerging denominational consciousness in Conservative Judaism is accurate, then we would expect to see evidence in the attitudes of Conservative synagogue members. In particular, we would expect younger members to express what we may call a "Conservative ideological affirmation" more often and more passionately than older members who matured in a less denominationally oriented period in American Jewish history.

To test this prediction, this analysis conceives of Conservative ideological affirmation as consisting of the following components:

1. Identification with Conservatism rather than Orthodoxy or Reform.
2. More positive images of Conservatism than of Orthodoxy or Reform.
3. In contrast with Orthodoxy, support for the equal participation of women in the rabbinate and liturgical life.
4. In contrast with Reform, rejection of rabbinic officiation at intermarriages and of patrilineal descent as a basis for Jewish identification.
5. Support for a variety of other positions consistent with the teachings of Conservative Judaism, as embodied in such catch-phrases as "tradition-and-change" or "dynamic halakha." In other words, we should find evidence of some dualities, or commitment to principles in tension that, when taken together, amount to a centrist position on the modernity-tradition continuum.

Indeed, as table 1.7 details, most Conservative respondents endorsed these sorts of positions, albeit with some notable exceptions. Thus, they clearly identify as Conservative Jews and reject Orthodoxy and Reform Judaism. A large majority reject the respective central claims of Orthodoxy (to being more authentic) and Reform (to being more relevant). In fact, the sample readily endorses views critical of these two movements (the Orthodox are too shut off, and the Reform are too much influenced by the surrounding culture), while rejecting a frequent criticism of Conservatism (that it is too wishy-washy). They balance a commitment to halakha with a commitment to voluntarism and personalism (as embodied in one of our questionnaire items that read, "Conservative Judaism lets you choose those parts of Judaism you find meaningful").

At variance with Conservative teaching, an overwhelming majority agree that "a Jew can be religious without being observant." This item is one of only two in the list of seventeen questions where a majority departed from what may be considered the views of elite members of the Conservative movement. The other departure came in response to the question on patrilineality, where a more than three-to-one majority would accept as Jewish someone whose lineage does not meet the halakhic definition of who is a Jew, as understood by both Conservative and Orthodox rabbis. Interestingly, both questions tap a sense of American individualism, personalism, and voluntarism, themes that run contrary to halakhic Judaism, as traditionally understood.

With respect to personal status issues that divide Conservatism from Reform, the sample leans one way on one issue, and in the opposite direction on the other. Consistent with the Conservative position, a majority oppose their rabbis officiating at intermarriages. But as noted above, in a rejection of Conservative teaching, a majority would also accept a claim to Jewish identity on the part of a "patrilineal Jew" (someone born of a non-Jewish mother, but a Jewish father, and raised as a Jew).

Table 1.7
Conservative Affirmation Items

Do you agree or do you disagree with each of the following statements? "Not Sure" responses are excluded from this table.

	Agree	*Disagree*
DENOMINAL IDENTIFICATION		
I don't think I could ever be Orthodox	71	22
I don't think I could ever be Reform	26	28
I don't really think of myself as a Conservative Jew	23	72
DENOMINATIONAL ATTITUDES		
Orthodoxy is "more authentically Jewish" than Conservative Judaism	21	73
Reform is "more relevant" than Conservativism	9	83
Orthodoxy is too shut off from modern life	55	36
Reform is too much influenced by non-Jewish culture and ideas	47	38
Conservative Judaism is too "wishy-washy"	9	86
Conservative Judaism lets you choose those parts of Judaism you find meaningful	65	22
Conservative Jews are obligated to obey halakhah (Jewish law)	63	23
Jews who don't ride on Shabbat should join Orthodox rather than Conservative congregations	10	83
OTHER ATTITUDES		
A Jew can be religious even if he or she isn't particularly observant	78	17
My being Jewish doesn't make me any different from other Americans	35	61
I don't find synagogue prayers especially moving or meaningful	33	61
In terms of Jewish religious services, women should have the same rights as men	85	10
My rabbi should be willing to perform intermarriages	28	54
Anyone who was raised Jewish—even if their mother was Gentile and their father was Jewish—I would regard personally as a Jew	69	21

How are we to understand these questions? What attitudinal substructure lies beneath the answers to these seventeen questions? One approach would be to regard them as indicators of a left-right or modern-traditional continuum. But in fact, an analysis of how the items cluster empirically suggests not one dimension embedded in the seventeen attitudes, but two. Interestingly, the two dimensions do distinguish "left" from "right," but the two dimensions themselves are not closely related to one another as one might expect if they were measuring the same concept. Rather, one dimension differentiates Conservative from Reform ideology, containing items that are critical of Reform Judaism and its positions, including the questions on intermarriage and patrilineal descent. The other dimension distinguishes Conservative from Orthodox affiliations, containing items that are critical of Orthodoxy, including the question on women's religious rights. In other words, the two dimensions measure one's position on the boundaries separating Conservatism from its counterpart movements to its right and its left. Those who prefer Conservative positions to those of the

Reform movement do not necessarily prefer Orthodox attitudes to those of the Conservative movement (as a simple left-right understanding of these seventeen attitudes would suggest). Rather, in many cases, Conservative preference vis-à-vis Reform Judaism is empirically coupled with Conservative preference vis-à-vis Orthodoxy.

In fact, both dimensions bear a similar relationship with age. That is, younger people express more sympathy for Conservatism over Reform, as well as more sympathy for Conservatism over Orthodoxy.

For the purpose of measuring an overall commitment to Conservatism, the analysis used an index that scores items in accord with what may be called conventional Conservative teaching. For those items that distinguish Conservatism from Reform, this implies items scored in a traditional direction. But for those distinguishing Conservatism from Orthodoxy, this implies scoring items in the less traditional direction. The table above lists in boldface the responses that contributed to higher scores on the index. All of this is to say that the Conservative Affirmation Scale measures commitment to the middle of the spectrum rather than to either extreme.

As figure 1.11 demonstrates, age is strongly and inversely related to the level of Conservative affirmation. That is, younger Conservative congregants are far more likely to affirm Conservative ideological principles than older congregants, and the level of ideological affirmation rises with almost every descent of age.

This datum provides a third leg of the tripod distinguishing younger from older Conservative congregants. We have seen that they are more Jewishly active at home and in the synagogue. We have seen that they have more often experienced more intensive forms of Jewish education. We now see that they have dramatically different views of Conservatism as against other denominations.

The Search for Explanations: Intermarriage and Jewish Education

Two seemingly contradictory phenomena seem to be operating at the same time. On the one hand, the Conservative movement membership seems to be poised to shrink in size, if not in absolute numbers, then relative to the other movements. Although still the leading denomination in terms of affiliated synagogue members, the Conservative movement currently (i.e., as of 1990) holds only a small lead over the Reform movement, and with many more elderly members, the Conservative movement is likely to decline in size. The shrinkage of Conservative membership has been forestalled by the maturation of the baby-boom generation. But with the further maturation of that generation, smaller numbers of Jews (and, therefore, of Conservative Jews) are following in their wake. As the Conservative market share shrinks, as the overall size of the Jewish birth

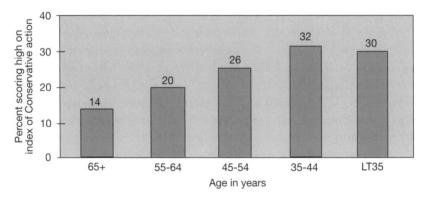

Figure 1.11. Conservative Affirmation by Age

cohort shrinks as well, and as the elderly meet their inevitable mortality, the Conservative movement will experience unavoidable declines in numbers of members.

At the same time, the Jewish "quality"—an admittedly ambiguous concept of younger Conservative members—generally surpasses that of the older members. They are more observant, more active in the synagogue, more Jewishly educated, and more committed to Conservative Judaism. Are these isolated phenomena, or are the two seemingly contradictory tendencies of decline in quantity and increase in quality somehow connected?

One key explanation linking the two phenomena lies with intermarriage. We asked respondents to report on whether their oldest children were married, and if so, whether they were married to Jews. We found a large discrepancy between the high rates of intermarriage reported by older respondents with reference to their young adult children and the far lower rate of intermarriage among Conservative congregants who are just as old as these grown children. For example, relying on reports of the older respondents, we learn that of their children ages 35–54 who had married, 28 percent had married non-Jews. Among Conservative congregants 35–44, just 7 percent had intermarried.

The contrast between these two figures implies that the vast majority of Conservative-raised young adults who have intermarried have failed to join Conservative synagogues. A small number may have joined Reform temples, and based on previous research on the mixed married (e.g., Medding et al. 1992) we can surmise that most probably joined no congregation whatsoever. We can also surmise that the intermarried, especially those who have failed to join Conservative synagogues, maintain lower than average levels of Jewish activity. We do know, from the data on their parents (and consistent with the research literature), that intermarried young Jewish adults come from weaker Jewish homes and had weaker Jewish socialization. In fact, the evidence here, even though restricted to Conservative synagogue members, shows similar patterns. Intermarriage is less likely among those whose parents were more Jewishly active and those who as children participated in such educational experiences as USY, Camp Ramah, or day schools.

Apparently about three out of four intermarried young people with Conservative movement upbringing leave the movement (or never join) as adults. However, the intermarried tend to derive from weaker Jewish homes and have undergone less intensive Jewish education. As a result of the departure of this selected group, the Conservative movement is left with more committed, better socialized, and more highly educated Jews. The selective impact of intermarriage, certainly, is part of the explanation for the changes in the character of Conservative Jews now underway.

Beyond intermarriage, the increased levels of Jewish education (formal and informal) among younger Conservative Jews have undoubtedly exerted an impact as well. To discern the extent of that impact, the analysis examined the cumulative effect of several forms of Jewish education upon the summary index of Jewish identity. The Jewish education index counted the occurrence of the following forms of Jewish education: Hebrew school or day school; attending services monthly as a child; USY; Ramah; visiting Israel before the age of 22; participating in Hillel; and taking at least one Jewish studies course as an undergraduate.

Figure 1.12 displays the impact of the number of Jewish educational experiences before the age of 22 upon adult Jewish identity, *after* the effects of the following confounding variables have been removed statistically: parents' ritual observance; parents' religious service attendance; denomination raised; age; and current family life cycle stage.

Obviously, even after extracting the influence of parental Jewish identity, age, and family life cycle, we see that Jewish education in its many varieties does indeed exert a long-term influence on adult Jewish identity.[9] The entries indicate the percent who would be expected to demonstrate high levels of Jewish involvement (scoring "high" on at least three of the six dimensions of Jewish identity) for each level of education, assuming that those with that level of education had the same type of parents, age, and family life-cycle status as all the other levels. These findings, demonstrating the effectiveness of Jewish education, are not at all surprising; a rather lengthy research literature points in the same direction (e.g., Goldstein and Fishman 1993; Fishman and Goldstein 1993; Cohen 1988, 1995a).

North American Jews in general and Conservative Jews in particular have been losing what may be called the elements of an "organic," geographically concentrated, and socially embedded community that could naturally socialize young

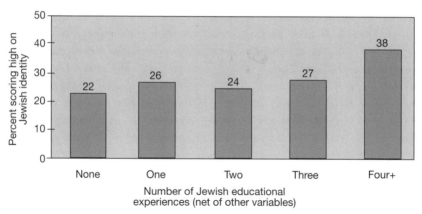

Figure 1.12. Jewish Identity by Number of Jewish Educational Experiences (MCA analysis)

Jews. Partly in response to this degeneration, they are turning increasingly to intentional instruments of Jewish education and socialization. Schools, synagogue participation, camps, youth groups, Israel trips, university study, extracurricular activities on campus, and more all serve to elevate adult Jewish involvement. With all their deficiencies and unevenness, these are generally effective tools of education and socialization. Clearly, they work for some and not for others, and some instruments or particular programs work better (or worse) than others. Taken all together, they serve to partially counter the adverse impact of intermarriage and of the forces that intermarriage represents.

With respect to numbers of members in the Conservative movement, Jewish education and intermarriage work in opposite directions. Jewish education increases Conservative movement retention rates, and intermarriage is a key factor in leading children of the movement to affiliate (if at all) elsewhere. However, with respect to those who remain affiliated, quality, education, and intermarriage paradoxically operate in the same direction: they both help enrich the quality of those who choose Conservative congregational affiliation. Jewish education enhances the skills, networks, and commitment of emerging Conservative Jews; and intermarriage is the vehicle utilized by the generally less committed and less involved to exit the movement, leaving behind a higher proportion of more committed and educated Jews.

We do not know the extent to which the opposing forces of Jewish education and intermarriage will prevail. But we can predict, with reasonable certainty, the consequences of these trends for the intermediate term. Among North American Jews generally and Conservative Jews in particular, intermarriage will continue to confirm and/or provoke the effective departure of large numbers of Jews from conventional, active Jewish life. At the same time, those who in-marry, and especially those who do so in a society in which many other Jews out-marry, are demonstrating evidence of an above-average involvement in Jewish social networks and, often, of a relatively more committed pattern of Jewish living as well. Aware of the rising intermarriage rates and concerned about their own families' chances for continuing as identifiable and committed Jews, these more active families (generally in-married and almost by definition synagogue members) have been turning to more intensive forms of Jewish education both for themselves and for their children. It may be presumed they will continue increasingly to do so.

What all this means for the Conservative movement is that its congregations will abide a growing number, albeit still a minority, of relatively observant, active, and learned Jews. This active core will grow partly in spite of and partly because of the growth in intermarriage, and its attendant shrinkage in the pool of potential members of Conservative synagogues among the younger generation.

Conclusion: Policy Implications

What are the appropriate policy responses to these trends? Which trends demand attention and which may be safely ignored? In the simplest of terms, the movement is shrinking in numbers and improving in quality. Ideally, movement leaders would want growth in both numbers and quality, but the ideal is not always attainable.

In fact, a case can be made that policies aimed at increasing numbers in the short term will also dilute quality. One way of increasing numbers would be to lower the formal and informal demands placed upon Conservative congregation members. "Demands" come in a variety of ways. They may be officially stated or informally conveyed. They entail such diverse issues as dues, volunteer time, observance, learning, years of Jewish schooling (or days per week) for one's children, and (to take a minor but telling example) observing kashrut at Bar/Bat Mitzvah celebrations. In the hope of recruiting new members, or retaining potentially disgruntled current members, some congregations and rabbis might be tempted to lower demands. Such a policy aims at maximizing numbers, albeit, arguably, at the expense of quality.

In the long run, which policy will ultimately produce a healthier movement: one with higher "standards" or one with lower "barriers"? (Of course, one Jew's standards are another Jew's barriers.) The correct answer, if there is a correct answer, may differ in different congregations. If there is a preferred policy direction, its formulation may be informed by a recent line of research in the sociology of American religion highlighted by an article entitled "Why Strict Churches Are Strong" by Laurence Iannaccone (1994).

Applying the tools of rational economic theory, Iannaccone analyzes the changes in numerical and qualitative strength of the major American churches over several decades. His conclusion is that churches can err by being too strict and too demanding of their congregants and, as a result, devolve into a small sect of highly committed adherents. At the other extreme—that exemplified by many liberal Protestant churches over the years—churches can err by demanding too little in the way of separation from the larger society and involvement in the community of the church. These low-demand institutions demoralize the most committed by abiding a large number of "free-riders," those who get the benefits of church membership without putting much of themselves into the community. The key to success is to strike the proper balance, to demand enough but not too much, to turn away (or turn off) some, but obviously not all.

It would seem that the Conservative movement is facing the same sorts of decisions faced by American churches for many years. Fortunately, the current numerical size of the movement (even the likely size after some anticipated shrinkage) is large enough for Conservative institutions to risk short-term numerical shrinkage if more demanding policies are instituted.

To elaborate, the current Conservative congregational membership is still so large that even if only a significant minority adopts a reasonably committed style of Conservative Jewish life, the movement will retain, if not enhance, its ability to significantly influence the contours of North American Jewry, and indeed, Jewish history more generally. In this regard, the Orthodox present an instructive model. With just 6 percent of American Jewry (according to the 1990 NJPS), the affiliated Orthodox population—capitalizing upon high levels of commitment, learning, and activity—certainly has exerted a dramatic cultural, spiritual, and political influence on North American and even world Jewry. Moreover, Orthodoxy's achievements have come in the face of two trends: a decline in the number of Jews who identify as Orthodox (a decline that is about to reverse itself) and an increase in the passion, commitment, involvement, and education of the small numbers who have been thoroughly socialized to an Orthodox way of life.

All told, Conservative congregations embrace a constituency currently three times the size of the Orthodox. As we have seen, prospects are bright for the emergence of an even more active and learned laity. If so, then Conservative Jewry stands poised to sustain and expand its contribution to Jewish life, even as it weathers a shrinking membership base. The key will be to maintain an emphasis on improving the quality of members, by way of increased education and retaining high formal and informal demands.

Such an eventuality, though, will require that Conservative leaders both lay and rabbinic work to nurture, mobilize, preserve, and expand the emerging younger cohorts of committed, educated, and potentially highly active Conservative Jews. The alternative is policies aimed primarily at slowing numerical decline, policies that put the Conservative movement in direct competition with

Reform Judaism. Such policies would lower demands (for ritual observance, learning, children's education, dues, commitment, conversion by non-Jewish spouses) in a well-intentioned but ultimately ineffective and inauthentic attempt to expand the membership base. In the long run, such policies may actually weaken the congregations rather than enlarging them. Instead, the movement would do well to consider sharpening and exploiting what may be Conservative Judaism's qualitative edge: an emerging group of highly educated and highly committed young Jewish adults.

Appendix: Questionnaire

Conservative Jews of North America: A Survey of Synagogue Members

1. Referring to Jewish religious denominations, were you raised
    - 52 Conservative
    - 26 Orthodox
    - 9 Reform
    - 0 Reconstructionist
    - 6 Something else Jewish
    - 6 Not Jewish (if you weren't raised Jewish, go to q. 7 on the next page)

2. When you were growing up, for how many years (if any) did you partici-
    pate in each of the following sorts of Jewish education? (If none, enter "0".)

	Number of Years One year or more:
a. Full-time Jewish school	11
b. Part-time Jewish school that met more than once a week	55
c. Sunday School or other one-day-a-week program	38

3. When you were 11 or 12 years old, how often did you attend synagogue
    services? And how often did your mother and father attend?

	You	Mother	Father
NOT AT ALL OR ONLY ON SPECIAL OCCASIONS (E.G., A WEDDING)	10	16	14
ONLY ON HIGH HOLIDAYS (ROSH HASHANAH, YOM KIPPUR)	24	31	29
A FEW TIMES A YEAR	21	25	22
ABOUT ONCE A MONTH	11	11	10
TWICE A MONTH OR MORE	34	17	25

4. Did you ever . . .

	Yes
a. attend Camp Ramah?	4
b. attend another overnight camp with kosher food or Shabbat services?	35
c. participate in USY or LTF?	20
d. participate in another Jewish youth group?	48
e. visit Israel before the age of 22?	20

5. When you were in college or university, did you . . .
   a. take any courses in Jewish Studies? — 18
   b. take part in any activities of a Jewish campus group like Hillel? — 32
   c. take part in activities of a Conservative Jewish campus group? — 5
   d. attend Shabbat services at least once a month? — 17

6. When you were 11 or 12 years old, did one or both of your parents . . .
   a. usually light Shabbat candles? — 68
   b. use separate dishes for meat and dairy? — 52
   c. have their own Succah? — 10
   d. refrain from eating meat in non-kosher restaurants? — 33
   e. fast on Yom Kippur? — 88

Now, we have some questions about you and your congregation.

7. For how many years have you been a member of your current congregation?

LESS THAN ONE YEAR	1
ONE YEAR	3
TWO YEARS	5
THREE TO FIVE YEARS	14
SIX TO NINE YEARS	17
TEN TO NINETEEN YEARS	23
TWENTY OR MORE YEARS	39

8. Five years from now, how likely is it that you will continue to be a member of your current congregation?

VERY LIKELY	73
SOMEWHAT LIKELY	19
NOT LIKELY	8

9. Have you served on the board of your current congregation?

Yes	31
No	69

10. During the last 12 months, how often (if at all) have you attended the following programs sponsored by *your* congregation?

	Once or more
Synagogue Board meeting	26
Synagogue committee meeting	36
Lecture or other cultural activity	67
Class in Jewish Studies	31
"Social action" program	36

Men's Club, Sisterhood, or Couples Club activity	49
Family program	54
Social activity at the synagogue	71
Celebration such as a baby-naming, bris, bar/bat Mitzvah, or wedding of congregants or their family members	81
A family Shabbat service	65

11. Among the people you consider your closest friends, how many would you say are members of your congregation?

NONE	18
A FEW	32
SOME	23
MOST	20
ALL OR ALMOST ALL	7

12. In the past year, about how often did you have a Shabbat meal with friends *who are members of your congregation*, either at your house or theirs?

MORE THAN ONCE A MONTH	4
ABOUT ONCE A MONTH	7
LESS OFTEN	36
NEVER	53

13. Thinking back to when you first joined this congregation, how important were each of the following reasons in your decision to join?

	Very important
It was geographically close	46
It was affordable	24
It was Conservative (rather than Orthodox or Reform)	71
My spouse wanted to join this congregation	49
My (or my spouse's) parents were members	24
Friends were members	29
Liked the community, the congregants	46
For the pre-school or nursery	25
For the religious school	51
For the youth program	30
So that my child(ren) could have a bar/bat Mitzvah	56
Liked the rabbi	49
Liked the cantor	34
Liked the style of worship	56
Liked the policy regarding the participation of women in religious services	43

The next group of questions concerns your participation in religious services.

14. During the last year, in your congregation, have you

accepted an aliya to the torah?	52
chanted the haftarah?	9
chanted the torah reading?	8
led services (as the cantor)?	6
given the *d'var torah* or sermon?	6

15. How often do you attend Jewish religious services? And (if married) how often does your spouse attend?

	You	Spouse
NOT AT ALL OR ONLY ON SPECIAL OCCASIONS (E.G., A WEDDING)	6	9
ONLY ON HIGH HOLIDAYS (ROSH HASHANAH, YOM KIPPUR)	16	18
A FEW TIMES A YEAR	35	36
ABOUT ONCE A MONTH	15	15
TWICE A MONTH OR MORE	29	23

16. How important is each of the following reasons for why you attend services?

	Very important
My spouse wants me to attend religious services	12
For my children—to bring them or set an example	40
To prepare my child for his/her bar/bat Mitzvah	28
To see or make friends, or to be involved with a community	32
To express my relationship with God	45
For spiritual reasons	52
I like the chance to play a leadership role in the service	4
I like the sermons or the discussions	28
I like the rabbi	44
I like the cantor's singing	30
I like the congregation's singing	29

17. Would you attend Shabbat services more frequently if . . .

	Yes
the services were shorter	28
the services were more meaningful	39
the sermons were better	28
the services were more spiritual	24
you felt more competent with your prayer skills	27

you felt closer to God   27
your family would want to go more often   49
more of your friends would go   29
people were friendlier   20
child-care were available   9

Now we would like to learn something about your participation in other Jewish activities.

18. Among the people you consider your closest friends, how many are Jewish?
    NONE   2
    A FEW   9
    SOME   18
    MOST   44
    ALL OR ALMOST ALL   27

19. Do you personally fast on Yom Kippur?

    YES   79   NO   21

20. Does your household usually light Shabbat candles?

    YES   56   NO   44

21. Does your home use separate dishes for meat and dairy?

    YES   30   NO   70

22. Do you refrain from eating meat in non-kosher restaurants?

    YES   15   NO   85

23. Does your household usually have its own Sukkah?

    YES   12   NO   88

24. Are you able to read the prayer book in Hebrew (not necessarily understanding the prayers)?

    YES   74   NO   26

25. Have you ever seriously considered living in Israel?

    YES   22   NO   78

26. About how often do you engage in the study of a Jewish text (e.g., bible or Talmud) in a class or group? (Do not count Shabbat services.)
    MORE THAN ONCE A MONTH   8

ABOUT ONCE A MONTH	5
LESS OFTEN	26
NEVER	61

27. How many times have you been to Israel?

NEVER	36
ONCE	27
TWICE OR MORE	35
I WAS BORN IN ISRAEL	2

28. During 1994, about how much did your household give in voluntary contributions to your current congregation? (Please do not include dues, tuition, or any mandatory contributions.)

$0	9
$1–99	22
$100–499	44
$500–999	16
$1,000–1,999	9
$2,000+	1

29. In 1994, about how much did your household contribute to other Jewish charities or causes (aside from the synagogue)?

$0	5
$1–99	18
$100–499	35
$500–999	14
$1,000–1,999	11
$2,000+	18

30. And, in 1994, about how much did your household contribute to charities or causes which are *not* under Jewish auspices?

$0	5
$1–99	25
$100–499	38
$500–999	14
$1,000–1,999	8
$2,000+	10

31. How old is your oldest child?
    Median = 24 years old

32. Did this child ever . . .

	YES	NO
attend a full-time jewish school (day school)	28	72
attend Camp Ramah?	14	86
participate in USY?	41	59

33. This child is:

NOT MARRIED	65
MARRIED TO A JEW	24
MARRIED TO A NON-JEW	11

Now, we have several questions about your beliefs and attitudes.

34. Do you agree or do you disagree with each of the following statements?

	Agree	Disagree
A Jew can be religious even if he or she isn't particularly observant	78	13
My being Jewish doesn't make me any different from other Americans	35	61
I don't find synagogue prayers especially moving or meaningful	33	61
In terms of Jewish religious services, women should have the same rights as men	85	10
Orthodoxy is "more authentically Jewish" than Conservative Judaism	21	73
Conservative Judaism is too "wishy-washy"	9	85
Reform is "more relevant" than Conservativism	9	83
Orthodoxy is too shut off from modern life	55	36
Reform is too much influenced by non-Jewish culture and ideas	47	38
Conservative Judaism lets you choose those parts of Judaism you find meaningful	65	22
I don't think I could ever be Orthodox	71	22
I don't think I could ever be Reform	62	28
I don't really think of myself as a Conservative Jew	23	72
Conservative Jews are obligated to obey halakha (Jewish law)	63	27
Members of my congregation are friendly to newcomers	75	16
I feel included in the life of my congregation	69	26

There's a group of people in my congregation with whom I feel very close	66	27
My rabbi should be willing to perform inter-marriages	28	54
Jews who don't ride on Shabbat should join Orthodox rather than Conservative congregations	10	83
Anyone who was raised Jewish—even if their mother was Gentile and their father was Jewish—I would regard personally as a Jew	69	21

35. How important would you say that being Jewish is in your life?

VERY IMPORTANT	78
SOMEWHAT IMPORTANT	20
NOT IMPORTANT	1
NOT SURE	1

36. How important would you say religion is in your own life?

VERY IMPORTANT	42
SOMEWHAT IMPORTANT	47
NOT IMPORTANT	9
NOT SURE	2

37. Do you believe that . . .

	Definitely yes	Probably yes	Probably not	Definitely not	Not sure
a. there is a God	57	23	6	3	11
b. God will reward you for your good deeds	18	27	20	9	27
c. God answers your prayers	16	26	19	10	29

38. In thinking about your ideal rabbi, how important would you rate each of the following roles?

	Very important
a. Public speaker	70
b. Teacher (of adults)	79
c. Scholar	64
d. Pastor to the sick, bereaved	76
e. Counselor	67
f. Representative of Jews to the larger community	76
g. Administrator	15

h. Initiator of activities and programs   47
i. Model of religious piety   51

39. Would you object to having a woman as a rabbi of your congregation?
        YES (I WOULD OBJECT)   15
        NO (I WOULD NOT)   71
        NOT SURE   14

40. During each of the following periods or events in your life, did your involvement in Jewish life increase, decrease, or stay about the same?

	Increased	Decreased	Stayed the Same
a. During your teen years	31	24	45
b. During your college years	14	46	41
c. When you first married	44	14	42
d. Birth of your first child	57	3	40
e. When your first child reached school-age	71	1	28
f. Bar or bat mitzvah of your child	73	1	27
g. Trip(s) to Israel as an adult	46	1	54
h. Death of a loved one	46	3	51

Finally, some basic background questions:

41. Are you:

        Male   45   Female 55

42. Your age:
        Median = 52 years old

43. Are you:
        MARRIED   79
        NEVER MARRIED   4
        DIVORCED OR SEPARATED   5
        WIDOWED   11

44. How many children do you have?
        NONE   8
        ONE   11
        TWO   47

THREE	26
FOUR+	8

45. How old is the youngest? MEDIAN = 20 years old

	YES	NO
46. Were you born in the United States or Canada?	89	11

47. Were BOTH your parents born in the United States or Canada?

47   53

48. Were at least three of your grandparents born in the United States or Canada?

10   90

49. Were you raised as a Jew?

94   6

50. Was your spouse raised as a Jew?

86   14

51. Is your spouse now Jewish?

86   14

52. Your zip code

53. For about how many years have you lived in the same town or neighborhood? Median = 21 years

54. Your highest educational degree:
HIGH SCHOOL	10
SOME COLLEGE	16
BACHELOR'S DEGREE	24
PROFESSIONAL OR GRADUATE SCHOOL	49

55. Your spouse's highest educational degree:
HIGH SCHOOL	14
SOME COLLEGE	16
BACHELOR'S DEGREE	24
PROFESSIONAL OR GRADUATE SCHOOL	46

56. Do you work outside the home?
    NO   29
    YES, PART-TIME   20
    FULL-TIME   51

57. Does your spouse work outside the home?
    NO   29
    YES, PART-TIME   16
    FULL-TIME   55

58. Are you (or your spouse) employed by a Jewish communal agency?

                          YES   6   NO   94

59. In 1994, your total family income was approximately:
    Under $30,000   11
    $30,000–$49,999   13
    $50,000–$74,999   18
    $75,000–$99,999   18
    $100,000–$150,000   20
    OVER $150,000   21

Notes

1. The items included the following: attending High Holiday services, fasting on Yom Kippur, lighting Shabbat candles, maintaining two sets of dishes for meat and dairy, eating only kosher meat, celebrating Purim, celebrating Israel Independence Day, never having a tree on Christmas, belonging to a synagogue, belonging to a Jewish organization, belonging to two or more Jewish organizations, volunteering at least three hours a month for a Jewish cause, having been to Israel, having mostly Jewish friends, having some Jewish friends, living in a neighborhood that is at least "a little Jewish," reading a Jewish periodical, contributing at least $100 to Jewish charities, contributing at least $500, and contributing at least $100 to the local UJA or Federation campaign.

2. The data are weighted in this table using two sets of weights. One set is the "household weights" developed by the NJPS data collection company to take into account number of telephone lines, demographic variations in response rates, and other concerns (Waksberg 1996). The second set of weights takes into account the number of Jews per household. In other words, the findings reported refer to the percent of individual Jews who live in a certain denomination's households who perform a certain practice (e.g., attend a Passover seder). Homes with fewer Jews, such as single-person households or mixed-married homes, perform fewer rituals than those with many Jews, such as those where both spouses are Jewish and with many Jewish children. Therefore, the percent of Jewish *individuals* who observe certain practices, or who are resident in homes where the specified practices are observed (e.g., Shabbat candles are lit), as reported in the table, is generally *greater* than the percent of Jewish *households* observing the same practices. To take a concrete illustration, 35 percent of Conservative households usually light Shabbat candles. In contrast, as reported in the table below, 38 percent of individual Jews living in Conservative households are in homes where Shabbat candles are usually lit.

3. As demonstrated earlier, synagogue members are far more observant than nonmembers, even across denominations. The gaps between the two movements among members only are smaller than that between all Conservative- and Reform-identifying individuals. Hence, for the purposes at hand, examining the differentiation between Conservative and Reform constituencies, the restriction to synagogue members provides a "conservative" portrait, with smaller rather than larger gaps. The decision here to exclude nonmembers from these calculations partially derives from the focus of this study, which is the Conservative synagogue member. In addition, whereas denominational affiliation may be meaningful for a member of a synagogue of that denomination, the meaning of denomination to nonmembers is elusive. When respondents who belong to no synagogue say they identify as Conservative or Reform, is that response a reflection of their upbringing, their earlier affiliation, their expectation, or their aspiration? Alternatively, are such answers an offhand abbreviation for intensity of Jewish commitment, drawing upon the public image of the denominations arrayed on a continuum from most intensive to least intensive? Moreover, when presenting findings for the public on particular denominations, does it make sense to conflate data from those who belong to the denomination's congregations with those from nonmembers who claim to identify with the denomination? However ambiguous is the meaning of denominational attachment for members, it is even more ambiguous in the case of nonmembers.

4. The entries in the table refer to the percent who answered "always" or "usually" with respect to the performance of the specified ritual practices.

5. Each of these activities was reported by only 6–9 percent of the sample, and, truth be told, correlations among them were rather weak. Normally, one would demand moderate correlations among items combined into a single index, on the assumption that correlations indicate the measurement of a common underlying factor and

that the indicators come from the same domain or pool of items. However, in a few instances that are theoretically justifiable, one can conceive of items as representing alternative ways of representing the same underlying concept, and such is the case here with liturgical activities.

6. The analysis examined alternative measures of charitable activity, including alternate combinations of the questions on donating to the congregation and to other Jewish causes, as well as extracting the influence of income. None of the indices bore markedly stronger relationships with the other six dimensions of Jewish activity.

7. Just under a third of the respondents said that they "had served on the board of [their] current congregation." We cannot distinguish current from former board members.

8. Preliminary analyses used two alternative ways of presenting the data on Jewish activity: z-scores (standard deviation: units above or below the means), and percentages (the proportion scoring high in any given dimension). The results are substantively the same whichever method is used. Z-scores are more precise and more appealing to the statistically oriented reader. Percentages are more readily comprehended by the lay reader and are utilized throughout this study.

9. The sampling design of this study operates to minimize the apparent impact of Jewish education upon adult Jewish identity. Recall that we sampled only Conservative synagogue members, excluding everyone else. As a result, we have missed those on the Jewish identity extremes: the Orthodox and the intermarried, to say nothing of the nonaffiliated and Reform Jews. As a result, we have narrowed the possible outcomes of Jewish socialization to a small portion of the Jewish identity spectrum.

Bibliography

Adler, Morris. 1958. "New Goals for Conservative Judaism—An Address [1948]." In Mordecai Waxman (ed.), *Tradition and Change: The Development of Conservative Judaism.* New York: Burning Bush Press.

Cohen, Steven M. 1983. *American Modernity and Jewish Identity.* New York: Methuen.

———. 1985. "Outreach to the Marginally Affiliated: Evidence and Implications for Policymakers in Jewish Education." *Journal of Jewish Communal Service* 62, no. 2 (winter): 147–157.

———. 1988. *American Assimilation or Jewish Revival?* Bloomington: Indiana University Press.

———. 1991. *Content or Continuity? Alternate Bases for Jewish Commitment.* New York: American Jewish Committee.

———. 1994. "Why Intermarriage May Not Threaten Jewish Continuity." *Moment* (December): 54ff.

———. 1995a. "The Impact of Varieties of Jewish Education Upon Jewish Identity: An Inter-Generational Perspective." *Contemporary Jewry* 16: 68–96.

———. 1995b. "Rejoinder." *Moment* (April): 68–69.

Fishman, Sylvia Barack, and Alice Goldstein. 1993. *When They Are Grown They Will Not Depart: Jewish Education and the Jewish Behavior of American Adults.* Research Report 8. Waltham, Mass.: Brandeis University, Cohen Center for Modern Jewish Studies.

Goldstein, Alice, and Sylvia Barack Fishman. 1993. *Teach Your Children When They Are Young: Contemporary Jewish Education in the United States.* Research Report 10. Waltham, Mass.: Brandeis University, Cohen Center for Modern Jewish Studies.

Goldstein, Sidney. 1992. "Profile of American Jewry: Insights from the 1990 National Jewish Population Survey." *American Jewish Year Book, 1992,* vol. 92. Philadelphia: The Jewish Publication Society of America, 77–173.

Heilman, Samuel C. 1996. *Portrait of American Jews.* Seattle: University of Washington Press.

Heilman, Samuel C., and Steven M. Cohen. 1989. *Cosmopolitans and Parochials: Modern Orthodox Jews in the United States*. Chicago: University of Chicago Press.

Iannaccone, Laurence. 1994. "Why Strict Churches Are Strong." *American Journal of Sociology* 99, no. 5 (March): 1180–1211.

Kosmin, Barry, et al. 1991. "Highlights of the CJF 1990 National Jewish Population Survey." New York: Council of Jewish Federations.

Liebman, Charles S. 1979. "Orthodox Judaism Today." *Midstream* 20 (August): 1.

Liebman, Charles S., and Saul Shapiro. 1979. "The Conservative Movement Today." Unpublished report submitted to the chancellor of the Jewish Theological Seminary.

Medding, Peter, et al. 1992. "Jewish Identity in Conversionary and Mixed Marriages." *American Jewish Year Book*: 3–76.

Ritterband, Paul, and Harold Wechsler. 1994. *Jewish Learning in American Universities*. Bloomington: Indiana University Press.

Sarna, Jonathan. 1987. "The Debate over Mixed Seating in the American Synagogue." In Jack Wertheimer (ed.), *The American Synagogue: A Sanctuary Transformed*. Cambridge: Cambridge University Press, 363–394.

Sklare, Marshall. 1972. *Conservative Judaism*. New York: Schocken.

Soloveitchik, Haym. 1994. "Rupture and Reconstruction: The Transformation of Contemporary Orthodoxy." *Tradition* (summer): 64–130.

Waksberg, Joseph. 1996. "The Methodology of the National Jewish Population Survey." In Sidney Goldstein and Alice Goldstein (eds.), *Jews on the Move: Implications for Jewish Identity*. Albany: State University of New York Press, 333–359.

Wertheimer, Jack. 1987. "The Conservative Synagogue." In Jack Wertheimer (ed.), *The American Synagogue: A Sanctuary Transformed*. Cambridge: Cambridge University Press, pp. 111–149.

———. 1993. *A People Divided: Judaism in Contemporary America*. New York: Basic Books.

Chapter 2

SIDNEY GOLDSTEIN
ALICE GOLDSTEIN

Conservative Jewry

A Sociodemographic Overview

As a major denomination in American Jewish life, Conservative Judaism constitutes a critical dimension in any assessment of the vitality of American Judaism as a whole. Conservative Judaism evolved over a century ago in response to the need to integrate waves of Eastern European immigrants into American life while enabling them to maintain their sense of ethnic and religious identity.[1] Conservative Judaism was intended to preserve traditional Judaism but in a modified form, to parallel predominant styles of worship in the United States. The movement drew heavily from the Orthodox population, providing these new adherents to Conservative Judaism with a familiar context but without the insistence on stringent observance.

By 1950 Conservatism's "historic mission" to prevent the religious alienation of the Jews originating in Eastern Europe seemed to have been accomplished.[2] The next two decades saw unprecedented growth for the Conservative movement and its assumption of numerical primacy among the three major denominations. A key factor in the change was the dramatic population movement—Jewish and general—from cities to suburbs and the subsequent spurt of synagogue building in these new areas. At the same time the movement developed a series of auxiliary institutions, including the Ramah camps and some day schools, that strengthened the sense of Conservatism as a movement among the laity.

Nonetheless, many of the problems that plagued the movement at mid-century continued. The lack of congruence between official ideology and individual observance remained. And assimilation was posing an increasing threat to Jewish continuity in the United States generally, forcing leaders of the movement to question Conservatism's appeal to younger Jews. In the large metropolitan centers a significant number of Jews identified themselves as "Conservative" but remained unaffiliated. In particular, the disruptive changes that swept American religious life in general in the 1980s did not leave American Jewry untouched,[3] making any predictions about the strength of a particular denomination particularly problematic.

The unprecedented freedom that America has offered Jews to determine the content and form of their religious practices and behavior has thus simultaneously helped to insure the movement's success and created the context within which threats to its future can develop. Religious freedom for Jews in America has created a fluid, dynamic situation, both between and within denominations.

Since its inception, Conservative Judaism's response to the larger surrounding society has led to changes in some of its religious positions, as well as in its organizational format. These have included incorporation of activities (like men's clubs, youth organizations, social action groups) other than religious services. Its constituency has also changed, reflecting both general sociodemographic changes in the American population as a whole and the flow into and out of the denomination of selected segments of Jews. As we move into the twenty-first century, continued responsiveness to the changing context is essential if Conservatism is to retain its strength and numbers. A successful response must be based on a firm understanding of the current situation that includes an accurate demographic profile of Conservative Jews and an understanding of their religious practices and attitudes. This study is intended to provide such a basic understanding.

Using data from the 1990 National Jewish Population Survey (NJPS-1990), supplemented by local community surveys undertaken in the 1980s, we provide a profile of persons who identify themselves as Conservative Jews in the United States. We delineate their sociodemographic composition, examine some of their religious/ritual behavior and beliefs, and assess the trends in movement into and out of Conservatism. The data thereby provide the basis for evaluating changes during the 1980s and for future planning and programming.

The NJPS-1990 data have the great advantage of including persons who are both affiliated and unaffiliated with synagogues/temples. Most studies of a particular denomination, including earlier studies of Conservative Judaism and other reports in this volume, have relied almost exclusively on information provided by synagogues or on respondents drawn from synagogue membership lists. With synagogue/temple affiliation rates among Jewish Americans at only 41 percent nationally,[4] the large unaffiliated segment of the population who identify themselves as adherents of a denomination is overlooked. Any comprehensive analysis of the members of a denomination must therefore include both those formally affiliated and those who identify with the movement but are unaffiliated.

The representativeness of the NJPS data also allows simultaneous comparisons

Table 2.1
Denomination of Adults by Household Synagogue/Temple Membership

	Total Number	Percent of Jewish Population	Synagogue Members (%)	Non-members (%)
Conservative	1,588,000	35.0	47.0	28.3
Orthodox	275,000	6.1	10.7	3.4
Reform	1,722,000	38.0	35.3	39.4
Reconstructionist	60,000	1.3	2.0	0.9
"Just Jewish"	457,000	10.1	3.4	14.0
Other[a]	428,000	9.5	1.6	14.0
Total	4,530,000	100.0	100.0	100.0

[a] In this and subsequent tables in this chapter, those whose denominational identification was unknown are omitted from the tabulations.
Unless otherwise specified, data are for adults only.

of the Conservative population with those who identify with other denomina-tions or with no denomination. In this way, we can determine the degree to which Conservative Jews are centrist or exceptional in the spectrum of Ameri-can Jews in general. Most of the focus for this aspect of the analysis draws com-parisons with Orthodox and Reform, but we also give attention, where possible, to Reconstructionism and to those who identify as "just Jewish" or "other."

At both the national and the community level, an overwhelming majority of adult Jews,[5] four in every five, identify themselves with one of the four reli-gious denominations of American Judaism: Orthodox, Conservative, Reform, and Reconstructionist. Of these, an estimated 1,588,000 identified as Conser-vative, constituting 35 percent of the total adult Jewish population (table 2.1). They were surpassed slightly by adults who indicated they were Reform, 38 per-cent of the total. The Orthodox constituted 6 percent of Jewish adults, and Reconstructionists just over 1 percent. Almost 20 percent did not identify with a specific denomination, reporting instead that they were "Just Jewish" or some-thing else. In addition to the 1.59 million Conservative adults, some 270,000 children under age eighteen live in households with Conservative affiliation.

While adult Conservative Jews constituted a slightly lower proportion of the total Jewish American population than the Reform, when the affiliated and nonaffiliated are considered separately, a different picture emerges. Among those who are affiliated with a synagogue/temple, 47 percent identify as Conservatives and only 35 percent are Reform. Conversely, among the nonaffiliated, a smaller percentage are Conservative than Reform: 28 percent compared with 39 per-cent. Thus, in considering the relative size of the various denominations, it is important to distinguish between members and nonmembers.

Within the Conservative population, socioeconomic variables differ among the various age segments and between those who are members of households with a synagogue/temple affiliation and those who have no such membership.[6] Regional patterns are also apparent, and switching into and out of Conservative Judaism is quite selective on a variety of characteristics and behaviors.

Several major themes emerge from our analysis:

1. Conservative Jewry generally occupies a centrist position between Orthodox and Reform on a wide array of characteristics.
2. Age (as a proxy for generation status) is an important differentiator of religious practices and strength of religious identification.
3. Respondents living in households with synagogue memberships are significantly different on many dimensions of socioeconomic characteristics and Jewish behavior from those in nonmember households.
4. Regional differences are strong, with Conservative Jews in the South and West generally showing lower levels of Jewish commitment than those in the Northeast and Midwest.
5. The inflow of persons not raised as Conservative Jews and the outflow of persons who were raised as Conservative Jews but who by 1990 identified with another denomination or no denomination at all have dramatically altered the sociodemographic and Jewish behavioral profile of Conservative Jewry.

The discussion that follows assesses each of these themes, highlights our major findings, and points to implications for future developments. Our discussion in this essay is based on extensive statistical analyses, but only key tables can be presented here because of space limitations. Some of the data discussed below will therefore not appear in the tables. These data, as well as other statistical materials, are available in a fuller monograph on Conservative Jewry using the NJPS data.[7]

The Centrism of Conservative Jewry

As Conservative Judaism has evolved, it has taken some positions on halakhic concerns that are less stringent than those held by the Orthodox. At the same time, it has maintained a much more traditional stance than Reform Judaism. Conservative Judaism is thus often considered to be a religion of the middle of the road and as such has appealed to persons of widely differing backgrounds and expectations. We anticipated, therefore, that persons identifying as Conservative Jews would show levels of religious identification and commitment that fall somewhere between those of the Orthodox and Reform. And indeed, the NJPS data confirm our assumption. Somewhat surprisingly, they show that

Table 2.2
Interdenominational Comparisons: Selected Socioeconomic Characteristics

	Conservative	*Orthodox*	*Reform*	*Reconstructionist*
Education (age 25 and over)				
High School or Less	32.4	42.5	14.6	11.2
Some College	19.7	12.4	25.7	5.5
College Degree	25.0	25.2	31.5	23.3
Graduate School	24.9	19.9	28.1	60.0
Total Percent	100.0	100.0	100.0	100.0
Occupation (of those in labor force)				
Males:				
Professional	42.2	47.3	39.1	*
Manager	18.3	9.8	18.8	*
Clerical/Sales	25.1	21.0	31.1	*
Blue Collar	14.4	21.8	10.9	*
Total Percent	100.0	100.0	100.0	*
Females:				
Professional	37.1	51.5	49.7	*
Manager	17.5	10.0	13.5	*
Clerical/Sales	36.5	33.8	29.5	*
Blue Collar	8.9	4.7	7.2	*
Total Percent	100.0	100.0	100.0	*
Five-Year Migration Status				
Non-migrant	78.9	88.2	74.9	70.4
Intrastate	9.7	5.0	11.0	5.2
Interstate:				
Within Region	4.5	1.3	4.3	9.3
Between Regions	6.6	2.5	9.0	12.5
International	0.3	3.0	0.8	2.7
Total Percent	100.0	100.0	100.0	100.0

* = fewer than ten unweighted cases.

Conservative Jews also have sociodemographic characteristics that in many respects lie between the other two major denominations.

SOCIODEMOGRAPHIC CHARACTERISTICS

Illustrative of their centrist position, the educational achievement of Conservative Jews is higher than that of the Orthodox but lower than that of the Reform (table 2.2). Similarly, the percentage of Conservatives in midlevel occupations (managers and clerical/sales) is higher than that of the Orthodox but lower than for the Reform; conversely, the Orthodox have a higher proportion of blue-collar workers and professionals, and Reform have lower percentages of each.

Even the level of geographic mobility of the three groups, as measured by migration in the five years preceding the survey, follows a similar pattern: Reform are the most mobile and Orthodox the least; Conservatives fall between the two but tend to be more like the Reform than the Orthodox. This differen-

Table 2.3
Denominational Comparisons: Age Distributions

	Conservative	*Orthodox*	*Reform*	*Reconstructionist*
0–5	6.7	11.7	9.1	12.3
6–17	13.8	19.8	14.9	18.7
18–24	5.0	6.0	3.6	1.7
25–44	32.5	24.2	41.0	43.3
45–64	17.5	10.5	17.6	22.4
65 and over	24.5	27.8	13.8	1.6
Total Percent	100.0	100.0	100.0	100.0
Median Age	40.1	35.3	35.9	33.0

NOTE: Children under age 18 were assigned the denomination of the household; adults' denominational identification refers to their reported current denomination.

tial pattern of mobility suggests that the need of Orthodox Jews for specific facilities and services (such as kosher butchers, mikvahs, and day schools) plays a larger role in determining where they live than is true for Conservative Jews. For the latter, other considerations, like economic opportunities or lifestyle amenities, may be more important determinants of residential location.

Age distribution is the one important area where the centrist position does not characterize Conservative Jews (table 2.3).[8] Not only is the median age of Conservative Jews (forty years) older than that of the Orthodox and Reform (about thirty-five years), but the configurations of the age distribution within each denomination also differ sharply. Conservative Jews have a dearth of children under age eighteen compared with the other two denominations, and they have more persons age forty-five and over. A combination of low Conservative fertility, the strong attraction of the movement in the past to persons raised Orthodox (see below) who are now in the older age categories, and its lesser attraction to families with young children have together created a situation that has serious implications for future Conservative vitality.

JEWISH PRACTICES AND BEHAVIOR

On every indicator of Jewish practices and behavior we have examined, the Conservatives exhibit a level below that of the Orthodox and above that of the Reform.[9] Those who identified as "Just Jewish" or "Other" have consistently lower levels of Jewish practices and behavior than those with denominational identification. The pattern for the three major denominations is consistent for variables ranging from Jewish education to ritual practices, from intermarriage to community involvement, although the differences put Conservatives closer to the Orthodox in some instances and closer to the Reform in others (table 2.4). The varying levels of Jewish education illustrate the mixed pattern of differences among the denominations. The Orthodox have by far the highest levels of Jewish

Table 2.4

Denominational Comparisons: Selected Aspects of Jewish Practices and
Behavior

	Conservative	Orthodox	Reform	Reconstructionist
Index of Jewish Education[a]				
None	23.0	15.0	28.0	11.2
Low	11.8	10.1	19.4	16.4
Medium	31.3	22.7	35.2	25.5
High	33.9	52.3	17.4	46.9
Total Percent	100.0	100.0	100.0	100.0
Synagogue Attendance				
Never	14.2	8.6	19.7	11.1
Often[b]	29.3	53.7	16.8	57.0
Selected Ritual Practices[c]				
Sabbath Candles	23.2	51.4	10.1	22.6
Kashrut	14.7	60.1	2.1	8.8
Fast on Yom Kippur	70.2	85.1	51.7	81.9
Attend Seder	73.7	72.5	69.5	80.6
Hanukkah Candles	72.8	77.1	65.8	70.4
Community Involvement				
Belong to Jewish Organization	39.2	43.4	28.2	30.7
Engage in Jewish Voluntarism	23.7	32.9	16.2	35.0
Contribute to Jewish Causes	63.0	72.3	49.9	67.6
Been to Israel	36.7	53.3	23.0	39.3
Percent in a Mixed Marriage	20.9	7.0	37.5	50.9

[a]   None = No Jewish education.
    Low = 1-2 years of any type school.
    Medium = 3 or more years of Sunday school or 3-5 years of supplementary or day school.
    High = 6 or more years of supplementary or day school.
[b]   Once a month or more.
[c]   Percent of respondents answering "Always" or "Usually."

education (over half had six or more years of day school or supplementary schooling). This was true, however, of only 34 percent of the Conservative, placing
them midway between Orthodox and Reform (17 percent) in the percentage
who had a high level of Jewish education. The percentages reporting no Jewish
education among the Conservative and Reform were, however, quite similar (23
percent and 28 percent) and higher than among the Orthodox.

These mixed patterns characterize other aspects of Jewish behavior and practices. On the one hand, for example, the percentage of Conservative Jews belonging to a Jewish organization is closer to that of the Orthodox than to that
of the Reform. On the other hand, the 15 percent of Conservatives who keep
the laws of kashrut is much closer to the 2 percent of the Reform who do so
than to the 60 percent of the Orthodox reporting kashrut observance. Since

maintenance of kashrut is a central tenet of Conservative Judaism, the great deviation here, as in the observance of lighting Shabbat candles, points to the diversity of belief and divergence from the stated Conservative norm in much of
the religious behavior of those who identify with the denomination. Our findings highlight the inclusiveness of Conservative Judaism, which encompasses
adherents with widely differing levels of religious observance.

Perhaps the most discussed statistics to emerge from NJPS-1990 have been
those related to intermarriage, in particular the high level of intermarriage in
1985–90. Here, too, our data indicate a centrist position for Conservative Jews.
Whereas overall some 21 percent of Conservative respondents reported that they
were married to a non-Jew, this was true of 38 percent of the Reform and only
7 percent of the Orthodox. When we focus on the most recent marriages—those
that occurred between 1985 and 1990—a similar pattern emerges, although the
levels are much higher: Just under half of the marriages involving a Conservative Jewish respondent are mixed, compared with about one-fourth of the Orthodox and almost three-fourths of the Reform. This pattern is directly related
to attitudes toward intermarriage; a much larger proportion of Conservative Jews
are opposed to it than is true among Reform, with the Orthodox most strongly
opposed of all.

The range of denominational differences is somewhat narrower for variables
related to involvement in the formal structure of the Jewish community. Nonetheless, the level of membership in Jewish organizations, voluntarism for Jewish
causes, and household giving to Jewish charities among Conservative Jews is consistently intermediary between that of Orthodox and Reform Jews. The same
pattern characterizes visiting Israel and the importance attached to living in a
Jewish milieu (i.e., having Jewish friends and living in a neighborhood that is
heavily Jewish).

One additional interesting insight provided by these data on denominational
differences is the exceptionalism of Reconstructionist Jews, who constitute less
than 2 percent of the adult Jewish population in the United States. The movement, a relative newcomer on the denominational scene, began to grow only in
the 1980s; because their numbers are still very small, the patterns can be sug-
gestive only. Since many Reconstructionists come from Conservative backgrounds, however, their profile may be an important portent of future trends.

On many indicators Reconstructionists are more involved and more strongly
Jewishly identified than their Conservative counterparts. For example, compared
with Conservatives, they have somewhat higher levels of Jewish education, attend synagogue more regularly, and have higher levels of voluntarism and Jewish organizational membership. Like the Conservatives from whose ranks many
of them came, Reconstructionists occupy an intermediary position between Reform and Orthodox, but they tend to be closer to the Orthodox than are the

Conservatives. Since so many of them were raised as Conservative, this finding suggests that persons switching into Reconstructionism are selective of the more Jewishly identified and committed. Their leaving the Conservative ranks may thereby serve to weaken Conservative Judaism somewhat.

THE IMPORTANCE OF AGE

Previous studies of Jewish identification and commitment have pointed to the importance of generational status.[10] Strength of identity, as measured by a variety of indicators of behavior and attitude, diminished directly with distance from the immigrant generation. Since the immigrants had largely arrived in the decades around the turn of the twentieth century, this implied that younger persons were generally less observant and less involved in the Jewish community than older cohorts.

Another concern related specifically to age is the stance of the baby-boom generation. This exceptionally large cohort has had a profound effect on American institutions, from schools to political parties, and on the role of religion as well.[11] As they move into the later adult years and into retirement, they can again be expected to alter demands for services and affect the climate of opinion on a large number of important issues.

Cognizant of these concerns about generation status and age, one segment of our analysis focuses on age differentials within the Conservative population. Sample size has necessitated broad age categories for most analyses (18–44, 45–64, 65 and over),[12] but even within this constraint, real differences emerge between groups. The youngest group is indeed further removed from immigrant origins than the two older ones; only half of those under age forty-five have all foreign-born grandparents, and 15 percent have all U.S.-born grandparents—indicating that they are at least third-generation Americans. This contrasts with over 80 percent of those age forty-five and older with all foreign-born grandparents and no more than 2 to 4 percent with all U.S.-born grandparents. The youngest group can thus be regarded as a much more American generation. Persons in this age cohort differ from the older groups in both their sociodemographic characteristics and their Jewish practices and involvement.

AGE DIFFERENCES IN SOCIODEMOGRAPHIC CHARACTERISTICS

Among Conservative Jews, age is directly related to level of secular education, with the 25–44 age group clearly being the most educated (table 2.5).[13] Over one-third of younger persons have had postgraduate education, compared with fewer than one in ten of the elderly. Nonetheless, the younger males are no more likely to hold high white-collar positions than are those in the middle age group, and in fact are more likely to be found among clerical/sales and blue-collar workers. About one-quarter of the men ages 25–44 are clerical/sales workers. Women

Table 2.5
Age Differentials for Selected Socioeconomic Characteristics of Conservative
Jews

	25–44	45–64	65 and over
Education			
High School or Less	13.9	29.9	53.5
Some College	18.8	18.3	23.4
College Degree	29.5	23.3	14.5
Graduate School	37.8	28.5	8.5
Total Percent	100.0	100.0	100.0
Occupation (of those in labor force)			
Males:			
Professional	42.0	42.8	39.1
Manager	18.1	24.3	2.3
Clerical/Sales	24.2	19.5	52.0
Blue Collar	15.7	13.5	6.6
Total Percent	100.0	100.0	100.0
Females:			
Professional	48.5	25.7	22.4
Manager	15.4	30.9	—
Clerical/Sales	26.8	37.1	71.1
Blue Collar	9.3	6.3	6.6
Total Percent	100.0	100.0	100.0
Five-Year Migration Status			
Non-migrant	64.5	91.2	92.0
Intrastate	16.6	3.6	3.6
Interstate:			
Within Region	7.3	1.9	1.3
Between Regions	11.1	3.3	3.1
International	0.6	—	—
Total Percent	100.0	100.0	100.0

ages 25–44 much more clearly reflect their high educational achievements. These women are heavily concentrated among professionals, with very few in the blue-collar group. This is in sharp contrast to older women, who are much more likely to be managers and clerical/sales workers.

Particularly notable among younger men and women, compared with those ages 45–64, is the low percentage reported as managers—positions that often require on-the-job experience. The situation may therefore change as these persons move through the life cycle. It is also clearly related to the national economic situation and to job opportunities.

Almost one-quarter of the 18–44 age group are not married.[14] And the younger married, in sharp contrast to older respondents, are most likely to be living in households with children under age fifteen. Among Conservative Jews who are married, those married in the 1980s were much more likely to be intermarried than those who married earlier: almost half of the more recent marriages were mixed, compared to just over one in ten of the earlier ones. Concomitantly, attitudes supportive of intermarriage are inversely related to age: older persons are much less likely to be supportive than younger ones, except that more of the very youngest group (ages 18–24) of respondents are opposed to intermarriage than those ages 25–44. Whether these younger persons represent a backlash against the more assimilationist attitudes of the somewhat older age cohort, possibly as a result of better formal and informal Jewish education, needs to be assessed.

Studies around the world have documented that migration is associated with those ages at which persons are obtaining higher education, entering the labor force, and entering the family-formation stage of the life cycle. It is not surprising, therefore, that Conservative Jews ages 25–44 also have heightened levels of five-year migration. One-third of the youngest group had moved in the five years preceding the survey, compared with less than one in ten adults age 45 and over; moreover, about 10 percent of younger persons had moved between regions. Younger persons are thus moving more often and longer distances, away from the influence of family and their institutions of socialization (such as synagogues and schools) at stages in the life cycle that are particularly critical to their formation of ties to a given community and set of institutions. Since this group is also the most likely to have families with young children, moving may be especially disruptive of their children's Jewish education.[15]

AGE DIFFERENCES IN JEWISH IDENTIFICATIONAL VARIABLES

The youngest group of Conservative respondents is distinctive in having not only very high levels of secular education but also relatively higher levels of Jewish education (table 2.6). More score high on the Index of Jewish Education (42 percent) than either of the older groups. The elderly have notably low levels, due in large part to the lack of women's Jewish education in the past. The higher levels of Jewish education among younger Conservatives do not, however, always translate directly into higher levels of synagogue attendance, ritual observance, or involvement in the Jewish community. Only about one-quarter of younger persons reported that they often attended synagogue, compared with one-third or more of the older groups. Those ages 25–44 also have generally lower levels of ritual observance than do the older groups.

In a few instances, however, the very youngest group (ages 18–24) seems to have turned this trend around; their levels of observance for some ritual practices are often as high as those of the older groups. For example, whereas fewer than 10 percent of Conservative Jews ages 25–44 observe kashrut, the one in five who does of those in the 18–24 age group matches the level of older respondents. Somewhat more of the younger respondents also attend seders and light Hanukkah candles in comparison with the next age cohort, but fewer light Shabbat candles and fast on Yom Kippur. Since some of these younger respon-

Table 2.6
Age Differentials in Jewish Practices and Behaviors of Conservative Jews

	18–44	45–64	65 and over
Index of Jewish Education[a]			
None	17.7	17.2	36.6
Low	10.0	14.5	18.2
Medium	29.9	33.9	30.3
High	42.4	34.4	20.3
Total Percent	100.0	100.0	100.0
Synagogue Attendance			
Never	15.2	6.3	18.5
Often[b]	24.7	32.6	33.5
Community Involvement			
Belong to Jewish Organization	30.7	44.5	48.4
Engage in Jewish Voluntarism	21.3	27.4	24.0
Contribute to Jewish Causes	49.5	73.1	77.5
Been to Israel	30.6	36.3	46.0
Jewish Milieu[c]			
Low	34.5	23.1	20.5
Medium	42.1	40.0	29.5
High	24.3	36.8	50.0
Total Percent	100.0	100.0	100.0

	18-24	25-44	45-64	65 and over
Selected Ritual Practices[d]				
Sabbath Candles	17.0	19.0	27.0	26.8
Kashrut	19.0	9.2	18.0	18.0
Fast on Yom Kippur	63.7	70.4	72.4	69.9
Attend Seder	81.4	71.7	82.7	68.2
Hanukkah Candles	73.1	70.9	80.0	69.5

[a] None = No Jewish Education.
Low = 1–2 years of any type school.
Medium = 3 or more years of Sunday school or 3–5 years of supplementary or day school.
High = 6 or more years of supplementary or day school.
[b] Once a month or more.
[c] Based on responses to questions about number of Jewish friends, Jewish diversity of neighborhood, and importance of living in a Jewish neighborhood.
[d] Percent of respondents answering "Always" or "Usually."

dents are adult children living with their parents, the reported levels of household ritual practices may, in fact, reflect the practices of the older generation. For those who have their own households, however, these patterns may augur a heightened level of ritual observance. Such behavior would be consistent with their higher levels of Jewish education and youth group/camp experiences.

The younger group thus has a very mixed pattern, more observant in some instances and less in others, and with many having high levels of nonobservance.

Younger people appear to be choosing their ritual practices to meet certain life-style or family needs, rather than following all of them as part of an overarching set of beliefs. Whether exposure to a more intensive Jewish education in the Solomon Schechter day schools will have a strong impact on this pattern remains to be seen, as the growing number of Conservative day school graduates move into the family-formation stage and set up their own households.

Especially notable is the sharply lower level of community involvement of younger Conservative Jews. The percentages who belong to Jewish organizations, volunteer for Jewish activities, and contribute to Jewish causes are all lower among those ages 18–44 than among the two older cohorts. Whereas almost half of those 65 and over belong to at least one Jewish organization, only one in three younger Conservative Jews do so. Of particular concern may be the low level of giving: only half report contributions to Jewish causes, compared with about three-quarters of the older groups. These patterns are quite likely related to life-cycle stage, in which case they may change as careers develop and family situations are altered. They may also reflect perceptions by some younger Conservative Jews that the formal institutional structure of the Jewish community is the domain of older, well-established Jews and that it has little room or tolerance for younger persons.

These patterns are echoed in two other measures of Jewish identity: having been to Israel and the importance of Jewish milieu. In both instances younger Conservative Jews (ages 18–44) score lower than their older counterparts. Only one in three has ever been to Israel (despite the proliferation of youth programs in Israel for American teens), and only about one-quarter score high on the Jewish Milieu Index. By contrast, almost half of the elderly have been to Israel, and half score high on Jewish milieu.

Conservative Jews who are under 45 are clearly different from older respondents. Although more Jewishly educated, they seem to be quite selective about what they choose to observe and how they choose to identify with the Jewish community. They are much less connected to the formal institutional structure than older Conservative Jews. Whether this pattern will change as these younger persons grow older warrants careful follow-up. The direction of change, if there is any, will have a significant effect on the strength of Conservative Judaism.

THE IMPORTANCE OF SYNAGOGUE MEMBERSHIP

The information on denominational identification in NJPS-1990 relies solely on the respondents' own perception and reporting. As we have seen, nominal Conservative identification does not mean behavior that is in full accord with Conservative doctrine. Jews identifying themselves as Conservative cover a broad spectrum of behavior, from the very observant to those who are only marginally connected to Judaism.

A more selective Conservative population, one that might be expected to act concretely on its identificational distinction, would refer to Conservative Jews who are affiliated with a synagogue. As noted earlier, NJPS does not provide entirely direct information for the synagogue/temple membership of individuals, since the survey asked only whether anyone in the household is affiliated with a synagogue/temple. Among persons identified as Conservative, just under half of all adult Jews live in households with synagogue/temple affiliation. But not all persons who identify as Conservative belong to households whose affiliation is with a Conservative synagogue. Nonetheless, the correlation between individual identification and household membership is high; seven out of ten persons who identify as Conservative Jews and who report a household synagogue membership are affiliated with a Conservative synagogue. We have therefore classified all Conservative Jews who report a household synagogue membership as affiliated, regardless of denomination.

Membership makes a dramatic difference in the profile of Conservative Jewry. Members tend to be older, married, and with children age 15 and older living in the household. Conversely, nonmembers are more concentrated among the young, never married, or divorced. Regional differences in affiliation are also strong. Members are even more concentrated in the Northeast than nonmembers and also live disproportionately in the West. By contrast, nonmembers are more likely to live in the South and Midwest. These findings are consistent with the general differences characterizing the four regions (see below). Both higher secular education and more Jewish education lead to higher membership rates, while nonmembers are more likely to be characterized by education below the college level and lower scores on the Index of Jewish Education.

Clearly, synagogue affiliation is attractive to families and much less appealing to persons not in traditional family configurations (table 2.7). Quite likely, it is the Jewish education of children, especially in connection with bar/bat mitzvah preparation, that encourages families to join synagogues; once members, they often remain affiliated beyond the bar/bat mitzvah of their youngest child. Among the married, intermarriage is sharply lower among members than nonmembers—6 percent compared with 36 percent (table 2.8), suggesting either that nonmembers are much more predisposed to intermarriage because of their more marginal attachment to Judaism, or that they do not feel welcome in a synagogue once they are intermarried and therefore do not affiliate.

Membership is clearly and unsurprisingly associated with much higher levels of ritual practices. About four times as many members as nonmembers light Shabbat candles and observe kashrut; only two-thirds as many of the nonmembers as members participate in such popular rituals as seders and lighting Hanukkah candles. And members much more than nonmembers consider a Jewish milieu to be important for them. Especially strong differentials are also apparent

Table 2.7
Selected Socioeconomic Characteristics of Conservative Jews by
Membership Status

	Synagogue Members	Nonmembers
Age		
18-24	9.9	8.4
25-44	33.1	44.7
45-64	26.7	21.6
65 and over	30.3	25.3
Total Percent	100.0	100.0
Life-Cycle Stage		
Single, under 45	5.6	15.2
Single, 45+	17.2	15.6
Adults only	32.0	38.1
Parent(s) with:		
Children under age 15	23.8	20.3
Children age 15+ only	21.5	10.8
Total Percent	100.0	100.0
Region of Residence		
Northeast	51.5	38.9
Midwest	12.4	8.3
South	20.8	28.3
West	15.2	24.4
Total Percent	100.0	100.0

in measures of community involvement. Not surprisingly, synagogue attendance differs significantly between members and nonmembers. Whereas half of the members report that they attend once a month or more, only about one in ten of the nonmembers attend this often. Conversely, while one-quarter of the non-members never attend, this is true of less than 2 percent of the members. Only one-quarter of nonmembers belong to a Jewish organization, while six out of ten members do; only one-fourth as many nonmembers as members volunteer in Jewish activities; and only half give to Jewish causes, compared with four out of five among members. Having been to Israel is also associated with higher membership rates.

Since the affiliated Conservative Jews are the ones most visible to the Conservative leadership, their characteristics and behavior have often been assumed to be representative of Conservative Jewry as a whole. This assumption is clearly misleading. Great variation exists between members and nonmembers. Nonmembers are significantly more marginal and therefore represent a population in need of outreach through special programming geared specifically to younger persons, to those not in traditional families, to those who may be financially constrained, and to those alienated from the formal structure of the Jewish community. In his assessment of Conservative Judaism in the 1970s, Marshall Sklare suggested that all that was needed to further augment the primacy of Conservative Juda-

Table 2.8
Selected Jewish Identificational Variables of Conservative Jews by
Membership Status

	Synagogue Members	Non-members
Percent with High Jewish Education Index[a]	44.8	24.6
Synagogue Attendance		
Never	1.5	25.4
Often[b]	49.8	11.3
Percent in a Mixed Marriage	5.8	36.3
Selected Ritual Practices[c]		
Sabbath Candles	37.4	10.9
Kashrut	24.5	6.3
Fast on Yom Kippur	87.6	55.6
Attend Seder	89.7	59.7
Hanukkah Candles	90.0	56.9
Community Involvement		
Belong to Jewish Organization	57.6	23.4
Engage in Jewish Voluntarism	39.1	10.6
Contribute to Jewish Causes	79.5	49.2
Been to Israel	49.0	26.2

[a] High = 6 or more years of supplementary or day school.
[b] Once a month or more.
[c] Percent of respondents answering "Always" or "Usually."

ism was to induce nonmembers to activate a commitment they already had.[16] Two decades later, the problem apparently remains. Whether Conservative Judaism can, in fact, draw these individuals into active participation remains a key question. It presents a particular challenge, since the earlier reservoir of potential members in the Orthodox community has diminished.

THE GEOGRAPHIC FACTOR

An important dynamic of the American population has been its redistribution across the continent. Jews have participated fully in this movement, so that the older areas of Jewish settlement in the northeast and midwest now share more of the Jewish population with the south and west. These major population shifts have involved Jews with certain characteristics, and, in turn, have provided a particular community context within which the Jews settled.[17] The participation of Conservative Jews is reflected in this redistribution, and there are clear regional differences in their characteristics and behavior. The differentials are not only regionwide, but they also often apply to individual communities as well, although the patterns are not as clear for the more specific areas.

Table 2.9
Regional Distribution and Migration Experiences of Conservative Jews

	Northeast	Midwest	South	West	Total Percent
1990 Regional Distribution	44.8	10.2	24.8	20.1	100.0
Lifetime Migration Status					
Nonmigrant	22.7	21.4	5.6	7.2	
Intrastate	37.4	30.9	6.7	18.8	
Interstate	29.4	37.3	77.0	65.5	
International	10.6	10.4	10.8	8.5	
Total Percent	100.0	100.0	100.0	100.0	
Five-Year Migration Status					
(U.S. Born)					
Nonmigrant	81.8	79.0	78.1	73.2	
Intrastate	9.8	10.1	6.3	13.4	
Interstate	8.4	10.9	14.9	12.7	
International	—	—	0.9	0.6	
Total Percent	100.0	100.0	100.0	100.0	

Lifetime migration patterns show the dramatic growth in the population of Conservative Jews living in the South and West. While nine out of ten Conservative Jews living in the Northeast in 1990 were born there, this was true of only one-quarter of the Conservative Jews in the South and one-third of those in the West. The pace of change slowed during 1985–90, with the South and West both showing much greater stability. Nor has migration, either lifetime or over five years, been unidirectional; all regions have participated in exchanges with each other. In the process, regional differences have been heightened.

As a result of these interregional streams, the lifetime and five-year migration experiences of the Conservative Jewish populations in the various regions differ considerably (table 2.9). The Northeast and Midwest have strikingly higher proportions of nonmigrants and intrastate migrants than do the South and West. These two newer regions of settlement, by contrast, include especially high percentages of interstate migrants: two-thirds to three-fourths of their populations were born in a state different from their state of residence in 1990. Not all of this movement was interregional, but such high levels of mobility have certainly contributed to the growth of the South and West.

While the five-year migration rates are much lower than lifetime rates in every region, some regional differences persist. The Northeast contains the most stable Conservative Jews; over eight in ten had not moved between 1985 and 1990. Conservative Jews in the West have clearly been the most mobile. Some one-quarter had changed residence, either within the state or to another state.

Not surprisingly, Conservative Jews in the South include a much higher proportion of elderly than do the other regions (table 2.10). Southern Conserva-

Table 2.10
Socioeconomic Characteristics of Conservative Jews

	Region of Residence			
	Northeast	Midwest	South	West
Age Distribution				
18–44	44.4	50.1	47.5	51.4
45–64	27.3	25.4	13.5	19.2
65 and over	28.3	24.5	39.0	29.4
Total Percent	100.0	100.0	100.0	100.0
Life-Cycle Stage				
Single, under age 45	10.6	8.5	12.2	9.9
Single, age 45+	19.3	10.8	19.4	8.9
Adults only	32.0	45.5	33.4	39.8
Parent(s) with:				
Children under age 15	18.3	26.7	21.5	28.1
Children age 15+ only	19.7	8.6	13.6	13.3
Total Percent	100.0	100.0	100.0	100.0
Marital Status				
Never married	22.2	23.8	17.2	18.1
Married	53.9	64.7	53.3	62.8
Separated/Divorced	9.6	6.7	15.1	8.4
Widowed	14.4	4.8	14.4	10.7
Total Percent	100.0	100.0	100.0	100.0

tive Jews also have an exceptionally high percentage of households consisting of adults only.

Other socioeconomic characteristics do not show a clear relation to region of residence, but some differences are noteworthy. Because of its large numbers of older persons, the South includes a disproportionate number of clerical/sales workers (occupations that are often used to supplement retirement income) and very few in managerial positions. The Midwest, with its relatively young population, has few widowed; a very high proportion in its Conservative population have had postgraduate education (44 percent compared with only about one in four in the other regions); and the Midwest includes a disproportionately high percentage of male professionals and female managers.

In general, the Conservative populations of the Northeast and Midwest are more traditional in their orientation and more strongly Jewishly identified than are those in the South and West (table 2.11). The Jewish Education Index and the Ritual Scale show a clear difference between the older and newer regions of settlement, with more persons in the Northeast and Midwest than in the South and West scoring medium or high on these two indexes. Strikingly fewer in the West also indicate that a Jewish milieu is of importance to them. Intermarriage levels are especially high in the West, where almost one-third report a mixed marriage; below one-fifth do so in the other regions.

Table 2.11
Jewish Identificational Characteristics of Conservative Jews

	Region of Residence			
	Northeast	Midwest	South	West
Index of Jewish Education[a]				
None	18.8	25.3	25.2	28.1
Low	12.8	7.5	12.2	11.2
Medium	32.7	33.0	29.9	29.2
High	35.7	34.3	32.7	31.3
Total Percent	100.0	100.0	100.0	100.0
Ritual Scale[b]				
None	2.0	14.8	7.0	7.2
Low	18.0	7.0	30.5	32.3
Medium	49.8	53.5	39.3	44.6
High	30.2	24.7	23.2	15.9
Total Percent	100.0	100.0	100.0	100.0
Community Involvement				
Belong to Jewish Organization	43.3	47.2	37.8	27.9
Engage in Jewish Voluntarism	22.2	45.5	3.8	16.1
Contribute to Jewish Causes	57.5	61.0	57.7	61.4
Been to Israel	37.1	38.4	42.5	31.2
Jewish Milieu[c]				
Low	22.0	20.0	28.2	44.9
Medium	35.1	49.2	31.6	43.1
High	42.9	30.8	40.3	12.1
Total Percent	100.0	100.0	100.0	100.0
Percent in a Mixed Marriage	19.3	16.3	16.9	31.1

[a] None = No Jewish Education.
Low = 1–2 years of any type school.
Medium = 3 or more years of Sunday school or 3–5 years of supplementary or day school.
High = 6 or more years of supplementary or day school.
[b] The Ritual Index consists of the sum of weighted values for lighting Shabbat and Hanukkah candles, fasting on Yom Kippur, attending a Passover seder, and keeping kosher. A score of 0 = none, 1–4 = low, 5–8 = medium, and 9–16 = high.
[c] Based on responses to questions about number of Jewish friends, Jewish diversity of neighborhood, and importance of living in a Jewish neighborhood.

The west is also noticeable for having fewer than one in three belonging to a Jewish organization and only 16 percent volunteering in a Jewish activity. At the other extreme, almost half of those in the Midwest are members of Jewish organizations and 45 percent volunteer in Jewish activities.

An outstanding exception to the regional split is the percentage contributing to Jewish causes. Only small differences characterize the four regions, and not in the expected direction. Conservative Jews in the West are just as likely as those in the Midwest to contribute; those in the Northeast and South are slightly less likely to do so. Perhaps solicitation methods are equally effective in all regions; perhaps those in the West prefer to show their identification through monetary donations rather than giving of their time or through formal affiliations with the organized Jewish community. It is also possible that giving opportunities within the Jewish community are more varied in the West so as to appeal better to its distinctive population.

THE DYNAMICS OF CHOICE

As we have seen, geographic mobility of the Conservative population has been a prominent factor in determining the current configuration of Conservative Jewry. Other forms of mobility are important as well, in particular the entry and exit of persons into and out of Conservative Judaism. Who is raised a Conservative Jew and remains one throughout his or her lifetime, who joins the movement, and who leaves have a significant impact on the profile of Conservative Jewry.

Because the denominational identification for American Jews is a matter of choice, it is easy for a person to switch out of or into Conservatism or any of the other denominations, or out of any specific denomination altogether. Such changes may be a matter of religious belief, but more often other factors are salient. A switch may occur because one denomination is seen as a more "Americanized" or a more traditional form of religious worship; because only one or two options are available in a given community; because of convenience and proximity of facilities; because of marriage, family, or friendship networks; because switching is seen as part of upward social mobility; or because of a host of other reasons. While NJPS-1990 does not provide information on why denominational change did or did not occur nor on when it occurred, it does allow some measure of that change. Questions asked about the denomination in which the respondent was raised and about current denomination permit us to identify the past denominational identification of persons who reported they were Conservative at the time of the survey and the current denomination (or lack thereof) of respondents who indicated they had been raised as Conservative Jews.

Information on denominational switching shows the fluidity of such identification. At the time of the 1990 survey, an estimated 1.6 million adults identified as Conservative Jews (table 2.12). Of these, some 917,000 reported that they had been raised Conservative and about 651,000 said they had not been raised as Conservative (for some, denomination raised was unknown). Another 728,000 indicated that they had been raised as Conservative but now identified with another denomination or none at all. Thus, there are somewhat fewer persons who were raised non-Conservative and have become Conservative than the number of persons who were raised as Conservative and no longer identify with the denomination.

Examination of the losses and gains shows that the shifts have generally been from the more to the less traditional movements. The vast majority of the

Table 2.12
Denominational Changes of Conservative Jews

	Estimated Population	Percent Distribution of Gain/Loss	Net Gain/Loss
No change	916,770	—	—
To Conservative from raised as:			
Orthodox	492,400	75.6	+477,400
Reform	63,400	9.8	–365,700
"Just Jewish"	23,400	3.6	–59,900
Other	43,700	6.7	–32,600
Non-Jewish	28,000	4.3	–65,100
Total Gain	650,900	100.0	
From raised as Conservative to:			
Orthodox	15,000	2.1	+477,400
Reform	429,100	58.9	–365,700
Reconstructionist	31,100	4.3	–31,100
"Just Jewish"	83,300	11.4	–59,900
Other	76,300	10.5	–32,600
Christian	93,100	12.8	–65,100
Total Loss	727,900	100.0	
Net change			–77,000
Total current			
Conservative population	1,588,100[a]		

[a] Includes some for whom information on denomination raised is unknown.

gains to Conservative Jewry have come from the Orthodox, while the largest losses have been to Reform. The shifting clearly has serious implications for the size of the Conservative movement, since the reservoir of Orthodox Jews, from which so many came into Conservatism, has shrunk sharply and is unlikely to provide the mass of population from which to draw in the future. By contrast, becoming Reform or "just Jewish" or moving out of Judaism altogether, continues to be a viable option. The losses to Conservative Judaism identified as of 1990 may thus continue into the twenty-first century, unless the denomination is able to attract members from other denominations or from among those who have no denominational identity.

The shifts have had a profound impact on the profile of Conservative Jewry at the end of the twentieth century (table 2.13). Because much of the in-switching from Orthodox occurred several decades ago while out-switching to Reform is more recent, Conservative Jewry has become older: the in-switchers are disproportionately age 65 and over and in households without children, while the out-switchers are more likely to be young adults with children under 15. Because of these age differentials and because the in-switchers from Orthodox were more likely to be immigrants or the children of immigrants, those who adopted Conservatism are somewhat less educated than the out-switchers, who are concentrated among the college educated. Differences extend to occupation. Sur-

Table 2.13
Socioeconomic Characteristics of Jews Who Have Changed Denominations

	No Change	To Conservative	From Conservative
Current Age			
18–24	9.3	2.1	4.9
25–34	22.9	10.4	19.9
35–44	26.0	18.8	31.4
45–64	21.8	25.4	28.3
65 and over	20.0	43.3	15.6
Total percent	100.0	100.0	100.0
Life-Cycle Stage			
Single, under age 45	14.5	4.1	6.8
Single, age 45+	11.5	23.5	7.7
Adults only	28.2	40.0	33.6
Parent(s) with:			
Children under age 15	27.1	19.0	34.6
Children age 15+ only	18.7	13.4	17.2
Total Percent	100.0	100.0	100.0
Marital Status			
Never married	25.4	11.1	15.4
Married	52.7	61.3	68.3
Separated/Divorced	12.7	10.1	11.9
Widowed	9.1	17.5	4.4
Total Percent	100.0	100.0	100.0
Education			
High School or less	26.8	34.6	22.6
Some College	44.3	39.9	49.2
Post-graduate	28.9	25.5	28.2
Total Percent	100.0	100.0	100.0
Occupation (of those in labor force)			
Professional	40.6	38.9	34.0
Manager	19.1	15.9	13.4
Clerical/Sales	27.1	35.7	37.4
Blue Collar	13.2	9.5	15.2
Total Percent	100.0	100.0	100.0

prisingly, compared with the lifetime Conservative Jews—the stayers—both in- and out-switchers are heavily concentrated among clerical/sales workers, but probably for somewhat different reasons. The in-switchers may be lower white-collar workers because many are using such jobs to supplement retirement income; the younger out-switchers may still be developing their careers and eventually move to higher-level positions.

The data on intermarriage show that the in-switchers have particularly low levels of mixed marriages, with only 15 percent married to a non-Jewish spouse compared to one-quarter of the stayers. Notably more of the in-switchers are in conversionary marriages than either the stayers or the out-switchers. Of those who left Conservative Judaism, half are married to a non-Jewish spouse, and many of these no longer consider themselves Jewish. Our findings thus suggest

Table 2.14
Selected Jewish Identificational Characteristics of Jews Who Have Changed
Denominations

	No Change	To Conservative	From Conservative
Synagogue Members	38.7	49.3	24.0
Index of Jewish Education[a]			
None	31.9	24.6	33.6
Low	9.6	12.8	15.3
Medium	29.8	28.4	30.9
High	28.7	34.2	20.2
Total Percent	100.0	100.0	100.0
Ritual Scale[b]			
None	11.1	9.2	18.3
Low	27.3	17.3	39.0
Medium	41.0	45.1	34.0
High	20.6	28.4	8.6
Total Percent	100.0	100.0	100.0
Been to Israel	31.1	37.2	24.4
Jewish Milieu[c]			
Low	35.8	25.8	44.6
Medium	35.1	37.6	39.2
High	29.2	36.6	16.1
Total Percent	100.0	100.0	100.0
Percent in a Mixed Marriage	25.9	15.2	50.3[c]

[a] None = No Jewish Education.
   Low = 1–2 years of any type school.
   Medium = 3 or more years of Sunday school or 3–5 years of supplementary or day school.
   High = 6 or more years of supplementary or day school.
[b] The Ritual Index consists of the sum of weighted values for lighting Shabbat and Hanukkah candles,
   fasting on Yom Kippur, attending a Passover seder, and keeping kosher. A score of 0 = none, 1–4 = low,
   5–8 = medium, and 9–16 = high.
[c] Based on responses to questions about number of Jewish friends, Jewish diversity of neighborhood, and
   importance of living in a Jewish neighborhood.
[c] 52 percent of respondents who switched from Conservative and are included in the mixed-married
   category identified as non-Jews at the time of the survey.

that switching is very often related to intermarriage, and quite likely is the direct
result of intermarriage. If intermarriage levels continue at the high levels characteristic of the 1985–90 marriage cohort, then losses can be expected to continue at equally high levels unless some kind of direct and successful intervention
is developed.

Particularly important for the vitality of the movement is the impact that
the shifts have had on those characteristics that relate to Jewish identification
and involvement. Here, the movement has gained persons with higher levels of
Jewish education, ritual index scores, and Jewish milieu scores than were characteristic of those who had been Conservative all their lives (table 2.14). The
Orthodox pool from which so many of those who switched to Conservative Ju-

daism are drawn has clearly had a strong, positive effect on the level of Jewish identity and behavior among Conservative Jews. On the other hand, those switching out of the movement have tended to be less Jewishly educated and to score lower on ritual practices and Jewish milieu.

Persons who switched to Conservatism also have higher levels of household synagogue membership (half are members) than those who have been constantly Conservative (39 percent); the out-switchers are much less likely to belong to affiliated households (only about one-fourth do so). The net result has been to heighten the level of identification of Conservative Jews.

The continuation of the past trend of interdenominational flows into the future is unlikely. Just as American Jewry as a whole can no longer count on transfusions of Yiddishkeit from immigrants, Conservative Jewry can no longer count on large numbers of strongly committed Jews to switch into the movement from the Orthodox. It can, however, expect to continue losing members from among the more peripherally identified. While this would have the effect of continuing to increase the level of commitment of those remaining—if continuing members retain current levels of identification—it would also serve to reduce the size of Conservative Jewry. Such heightened commitment may also occur if Conservative Judaism attracts the more committed persons from less traditional denominations.

Another factor that has slightly affected the pattern of switching and that may have a more profound effect in the future is the growth of Reconstructionist Judaism. No adults in the sample identified as having been raised Reconstructionist, but some 2 percent indicated that they had been raised Conservative and now identify as Reconstructionist. While the numbers switching out of Conservatism to Reconstructionism are thus minimal, these persons are highly selective of the more Jewishly identified. If Reconstructionism continues to grow and the number of persons becoming Reconstructionist increases, their switching may serve to weaken the most committed core of Conservative Jews. The trend needs careful tracking over the next few years.

Entering the Twenty-First Century

The foregoing analysis of the sociodemographic and Jewish characteristics of the Conservative population in 1990 points to several areas that will pose major challenges to the movement in the coming decades. These challenges must be seen within the broad framework of American society and changes in its attitudes toward and acceptance of religious diversity. The changes that occurred from the 1960s through the 1980s have already profoundly affected how individuals relate to religious institutions and how they deal with private expressions of religiosity. Further transformations are inevitable.

At the most basic level, persons who identify themselves as Conservative Jews do not necessarily manifest this denominational identity by being members of households that belong to a Conservative or any other synagogue. That more than half are in unaffiliated households suggests that concerted efforts may be necessary to reach this segment of the population. The reasons for their lack of institutional membership may well be conditioned by factors beyond their control—economic constraints or lack of a Conservative or any other synagogue in the area where they live (especially if they have moved away from centers of Jewish concentration) or by purely personal preferences. Better understanding of the dynamics involved in membership are essential to understanding why so many Conservative Jews do not express their identity through membership and also to designing strategies to attract the unaffiliated and retain current members. The generally low rate of affiliation among Conservative Jews and the selective characteristics of those who belong to synagogues also suggest that relying exclusively on studies of synagogues and their members provides incomplete and possibly biased information about Conservative Jewry as a whole. The data we have analyzed from the 1990 National Jewish Population Survey, encompassing both affiliated and unaffiliated Jews, thus provide important, basic information on Conservative Jewry as a whole and on the differences between members and nonmembers.[18]

Conservative Jews vary widely in their religious practices, despite the overall halakhic positions taken by Conservative Judaism. This "pick and choose" approach to religion resembles that characterizing the general American population and even those Jews identifying as Orthodox. For Conservative Jews, the selectivity of practices may be exacerbated by the very nature of the movement. Conservative congregations have a great deal of autonomy in setting their own practices and formats, albeit within the confines of general Conservative ideology. Conservative congregations can therefore offer many entry points for individuals seeking affiliation. Moreover, since Conservative Judaism is seen as lying between the more traditional Orthodox on the one hand and the more liberal Reform on the other, many Jews may believe that, as Conservatives, they can personally opt toward one side or the other, choosing the practice that suits them best at any given time.

The permeable nature of the lines between the major denominations and the large overlap in practices makes it difficult to define a strictly Conservative position and may thus encourage individual choice. Individuals with widely varying practices and beliefs can feel comfortable within the Conservative movement and can choose to respond to encouragement to be more observant at their own pace or not at all. At the same time, Conservative Judaism may also be attractive to Jews from other denominations or with no denominational identity who are seeking a more structured religious experience than offered by Reform, but who are not generally halakhically observant.

There remains within the Conservative leadership some of the vagueness about matters of ideology that were identified by Sklare as a possible weakness in the 1950s.[19] That the leadership is aware of the inconsistencies between ideology and practice is suggested by efforts to delineate more clearly for Conservative Jews just where Conservative Judaism stands on a wide variety of beliefs and practices, including kashrut and intermarriage. *Emet v'Emunah* was one step in this direction.[20] More recently, in May 1996, the Conservative movement issued a policy statement on intermarriage that clearly delineates the movement's position on that issue. Achieving a balance between the official ideology of the movement and the need and desire to be inclusive of Jews who do not necessarily subscribe to most of the stated positions is a major challenge facing the movement.

Our analysis also makes clear that age is an important factor in determining individual religious behavior. In this respect, the baby-boom generation is of critical importance, most especially because of its size. As the baby-boomers move into middle age and beyond, their influence may have profound effects on the shape and content of Conservative Judaism. Although our analysis has not focused specifically on the baby boomers, we have found that younger Conservative Jews (ages 18–44) show a strong proclivity toward independence and largely avoid any formal affiliation with the organized Jewish community. They also appear to have put increasing emphasis on those rituals that are family oriented and observed only once a year (for example, Hanukkah candles and Passover seder); few keep kosher or observe Shabbat, as indicated by lighting candles. As they age and assume the responsibilities of raising children, their attitudes may change and they may become more involved in Judaic matters. This may be the case especially if they or their children have been exposed to a Conservative day school education and Jewish camping. Since both of these experiences are becoming more prevalent than was true in the past, they may have a strong impact on the future direction of Jewish involvement and identity.

There is little that the Conservative movement or the Jewish community as a whole can do to control the societal forces that have helped shape American Judaism. If large families are widely seen as a detriment to achieving personal life goals, then pro-family programs in the Jewish community will have little effect on raising the birthrate. Nonetheless, family support in the form of available childcare, subsidized Jewish education for children beyond the first child in a family, scholarships for Jewish camps, and Israel incentive programs are all ways in which Conservative congregations can enhance the Jewishness of families.

If economic opportunities shift from one region of the country or from one area to another, most Conservative Jews, like other Jews and Americans generally, will tend to move to the places where they can earn a better livelihood, regardless of the Jewish amenities available in those places. Others will move in search of a more desirable physical environment, motivated by such concerns as climate and ecology. It becomes important, then, for the Conservative movement to be responsive to mobility, at both the individual and the institutional levels. Especially useful would be programs designed to strengthen small and isolated Conservative congregations, as well as to support Jews living in areas where no congregations exist at all. Provision of visiting scholars and educators and dissemination of printed and electronic educational materials (such as video tapes and materials on the internet) are all ways to reach these communities and individuals. Facilitating transfer of membership from one Conservative congregation to another and/or credit for initiation fees would enhance continuation of membership among mobile individuals. Welcome wagons sponsored by Conservative synagogues might also be useful, as would tracking those who move—with the original congregation informing the Conservative congregation(s) at the member's destination that a new Conservative family/individual is arriving, so that contact can be made quickly. A central data bank of members of Conservative congregations might be useful in coordinating such an effort. In this way retention of Conservative Jews would be enhanced, and they would be helped to integrate into their new Jewish community quickly and more fully.

We have seen that in the past decades Conservative Jewry has lost adherents because they have shifted to other denominations, especially to the Reform and Reconstructionist movements, or moved out of Judaism altogether. Some of the losses are attributable to the appeal of less stringent practices and fewer demands on time and lifestyles. Many losses are the result of high levels of intermarriage, especially among the younger segments of the Conservative population. Whether these trends will continue at the same levels into the twenty-first century is difficult to predict. That they are likely to continue at least in the short run is quite probable. The challenge, then, is to develop strategies for intervention.

Some of these strategies have been indicated above. Others might involve concerted efforts to intensify Jewish education at all levels of both formal and informal experiences. The Orthodox emphasis on a vigorous and widespread day school movement serves as one example. Full day school education through the teen years may well help to retain the youth, particularly if it is coupled with stimulating youth group, camping, and Israel experiences. To be successful, however, day school education must also involve the parents. Moreover, since a large segment of Conservative Jewry is unlikely to be able or to want to send their children to day schools, supplementary education must also be improved and synagogue family education programs strengthened. Such efforts are already being made in some locations. Other congregations, including the smaller synagogues away from centers of large Jewish populations, must be encouraged and helped to institute similar programs. The national organizations of the Conservative movement may be especially helpful in this respect.

If the Conservative movement is seeking to retain its members, to strengthen their Jewish identity and commitment to Conservative Judaism, and perhaps to draw in those Jews who identify as Conservative but hold no formal synagogue affiliation, then it must develop programming that can be effective despite trends in the larger society. It must seek to speak to Conservative individuals and families on a personal, meaningful level. A first step toward realization of this goal is to know the characteristics of the constituency. The data from the 1990 National Jewish Population Survey have helped us to do so.

By identifying the sociodemographic and Jewish profile of Conservative Jews in relation to those identifying with other denominations, by recognizing the importance of both age and regional differences, by distinguishing between members and nonmembers, and by examining the dynamics of change within the Conservative population, the important first step has been taken to establish the basis for making informed decisions about planning and programming.

Notes

1. Marshall Sklare, *Conservative Judaism: An American Religious Movement* (New York: Schocken, 1972).
2. Ibid., 252.
3. Jack Wertheimer, *A People Divided: Judaism in Contemporary America* (New York: Basic Books, 1993).
4. Barry A. Kosmin et al., *Highlights of the 1990 CJF National Jewish Population Survey* (New York: Council of Jewish Federations, 1991).
5. The findings of NJPS-1990 often center on the core Jewish population, which is defined as Jews by religion, Jews by choice, or secular Jews (ibid.); here we refer to this population as Jews. Excluded from most of the analyses are those persons included in NJPS-1990 who were of Jewish descent but were not Jewish at the time of the survey; they are included when we discuss denominational switching.
6. The information on household synagogue/temple membership is based on a question that asked whether anyone in the household held such an affiliation. The respondent may thus have lived in a household in which only one individual held a membership or in a household that held a membership as a whole. When we speak of synagogue affiliation, therefore, we are referring to a general context within which the respondent is operating, rather than to membership of a specific individual. Moreover, in our analysis by synagogue membership we do not distinguish between persons who identify as Conservative Jews who indicate Conservative affiliations and those Conservative Jews affiliated with synagogues/temples of other denominations.
7. Sidney Goldstein and Alice Goldstein, *Conservative Jewry in the United States: A Sociodemographic Profile* (New York: Jewish Theological Seminary, 1998).
8. Unlike the data in the other tables on which our discussions are based, the data in table 2.3 include children under age eighteen.

9. As with synagogue/temple membership, many specific ritual practices refer to the household as a whole and not specifically to the respondent. Readers should be aware that the only aspects of ritual practice we discuss that relate directly to the respondent are fasting on Yom Kippur and synagogue attendance. To the extent that household practices set a context, however, particularizing them to individual household members seems justified.

10. Sidney Goldstein and Calvin Goldscheider, *Jewish Americans: Three Generations in a Jewish Community* (Englewood Cliffs, N.J.: Prentice-Hall, 1968).

11. Wertheimer, *A People Divided*.

12. For some analyses, we distinguish between persons age 18–24 and those age 25–44, but the small number of younger persons represented among respondents precludes consistent use of this youngest age category.

13. Completed education was ascertained only for persons over age 25, since many younger persons continue their schooling into their twenties.

14. Data on marital status and intermarriage are not included in the tables presented here.

15. Cf. Sidney Goldstein and Alice Goldstein, *Jews on the Move: Implications for Jewish Identity* (Albany: State University of New York Press, 1996).

16. Sklare, *Conservative Judaism*, 260–261.

17. Goldstein and Goldstein, *Jews on the Move*; Paul Ritterband, "The New Geography of Jews in North America," *New Insights on a Changing Jewish Community*, Occasional Paper No. 2 (New York: North American Jewish Data Bank, Graduate School and University Center, City University of New York, 1986).

18. See also Bernard Lazerwitz, J. Alan Winter, Arnold Dashefsky, and Ephraim Tabory, *Jewish Choices: American Jewish Denominationalism* (Albany: State University of New York Press, 1998).

19. Sklare, *Conservative Judaism*.

20. *Emet v'Emunah* (New York: Jewish Theological Seminary, 1988).

Chapter 3	Holding Firmly with an Open Hand

SAMUEL C. HEILMAN

Life in Two
Conservative Synagogues

1: Prologue

Societies, like lives, contain their own interpretations. One
has only to learn how to gain access to them.

—Clifford Geertz

WHILE MOST of the attention devoted to Conservative Jews in the current large-scale study has been given to counting those nearly 40 percent of American Jews who identify with the movement and surveying a broad array of their opinions and practices, the purpose in these pages is to provide readers with a sense of the inner life, the blood and tissue of Conservative congregations. Toward that end, I chose to enter into that life as a participant-observer, an insider who never quite loses his outsider perspectives even as he shares the view from inside. I expected to discover people whose lives would teach me not only about what they understood to be Conservative Judaism, that denomination that fills the vast middle ground between the traditional and liberal wings of American Jewish life, but also something about how and why they are connected to it. While my initial inclination was to select only one congregation, I was persuaded by the Ratner Center's director that by selecting two congregations I would be able to draw a richer, more textured portrait.

Complicating my plans was the fact that as an observant Jew myself, one who does not drive on Shabbat, I would have to find two synagogues within walking distance of my home. I was indeed fortunate to find two synagogues that I have called "Kehillath Achim" and "Central Synagogue." (All names are fictitious, as are identifying details, in order to ensure anonymity.)

Although I spent more *Shabbatot* at Kehillath Achim because of its greater

95

proximity to my home, I divided my research time primarily in interviews and examinations of weekday life more or less equally between the synagogues. From the summer of 1995 until the late spring of 1996, I spent whatever time allowed at these synagogues. I tried to remain as unobtrusive as possible but always made it clear to whomever I spoke that my interests were ethnographic. And when I stopped the active phase of fieldwork, I continued to receive mailings from the congregations while a number of members expressed the sentiment that my presence was missed.

To be sure, I could have spent much more time in both synagogues, could have written volumes about education, institutional organization, and a variety of programs the congregations sponsored, could have given a greater voice to the rabbis in both synagogues, both of whom were generous with their time and extraordinarily helpful to me, and to the rest of the professional staff. In short, there is more to the story than what is in these pages—but that is always the case in the study of living and vital communities.

My organizing principle has been to offer an interpretive portrait of the synagogue landscape, to reveal something of what Clifford Geertz calls "the socially established structures of meaning,"[1] or how people understand their Jewish lives in the synagogue and the Conservative movement.

More specifically, my ethnography, an account of several parts, is organized as follows. I begin with a brief account of the distinctive features of each synagogue's story, in particular those details that illuminate its collective character. Next, I provide a series of biographies of a sample of members from each congregation. These are the voices of the congregants, covering the spectrum from the most to least active, the young and old, newcomers and veteran members. They offer entrée to the nature of these people's attachments to the synagogue and Conservative Judaism. Finally, I offer a series of thick and detailed interpretive descriptions of a variety of cultural performances, events and activities at which synagogue members reveal themselves to themselves and to the careful observer. These are opportunities to see heaven in a grain of sand, to discover the essence of the culture of Conservative synagogue life in a particular moment. Included here are a board meeting, a synagogue breakfast marking the completion of kaddish recitations, and Shabbatot when children play a prominent part in the services.

The sum of what emerges is one representation of the Conservative synagogue, a depiction meant to be placed on the broad canvas of the larger study, read along with Riv-Ellen Prell's portrait (chapter 6) and the account that emerges from the demographic analysis and surveys that are part of this overall project. What surfaces in these pages is a Conservative Jewry and a synagogue life that have much to teach us.

2: *Central Synagogue: Rebuilding the Congregation*

Driving northward along the verdant county road that passes through some of the wealthiest suburban neighborhoods in the nation, one passes a large private golf course and then the Heavenly Church of God, situated prominently among the many impressive private houses and estates that line the roadway. Just a few tenths of a mile farther along the same road, one finds Central Synagogue, nestled discreetly behind a thick grove of trees.

The congregation has long been an important Jewish presence in the county, tracing its origins to 1907, and has been on this site since 1948, when the Jewish move to suburbia began in earnest. Having survived the struggles during which a more Orthodox element of the congregation left to erect a second synagogue in the community and a more liberal group split off to form a Reform temple, the remaining Conservative Jews experienced some lean years and a dwindling membership. But by 1958, when they celebrated their jubilee and the tenth anniversary of their new building, they had rebuilt and could count a thousand member families. At the time of those celebrations, the congregational rabbi reaffirmed the essential Conservative character of the synagogue, "founded on the conviction that traditional Judaism can function as a vital spiritual force in this country in complete harmony with the best in our American culture." This echoed the charge given the congregation by a visiting rabbi nearly a half century earlier, at the dedication of their very first new building, to be "true to the traditions of their race and the religion of their fathers" and "also never to forget they are American citizens."

From its modest beginnings, the congregation had evolved in its first fifty years from simply being a synagogue to being, as their rabbi put it, the incarnation of "a new concept—so uniquely American—the 'synagogue-center.'" This, he explained, was "a religious institution that serves not only as a House of Worship but also provides a whole complex of programs to meet the needs of every age level of the family—spiritual, educational, cultural, social and recreational." The emphasis on the family is critical, for then as now, it is the family that is a key stimulus for synagogue affiliation and involvement. People attend with their parents (or in remembrance of those parents) or with their children. Indeed, without the family connection, the synagogue often feels empty.

Nearly forty years later, Central Synagogue, the "Temple on the Hill," as some now call it, was still trying to be all these things while remaining "dedicated to the task of 'conserving' and transmitting the high traditions" of Judaism. But in the intervening years, Conservative Judaism, like the population it served, was being transformed. The life of the synagogue, like Conservative Judaism generally, was in the hands of an increasingly American-born and bred membership.

Moreover, the European-born rabbi, a graduate of both Orthodox and

Conservative rabbinical seminaries, who had done so much to shape the character of the synagogue, stepped down in the early 1970s after more than thirty years there. Much had changed, but perhaps nothing more so than the fact that many found life outside the synagogue more engaging, and those who remained inside expressed a growing desire for greater empowerment. One desired area of empowerment related to political matters. As one member recalled, when he first joined about thirty years ago, he was told by one of those who "welcomed him" that a select few members of the synagogue really ran the place. For a time, this was indeed the case. But eventually more and more people who chose to be members wanted a say in what went on in the congregation, a change in the lay power structure. Intertwined with these struggles, moreover, especially in the years of the late 1970s, 1980s, and 1990s were divisions over issues related to the emergent Conservative Jewish trends toward greater gender egalitarianism in matters of religion and public ritual, especially in the synagogue. For traditionalists, giving women the same rights and responsibilities in synagogue life as men was a radical, undesirable break with the past, while for those on the other side it signaled the tearing down of the final obstacle to full participation by all members of the movement. Together, the matters of egalitarianism and a more open synagogue often became articulated as a question of who was for egalitarianism and who opposed it. The struggle was most acute among those who made up the core of regular synagogue attendees, a group that often included the more traditionalist elements of the congregation.

To complicate matters further, congregants became polarized over the person of the rabbi who, in the pulpit for more than twenty years, tried to navigate between the Scylla of the movement's attachment to tradition and the Charybdis of its embrace of change. For some he was all a rabbi should be, while for others he embodied much that was wrong with the congregation. Moreover, adherents of both positions were not happy with the rabbi's handling of the conflict. When his contract came up for renewal, many of these festering divisions in the congregation came to center on whether to reappoint him. Into this mix entered a variety of other unrelated concerns, including the question of whether or not the complex of buildings that for forty years had housed the Temple on the Hill should be redesigned, refurbished, or even torn down and rebuilt. Supporters of the project believed it would signal renewal and change as well as require a significant infusion of funds. But no rebuilding could take place, no new funds successfully gathered, as long as the rifts remained. Again the congregation stagnated and membership rolls dwindled. As it had in its distant past, the synagogue again lost members to other congregations. Gloom, resentment, and demoralization took over.

In the end, the rabbi was given a new contract, which nevertheless led to his imminent retirement. Many members disaffiliated or else diminished their level of synagogue activity, while those who remained resolved to rebuild. A search was on for a new rabbi, and there soon followed a decision to hire a new chief administrator as well.

When the dust settled, the congregation selected the current spiritual leader, an Ivy League graduate who, while an ordained rabbi, had never had a pulpit while pursuing another profession. Now into his forties, he paradoxically still possessed all the enthusiasm of someone in his first pulpit but the maturity of someone who had been out of training for a while. He appeared ready to move the congregation in a new direction.

The new rabbi carefully established himself in what was now a post-conflict, affirmatively egalitarian congregation and helped reshape it in a new and more inclusive image. The lay leadership could now turn its attention to other matters. The person who had served as synagogue administrator had not been performing well in areas such as staffing and billing, so the congregation replaced him on an interim basis with one of its own members. Next, they again took up the plan to refurbish the synagogue building. Together with their new leaders, both spiritual and lay, they were, under the leadership of a woman president, ready to take the Temple on the Hill out of the doldrums and rebuild it yet again.

It was during the early stages of rebuilding and renaissance, after the struggles had been resolved, that I began my visits.

3: Kehillath Achim: The Shul within the Synagogue

Standing atop a grassy hill flanked on the north by a Catholic girls school and on the south by a shopping center, Kehillath Achim synagogue is an imposing structure. This building is not the first home of the congregation, which was founded in 1909 by fifteen men who filed for incorporation as a religious institution; rather, it is its fourth, completed in 1971 but part of a complex constructed over a forty-year period. Marked by a white stone pillar set against a series of high brick walls, on which a golden menorah and an English version of the Ten Commandments are carved in stone, the front of the synagogue building on the main avenue of town is an impressive sight. To enter the world of Kehillath Achim, however, one diverges from the front and follows a small lane between the synagogue and the shopping center and enters a cul-de-sac that leads to glass doors that open on to a large vestibule. Here too, as at Central Synagogue, only the informed can find the way in. Once inside, one may turn one direction and wander past a few glass vitrines that make up the synagogue museum treasury and find one's way into either the main office or beyond it into an older wing, where the three-day-a-week religious school and the high school hold classes. Or, turning left and descending some stairs, one comes upon the nursery school, which serves as a gateway for many who will in time become members but whose initial interest is in a congenial place for their toddlers. Downstairs, the visitor will also find a chapel in which daily services are held, a small synagogue library, several function rooms, another chapel where a junior (youth) congregation holds Shabbat services, and the offices of the rabbi, the cantor, and their administrative assistant.

Should one go up a few stairs from the entry doors, one will come into both the large social hall and the main sanctuary, the two largest rooms in the complex, which are separated by movable walls that can be slid aside to make one huge space. The sanctuary itself, with plush pews, holds about five hundred, but when combined with the social hall it holds more than twice that number. This happens on the High Holidays and other special occasions when especially large crowds attend.

By far, the most dramatic aspect of the sanctuary is its eastern wall, made of what looks like large hewn limestone of the sort used in the Western Wall in the Old City of Jerusalem. Placed among these stones is the holy ark, a modernist-looking design covered by a golden grate; beside the stones are seats for the rabbi, officers, and other notables. Also along the eastern wall is a large stage with two podiums that, in the emergent style of the last twenty years, face the congregation, as well as a table for reading from the torah scrolls that faces east and toward the site of the ancient holy temple in Jerusalem, according to the ancient Jewish custom.

In a sense this combination of the ancient stones with the modernist ark, podiums facing the congregation, and a torah table facing the ark seems to capture an essential goal of this Conservative Jewish synagogue: as the rabbi put it in a letter to his congregation, to "combine the very best of our sacred traditions together with the sensitivities and concerns of modernity."

But the main sanctuary is not the only place of prayer in the synagogue. There are many others. These include the "alternative service" in which worshipers (especially women) are given a greater role in conducting the prayers; the "parallel service," which, in deference to the congregation's traditionalists who object to women on the pulpit, meets on those Shabbatot when a bat mitzvah is being celebrated in the main service; and the "learners' service," where on average twenty people gather to discuss the torah portion or some aspect of prayer and Judaism. Then too there is a youth service, the junior congregation, as well as the occasional special services organized by the synagogue school according to grade.

In a sense the plethora of holy arks throughout the building accommodating the various services held there can be viewed as symbolic of the many sorts of constituencies that coexist at Kehillath Achim. Some might call the synagogue a kind of spiritual supermarket, where every worshiper can find the sort of religious services that fulfill his or her own needs. The rabbi, in that same letter, spoke of this as a congregational principle of "unity in diversity." This value might be said to be central to the congregation's sense of itself.

To some extent, this division into many parts and many Jewish activities allows Kehillath Achim to maintain two, in some ways contradictory, identities. On the one hand, with its eleven hundred member families, Kehillath Achim Synagogue is a large congregation. On the other, with its various services, it allows many of its most active participants to feel they are part of something small, personally tailored to their needs, and intimate.

But there is more to the dualistic character of the synagogue than the building. Despite its ample membership of more than eleven hundred member families, on Shabbat mornings, the largest service of the week, Kehillath Achim is actually attended by a core group of only about two hundred people (about 16 percent of the membership, according to a random survey), who are there at least one Shabbat a month and often more. In a sense, these people constitute a small core congregation, the beating heart of the larger institution. These are the people who make up most of the leadership corps of the larger organization, who shape the character of its social life, and who in concert with the religious and educational staff determine its Jewish orientation. For this core group it is not the many who come a few times a year (and whose dues and financial donations help sustain the large building, staff, and institution) but rather the familiar faces they see and worship with regularly, who serve on its many committees, who are the real Kehillath Achim. Indeed, those who are part of the core often refer to the synagogue as their "shul," a term commonly associated with smaller, more intimate synagogues. Yet these core people who make up the "shul" also recognize that they are part of a larger synagogue that includes many others who will make an appearance only occasionally: on the High Holidays, on special occasions like the anniversary of a kaddish recitation, for a bar or bat mitzvah or some other rite of passage, or for Homecoming Shabbat, when college youngsters return home for Thanksgiving and are invited to play a prominent role in the service, or similarly Teen Shabbat, when high school youngsters lead the services, or one of the special school Shabbat services.

Beyond these passive and largely peripheral members, whose membership is essential to the "largeness" of the institution and whom everyone recognizes to be a legitimate part of the greater congregation, there are also people whose synagogue involvement has been dormant but who become active because of a change in their lives: when their children start nursery or religious school, or when they find themselves facing an empty nest, or when they recite kaddish during their period of mourning. The core is prepared to embrace these returning members. By the same token, there are also people who cease coming regularly when their children are grown and out of the house or when they enter adolescence or go off to college. These adolescents may themselves return after marriage and the onset of parenthood, although often to another congregation wherever they make their lives.

In keeping with the tolerant ethos of Kehillath Achim in particular and Conservative Jewry in general, the inflow and outflow of such people is expected and accepted. In fact, many of the current core members may themselves have had long periods when they were not very involved and understand that it could happen again. As one member put it: "There is a life-cycle character to involvement."

4: This Is Who We Are

BIOGRAPHY AND OUTLOOK ON LIFE AS A MEANS OF DISCOVERING CONSERVATIVE JEWRY

Thus far, the focus has been on the congregations and the central themes of their identity: rebuilding a congregation in the case of Central Synagogue and finding unity in diversity in the case of Kehillath Achim. But the blood and tissue of those congregations are their people, who they are and how they have come to be the Jews they are. It is therefore to them that we turn next.

In his classic exposition of the "several ways in which the organized life of man can be viewed and understood," Robert Redfield has suggested that one useful approach involves the examination of a "typical biography."[2] This approach recognizes that while "particular men and women come and go, and make life's passage in varying ways," nevertheless, "in any stable community there is a characteristic passage."[3] The ethnographer's role is thus to present "what is general and characteristic about these life experiences" and thereby to make the character of the community visible and comprehensible through the life of its members.[4] In a sense, the synagogues I have observed constitute a sort of stable little community, and the particular biographies that follow provide some insight into what they are about.

Asking members to provide a narrative account of how their lives brought them to the synagogues, I was able to explore (both in individual interviews and as part of focus groups of six or seven people, sometimes in the synagogue and sometimes at people's homes) the meaning that both the synagogue and Conservative Judaism had for them, how and why both attracted them, and what about both or either continued to hold their allegiance. Often, the narratives reveal how the synagogue either nurtures and furthers religious commitments or how it undermines them. In some accounts these understandings remain implicit; in others they are an explicit aspect of the telling.

To be sure, there are some risks. As Redfield reminds us, "If the native is induced to sit and reflect, if he finds it interesting to arrange his thoughts so as to communicate them to someone, perhaps an ethnologist, the structure of the world view grows and develops."[5] Certainly that happened here. Indeed, sometimes my conversations with members made explicit matters that until then remained implicit or hidden. As anthropologist Renato Rosaldo has correctly observed, "Stories often shape, rather than simply reflect, human conduct."[6] Some people, a bit reticent at first, ended up going on and on, stretching the interview to twice or even three times its projected length. Others, after reflection, called me at home to add to their interview. Still others, at the end of a long evening of talk, followed me to the parking lot to share more in the privacy of darkness. Many claimed to find the very act of such review "moving and fascinating." And in the focus groups of six or seven, people were so engaged by the narratives of their fellow congregants (often people whom they did not know well) that the sessions went on late into the night.

Some of these meanings that the synagogue and Conservative Jewry had for the people I talked to had changed in the course of their lives. Sometimes they changed because the people changed; sometimes they were recast because the synagogue or the character of Conservative Judaism changed. As Redfield reminds us: "To tell of a human life and its development it is necessary to tell of the changing states of mind of the person who lives that life."[7]

Those changing states of mind encompass what Redfield called "an outlook on life." Hence the pages that follow offer not only "objective details" of typical biographies but also present "subjective details." Arguing for the ethnographic examination of such states of mind or outlooks on life, Redfield suggested that only after one has seen life "from the native's point of view may the investigator change his viewpoint" and then observe and understand "according to the demands of a more detached and abstract understanding."[8] In other words, the ethnographer must understand the insider-native's point of view before he or she can formulate a more informed outsider's understanding.

"The outlook on life," Redfield concludes, "is one dimension of the common human"—with the biography, a sort of nodal point in the group personality.[9] In their book on American religious congregations, James Wind and James Lewis apply this insight: "Congregations should be viewed as human . . . entities," breathing with "memory, interpretation, understanding, belief, and action."[10] One might argue further that it is the individual members of those congregations whose memories, interpretations, understandings, beliefs, and actions make the congregation the human entity it is. What better way to discover this than through their biographies, which provide, in Stephen Warner's words, "the personal element that gives congregations their rich, many-layered, and emotion-laden texture."[11]

The aim in the sketches that follow is to provide for that opportunity. By framing and editing them, by juxtaposing and glossing them, they become more than repetitions of conversations; they become ethnographically descriptive.

They become Conservative Judaism, "as felt," experienced, "good or bad, desirable or not to be desired" by the people of the congregations studied.[12]

By choosing a variety of narratives one perceives the synagogue from a variety of perspectives: those of the young and the old, those of people who grew up in the movement and of people who came to it (or even Judaism itself) later in life. They are the stories of those who are active in synagogue life and those who are not, stories of men and women, stories of people who have raised their children and of people who are about to do so. Indeed, the synagogue is not any one thing; it is as diverse as these members.

One final personal note by way of introduction. When I was in the midst of the fieldwork the narrative thread was not always apparent to me. Rather, the analytic framework for a set of stories "[made] sense only after the fact."[13] Hence the patterns and themes that emerge from all these biographies and associated outlooks on Conservative Jewish life only became discernible for me in the course of actually writing this ethnography. Moreover, readers may discern even more than this observer was able to see. But that is precisely what ethnography is meant to facilitate: to give readers a chance to look over the researcher's shoulder and sometimes see even further into the field.

THE PEOPLE OF CENTRAL SYNAGOGUE

While it is difficult to capture the character of a congregation or community in a few words, there are nevertheless repeated phrases and conceptualizations that offer a key to unlocking the way its members perceive Central Synagogue. Stephen Q., both a long-time synagogue member and a trained social scientist, provided insights that ring true. For Stephen, the Central Synagogue and Conservative Judaism were largely identical. He saw in both the capacity for "holding firmly with an open hand"—by which he meant that his synagogue and the kind of Judaism it sustained provided people simultaneously with a strong sense of being held to something concrete and with a great deal of freedom to move away and broadly interpret the nature of their attachments and commitments. Put differently, both the synagogue and the movement created an environment where people could feel "comfortable" rather than constrained about the way they did or did not practice being Jewish. They were free to be inconsistent in their Jewish lives if they wanted to be. They could guiltlessly diverge from ideological boundaries set either by the movement or the rabbi. They were offered the opportunity for Jewish growth, even if that happened in irregular spurts. They could feel good about their level of commitments, without regard to the level of those commitments. And however they chose, their affiliation and belonging were never questioned.

After a long period of *Sturm und Drang*, of struggles over what it would allow in Jewish and institutional norms, Central Synagogue was now a revitalized congregation at ease with itself. It no longer looked upon its staff as employees or its officers as *machers*, that is, the only ones empowered to make decisions. Many of the hard-liners and those with the *macher* mentality had left. There was a new rabbi who was at once a dedicated Jew and scholar, yet who was comfortable with those who were far less Jewishly engaged or dedicated, even as he encouraged them to do more. Old and new members looked upon one another as friends and shared a common and generally egalitarian community. The emphasis was on a community rebuilding itself with a maximum of tolerance. As Stephen put it: "Most of the people in this congregation do not feel that they're bad Jews or bad Conservative Jews if they're not doing everything. . . . There's a sense in which this is their place, and these are their friends. You flow in and flow out."

The congregation and Conservative Judaism had their syncopated rhythms. Episodic engagement was all right: do what you will and what you can; you shall be welcome. At the same time, of course, intensive commitment was also encouraged, but it was its own reward. This was not a Reform temple; the congregation could count on the fact that its members, or at least a significant number of them, would always do something strongly linked to the tradition. And they would try to see to it that their children continued and maintained that same sort of Judaism. These values revealed themselves in the story lines of the congregants.

ELIOT F.: AN ADULT EMBRACE OF CONSERVATIVE SYNAGOGUE LIFE

Now in his sixties, Eliot F. is a former synagogue officer and a member of Central Synagogue for twenty-two years. Among his special interests is Civil War history and along his den wall is his impressive collection of vintage rifles and pistols. But Eliot is also a man whose passions are Jewish. Although he remains active and successful in his business, the synagogue which once took up most of his energy and public time still occupies a large place in his life. He attends Shabbat services regularly, participates actively in board meetings, and is now helping plan the synagogue's restoration. Most of Eliot's friends and certainly his closest friends are from the congregation. By his own admission, he could not now imagine belonging to any other congregation or religious movement. But Eliot was not always so caught up in Conservative synagogue life.

With roots that go back to Austrian Jewry (although his father was already American-born), Eliot grew up in a well-to-do Long Island family that was affiliated with large, well-known Reform temples. Although he celebrated his bar mitzvah, he did not receive much in the way of Jewish education ("I went to Hebrew school for too long") or acquire anything more than the most rudimentary of childhood attachments to his Judaism or the Jewish community. Indeed, in 1946, at a time when the world was just beginning to recognize the enormity

of the Holocaust and on the eve of Israel's independence ("If I ever meet my
late father [again], I'll ask him why he didn't tell me about Israel and the Holocaust"), Eliot's parents chose to send him to a Christian boarding school. To be
sure, he was not the only Jew at this prep school. At least "9.8 percent of the
students, never 10.1 percent," were Jews. It was a place where anti-Semitism
was endemic, such that Eliot tended to downplay his Jewish attachment, even
going so far as to wear a crucifix and agreeing on a number of occasions to lead
the obligatory chapel sessions. As Eliot sums up the experience: "It was a very
good education; it was a very difficult environment to be in."

Still, the school helped lead him to his next stop: Yale University. The Yale
of Eliot's education was institutionally resistant to Jewish admission and barely
tolerant of Jewish life. For the most part this did not seem to bother Eliot, who
was not looking for Jewish connections at college. Indeed, the only positive,
vaguely Jewish experience that made an impression during his beloved Yale years
was a talk by the social historian Will Herberg, author of the then-popular book
Protestant, Catholic, Jew.

Following Yale, Eliot joined the United States Navy because of the Korean
War. Here too his Jewish connections were tenuous. He recalls celebrating Passover, or at least attending a seder, in Cannes, France. And he remembers a curious encounter with a French bar girl who asked him if he was a Jew (he still
marvels over the fact that she picked him out, especially given his socialization
and ability to pass as a nonaffiliated American, to say nothing of his uniform).
When he admitted his Jewish identity, she took him to the back of the bar and
showed him a little packet of soil from Israel that she was saving. "It was her
dream that when she finished being a bar girl to go and make aliya to Israel."
This encounter and the girl's Jewish aspirations so impressed him that he took
a bit of the earth and mailed the packet along with a long letter in which he
expressed his Jewish sentiments to his family's congregational rabbi on Long
Island.

Eliot married after leaving the navy. His wife, Irma, came from a not terribly active Reform Jewish New York background. When they had children, they
followed the family pattern and joined a small Reform temple in their city neighborhood, though their involvement in synagogue life mirrored the limited sort
of attachments their parents had made: "We wandered in and out." Throughout much of their children's youth, even when they moved to the suburbs, Eliot
and his wife remained loosely affiliated with a series of Reform temples, primarily to meet people like themselves. For High Holidays Eliot and his young family would return to Long Island.

An avid reader, Eliot had been swept up by Leon Uris's novel *Exodus.* No
sooner had he completed reading the book in 1964 than he decided to make
his first trip to Israel. His Jewish consciousness awakened, he resolved to

strengthen his Jewish connections. Unfortunately the nearby Reform temple, whose rabbi was the son-in-law of Eliot's parents' rabbi on Long Island, was not taking new members, as its religious school could not accept any more students. Eliot and his wife decided to join another Reform temple a bit farther away, but they would much have preferred something in their neighborhood.

This Reform congregation did not answer Eliot's growing Jewish interests, but Shlomo Bardin, founder of the Brandeis Institute in California, an early Jewish outreach organization, did. A friend had urged Eliot to meet with Bardin, who happened to be visiting the area. Bardin and the Judaism he promoted fascinated Eliot, even though, as Eliot explained, "He had a very great failing; he spoke with a Yiddish accent, and I spent my whole life running away from that and looking down at people like that."

Bardin persuaded Eliot and his wife to visit his institute, and they found it very attractive. Indeed, they would return many times. Eliot explained that he learned from Bardin "that we were the people of the book, and that placed the torah in some framework for me that it never was, and that Judaism was for adults."

Adulthood was very much on his mind then. Not only were his three daughters growing up, but he had just lost his father. It was a time to make some mature religious choices, to move beyond his childhood Judaism. Eliot became more active in the Reform temple and was put on the ritual committee. Although his ritual synagogue skills were limited, he nevertheless worked at involving himself and considered it a great achievement to author a "creative service" commemorating the deliverance from the Holocaust of the Jews of Denmark.

He was perplexed to discover, however, that while everyone loved the service, they wondered why it had included a reading from the torah, which they found "most boring." Having just returned from Bardin with the idea that torah was specifically what kept the Jews alive, this reaction suddenly alienated Eliot from his fellow Reform Jews.

Around this time, someone took him for a Simchat Torah service at the nearby Conservative congregation, Central Synagogue. He found to his surprise that he was "very moved" by what he considered to be an "adult service," and the rabbi and cantor struck him as "real, legitimate educated men." With his wife's acquiescence, they joined this synagogue. The time was right. His middle daughter was near bat mitzvah age and expressed an interest in having such a celebration (his oldest daughter had had none in the Reform temple). Central Synagogue arranged for her to be tutored and "brought up to speed," a commitment that solidified the family's attachment to this new congregation. (For this daughter, who later would become the first Judaic studies major at Yale, this family move and the Jewish education that came with it obviously had long-term positive Jewish consequences.)

With this affiliational change, Eliot's family, like him, gradually expanded their Jewish commitments. They increased their Shabbat observance, attending Shabbat services and especially staying home on Friday nights, lighting candles, and "making Shabbat." Additionally, Eliot went to the cantor to learn about the Hebrew prayer book, attended some of the rabbi's classes, and read more on matters Jewish. He and Irma began reciting an increasing number of prayers in Hebrew, which they came to prefer to the Reform English service. As Irma put it: "Now when we go to a bar mitzvah or something at a Reform temple I think, 'My goodness, all this English, and there's no feeling here, and it's not authentic.'" In time, they simply no longer thought of themselves as Reform Jews. So they made the move emotionally and socially to embrace a Conservative Jewish identity.

"We stumbled along, and the kids too," Eliot explained. Eliot and his family tried to make "Shabbat fun." They invited many of their children's friends for a meal and "we would sing." To be sure, it was hard for him as an adult to get fully "up to speed," as he put it, much harder than for his younger daughters who were growing up with this level of observance. Even the recitation of grace after meals remained difficult: "I can't do it all," Eliot said, "but I can do about 70 percent of it." But that was an enormous leap forward for the young prep school student who once wore a crucifix and led chapel services. This more active Judaism became a permanent part of Eliot's life. "And that became our routine; we've kept it up. We've done it on boats in New York harbor; we've done it at the ski place, wherever we go."

In the meantime, Central Synagogue also took on a larger role in the family's life. "I liked the people; I liked the service." The rabbi even asked him to occasionally speak from the pulpit: at last, Eliot was leading the service in his own Jewish chapel. He wanted to "touch" his fellow Jews as he himself had been touched.

Eliot was ready to soak up all the Judaism he could. As a "seeker," he found many a rabbi ready to reach out to him. Some were Orthodox, and he established warm and supportive ties with them. But in the end, the Conservative movement, with its Jews in the center, in place between the extremes, was where he felt most "comfortable." It was most "authentic," attuned to the contemporary Jewish experience, and solidly in the Jewish mainstream:

> I think the majority of Jews are Conservative Jews; I think the majority
> of Jews have lived somewhere in the middle, whatever they've said to
> themselves. They weren't hasids way out here with their *shtreimels* and
> they weren't the super-liberals who weren't doing anything. They were
> somewhere, finding themselves in the middle. I think Conservative
> Judaism tries to move tradition forward; it's not frozen. It wrestles with
> tradition, and I like that wrestling. I don't always like what happens or

doesn't happen, that it's not fast enough or slow enough; but I like the fact that it wrestles with tradition. And finally that it tries to be historically accurate. It tries to look at the reality of the Jewish experience.

To this his wife added: "I just feel comfortable with it now, to me it makes sense and it feels right. I think we've imbued our children's lives with it, and I can't imagine anything else."

Still, for Eliot and Irma, this commitment and the identification of Judaism and synagogue life with family life had limitations. After their children left the house, they dropped some rituals and involvements, for example, building a sukkah. As he explained, after the children moved away, "It lost its charm." And he increasingly found "the High Holidays burdensome; they're long and repetitive," although he still celebrated them. Yet other practices continued: Hanukkah remained his "favorite holiday."

Moreover Eliot and Irma were never interested in keeping kosher. "We don't think Conservative Judaism demands that. I think we can be good Conservative Jews the way we are." Yes, they knew their rabbi would not agree with that judgment, but they believed that Conservative Judaism allowed them to make choices about which commitments to embrace. "Judaism should survive . . . and kosher is part of that—not all but part of that." Eliot and Irma simply did not choose that particular part. Besides, Eliot was convinced that in fact the price of kosher food was "an outrageous rip-off." He was fighting back by not keeping kosher.

As for the formal commitment that Conservative Judaism had to halakha (Jewish law) more generally, Eliot was by no means opposed to it. But for him, "every Jew has to find out where they are and who they are." The contemporary American ideal of personal choice was sacrosanct.

Eliot and Irma's personal religious commitments could be minimal. Thus, for example, as Irma explained, on the eve of a weekend ski trip to Utah: "We do Shabbat on Friday nights wherever we are. . . . We take time out. We're going to Utah. Friday night we'll be in a restaurant somewhere; we will have stopped a moment—sometimes I even take candles, if I remember—we will stop with our friends and our daughter and we will say, 'it's Shabbat,' even though Saturday morning, we'll go skiing." Half giggling, and perhaps aware of how this decision to ski on Shabbat might appear inconsistent with Jewish commitment, Eliot explained, "For what it costs, we'll go skiing." Later he would add that skiing, and the great awe of God's nature that it inspires, is for him a religious experience. He also admitted: "I know it's inconsistent," and then repeated his mantra: "Every Jew has to find out where they are and who they are."

That kind of tolerant, live-and-let-live attitude that allowed him to live with contradiction was something he and his wife appreciated about the movement and particularly about their synagogue. He quoted Bardin: "There are 613 commandments; find one and begin." He was an adult Jew, and that is what he did, even if it left him significantly short of 613. Not that Eliot and his wife were unwilling to do what was required of them as Conservative Jews. As Irma articulated it: "If someone said to me, 'You can't be Conservative unless you're kosher,' then I would be kosher. But I don't think that's what they say." Eliot agreed. Indeed, the people they found in the Conservative movement and their synagogue were ready to accept them exactly as they were. And that was just the way they wanted it.

Although Eliot was happy with his Conservative Judaism, there were still some spiritual matters with which he was not completely at ease. God was one of them. Asked if he believed in God, Eliot answered, "Oh, that's a bad question. . . . I don't know," and concluded vaguely, "God figures in my life." Irma was more direct: "I don't believe there's a God." Yet this did not keep her from the synagogue: "I go to synagogue because it's uplifting. I like the people; I like the music; I like the rabbi."

Yet when Irma prayed she claimed, "I don't believe anyone's listening; it's comforting but I don't think anyone's answering me." This was not all that far from Eliot's attitude: "I do not believe in the world-to-come; I do not believe that life goes on. I'd like to; it would be nice, but I just don't believe it." He added: "I don't believe God answers penitential prayer; I can't do that after the Holocaust. I just don't believe in it. But I pray anyhow, 'cause it can't hurt."

These theological matters were not at the heart of Eliot's Conservative Judaism. The synagogue was. "The synagogue brought me a long way," he says. Perhaps that is why so much of his Jewish life these days has to do with rebuilding and sustaining Central Synagogue. He had already helped lead the institution following the difficult and sometimes divisive transition to egalitarianism, whereby men and women were afforded equal rites and obligations in line with the Conservative movement's changing ideology, and he had helped the move from one rabbi to another. Now he turned his attention to rebuilding. As he put it, speaking for the planning committee, during a board meeting considering plans for the building's renovation: "We need your help. We need your support, and we want you to feel the same sense of being involved as we do."

This was not always easy because, as he saw it, for many Jews, "synagogues are like hospitals. People come for crisis management. And when they have a crisis, you have to stop everything for them. Death in the family. Rabbi has to stop everything, boom." But though many people count on their synagogue and rabbi to be there for them, "when you ask something from them, they think it's too much to ask."

Eliot and Irma, by contrast, worked tirelessly for the synagogue. As Eliot explained, his motives were not just local. "Synagogue is community. We have to rebuild the synagogue in America if we're going to rebuild the community.

Israel and bonds and everybody else can't siphon our money and everything else and take it all away from us. If we don't have synagogues and communities, we're going to suffer." That's why the synagogue "is my thing."

Indeed, the measure by which Eliot would evaluate a synagogue is whether or not it succeeds in producing a warm caring community, collecting money and producing actively engaged Jews. Aware that a majority of the members do not attend the synagogue regularly, he believed, "it would be good for them and good for us if they came a bit more frequently." But neither he nor his wife would ever say this to such people; "You don't want to make them feel guilty. . . . You have to tell them what they're missing."

In sum, Eliot concluded: "The American Jewish community needs the synagogue more than we need them. The people we're trying to seduce to come in—they need us."

SHERRY H.: FROM CONSERVATIVE CATHOLIC TO CONSERVATIVE JEW

An attorney in her thirties, married to another attorney, and mother of three children under ten, Sherry H., trim and professional looking, has been a member of Central Synagogue for about five years. She and her husband, Danny, are strongly committed to the synagogue and to the Conservative movement. He is active on the board of the synagogue school to which they send their children. Two years ago when they moved to the large house in which they now live, they decided, at Sherry's urging, to make their kitchen kosher, something that both view as a major Jewish commitment and that Sherry describes as a most difficult adjustment, "because I entertain a lot and it's very hard when you have people over and they can't bring food; it makes them feel bad. And it's also a tremendous amount of work. I have friends over all the time."

For Sherry, the sort of Jewish life that she has embraced and its commitments seem ironic. Yes, she grew up in a "religious home," but the religion was Catholicism. That she now has a religious Jewish home is at once both a continuity and a discontinuity with her past.

To be sure, even as a Catholic Sherry was not altogether unrelated to Jews. Her paternal grandfather (who died when she was very young) was a Jew, a fact she grew up knowing. So, like her Catholic grandmother, Sherry too had married a Jew. But unlike her grandmother, when Sherry married *her* Jewish husband, nearly fifteen years ago, she decided to convert to Judaism.

While Sherry admitted feeling a powerful commitment to her Judaism, that attraction did not come out of nowhere or even out of some lifelong spiritual seeking. Rather, when asked why she had converted, she replied: "I certainly wouldn't have considered it if it hadn't been for Danny."

Sherry's transition to Judaism was not without difficulties. For starters, her Catholic family was not happy about her conversion. ("But they really do love

Danny and it's been a long time anyway. They've made peace with it, but they don't love it.") Then there was the matter of ritual. She always liked ritual, but in Judaism, as she discovered, "The rituals are very different."

However, after fifteen years, the last two of which she has kept a kosher home, she felt herself personally committed to and engaged by her Judaism. There was something in her Judaism that resonated from her upbringing, the idea of "religion being a very important part of life." She found that for all the difference there was also something comfortably familiar in the framework of practicing a religion, home rituals, and the family, like going to the synagogue and sitting together: it fostered "a very strong connection to family."

Now that Sherry was Jewish, she was no longer troubled by some of the theological problems she had while growing up in the Catholic Church: "Views on abortion, and women in the Church, and papal infallibility. I never really bought that stuff." As for synagogues, she said, "I wouldn't consider joining a synagogue where women aren't given the same opportunity to pray publicly as the men, which is why I have a lot of trouble with the Orthodox movement."

Instead, she had to come to terms with Judaism's demands, as she understood them. "Obviously there are rules, but I decide for myself in a way whether or not I'm fulfilling my obligations as a Jew. I don't like the idea of a person telling me that they've got the rules. It's no surprise that so many Jewish people are lawyers. I mean, you know, the torah is basically arguing every issue in the world, and so I feel comfortable in that."

As Sherry saw it, she had become, in particular, a Conservative Jew, following her husband's affiliation. Even before her children were born, while she and her husband still lived in the city, they had been members of a revitalized Conservative synagogue on the Upper West Side of Manhattan. There Sherry, newly Jewish, had absorbed some of the ethos and worldview of a young and activist Conservative Jewry, many of whose members became her friends. "I've certainly been to Orthodox synagogues; I'm not at all comfortable in them. And I've been to Reform synagogues, and I feel like I'm in church. . . . I suppose the reason I feel more comfortable [in Conservative Judaism] is because that's just my experience."

No less than with her conversion, her attachment to Conservative Judaism was neither automatic nor lacking in personal commitment. It was a combination of both. Although she had come in through an accident of marriage, she had over time made Conservative Judaism her own through conscious and deliberate choices. Indeed, in talking of these, she sounded not unlike her Jewish peers in the synagogue who had also made their Conservative Judaism a matter of choice rather than fate. She was under no illusions, however. She realized that her brand of Conservative Judaism might fall short of the ideal: "Certainly there is an agenda in Conservative Judaism, and there are things you theoretically do as a Conservative Jew, and I obviously don't do all of them," she admitted candidly. But even though she was certain that the Jewish Theological Seminary of America, where the movement trained its rabbis, "would not agree with my choices," nevertheless, "I feel comfortable choosing to do what I want to do." Then she added: "Judaism is significantly different [from] any Christian or any other religion. And I think in many ways it's more difficult. You need to find your own comfort. . . . You have to do the organizing yourself."

Sherry had learned well the lay of the Jewish landscape and knew that, for example, one could even go into an Orthodox synagogue (where the claims of Jewish law are presumably maximal) and find many who do not follow all the laws to which Orthodoxy is nominally committed. Yet these people, some of whom she saw when she visited her sister-in-law's Orthodox congregation, still call themselves "Orthodox" or feel comfortable worshiping in an Orthodox synagogue. So yes, she admitted, people "could look at me and say 'she doesn't keep Shabbat, doesn't go to a mikvah,' I mean you could find plenty of things we don't do. But, if you talk to my kids, you would be absolutely certain that they feel Jewish and that they know that. And I would be surprised if they don't continue that as they get older. Her children's explorations of their Jewish identity were, she asserted, "important"; they were of course confirmation of her own successful transition to a Jewish identity.

And then, she and her family moved to the suburbs. But by now, she looked at the prospect of the move through the prism of her Jewish identity. "We wouldn't move to a place where there wasn't a Conservative synagogue."

When they first moved to their current home, Sherry and her husband affiliated with the Conservative synagogue a few towns over. But that turned out to be too far away, or perhaps it was because, as she put it, "the congregation didn't reach out to us." And so, "we never made connections there." Another nearby Conservative synagogue was in her judgment "hostile to women," not committed to egalitarianism. That was unacceptable. And although she sent her children to a Reform temple's nursery school that she liked, the synagogue turned her off. "It was all in English. The rabbi was kind of boring. The level of observance among the people there wasn't very good." At last she and her husband came to Central Synagogue just at the time it was rebuilding itself and found that the people "reached out" to her husband "the first time he walked in." So they affiliated.

Whenever possible, Sherry tried to get to Shabbat morning services. She also wanted to get more involved in synagogue life because of her children. But for all her intentions, getting to services was not easy. Paradoxically, the same children who enhanced her desire to go were also, in many ways, the greatest obstacle to her becoming more engaged. "I think the services are really long in terms of children; I have problems with that. That's why [I don't go on a regular basis]. It's really hard with the kids, but when I *do* get a chance to go, I enjoy it."

The fact was, as she admitted, her children often give her and her husband "a hard time about going," but she believed that "once they're there they enjoy it." For the present, she could report that "the ten-year-old is awfully good at prayer; the eight-year-old is fine." But bringing her hyperactive five-year-old just would not allow her to participate: she or her husband has to spend most of the time in the hall with him. Still, the decision to go was not the children's to make: "They have to go. They don't get a vote."

The votes were Sherry's and her husband's. Yet here too there were difficulties. Speaking of her husband, she explained: "He works probably eighty hours a week. He's very involved in the synagogue and how to get things done for it. He's very exhausted at the end of the week. It is a major fight to get [the children] out of the house and to the synagogue, and he doesn't want to spend his life fighting." Weekends were, after all, busy times, between birthday parties and business obligations. So her husband wanted and deserved "a little bit of a break." Synagogue services were not that break. "We're not great at this," she concluded, almost reflectively. "I would like to go to the synagogue and get through some of the service; that would be nice. I find comfort in going to synagogue when I get to do it. You know, I like praying. And also I have a lot of friends there." But it just did not work out often enough. And if they failed to go to the synagogue on Saturday morning, she admitted with a half shrug, "We don't do anything Jewish Saturday morning."

Sherry was nonetheless ready to make some serious ongoing commitments. She fasted on Yom Kippur and lit candles every Friday night, and the family recited the Shabbat kiddush. She had tried to learn Hebrew and would try again. Yet perhaps foremost in her mind among her Jewish commitments (and almost the first thing she revealed about herself after talking about her conversion) was her decision to make her home kosher. Even her husband had been reluctant to take on this commitment. "When we first got married, he would have liked to have a kosher home, but I was not ready for that. But then *I* did it; I made him change." And, she added, her husband "supported the change." This act of commitment put her, she felt, among the more ritually observant in the congregation. As a result, ironically, a number of her friends thought she was Orthodox which, she hastened to point out repeatedly, "I'm not."

So why did she make her kitchen kosher? Her answer reflected a common theme among many of the members of the synagogues: she did it for her children, to remind them they were Jews "and teach them a way of life." And as already noted, when they acted or thought like Jews, they confirmed her identity as a successful Jewish parent. "I mean, they know they're Jewish—don't misunderstand me. I just think it like puts it in a block." That block was necessary, she believed, not simply because America was out there, somehow capable of eroding their Jewish commitments and attachments. It was especially necessary, she believed, because of who she was. "I'm very close to my family. You should hear what goes on at Christmas when they're talking to their cousins, my nieces and nephews. So they need a reminder." And keeping kosher was that reminder that they were Jews.

Yet Sherry's kosher commitment was limited to the house, to her kitchen. When they left home, they left the demands of kosher behind. "There are only so many stands I can make," she explained. She realized this life pattern put her at odds with the formal demands of Conservative Judaism. Still, as she asserted, moving toward complete kashrut "is not one of my goals at the moment." Where did all this put Sherry in comparison with others in the congregation? She didn't know how many kept a kosher home, but supposed relatively few. Yet there were many more who went to Shabbat services more than her. "So you tell me who's more religious," she concluded.

As much as Sherry and her husband tried to do to involve their children Jewishly, there was one real obstacle to a greater engagement on their part: Jewish education. Like many families taking a journey toward Judaism when their children were young, Sherry and her husband never thought about giving their young children anything beyond a synagogue-school Jewish education. They assumed it would be adequate. Moreover, they felt strongly about the need for a good secular education and had moved to this suburb because of its superior public schools. They had never given any thought to the alternative of a Jewish day school.

"We live in the United States of America. This is a secular society. The reason that we originally decided to send our children to a public school—and we both know a lot about day schools and religious schools and secular education as well—is because this is the world they will function in, and it is a superior secular education." Later she added that she thought that their going to a day school "would not have made them better Jews; it would just have made their lives less complicated."

However, as Sherry's and her husband's Jewish engagement and awareness grew, they became concerned that their children were "not learning enough." That was one of the reasons her husband became active on the synagogue school board. While she wanted her children to get more Jewish learning, she could not see how to do it. "There's certainly no more time in the day," as she put it. Her children were already "under a lot of pressure" in school, and they were involved in sports.

She looked at the Schechter Day School that some of her friends had selected for their children. It was a successful, over-enrolled school. The only way to get in was to start in kindergarten, an option her two older children had missed. "If I had it to do over again, I would definitely send them to a day school, but I can't do it now."

The summer might be a time to help them make up some of what they had missed, but the Conservative movement's Camp Ramah was out; her husband had once had a bad experience there and did not want to send their children. Besides, Sherry added, "the lack of sports and crowded bunks" that she believed was the Ramah experience ruled it out. She and her husband agreed camp should above all else be fun. "In the summer, they just cool out."

Bar and bat mitzvah remained on the horizon. After that rite of passage, however, Sherry would no longer make her children continue their Jewish education, even though she fully expected to remain a member of the congregation and hoped that her children would go to services with her and her husband. "I will not make them go to Hebrew high school."

Clearly her commitment to Jewish education was qualitatively different from her attachment to secular education. Almost wistfully, seemingly as an afterthought, Sherry added, "My guess is, it wouldn't surprise me if [my eldest daughter] decides to go on to some sort of Hebrew high school." And several months afterward, Sherry expressed second thoughts about her educational decisions, asserting her children would indeed go to the Hebrew high school; clearly her Jewish commitments were continuing to evolve and develop.

Israel was also part of Sherry's Jewish life. Her husband's family was very much involved in Israel and Jewish philanthropy and that had been the way she was introduced to the country. She had already visited twice, once with her entire family. As she saw it, her ten-year-old was "an ardent Zionist" who wanted to have her bat mitzvah on Masada (something Sherry assumed would happen in addition to a synagogue celebration). Yet for all these connections, Sherry would "never consider living in Israel," because "my family is here," and as a convert by Conservative standards, she guessed, "I also wouldn't be particularly welcome there."

In spite of her assimilation into Jewish life, Sherry was well aware of the obstacles she still faced as a neophyte. Yet she was confident in her Jewish identity, comfortable in the congregation and the movement.

BETH G.: LOOSELY HELD

Beth G., thirty-something wife of a second-generation Central Synagogue member, is also a mother of three who recently made her kitchen kosher. Articulate and intelligent, she, like Sherry, represents the new generation of congregants, the mainstays of the synagogue and the laity of Conservative Judaism in the next decade. As if recognizing this, she has joined the congregation's membership committee.

Although she has not made quite as long a religious journey as Sherry on her way to Conservative synagogue life, she did travel some distance from her Reform Jewish childhood in the Midwest, noting, "I know I need something more than Reform Judaism." That something more turned out to be membership at Central Synagogue. In fact, Beth's encounter with Conservative synagogue life began long ago as a child, when she sometimes attended synagogue with friends who were affiliated with Conservative Judaism. She "liked" what she found there, and the ambience of the place also "felt right."

But her parents did not share this interest or perception and refused to switch denominational affiliation or to send her to the Conservative Hebrew school she wanted to attend, enrolling her instead in a one-day-a-week Reform Sunday school. They did not celebrate her bat mitzvah. And when she expressed an interest in learning Hebrew, her parents "flat out refused," because they said they knew nothing about it.

As a teen, Beth wanted to join the United Synagogue Youth at her friends' Conservative synagogue, but the local rabbi there gently informed her that her parents had to join the congregation in order for her to be able to be a member of its youth group. He then tried briefly to nurture her Judaism, but his synagogue was just too busy for a youngster whose parents were not interested in joining. Beth's reaction was to be angry at her parents (and although she did not say so, one suspects that her feelings toward this rabbi were at best mixed).

In the meantime, she went to a summer camp that was ethnically Jewish but that lacked Jewish content. In time, she learned to still her interests in Conservative Judaism. During high school, she joined a B'nai Brith-sponsored summer tour of Israel. It was her only trip to the Jewish homeland, and as she recollected it years later her face lit up. "It was wonderful; I recall wanting to move there," she laughed. Nevertheless, she has never returned to Israel. As an adult, she lost the desire to go to a place she now perceived as most Americans did, as a war-torn region: "At this point, I think, 'I'm a mother and I have three small children'; the danger of going there is what I see most."

In college, except for the trip to Israel, her Jewish life remained largely dormant. But her marriage, and in particular her husband, changed all that. He had celebrated his bar mitzvah at Central Synagogue and so naturally brought his new wife to visit. And recently they moved back to his old neighborhood and reestablished a personal connection to the synagogue, independent of his parents' ties.

Like so many other young parents, Beth had been moved to intensify her Jewish engagement with the birth of the children. When their first child was eighteen months old, she and her husband began the search for a synagogue with which to permanently affiliate. And as the children grew older, Beth continued to feel moved to do more. Thus, before the children were in school, she want to an occasional Shabbat service, lit Shabbat candles about twice a month "if we were home and weren't working," and attended synagogue on holidays. But once the children reached school age, Beth and her husband took additional Jewish steps. Half a year ago, when their oldest child reached the age of six, they made their home kosher.

It was something Beth chose on her own; no one in the synagogue suggested it. "From my perspective," she explained, "I like the idea of a discipline and a constant reminder that I'm Jewish . . . and since I do a lot of things that I *shouldn't* be doing, this is something I do that makes me feel good and it's not placing tremendous restrictions on my family." If it proved too difficult a discipline, however, she knew there was an escape. After all, her in-laws had kept a kosher home for five years when their children were young, until it "became too difficult." That example taught Beth that in practice, at least, kashrut *is* reversible in the Conservative movement.

Like Sherry and her family, Beth's observance was limited. The family did not keep kosher outside the home. But Beth was not certain that this would continue. "We'll still take the kids to McDonald's. My husband doesn't eat bacon anymore." She concluded: "There's something going on there." She was feeling different—not quite at ease—about eating nonkosher outside of the house.

Beyond the matter of making her home kosher, Beth was also focusing more on her children's Jewish education. She anticipated sending them to the synagogue school, although her six-year-old had recently expressed a desire to attend the Solomon Schechter Day School. But Beth was sure that this was "for all the wrong reasons," that is, "because his friends were going there, not because he would learn more Hebrew and Judaism." It would be the synagogue school for him and her other children as well. (In a sense, Beth's response to her son's desire to move beyond where she had placed herself Jewishly was a reprise of her parents' reaction to her own childhood desires to move beyond their Reform Judaism and attend the same Conservative Hebrew school as *her* friends—but she did not seem conscious of the parallels.) Rather, Beth simply felt she was not ready for the implied parochialism of a day school education. That was not where she believed Conservative Judaism was supposed to take her. Articulating the fundamental aspect of her resistance to sending her son to a day school, she explained: "We also feel fairly strongly that we've isolated ourselves in [our choice of suburb]. We've further isolated ourselves in this neighborhood [but] we like the idea of our children being exposed to many different kinds of people." She wanted to minimize the isolation created by their being Jews. Accordingly, she and her husband sent children to school on Jewish holidays like Sukkot. "And I don't anticipate ever changing about that." Part of her reasoning was that "we moved to [this suburb] because of the [good] schools," but no less important was the fact that "we also want our children exposed to other backgrounds, different religious backgrounds, different ethnic backgrounds, different socioeconomic backgrounds. They're going to have that much more in the public schools in [this suburb] than they're going to have that at Schechter." Given that the suburb was among the most affluent and white in the region, and that the school district was heavily Jewish, the likelihood of such multiethnic, multiclass exposure was probably a liberal fantasy.

What propelled Beth away from day school was probably a combination of her own inbred attitudes, gleaned from her own childhood experiences, and a conviction that the combination of public and supplementary Hebrew schools would be adequate to meet her children's needs. Her children would be prepared to live the sort of life Beth and her husband had chosen. In a sense, Beth wanted to be actively Jewish but not separated from America. So she had a kosher home but took the kids to McDonald's, would send them to Hebrew school but also public school (even on the Jewish holidays). For the time being, she was ready to walk both sides of the street.

Beth's attitude toward the synagogue reflected this dualism as well. When her husband had first brought her to his childhood congregation, she was "very adamant about *not* joining." To her it seemed like "too large a congregation, and that was a turn-off. It seemed too impersonal, even though there are outreach people who gather in the stragglers, but it just felt too large." Furthermore, the rabbi "wasn't quite right for us. He'd been doing this too long . . . and very intolerant of anything other than this narrow path. And that's not who we are."

But that rabbi retired and was replaced by a new one who for her was "approachable and encouraging." And then as the children grew, "I became adamant *about* joining." To Beth, the synagogue affiliation was at the outset inextricably bound up with good parenting. This meant embracing activities like nursery school Shabbat, various holiday events, Sukkot, Purim. In time, however, all this stimulated in her something more.

"At first it was good parents doing this because this is something you do for your child. And then it just woke up something inside of me." This awakening was not simply religious and spiritual. It also included "being together with people who had similar type backgrounds and who felt they missed out on something and want more for their children. A lot of us are sort of struggling through this together. My six-year-old knows more Hebrew than I do. Yes, it's embarrassing, but I'm doing something about it which my parents didn't do. They were just embarrassed."

Her husband, perhaps because he was a young physician busy with rounds on Shabbat mornings or because he knew the congregation as a youngster, was not as quickly moved. At first, he "couldn't care less" about these matters. And yet, as she and the children had awakened Jewishly, Beth believed that at last "he's just starting to wake up to some of this now."

As with her resistance to day school, there were, however, limits to how much Beth expected to be awakened Jewishly. She did not, for example, expect her husband to do his Saturday morning rounds in a way that would weekly "give me the luxury of going to services," nor was she prepared to allow Jewish involvements "to take away from family time," which she believed to be somehow different. Judaism remained in the service of her family life rather than the reverse. In those situations where in her judgment family considerations seemed to clash with Jewish involvements, Beth came down for what she judged to be best for her family.

For Beth, the synagogue's greatest appeal was that it was becoming like an extended family. Although most of her friends were not from the congregation, her "dear friends, the people you feel like you've known for a long time," were in the synagogue. Moreover, her children "felt comfortable in the Temple" and she did too, for the first time. She was still bothered by some of the aspects of the place that had put her off at first: its size and the formality of dress, yet once she became part of the congregational family, these matters did not loom as large as they once did.

Like Sherry, Beth found her children at once the cause of her greater involvement in the synagogue and the greatest obstacle to it. She joined because she was a mother, but she did not go to Shabbat services because her children found it hard to sit still for so long. She had, however, come to terms with this fact and concluded: "I don't feel I'm missing something by not attending Shabbat services; I really don't." Yet at another point, she noted that when she did go to a service and all went well with the kids, then "the day feels better, more relaxed."

Beth's relationship to God and the idea of commandments was also dualistic. "I believe in God," she said and then quickly added, "I question a lot; we've had a lot bad happen in our life and that makes one question that type of thing." She was unable to connect her belief in God with the idea of being commanded. Still, she had a young person's optimism that even these difficulties would eventually be worked out. "Down the line in my life, the questions will change, the answers will become easier."

The idea that "down the line" she might evolve into a more intensive Jewish life was a basic part of her outlook on life. This was why Beth was sure that she would start going to Shabbat services more frequently as her children grew and that her Jewish attachments would also grow. She thought she might even become part of the ritual committee one day. For now, however, Beth was content to live with her dualism. "If I felt commanded to do certain things there would be a lot more I would be doing. I would be going to Shabbat services; I wouldn't be driving [on Shabbat]; there's a lot more that I could do." The fact that she was not observing these commandments she explained simply by virtue of her self-identity: "I'm not an observant Jew."

For Beth, as for so many of her peers, it was simply a reality to be acknowledged without guilt, a reality that the Conservative movement and the synagogue allowed for as well. This elasticity meant that the synagogue was not necessarily a Jewishly protective environment. This was apparent in the way Beth spoke about intermarriage. Although in her younger years Beth had dated "many non-Jewish boys or men," she did not believe that this would necessarily lead to her marrying one of them. She hoped, perhaps even assumed, that her children would be able to live the same sort of double life and reach the same conclusion. To be sure, if her children married non-Jews she would be "disappointed." But Beth did not have much in the way of a plan for preventing her children's assimilation, nor did she believe that the synagogue could serve as a protective membrane. Indeed, she embraced the outside world—was that not why she was so much in favor of their attending public schools? In sum, Beth was all for nurturing a positive feeling for Judaism but had no intention of abandoning the mainstream of the American culture.

SYLVIA Y.: LESS CAN BE MORE

Like Beth, Sylvia Y. was raised in the Reform movement and became a member of a Conservative synagogue nine years ago, at the urging of her husband. But for her the transition was not at all easy. For several years, "I felt like a real outsider." She could not read Hebrew and could not understand what was going on in the service. Moreover, unlike Beth, she had always "liked the Reform service."

For three years, Sylvia had very little involvement. When her children started going to school, however, she "decided to stop feeling like an outsider and to become involved." For her the way in was through the organization rather than through the services, where she was still hopelessly disempowered by Jewish ignorance. Because her children were enrolled in the synagogue school, Sylvia decided to join the school board. She put in long hours and worked hard at it. As Sylvia saw it, "the synagogue is not just the services. . . . The school is very important to me because that's where my kids are and that's what brought me in. The synagogue is a community, . . . a Jewish home." One of her initiatives had been to launch a family service on Shabbat and on Yom Kippur. This was a service geared to those like herself who needed some coaching and who preferred something that even the youngsters could tolerate, both in length and content. Through her involvement in the service Sylvia became a bigger player in her synagogue's life and was eventually asked to serve on the synagogue board.

In the meantime, Sylvia acquired some of the basic skills she needed to be more comfortable as a Conservative Jew. Studying with the rabbi, she learned to read Hebrew and over time came to prefer a service with Hebrew in it. She liked the Hebrew service precisely because she understood so little of it. It was a kind of musical mantra: "I just find it kind of relaxing because I can get into the rhythm of it and don't have to read all the words. . . . I have to pay too much attention to the Reform service because I understand all the words. And that bothers me."

There had been years when Sylvia came to services "fairly frequently" and others when she did not. When she did come, however, she preferred to come late. "It's sometimes scary to arrive between 9 and 9:30 [around the time services begin] because they might ask you to do something because there's nobody in there." That would make her feel incompetent and uncomfortable. For Sylvia, less was definitely more.

These days, as her daughter's bat mitzvah was approaching, she was still not coming to pray very often, but that did not bother her. She was still "in the building" three to five days a week. In fact, Sylvia described herself as a board member who represented that large segment of the congregation who did not come to services often. These people included her husband, who was not even as active as she was. And he was the one who had grown up in a Conservative synagogue.

Most of Sylvia's friends were not from the congregation, though some of her closest ones were. The synagogue was not the center of her social life, and although Sylvia would now "definitely" identify herself as a Conservative Jew, it was an identification that allowed a great degree of disengagement. She was happy for that identity to be relatively vague and loose, and her notion of the synagogue reflected that: for Sylvia the synagogue was a vehicle for expressing a general Jewish affiliation, "a place for those who want to identify as Jews to be Jewish, to do Jewish things."

CHARLOTTE AND BEN: RARE VISITORS

Charlotte and Ben L., now in their late sixties, are products of the American Conservative movement, even as it was emerging from the shadow of Orthodoxy. For Charlotte this meant growing up in the inner city in a kosher home and even going to a Hebrew school/Talmud Torah at a time when "girls did not have to attend." Ben's background was similar, if only vaguely recalled.

They had been members of Central Synagogue for thirty-six years. Their children had gone through the synagogue school, and some even enrolled for one year of the high school. Ben encouraged their attendance and for a time played an active role in the synagogue youth group, mostly as a kind of sports coach. Their children also celebrated their bar and bat mitzvahs in the synagogue, a rite of passage that they "enjoyed" and found meaningful. Nevertheless throughout nearly four decades of affiliation with Central Synagogue, Charlotte and Ben saw it primarily as the place they came to on the High Holidays, those three days in the year when just about all members felt the tug of their Jewish conscience. She could read Hebrew, and staying in the synagogue throughout the whole day on the High Holidays had a "very special meaning" for her. "It relates also to the past, so it brings back a lot of memories." Nostalgia played a large part here. These limited visits were enough, as Charlotte explained, to give her "the meaning of Judaism."

In a very real sense, Charlotte and Ben saw their connection to the synagogue as a kind of background, almost quiescent, element of their lives. As Charlotte articulated this affiliation, it was part of her history more than of her present. It was "what I grew up with. It had meaning to me as a child. It had meaning to me when my parents died."

Over time, however, they "moved away from the temple as any kind of central focus." As both husband and wife saw it, their synagogue affiliation had done its job: "Our children have married and are in temples in their own communities, and their children are in Hebrew schools."

"I've been here for thirty-some-odd years," Ben explained, "and look at the results. All four of our children are involved in one way or another in a Conservative or Reform temple." This was enough for Charlotte to conclude that "Judaism has a very basic meaning to all of us." But "basic" was not the same as active participation. "In fact," Charlotte observed, "we are more likely to attend services at our children's temple than at Central Synagogue."

Moreover, she added, Jewish continuity and meaning displayed itself not only in the time spent in their children's places of worship—both Reform and Conservative—but also in their numerous trips to Israel, which became an important vehicle for their Jewish expression and a means for passing on that Jewish feeling to the next generation. Thus, as each grandchild reached bar or bat mitzvah, Ben and Charlotte took him or her on an extended trip to the Jewish homeland. These trips afforded them an opportunity to relate to their grandchildren, as well as to demonstrate to them the regard they held for their Jewish identity.

Would they ever become more engaged in the life of the synagogue? In fact, both were sure that the synagogue would be "helpful" to them in times of crisis. Like an insurance policy, it was an important investment, assuring some level of continuity, available in a crisis, renewable each year, and always valuable. But one rarely needed to use it, these days. Charlotte did not like the insurance metaphor. Instead she preferred to think of the synagogue as an extended family: you might not always be in touch or visit, but it was always there when you were ready to return.

OPAL A.: BACK INTO THE SYNAGOGUE WEB

Opal A., a forty-something doctor and mother, grew up in suburbia where her parents were nonobservant members of a Conservative synagogue. They did not observe Shabbat or the dietary laws. As she was growing up Opal never felt disturbed with this limited level of Jewish observance and engagement. All that changed during the summer she received a scholarship to go to Camp Ramah. The experience was transformative, even conversionary. Opal returned home fired up with Jewish interest and engagement. Among other things, she wanted to keep kosher, "much to everybody's dismay."

For a while, Opal tried to keep up her intensified Jewish practice and enthusiasm, but as the months and years wore on, it was difficult to do so alone, without the support of her family. And in the meantime, she became caught up with the normal concerns of middle-class American adolescence. Soon enough, her Ramah conversion eroded and she "just sort of dropped out of it."

Although she went to Brandeis University, a college rich in Jewish life and opportunities, Opal did not get actively involved in Jewish life there—although, as she put it, she maintained something of a distant "interest" in it. She generally avoided the Jewish religious activities and participated instead in the "political" and "cultural" ones. By the time she graduated, this Ramah convert "wound up marrying somebody who comes from a very Reformed background."

At the start of their married life, these two professionals lived in the city and did not affiliate with a synagogue until they became parents. Her husband, she thought, would have been happy to join a Reform congregation, but with Opal "pulling and tugging" they ended up at a large and prestigious Conservative congregation in the city.

In time, they decided to move to the suburbs and their current home. Although they would have preferred joining another Conservative synagogue, they opted to join the nearby Reform temple, rather than a more distant Conservative congregation "where they would not know anybody." They figured that a synagogue was above all else about community and neighborhood, and how big were the differences between Reform and Conservative anyway? Besides, Reform Judaism was a part of Opal's husband's background.

But, as Opal discovered, the Reform temple "was not a very good match for me." After almost two years, she was still uncomfortable with the style of services: "There's no participation; you're an observer and it's almost like a Protestant service. You don't really sing along; you're not part of it." And she found herself increasingly alienated by the laxity of people's religious and Jewish commitments and by what she saw as the coldness of the congregational community. Even her husband referred to it facetiously as "Our Temple of the Highway"—a place as impersonal as a rest stop on the interstate. So once again they sought out a Conservative synagogue. For Opal finding a gender-egalitarian synagogue was important. Central Synagogue seemed the right choice; it was also the Conservative synagogue closest to where they lived.

Although Opal found the services and the general character of the synagogue comfortably familiar, she and her family found it a bit difficult to break into the congregation. All that changed, however, when they decided to go on the congregation's first retreat, a Shabbat away with a group of about 110 self-selected members of the congregation—"a third religious school families, a third Schechter day-school families, and a third older couples with grown children, and interspersed in those three were five or six new families," according to a report to the synagogue's board. Overnight, Opal and her family felt like insiders, not an atypical response. Commenting on the value of the retreat, and particularly its impact on new members, one participant noted afterward: "There was one new family with one foot out the door [to another congregation], who was really disenchanted with the synagogue, who ended up being encouraged to go [on the retreat]. They called me this morning to say what a wonderful time they had, they met such wonderful people, and it was a terrific experience for them. People were very enthusiastic, in a very good frame of mind; people got to know people that they didn't know before."

When, a few weeks after the retreat, Opal and her family attended a Friday night dinner and service with about 130 synagogue members (all families like them, with sixth graders), they felt at ease both with the ritual and with the others who attended. More and more Opal felt herself and her family wanting to be part of what she perceived as a close-knit community.

The rabbi was quite important to her: he was approachable as well as knowledgeable. As Opal explained: "Everybody in my family relates" to him. More than that, she added: "I've learned a lot of things from him, even things that I thought I knew how to do, things like lighting Hanukkah candles. Now everybody has his own menorah, his own kiddush cup—stuff like that. And it feels good." For Opal's husband, too, there was a new feeling of competence in negotiating his way through the service and its ritual, which made him an ally to his wife's synagogue inclinations.

Both Opal and her husband were pleased that their children were also beginning to enjoy Shabbat more than before and to feel more at ease with Judaism. "I think being a member has changed our lives a little bit," Opal explained. "I'd like to get a sukkah. I think we'd like to start adding more ritual to our lives that we really have not done before. For our kids who did not go to Ramah the [congregational] retreat was a little bit of a turning point in terms of, 'This feels great. This is not all geeky and why are we here?'" To be sure, her home was still not kosher and they only went to services about once a month. Yet they always lit Shabbat candles, drank wine and had "Shabbat dinner" with "family and whoever—friends or parents—is around." The synagogue was the vehicle for their becoming far more engaged in their Judaism. "The ritual really seems to matter." Opal added, "I didn't really understand that until we went to [the Reform temple] and it really seemed a little hollow to me."

Again, Opal could feel herself becoming Jewishly "converted" as she did in camp that summer long ago. But this time, she would not be alone. This time she was doing so with a family who joined her.

ALVAN AND CLAIRE U.: CONSERVATIVE JEWS IN SPITE OF THEMSELVES

Since she was fourteen, and except for a short period in college and graduate school, Claire U., daughter of one of the families in the congregation, has lived in the Central Synagogue community. As a teen, she was active in the synagogue youth group. She also went through the synagogue school, an experience that she characterized as "a disaster," the place where she did *not* learn very much about what was attractive about being Jewish. Part of this she attributed to an "Orthodox" tendency on the part of the rabbis who taught in the school. They were also, she believed, "interested in making money and not necessarily educating the kids, especially not the girls."[14]

Claire remembered being "pretty turned off" as a child and then "forced to go to Hebrew high school, which was terrible." Yet for all she criticized her Jewish education, she admitted that "when I took a year of Hebrew in college to keep my grade point average up against physical chemistry, I realized that I had learned a lot [more than I thought]. It was really fascinating."

In college she felt that being actively Jewish was "not the thing to do." Accordingly, her Jewish involvement there was limited to High Holiday services or celebrating Passover, if she found herself on campus at those times of year. Despite this limited involvement and the bad memories, she claimed that throughout the years at college, her "Jewish identity was still strong."

After graduating from college, she married Alvan, a man who had been raised in a "very religious" fundamentalist Protestant home. This marriage, which might have signaled the end of her Jewish involvement, in fact did just the opposite. It happened that Claire's estrangement from her Jewish background was mirrored by her husband's estrangement from Protestant fundamentalism. Although he had been raised with the notion "that religion encompasses everything; it's the focus of your life," and that as a Christian, he was "the successor to the Jewish people," as he got older he underwent a sea change. Having moved from a rural to an urban area, where most of his new friends were Jews—the first living Jews he had met—and as a result of his studies of science, he found himself increasingly distant from his fundamentalist roots. "I went from a state where I fully expected to become a minister, because my older brother was, to the point where I was just about a devout atheist."

Perhaps that was an exaggeration, for he found that he was not ready to abandon all religion forever. Actually, he was impressed with the Judaism he saw when he visited his friends' families. He resolved to marry a Jewish woman. When he married Claire, therefore, he was more than ready to accede to the wishes of her family that he convert—even though at the time, his new wife would not have forced him to do so, as by then she had "absolutely no interest in synagogue attendance and religion." Alvan, however, realized "that the family would not accept me unless I was converting."

Alvan took his conversion quite seriously, not simply as a formality. "So I spent a lot of time thinking about and studying it. And the more I studied it, the more I fell in love with it. I idealized it. As I evolved as a Conservative Jew, I started becoming a Jew, as opposed to a former Christian who fell in love with something that didn't really exist and then was disappointed." That is, he came to terms with and embraced a real rather than an idealized Judaism. That Judaism was the version he found in the Conservative movement.

For Claire, her husband's discovery of Judaism was the catalyst for her own rediscovery of Judaism. She now realized that her Jewish identity and religion "was more important to me than I had appreciated before." As she concluded: "There's nothing like teaching somebody what you take for granted yourself."

As they thought about having a family, Judaism came to play an even greater role in their lives. Alvan especially wanted his children "to have a religion. I can't give them the one I had." This meant becoming more actively Jewish. When at last they had both graduated law school, Claire and her husband moved to the suburbs and gravitated toward her old synagogue—a synagogue where they could "sit together." They became active in the congregation, and Alvan became a synagogue trustee. Their children went to the Schechter day school so they would not have the negative synagogue school experiences Claire had had.

But the early enthusiasms waned over the years. While Claire and Alvan continued to send their children to a Conservative day school, because it was "part of wanting to pass on Jewish identity," their attendance at synagogue became gradually more episodic—though Claire expected it to become more frequent with the approach of their son's bar mitzvah the next year.

Like Charlotte and Ben, Claire considered the synagogue a place to which she would return whenever she felt the need. "The temple is here for me when I need it. I will support it whether I come three times a year or fifty-two times a year." And when she came she could feel guilt-free about her failure to attend more often while still feeling "very much at home" in the synagogue. She expected others to carry the institution when she was otherwise engaged, not an unrealistic expectation in a synagogue as large as Central Synagogue.

Alvan put it this way: "You need to participate enough so that it [the synagogue] threads into your life." But once it becomes woven in, one can loosen the thread as needed so the bind of synagogue life does not become too tight.

Part of this was because, as he saw it, "in my concept of Conservative Judaism, the temple is not just a service, though that's important and it's there for you when you need it, and *in different stages of your life, you need it in different ways*: when you want to get married, it's important; when you want your kids to be bar mitzvah, it becomes important; when you lose someone, and when you happen to make friends there. But to me the center of Conservative Judaism is not the temple. The center of Conservative Judaism—and I've spent a long time thinking about it—is the home and the family. . . . The family comes first, but you reinforce it in that you're part of the community."

Alvan and Claire believed that they were "very, very active Conservative Jews because our home is kosher." More than that, the fact that they sent their children to a day school also meant that "our day-to-day family activities circle around Hebrew and Judaism and teaching the children what we want to teach them about the religion."

In a way, their son was now going through this same kind of episodic synagogue involvement. When he was young, he seemed to love coming to the synagogue. By the age of three, he knew every part of the Shabbat service. "It was like this magical thing." Now that he was at the Schechter day school, however, that youthful enthusiasm seemed gone. It was almost as if he wanted time off on the weekend from being so Jewishly involved during the rest of the week.

This concerned Claire somewhat; was her son going to become estranged as she had? She half-expected it. As she saw it, the Conservative movement was not always good at keeping "the kids here post-bar mitzvah." There were no guarantees, she knew. And yet, if she could come back in spite of an intermarriage and a less than perfect childhood synagogue experience, perhaps she could count on her children doing the same.

EVELYN V.: A SENSE OF COMMUNITY

Raised in a small town less than an hour north of where she now lives, Evelyn V., a woman in her late forties, has always been a Conservative Jew. She grew up in a small synagogue of no more than a hundred families, and from early on used her Jewish connections to foster a sense of who she was and to connect her to a larger Jewish world. She was active in the United Synagogue Youth and had gone through a classic synagogue Jewish education. But then, unlike most of her peers, she continued in Hebrew high school, traveling to a midsize city and its larger Jewish community. As a student at the state university, Evelyn participated in campus Hillel events and became part of a Jewish community that helped her cope with life on the large campus. At Hillel, she not only found friends but also met the man whom she would later marry. This man, who came from an Orthodox home, found in Evelyn someone whose commitments to Judaism and familiarity with its demands were close enough to his to enable them to build a life together.

By the time Evelyn and her husband had children, they were living in suburbia in New York. That was twenty-two years earlier. At Evelyn's initiative, they joined a Conservative synagogue. In part because of her childhood experience in a small synagogue, Evelyn wanted very much to be "part of a larger synagogue, where there were more options of programming, more people, more choices than what I had when I was growing up." After some synagogue shopping, she and her husband found a congregational home at Central Synagogue. They had come there on a Shabbat when a bat mitzvah was being celebrated. For Evelyn, the large crowd in the synagogue was an inspiration. Many of those whom she encountered, moreover, were regular attendees. Week after week, the congregation on Shabbat mornings was larger than anything she had seen before. This particularly appealed to Evelyn. By contrast, the other Conservative synagogue they had considered joining never had a very large turnout. As she put it, "When there's no bar or bat mitzvah there, the place is empty. But if you come here on an average Shabbat, it's hundreds of people." This was a community. Evelyn and her husband found it to be a community where they were "both comfortable."

Among the first families in the area to send their children to the Schechter day school, they became, by Evelyn's description, "very involved Jewishly." They became mainstays of the day school and board members of the synagogue; they also maintained a kosher home, visited Israel five times, observed all the holidays, and attended synagogue regularly. In addition, Evelyn had been working at a large Jewish cultural institution in the city for twelve years.

Yet in spite of the fact that by all measures Evelyn and her family would appear to be among the more observant and committed members of the synagogue and the movement, she suggested that "we're veering more toward being ethnically Jewish than toward observance." Increasingly what she found most meaningful about her Conservative Judaism was the community affiliation and sense of peoplehood or ethnicity that it granted her, and not the ritual or the services.

Her emphasis on this aspect of her Judaism derives in part from what she perceives as a growing problem: defining exactly what Conservative Judaism is. "We have a real problem in the Conservative movement: We tend to define ourselves by what we're *not*. 'The Reform do this; the Orthodox do that. We don't like that, so we're Conservative.' We don't seem to articulate what we truly stand for." And the movement's formal commitment to halakha did not speak to her. As she saw it, that commitment and indeed halakha are "not part of our vocabulary, of how we function on a daily basis."

In part, she added, her children's identities as Conservative Jews derived more from their experiences in day school than from their connection to the synagogue. "The one thing that kept my kids here [at the synagogue] was the basketball." And she quickly added, "For my family it was an important tie." It was a way of being part of the Jewish team. One youngster had even gone to shoot baskets with the rabbi. The team, the rabbi, the congregation, the community were all one.

On the other hand, Evelyn felt that Shabbat services in particular had become a drag. "I personally think the Jewish people wouldn't be around if services were always around $3^1/2$ to 4 hours long," she said, only half-joking. She was ready to "make the services shorter." Too much had been added by the tradition over the years. For this reason she saw herself "veering" toward what she called "ethnic Judaism" but was really community-based Judaism.

This orientation was in harmony with the congregational affiliation that was the core of her synagogue life, she thought. "When you're involved in a synagogue there's a sense of being part of a group in search of having a stronger spiritual dimension in their lives, which is why you kind of have something in common." As she saw it, the Central Synagogue community "is a wonderful place to be at the end of the twentieth century, in terms of the quality of Jewish life."

JOAN M.: IN LOVE WITH THE SYNAGOGUE COMMUNITY

Joan M., a woman in her thirties, also was most touched by the community character of the synagogue. She had grown up belonging to a Conservative synagogue, but "I don't think we went even three times a year." The only exceptions that she could recall were her brothers' bar mitzvahs. When she was living on her own for the first time in college, Joan slightly increased her level of Jewish participation: she went to the synagogue on High Holidays even when her family did not join her and she fasted on Yom Kippur.

It was not that her family did not care about Judaism or Jewish life. Rather, the connection was more ethnic and familial than ritual or religious. Thus they always had a family Passover seder and used Rosh Hashanah as an occasion to visit family. Later in life, Joan's mother had worked for many years as an administrative assistant in a university Jewish studies program and during those years also pursued both undergraduate and graduate degrees in Jewish studies. Although her parents were American-born, Yiddish (and Yinglish) expressions were part of the language of the house; and in spite of its minimal involvement in synagogue life, this was a family that was very open about its Jewish ethnic roots.

It is likely that Joan might have repeated this pattern except for several events in her life that turned her much more in the direction of Judaism and toward Central Synagogue in particular. First, she married the son of Holocaust survivors who had grown up in an Orthodox synagogue, gone to an Orthodox day school, and felt very strongly about his Judaism.

"Before we got married, we had a prenuptial agreement: our children had to go to day school." Joan was ready for this, but she wanted something that reflected her own proclivities as well. "I said, 'That's fine, so long as it's Conservative.'" She accepted the idea of more Judaism in her life but felt uncomfortable with Orthodoxy and with what she perceived to be insistence on keeping women subordinate and separate. And she wanted to be "comfortable" in her Jewish life. Conservative Judaism seemed to her to fit that need. Her husband agreed.

As newlyweds, Joan and her husband kept a kosher home and observed and celebrated Shabbat. But they did not join a synagogue during their first year of marriage, when they lived in the city. Instead, like so many other young couples, they went to their parents (mostly his) to celebrate the holidays and attend the synagogue.

Only when they had a son and moved to the suburbs did they begin to think about synagogue membership and making a Jewish home. "Somehow you become a parent and you feel like you need to join somewhere."

Joan's husband felt this need while his newborn son and wife were still in the hospital. He recalled the agreement he had made with his wife and went to Central Synagogue, the Conservative congregation closest to where they lived. It was a weekday morning, and there happened to be a bris that day. Although a stranger, he was warmly greeted by the congregation, especially when they discovered that he too would be celebrating his son's bris in a matter of days. Later, he told Joan about this greeting and within a month they became new members of the congregation, even though it was not within walking distance of their home and the idea of driving to synagogue on Shabbat seemed unthinkable for Joan's husband. Still, he wanted the affiliation and made the compromise about driving.

Over the years Joan became increasingly committed and engaged religiously. She fervently wished that everyone in the congregation could maintain a similar level of Jewish commitment and engagement, and in particular she wanted to make the three-day-a-year attendees more active, "to get people in" to the synagogue: "Your tennis cannot be more important than your synagogue life." In short, she wanted others to repeat her religious journey.

As Joan and her husband became more involved in parenting and synagogue life, they decided to move closer to the synagogue. Part of this had to do with her husband's residual commitments to halakha: although he had come to terms with riding to the synagogue on Shabbat, he did not under any condition want to drive there on the High Holidays (until then, they were still going to his parents on those days; now he wanted to stay at home). More importantly, their Conservative Judaism had become a habit of their heart and they wanted to bring it closer to home. Moreover, they knew that they intended to send their son and any future children to the Schechter school, which was located in the same suburb as the synagogue. The move therefore seemed a natural and significant indication of their growing commitment and Jewish involvement. Although they were still a distance from the synagogue, Joan's husband was at least now able to walk to the synagogue in nice weather and on High Holidays.

The synagogue community was becoming an increasingly important part of Joan's life. On Shabbat, for example, "we invite people or we go to someone else's house," she noted. "It becomes a whole outreach community thing." She guesses that 98 percent of her close friends were from the congregation; this was a network of people who observed ritual life. It was indeed a key feature of Conservative synagogue life. Yes, Joan admitted, an Orthodox congregation might offer the same social life, but it also treated women differently. The few times she had gone to an Orthodox synagogue, she felt like "a second-class citizen." It had been "a horrible, horrible experience for me as a woman."

Conservative Judaism, however, allows her a greater religious freedom because, she believes, it allows her to choose those rituals and observances that she finds meaningful and dispense with those she finds fossilized and empty prac-tices of Orthodoxy. For her, the new rabbi was a role model for the ideal to which she now aspired. She called him "a wonderful Conservative Jew. He keeps Shabbat; he's kosher; he does *everything*. But he's *Conservative*; he's not Ortho-dox." She meant that he had a positive connection to the particularities of Con-servative Judaism; he had not simply devolved from Orthodox traditions, as perhaps her husband had, to a Conservative lifestyle.

In short, Joan was in love with her Conservative Judaism, her congrega-tion, her rabbi, and the community that they created. And she felt that love returned. When one of her children fell ill and spent many months in the hos-pital, what saved her was "this place, this synagogue community—I would never have made it through [without them]. I mean, people helped. They reached out to us. We never spent a Shabbat alone. If I needed to get driven into the city [to the hospital], there were people who would drive me into the city. [W]hen I really needed it, it was really here for me."

ROBERT H.: DO-IT-YOURSELF CONSERVATIVE JEW

Now in his late thirties, Robert H. grew up in Central Synagogue, went to its school, and was part of its United Synagogue Youth program. Nevertheless, he saw his current membership as a new affiliation, because fourteen years earlier, when he and his wife (who had also grown up in a Conservative congregation) moved back to the area, his parents were no longer here. He was therefore join-ing the congregation on his own, establishing a separate and new relationship with the institution.

At the outset of married life, Robert and his wife, like many new couples, did not belong to a congregation; they could not find one that suited them. But when they were expecting a child and bought a house in the suburbs, they—like so many others whose lives are documented in these pages—joined Cen-tral Synagogue. At this time Robert began a new phase in his Jewish life too, in part because his wife was more observant than he had been. He did not come from a kosher home; now he lived in one. While he still did not keep kosher when eating out of the house (though his wife did), chances were, he guessed, that he would soon do so. He came to services regularly, found himself involved in some sort of synagogue activity almost every night of the week, and was be-coming increasingly interested in religious seeking. Of his four children, three were at the Schechter day school, and the youngest one was at Central Syna-gogue nursery. And although "until recently we soft-pedaled the commitment to halakha," he was ready to move toward greater observance. This was quite a change for someone who had grown up in a family of three-day-a-year attendees.

As Robert explained, he found Conservative Judaism, as practiced at his synagogue, "rich and meaningful," and "over the years it drew me in to get more involved both Jewishly and in the synagogue in general." Robert was becoming more affirmatively a *Conservative* Jew. He explained his attachment this way:

> It can be uncomfortable to be in the middle, but to me it rings truer in its historical and intellectual honesty about what it is to be Jewish. I look at Reform and I see them jettisoning for *convenience* sake ritual and observant practices that are traditional, that are a way for people to participate and to connect spiritually with their Judaism. And on the other hand, I look at Orthodox, [where] if anything I'm more comfortable in an Orthodox synagogue than I am in a Reform, but I look at them and I see a refusal in them to address the reality that Judaism, like anything else, has been an evolving, growing thing—something that lives. I see Judaism as something that lives, changes. . . . To deny that is to deny reality. And so, the triumphs of the Conservative movement dealing with an issue like egalitarianism is an intellectually honest process and something that to me rings truer to history as to what Jews truly have been.

Like Evelyn, he was proud of his congregation, especially when he contrasted it with the neighboring Conservative synagogue in a northern suburb. At Central Synagogue there were always many members ready to participate and engaged, while in the other congregation "not only is it that they can't get a minyan or close to a minyan if there's no bar or bat mitzvah, but when you go there for a bar and bat mitzvah, virtually the entire congregation there are invited guests." For him his synagogue was "a kind of extended family."

But Robert worried about his synagogue's success in holding on to those at the margins of that extended family. He believed the congregation needed to do more to engage congregants whose children were grown and out of the house. And he wanted to include more of those who were new to the congregation. Thus, he had been an enthusiastic participant in the highly successful synagogue weekend retreat, an occasion on which "people got to know people that they didn't know before." And he also cared about keeping the children engaged in synagogue and Jewish life. The retreat had been successful on that count as well. As he recalled, "That was really one of the most extraordinary parts; the interaction between the children."

Yet however much he cared about the synagogue community, for Robert, Judaism was a personal commitment, not something someone else did for you, not even the rabbi. "I adore the rabbi, but I personally think religion is a do-it-yourself thing."

And, in his view, life at the synagogue affirmed that approach: "The level of participation that is allowed and encouraged . . . is far beyond what is accepted or allowed by Conservative clergy in other places. A lot of what we have here is not necessarily easily replicated."

VERED AND BARRY J.: ORTHODOX DROPOUTS

Vered and Barry had started out in the world of Jewish tradition and Orthodoxy. Barry was American born and bred, part of revitalized Orthodox Judaism, and Vered was from a proud Orthodox Israeli family. Their biographies and expressed Jewish outlooks thus offer some instructive hints as to how Conservative Judaism can appeal even to those who have seen the "best" that Orthodoxy has to offer.

Vered, born in Israel into a family of Tripolitanian immigrants, grew up in a Sephardic Orthodox home and was a product of the public religious school system in a town not far from Tel Aviv, made up overwhelmingly of working class, religious immigrants. In her house next to the synagogue, Vered used to sit on the porch and hear the sound of services. After high school, she entered the army, a break with Orthodox practice and her family's wishes. In their world, army service for women was considered immodest and religiously perilous, for it placed these women in circumstances where they were surrounded by secular adolescents. This could lead to compromising situations, sexual intimacies, and social pressures to conform to the secular lifestyle of the majority. Indeed, the army did erode Vered's attachments to the sort of Judaism in which she had grown up. As she put it, "That's when I started to be less religious." This included, most dramatically, a decision to drive in a car and use electricity on Shabbat, transgressing in public the Orthodox rules of the day of rest. But she still kept kosher, something easily facilitated by the Israeli Defense Forces, all of whose food rations and kitchens are kosher. Moreover, Vered hastened to add, in spite of her lapses in religious observance, she still maintained a "strong belief" that the demands of Orthodox Judaism were legitimate and true. Her parents preferred not to know about Vered's lapses and so whenever she was at home, she acted as if she were still Orthodox.

"Until I came here." She arrived in America nineteen years ago and discovered that her brother, who had preceded her, ate nonkosher food in restaurants. "He told me chicken is all right," she said, laughing now at her religious naïveté in believing all chicken is kosher. "So that's when I started eating chicken and more nonkosher outside the house"—yet another step away from the Orthodoxy of her origins.

At work, Vered met Barry, who followed her when she went back to Israel and persuaded her to marry him. Barry's father was "basically assimilated. But my mother," who came from a Hungarian Jewish family largely decimated by the Holocaust, "ruled with religion," and "came from a very Orthodox background." Although the home and community in which Barry grew up was basically Orthodox, as was his education, he nevertheless felt that Orthodoxy had been imposed on him. Recalling his childhood Shabbatot, he mostly remembered "being dragged out of bed Saturday morning and going to shul, my mother haranguing me about going to pray." Barry felt his Jewish observances were done "out of compulsion." It was "an Orthodoxy that wasn't tested because we had our parents behind us" propping us up.

After attending a public university and before becoming an attorney, Barry found himself becoming less attached to Orthodox practices and beliefs. Although he and Vered came from two sides of a Jewish cultural divide—Sephardic/ Libyan versus Ashkenazic/Hungarian, one from Israel, one from America—their shared status as Orthodox expatriates, as well as their blossoming love, overcame these divisions. There were also some aspirations they shared, foremost among them to give their children a day school education that would guarantee their fluency in Hebrew and consciousness of Jewish history.

After marrying, they did not affiliate with any synagogue, but on holidays and special occasions they went to Barry's parents, to the same Orthodox synagogue he had attended growing up. In their own home (although not outside it), they kept kosher, lit candles on Shabbat, and recited kiddush, but on Saturday mornings no one dragged Barry out of bed to go to the synagogue. The day became "more like a weekend," Vered said. "We had fun."

Eventually, Barry and Vered moved to the suburb where they now live. Now they had to decide where to affiliate: they lived near both an Orthodox and a Conservative synagogue. But Barry's parents had moved to the same suburb and joined the Orthodox synagogue, so the young couple, who were now parents, felt tugged in that direction. For the first few years, they went to the Orthodox synagogue and even had their daughter's bat mitzvah celebration there. But increasingly they were feeling "more comfortable" in the Conservative synagogue, which they had begun to attend on their own. Vered found they "enjoyed the service," and she "liked the fact that we could sit together" in one pew. She was turned off spiritually by her experience in American Orthodox synagogues, where she had sat among women who came to services regularly but, according to her "[talked] all the time" and "never participated" in the worship. She felt culturally alienated from this kind of American Orthodoxy.

For Barry, it took some time to feel as comfortable in the Conservative synagogue. But he came to appreciate the openness of Conservative Judaism and the absence of what he saw as Orthodox hypocrisy, and he increasingly "liked the service." He found that "people who showed up for services participated and found great joy in it, while I found in the Orthodox services I had been to for many, many years, a lot of men caught up on the week's business and the women showed up around 10:30 to talk to each other. So this was more in line with my philosophy." As he understood Conservative Judaism, it had "a belief in tradition" but at the same time that tradition was "not necessarily cemented two thousand years ago; it evolves."

By the time their son became a bar mitzvah, they decided that, in spite of Barry's parents' wishes, the celebration would be at Central Synagogue, where Vered and Barry were now members. Their son's bar mitzvah thus became a time of the family's confirmation of its commitments to Conservative Judaism, a journey that had included moving the children from the Orthodox day school to the Conservative Schechter day school. Over the last few years Barry and Vered had been attending Shabbat services at Central Synagogue at least twice a month. Barry no longer had to be dragged to go. Once the children graduated from the Schechter school, they felt that it was "important to at least continue going" regularly to the synagogue. And they were sending their children to a Jewish high school program.

Reflecting on past years, Barry added: "We sent them to a Jewish day school because I felt it very important that they have a Jewish identity. Without a Jewish education you can't have the identity; without the identity, what does it mean to be a Jew? It's all hand in hand. . . . And once [the children get] to be of higher cognitive age, you can't very well send them without participating ourselves, so we made a decision actually last year that we'll come every second week [to synagogue services]. It turns out to be about once a month, and we bring the children." Vered affirmed this sentiment: "If you don't participate in Jewish life," the children "resent it even more."

Barry and Vered were both convinced too—perhaps never more than at their son's bar mitzvah—that Conservative Judaism suited them. Prior to that occasion, as Barry recalled, one of his "ultra-Orthodox cousins" from Brooklyn told his mother that she could not walk into the Conservative synagogue because that "was very wrong." His mother, deeply shaken, asked Barry to reschedule the bar mitzvah in an Orthodox synagogue. He told her, "I'm sorry; it's not going to happen." His mother came to the bar mitzvah and "loved the service." She was called up to close the ark and thought it very nice. The whole thing— the bar mitzvah celebration and in a symbolic sense, the shift in Barry's and Vered's affiliation that it publicly marked—"was a great success," he concluded.

SHERMAN I.: SAYING KADDISH

Sherman I., a man in his late fifties, grew up in New York City on the border between Conservative Judaism and a waning Orthodoxy. Although his parents were part of the former, his immigrant grandparents, who had lived with him for a number of years, were Orthodox. Their impact was powerful enough to ensure that all their sons and grandsons went to yeshivas—all except Sherman: "I was the black sheep."

He attended an Orthodox synagogue when he was very young, then went on to public school—although at the insistence of his grandfather (and in a trade-off with his mother, who wanted him to go to the "better" public school), he also went to an "old-fashioned *heder* where I learned to detest much of the teachings." In fact, looking back on his years in *heder*, he reported, "The only thing I didn't detest is that we were able to read stories in Yiddish."

All this Jewish education, such as it was, came to an end with Sherman's bar mitzvah ceremony, held in his parents' Conservative synagogue. During high school, he "intermittently" went to "temple," that is, on the High Holidays. During his university years, he did not become any more involved Jewishly. He dated some non-Jews but he never considered marrying one and eventually married a Jewish woman. His son, as he would later tell me, also dated non-Jews but was on the verge of marrying one, a woman Sherman did not think would convert to Judaism (something he said troubled him deeply).

After their wedding Sherman and his wife decided to make their home kosher, although he admitted the idea was more his wife's, but "after all, the kitchen was hers." But this commitment lapsed after about eight years. "My son had to have milk," he explained, and that milk was spilling over meat dishes and the like. Sherman and his wife decided the situation was "ridiculous" and gave up being kosher. Moreover, as Sherman added, "I also resented what some of the kosher butchers did, especially around holiday time when they would gouge you for meat that wasn't as good as other meat that was tastier and cheaper." But this was long ago. In fact, after some reflection, Sherman acknowledged that he was not certain whether they abandoned kashrut before or after his children were born and spilling milk.

In the early years of their marriage, Sherman and his wife moved around the northeastern United States. Though they kept something of a kosher home, they did not join a synagogue. Only about twenty-six years ago, when they moved to "this area" shortly after becoming parents, did they decide that "it's time to belong to a synagogue." Synagogue affiliation was the way to "put down roots."

Looking for a place to plant those roots, he concluded that "Orthodox was too Orthodox." The services offered "no English—while I can read Hebrew, I can't speak it or understand it." And Reform "temples were too left of center, too little Hebrew, too little that I grew up with, very little in the way of tradition, very little in the way of what I was familiar with in terms of melodies, songs, prayers and all that."

The Conservative synagogue, by contrast, seemed the right place, the "most comfortable," in great measure because he was "familiar with the service." Nevertheless, he did not very much change the level of his involvement in Jewish life after joining. Indeed, he found the rabbi at the time to be religiously uninspiring and lackluster. He was actually looking for another synagogue when he heard that the rabbi was retiring. He decided to stay. The new rabbi made all the difference. "I think that . . . the rabbi is a very, very important part of the temple." Although that rabbi has since also retired, Sherman and his wife stayed.

But Sherman remained part of the congregation's periphery. Even when his children were attending the synagogue school, he continued to attend services only on the High Holidays and a few other occasions. His wife occasionally lit Shabbat candles, and he occasionally recited kiddush. They had a seder, though it was more like a festive family meal than a Jewish ritual occasion. This did not change even after his children were grown and no longer living at home.

During the last year, however, Sherman's father passed away. That inspired a major change, as Sherman has tried to go to synagogue daily to recite kaddish, an obligation he felt duty-bound to fulfill. These days he finds himself among the first to arrive on Shabbat mornings, no matter what the weather. But even though synagogue attendance and prayer are now part of Sherman's daily routine, at home his level of Jewish observance is largely unchanged; he remains only marginally engaged Jewishly. By and large, Sherman was satisfied with a "combination of spiritual and traditional" involvement. He could not guess what the impact of a year's kaddish recitation would have on him. As much as he might in some way want to be changed by his year of kaddish, he did not believe he could be. Looking ahead to when his time of recitation would be over, he did not expect to continue to participate as much in synagogue life on a daily basis. As for Shabbat, he guessed that "I probably won't come every week."

Yet while Sherman expected not to change his own Jewish commitments and level of involvement, he desperately wanted his son to think more about Judaism and avoid a mixed marriage. He did not, however, know exactly what to say to him or how to demonstrate that concern. He was not even certain why he was concerned. In a sense, Sherman's kaddish may be his last and at the same time his most intensive contact with Judaism and the synagogue. It was a kind of debt that he was paying to his past. And given the fact that his son was about to intermarry, one might even suggest that in his kaddish Sherman was not only mourning a lost father but also a dying Jewish future.

THE PICTURE THAT EMERGES

In reviewing these stories, one is struck by both their common elements and their unique characteristics. One of the common elements is the profound impact that becoming parents has had on all these Central Synagogue members and on their Judaism and affiliation. All recognized that living as a family entails being in some way connected to a synagogue and the Jewish people and that at one point or another life must be shared with other Jews. They often speak in the "familiar language of exchange" and support the idea that religious "meaning is 'magnified' when it is shared with others."[15]

There is also the fact that all of them are attracted by a Judaism that they find "comfortable." Sometimes their use of this word may be a reflection of their inability to articulate the nature of their Jewish commitment. But the constant refrain of "comfortable" is also a way of saying that theirs is a relaxed Jewish attachment, tied to both an untroubled sense of community and rootedness, as well as a tolerance of one's right to make religious and affiliational choices, to be attached by personal preference and not by obligation. These are people who are content to be held firmly to a historical and particularistic Judaism, but to be held with an open hand, as one of them put it, a hand that will let them go when they want to go and will grasp them when they want to come back. These are people who are at ease with their Judaism and synagogue, both when they are in the process of making greater commitments to them as well as when they are reducing their levels of involvement. They see their synagogue and movement as a liberal institution, ready to accept them on their own terms. And while they are aware that it makes demands upon them—and they even appreciate that it makes those demands—and are repelled by a Reform Judaism that does not have the same expectations of its members, they also are pleased that it does not force its demands upon them. They like a Conservative Judaism that evolves and a synagogue that will always take them in whenever they arrive and however they choose to present themselves. Freedom and restraint, individual preference and Jewish as well as communal commitments, coexist in a comfortable mixture.

Yet these are also diverse people. Some have moved to Central Synagogue by turning religiously leftward, abandoning their Orthodox origins, while others have moved in the opposite direction, leaving Reform Jewish roots or even Christianity. Somehow they have found a place side-by-side at the center. Some are surprised at how far they have come and seek to move further, while others are happy to stop where they are. Yet all of them inhabit a pliant institution that shifts and moves with them, and never forces its demands upon them.

These people are successes in their adult lives; they live in an affluent area, have professions and careers, children and high social standing. The synagogue, when it works best for them, extends that sense of standing and empowerment; it gives them a stronger position both in heaven and on earth. This synagogue provides them with ways to extend their Jewish competence, either personally or vicariously through their children. It also offers them a way of participating in personal continuity that is interwoven with Jewish continuity. That is, they can act as good parents by being good Jews, and in being good Jews, they are forced to enhance their parenting—all of which guarantees continuity. Finally, for career people living in a suburban bedroom community, the synagogue offers them a community in which they can move beyond workaday lives and overcome the loneliness that is often part of suburban American life. For some, especially those in the active core of the congregation, this demands much activity, while for those in the periphery even a three-day-a-year involvement supported by the institutional prop of synagogue membership is sufficient. For the former, the synagogue and Judaism are always calling. For the latter, it is enough to know that the synagogue and its Judaism are there when they need them.

The People of Kehillath Achim: Called to Community

In many ways Kehillath Achim, among the oldest synagogues in the county, is caught in a struggle to maintain its strong sense of community and sociability while engaging in a congregational debate between those who are powerfully attached to tradition and those who are instead attracted to innovation, in particular in the matter of egalitarianism and the greater religious empowerment of women in the synagogue. The traditionalists trace their outlook to the congregation's previous rabbi who, now deceased for about twenty years, was ordained in an Orthodox seminary. The current rabbi, formerly his assistant, is a product of the Conservative movement but remains committed to many of these same traditions and is viewed as a moderate when it comes to change.

So well known is this congregation's traditionalism—most vividly represented by the continuing opposition to egalitarianism—that only a few candidates from the Jewish Theological Seminary applied this year for the position of assistant rabbi. Ultimately, a rabbinic intern was selected from among the more traditional graduates of this year's class (1996), most of whom embrace more change than this synagogue allows.

Those who seek change, and in particular push a move toward gender egalitarianism, are not necessarily opposed to Kehillath Achim's commitment to tradition in other areas. In fact, many of those who are most committed to high levels of Jewish observance are also in favor of egalitarianism. For them, the empowerment of women would simply increase the number of members who could express strong attachments to Judaism.

Yet while this debate goes on, it remains a disputation among people who are committed to the congregation and who see themselves as called to its community, which is at the heart of what makes this a successful synagogue. Both sides have shown restraint and kept the debate civilized and remarkably free of bitterness. Those who disagree have found ways to coexist. Thus, for those who embrace egalitarianism there is, as noted earlier, an alternative service that meets several Shabbatot a month, and those who oppose the principles by which the alternative service operates have taken a tolerant attitude toward it. In effect, Kehillath Achim offers everyone a way to participate in Conservative synagogue life. At the end of day, at the completion of Shabbat services, as noted, everyone gathers together for a sit-down kiddush, a meal at which the community is once again knit together religiously and socially.

Although its religious conservatism puts Kehillath Achim at odds with many congregations in the movement and may account for some potential members choosing not to join, the fact is that it is a large, very successful synagogue of eleven hundred member families. What marks its success is not only its size but the fact that a relatively large core of about two hundred member families are actively involved in its activities and can be counted on to appear on Shabbatot and holy days, whether or not there is a bar or bat mitzvah. This is the "shul" within the synagogue, about which I have already written. To understand the synagogue, one must first of all understand these people for whom the synagogue is, as one of them put it, "a second home." And even those on the periphery must be seen in contrast to the core. These then are the themes that serve as the background to the life histories that follow.

GLORIA AND HARRIS P.: CLIMBING THE LADDER OF OBSERVANCE
Gloria and Harris P. are among the active core at Kehillath Achim. They attend services regularly and volunteer for a whole host of congregational activities, from helping prepare the weekly sit-down kiddush to serving on the board. They have provided their two daughters with an intensive Jewish education, and both daughters, now grown, have themselves made these commitments their own. Indeed, one currently works as a university Jewish advisor, and the other spoke from the synagogue pulpit about her feelings of Jewish devotion. Gloria and Harris are personally committed to ritual practice and torah study and in fact moved to live within walking distance of the synagogue. They have an ongoing relationship to Israel, having sent both their children on year-long study programs there. In a sense, they seem to represent the ideal of Conservative Judaism. Even more than that, theirs seems to be a success story, for they are people who underwent a transformation from being marginally Jewish to being, in their own words, "totally involved in Jewish life."

This transformation was enormous considering the lives they led while growing up. Gloria, an energetic school teacher in her late forties, was the child of American-born parents who had come out of the Lower East Side of New York and were sympathetic to leftist and socialist causes. They moved to the suburbs when Gloria was eight. Theirs was "a secular home, in a town where there were no Jews," and during summers she was sent to a socialist camp. Nevertheless, there had been an occasional reminder of her Jewish identity. "I grew up not understanding what it meant to be a Jew," she explained. "But when I was in the seventh grade, I went and knocked on Tommy Ryan's door—he was my best friend. And his mother came to the door and said, 'Tommy can't play with you any more.' I had no idea why. I was devastated. But it was because I was Jewish and in the seventh grade was when you started dating." For most of her youth, however, Gloria remained quite ignorant of Jewish life—so much so that she only learned about the Holocaust in college.

Harris, a social worker, grew up on the margins of Orthodoxy. "My father, may he rest in peace," he explained, "kept a kosher home; he was observant." But his father died when Harris was eleven. The Orthodox congregation helped his American-born mother maintain their family's Jewish connections thereafter. Although Harris remained affiliated with the local Orthodox shul as a child and attended its Talmud Torah, he did not see himself committed to the Orthodox ideology. After bar mitzvah, he put on tefillin for a time, but this soon stopped in high school. Then, and even more so in college, his nominal Jewish attachments deteriorated. Nevertheless at Brooklyn College, where he studied history, the ambience remained heavily Jewishly ethnic, so that he could not altogether forget who he was. Still, from the age of seventeen until after his first daughter was born, Harris had, he claimed, managed to stay out of synagogues.

When Harris and Gloria married, "we didn't do anything," as Gloria put it. Indeed, they had been so unaffiliated in Canada during their first year of marriage that they could not even find a synagogue for Yom Kippur nearby. But when their older daughter was ready for school and Gloria was pregnant with another child, she and her husband decided that they wanted something Jewish for their children. Recalling what she had learned not long before about the Holocaust, Gloria explained her desire for such a Jewish education as follows: "I wanted my kids to know that if somebody ever knocked on *their* door to get them, they would at least know why." Considering three nearby possibilities—the local YMCA, the Stephen Wise Free Synagogue School, and the Manhattan Day School, an Orthodox institution—they decided on the last: Gloria "did not want a Christian organization educating my daughter," and she did not like the "dinginess" of the Wise school building. She had never been in an Orthodox school before, but when she walked into the Manhattan Day School, "I felt like I had come home."

For Gloria, there was something mystical about this encounter, and over time the affiliation began to work its magic on her: "I felt I belonged there." She began lighting candles on Friday nights, and "I learned the brachot." Right after Thanksgiving that year, in a change that Gloria wanted more than Harris, they made their home kosher. A year later, seeking a better quality of life, they moved to the suburbs.

They chose a community north of the city, along Long Island Sound. Gloria found a job teaching math in the local Orthodox day school where their older daughter was now a student. In selecting a synagogue, Harris at first favored a Reform congregation, because he associated Reform with social action, something that he pursued vocationally and also embraced personally. But Gloria wanted something more traditional, in keeping with her growing Jewish consciousness. Harris agreed and they joined a fledgling liberal Orthodox synagogue in the next town. The congregation, which still met in the rabbi's house, was welcoming of new members of all sorts, even those who were not fully Shabbat observant, like Gloria and Harris.

Gloria taught herself to read enough Hebrew in order to follow along in the services. Moreover, by virtue of being a teacher in the nearby day school, she also picked up other skills, like learning the grace after meals, which was sung aloud each day. Her extracurricular work in the school enhanced her Jewish consciousness, as did the friendships she made with some of the Orthodox staff. In short, Gloria believed she was on a path to becoming an Orthodox Jew.

Her husband worked on Saturdays and did not attend shul as much. Moreover, a bit of an iconoclast, he would sometimes make remarks that flirted with what the Orthodox might consider heresy. "I made reference to the Gospel once and that made people look askance at me." Still, as Harris put it, "a spark was still there." He recalled the cadences and rhythms of his Orthodox past and found a way to feel at home in their small Orthodox shul.

In the meantime the synagogue they belonged to relocated even farther from where they lived. Gloria and Harris now decided they could no longer live so far from a synagogue and started looking for a new place. They moved to a neighboring town and joined the Orthodox synagogue.

But Harris was still working on Saturdays and did not attend. And in contrast to how they had been greeted at other smaller Orthodox institutions, in this place, where there were many new members moving in weekly, Gloria felt they were getting the cold shoulder. No one sat near her; she felt that she and her family were treated like outsiders; she felt that what she did not do as a Jew counted for more than what she had already started doing. In a short time, both Gloria and Harris felt alienated from the Orthodox synagogue, in spite of the fact that many of the members sent their children to the school where Gloria taught.

Within six months the Orthodox synagogue hired a black-hatted rabbi, which Gloria interpreted as a tilt toward a more rigid Judaism. Thus on Simchat Torah she decided to go to Kehillath Achim, located a block north of their Orthodox synagogue. "We had a wonderful time." Her husband went to work, but she did not feel stigmatized because her husband was working on a holiday. After the service, Gloria and her daughter peeked into the social hall where the kiddush was held. But seeing how crowded it was, they turned to leave. "And somebody—I don't even know who it was—came out to get us and said, 'You're new here; please don't leave.'" As it often did for others, this sort of unanticipated welcoming response brought Gloria back. She and her family became regular attendees, and now "almost our entire social life comes out of that shul." The quest for community, so much attached to their Judaism, was finally satisfied.

There were many aspects of Jewish life at Kehillath Achim that they found satisfying. At the simplest level, Harris liked sitting with his daughters and wife during services. He liked the fact that he could come or not as he chose, without feeling stigmatized. Indeed, he sometimes preferred to attend the much smaller afternoon services rather than the main Shabbat morning ones, which for many years he had to skip while he worked. He liked the sit-down Shabbat morning kiddush, which provided him an opportunity to touch base with a circle of ever-closer friends. And he liked some of the people who led the religious life in the congregation. This included not only the rabbi, whom he found warm and supportive, but even more so the synagogue school director, whom Gloria called "the most important person in the synagogue." Although not a rabbi, Jim—as everyone called him—touched their children and themselves religiously, became a friend, and perhaps most importantly served as a "reachable role model" of the engaged, serious, and committed lay Conservative Jew.

Harris especially appreciated the pluralism of the congregation and its Judaism: he loved the choice of services available on Shabbat mornings. He saw this as the strength both of the movement and of the synagogue. He liked the synagogue's willingness to take a "critical approach" to Judaism even as it held fast to many old-time rituals. This contrasted with the Orthodoxy they had seen, where there had been people who did not observe everything strictly, yet these lapses had been hidden and denied. He did not like feeling like a sinner, as the Orthodox made him feel. He liked the revolutionary character of Conservative Judaism. Harris and Gloria preferred being among the more observant and committed in the Conservative synagogue rather than being counted among the less religious in the Orthodox one. The forthrightness of the Conservative group approach felt more spiritually honest. Moreover, in the Conservative synagogue, everyone could be open about not only what they did but also about what they did not do. "It's really a consensus type of thing," said Harris, a Judaism that left the people who practice it in control. And he liked that.

As Gloria summed up their situation: "We are conservadox because we are much more observant than the majority of Conservative Jews." In fact Gloria had become a kind of booster for Judaism: if there was anything that still bothered her, it was not that others in the congregation and the movement were not more observant but that they were Jewishly ignorant. And her daughters, who were even more learned than their parents about Judaism (something of which both Gloria and Harris were genuinely proud), had come to prefer a more traditional Judaism (at college, one of them attended the Orthodox services). When they came home and worshiped at Kehillath Achim, they eschewed the egalitarian alternative services, which their parents commonly attended.

Both Gloria and Harris were regulars at the alternative services. For Gloria the appeal of the alternative services was not so much its egalitarian character, though she certainly did not oppose that. "I don't go because women participate. . . . I find the intimacy of the alternative service far more spiritual than the large congregation." And she liked hearing from others besides simply the rabbi. "I find the *divrei torah* more interesting. I like the varied points of view. You get to learn about people and what they believe, because you hear from different people all the time. And I think the davening is just much more meaningful. People do it because they *feel* it. And that makes a big difference to me."

Harris also valued some of the egalitarian moves, however tentative, that the congregation was taking. But he so strongly valued a small service that he would abandon the large sanctuary even to attend the so-called "parallel service"—held for those traditionalists who would not worship in the main sanctuary when a bat mitzvah girl was called up to the torah. At the parallel service he could play an active part in running things; he could pray aloud and not simply be part of a passive audience. So much did he find the many bar and bat mitzvahs, with their pomp and circumstance, a distraction and a spiritual turn-off that he often skipped the big show on Shabbat mornings in favor of the smaller Friday night or Saturday afternoon services that reminded him more of the little Orthodox shuls of his childhood. Still, he was by conviction now a Conservative Jew, and both he and Gloria agreed that if there were no Kehillath Achim in town, they would move. For them, Kehillath Achim was a rich Jewish treasury, with its rabbis, role models, and others who took their Judaism seriously. It met their needs as spiritual seekers.

And participation linked them to their Jewish and personal pasts. In Gloria's conception, this was particularly important. Her parents had been aggressively unobservant, whereas she was now observant. She felt that she had somehow closed the circle. "I am doing something my grandparents and great-grandparents did." Now at last she was able to get past her parents. And both Gloria and Harris hoped to continue, as one of them put it, "climbing up the ladder of observance," in spite of the fact that their children were grown and no longer living at home.

NORA E.: CLOSE BUT NOT QUITE INSIDE

Now in her forties, Nora grew up in Newark with a father who, until she was three years old, was the head of a local Hebrew school and a mother who was from a "totally irreligious family." During her youth, she sometimes witnessed candle lighting, "vestiges of a Passover seder, but always with [an undercurrent of] tremendous anger." And she perceived High Holiday synagogue attendance as an "archaic obligation." In short, as Nora summed up her Jewish upbringing, the result was "tremendous religious tension in my house," which disturbed her greatly. She "promised" herself never to repeat that pattern.

She did not have much in the way of formal Jewish education, "never went to Hebrew school," in spite of her father's job. She had not been brought up in

a Jewish community and "just felt that my friends who were in a Jewish community and neighborhood had *tremendous* advantages over me; I always longed
for that." Nevertheless, in college she was not very active at Hillel, although "I
wouldn't even date a non-Jew." Nora's marriage (to a man who grew up Orthodox) came "very late." Her three children, however, came very quickly.

Nora felt it "was very important that we move to a community with a very
strong Jewish population and the ability to have access to everything that was
culturally and religiously Jewish." So thirteen years earlier, when her oldest was
three years old, her family moved to where they now live. As with so many others, her affiliation followed her children's Jewish schooling. At first, she chose a
local Reform temple, but within only a few weeks "it became very clear to me
that I couldn't tolerate the diluted atmosphere." She chose to switch to Kehillath
Achim because it was "close to home," and she thought the "Hebrew school
was superb, second to none," and the "social back-up" was there. That is, it was
part of a rich and varied Jewish community. "I am very happy at Kehillath
Achim." Today her oldest son is a junior in high school; her teenage daughter
is in Hebrew high school and U.S.Y., the national Conservative Jewish movement, and she has an eleven-year-old in the Hebrew school.

Yet for all this, as well as the rituals like Friday night dinner, Shabbat candles,
and kiddush, Nora believes "there are tremendous forces pulling us away from
synagogue." These are the forces of an American life that she and her family
have embraced. In particular, she cites a son who plays soccer. Her son is "not
just a player; he's an exceptional player." And soccer practice and games are always on Saturdays and Sundays, which competes with Shabbat and Hebrew
school, "and I can't deprive him of that because he'll become very angry about
being a Jew." She added, "I don't want to make [Judaism] a chore; I want to make
it a pleasure." After all, the boy is "here three days a week for Hebrew school."
She knew well what it felt like to experience a Judaism filled with tension, and
she did not want her children to have that sort of feeling toward Judaism or the
synagogue. Perhaps, she reflected, had she sent her children to day school, these
sorts of conflicts might not have emerged. But that was not the choice she made.

As she observed, "I did not know how much I was going to love the almost
daily experience of being Jewish until I really became involved in Kehillath
Achim." So if she had it to do over again, she says, she would send the children
to day school. "One of the difficult things about being a Jew," she added, "is
having to make decisions so early. I would have loved to have my daughter and
my son when they finished eighth grade to be able to go to a Hebrew high school,
but they didn't have the background." She regretted that "Jews are not allowed
to learn late," and this she believed would lead to losing a lot of children "socially." But now it was too late for her own children. Now soccer was in competition with Jewish education, and soccer was winning.

For Nora, too, there remain obstacles to greater involvement. As one who does not come to shul all the time, she feels it: "There's an intimidating character to Kehillath Achim because there are so many of the people here who have background and knowledge that if you don't have that you sometimes have to take a deep breath and walk in." She did not quite know what to do about this, but added, "I think there has to be some aspect of Judaism to bring in everybody from the wings." Then, almost as an afterthought she added, "I hope my children will feel comfortable here. What I'm worried about now is—will my children marry Jews?"

MARK AND STELLA W.: LOOKING FOR MORE

Speaking in the flat-voweled accents of his native New England, Mark W., the son of American-born Jews and today a respected local physician, described growing up in a city of about 55,000, about 10 percent of whom he believed were Jewish. As a boy, his neighborhood seemed in those days to be a sort of ghetto, with several synagogues, a kosher butcher, bakeries where the twisted loaves of challah were plentiful, and a general Jewish ambience. His maternal grandparents, who lived nearby, kept a kosher home, but his paternal grandparents, who were also a block away, did not. Nor did his own parents. Both sets of grandparents played a role in his life "for many, many years." The Jewish holidays Mark remembered observing were always with his grandparents. So on Rosh Hashanah and Yom Kippur they went to his grandparents' Orthodox synagogues, although, as Mark recalled, neither set of grandparents was "truly Orthodox." Mark's parents, however, joined the local Conservative synagogue where Mark celebrated his bar mitzvah. He recalled that shortly after his bar mitzvah, the synagogue changed its affiliation to Reform. His parents stayed in the congregation. The various local synagogues had joined to create a community-wide school, which Mark attended three or four days a week from the age of eight or nine until his bar mitzvah. "And that was pretty much like an Orthodox teaching," he remembered, "including use of a ruler to rap your knuckles." The pain of those raps was about all that Mark remembered. "And so when I was bar mitzvah in May of 1948 that finished my Hebrew education." For that bar mitzvah, Mark chanted the haftarah, which he had learned by rote from a recording. Other than that, he could read Hebrew slowly, "but I couldn't understand very much. And that was pretty much it."

As he entered his teenage years, Mark's Jewish involvement was essentially limited to going to the synagogue on the High Holidays, but neither he nor his father fasted on Yom Kippur. On Hanukkah, he lit some candles and on Passover went to his father's parents. And in college, he did not really identify Jewishly, though he thought that he had probably "joined" Hillel "but I wasn't a major participant." He guessed that he did not go to any Shabbat services "for many, many years."

Then he met Stella, to whom he has been married for over thirty-five years. She grew up in southern New England and attended a large Conservative synagogue. Like Mark, she too had celebrated major Jewish holidays at her grandparents' home. Like Mark's maternal grandparents, hers kept a kosher home and were nominally Orthodox but not very observant. But unlike Mark's experience, Stella's parents' home was also kosher, though they followed the fashion already common at the time, not keeping kosher outside their home. Stella attended Sunday school but had no after-school Jewish education beyond that. "At the time," Stella explained, "this was what you did. There was no weekday after school for women where I lived," and occasionally she attended Shabbat services, but did not celebrate a bat mitzvah. She did, however, become "confirmed" at the age of fifteen.

In college, Stella's Jewish life "didn't increase; it just stayed the same." Nevertheless, she felt a strong ethnic tie to her Jewishness and was unhappy at how few Jews were at the women's school where she began her college career. So she transferred to another school, where she eventually met Mark. Like him, she remembered going to Hillel only occasionally. And both recalled trying interreligious dating. For Mark, it came in medical school and for Stella in high school. "My mother was very angry, really angry. And that was the end of that," Stella recalled.

After Mark and Stella married in a Conservative synagogue, they lived in New England. They then moved to the community in which they still lived. For the first eight years of their marriage, neither had joined a synagogue. For holidays or Jewish needs, they went to Stella's parents. But now, with their oldest child, a son, six years old, they both felt, as Mark put it, "even though I hadn't been attending services, that we wanted our children to have a Jewish education." They had been in town for nearly five years.

They had sent their daughters to the nursery school at the nearby Reform temple, though not for any ideological reasons. In fact, as Stella explained, that congregation was a place she would never have considered joining "because it wasn't a place where I felt comfortable." Mark agreed. The choice of Kehillath Achim, however, seemed a natural one. Mark had been a member of B'nai Brith, Stella of Hadassah, "and that cluster of people that we had become friends with were coming to Kehillath Achim," as Mark explained. That was the majority of their close friends. In a sense, as they both agreed, before joining they had simply been unaffiliated Conservative Jews. Now they were formalizing that identification with the world from which they had come.

While Mark thought they had joined the congregation at Stella's instigation, she on the other hand remembered Mark coming home saying that he thought that joining the synagogue was the right thing to do. At first they were not certain Kehillath Achim was going to be a perfect fit, but they liked its *mechina,* the educational program that allowed youngsters to get into the Talmud Torah at an early age. Both Mark and Stella wanted their children to go to the synagogue school.

While they had joined the synagogue out of these child-centered concerns and for the social contacts, the experience began to have an impact on their own Jewish life, a change that Mark attributed largely to his wife. "We have become, with Stella's instigation, much more observant about things. More and more Shabbat at home, coming to services certainly much more frequently." The fact that both their parents died at this time intensified things further, as Mark and Stella became "fairly regular kaddish" reciters, a practice that brought them to far more services than they had ever attended before.

As their children were growing up, Stella came for Shabbat services every week. Because of his medical practice, Mark did not attend as frequently. Stella also began a campaign to persuade other Talmud Torah parents to come with their children. She wanted to build the junior congregation as a place where children could learn how to connect what they were learning in the Talmud Torah with the experience of Jewish worship. Later, the parents would move to the main sanctuary, while the "juniors" became increasingly comfortable in their own congregation. From there they would move on first to a teen service and ultimately as young adults to the main sanctuary. Behind this was the conviction that the children were "the future."

While she never made her home kosher, as her mother had done, she tried at least to keep obviously non-kosher foods out. The basic rituals that have become an accepted feature of American Jewish life—Hanukkah candles and Passover seders—were always celebrated, and Stella lit Shabbat candles and saw to it that kiddush was recited every Shabbat. Even after her children had largely moved out of the house, Stella kept coming to the synagogue weekly, and Mark was able to take more Saturdays off and come as well.

Today, both saw the synagogue as an "anchor" in their lives. "You know," Stella explained, "our friends now are thinking of moving to warmer climates to Florida, here and there and the other place. And we've talked about this a lot." But, she concluded, both the town community "and the Kehillath Achim community are exceedingly important to us."

Yet as much as Stella and Mark loved the synagogue, there were things that bothered them about it. In particular, they wanted a place that was more progressive and in tune with the times. And more than anything else, the matter of women in the synagogue weighed on their minds. Stella articulated the matter this way: "It's been very comfortable here and it's been a major part of my life. I come frequently; I participate; I've said kaddish for both parents every day for a year. However, I still feel the same that I would like very much to be able to participate equally in the service and in the religious aspects."

The alternative service, which she had played a part in starting, was not enough to satisfy her. There, women could lead the service, read from or be called to the torah, and more, but they could not be counted in the quorum. She wanted equal rights in the main sanctuary, where, "particularly since my parents have died, I prefer to go and say kaddish." As Mark pointed out, his grown daughter participates in a Conservative synagogue where she is counted as part of the minyan. But here, "we haven't been as inclusive as the Conservative movement allows us to be." Stella vigorously agreed. "Why deprive a woman from learning more or caring more about her Judaism? What have we accomplished by limiting women?"

To Mark, those who claim that women's full participation in Judaism is religiously threatening were missing the point. Why not let women do as much as they are willing to do, which was a great deal more, he reasoned. "So long as the movement is saying there is more that is allowable," he concluded, "let's get there."

MIMI M.: MARGINALLY INVOLVED BUT STILL PART OF THE CONGREGATION
Mimi, an attorney in her early thirties, was raised in an urban neighborhood "in transition" (read: in which whites were in the process of flight to the suburbs). Many of her Jewish neighbors were not comfortable sending their children to the public schools; neither were her parents. They were what she called "right-wing Conservative" rather than Orthodox, but nevertheless sent Mimi to a yeshiva in the neighborhood. Although traditional Jewish practices and worldviews were familiar to her, Mimi always felt "different" from the other children in school with her, most of whom were part of the Orthodox world that dominated the Jewish life in the neighborhood. She offered examples of her "differentness," speaking in the vocabulary of contemporary Orthodoxy: "We turned on the lights on Shabbos; we ripped toilet paper, we watched television on Shabbos. My friends' parents wouldn't do that. I remember there were some parents who would not let their children eat at my home, even though our home was kosher."

In the middle of seventh grade, she switched to a Conservative day school to which she commuted in northern New Jersey, where "the people were more like me" and she "felt a lot more comfortable" because it was "less strict." After the eighth grade she went for one year to a public high school in New York, until her family finally moved to the suburbs where they joined Kehillath Achim. In this suburb, where the schools were first-rate, Mimi continued in public education and ended her full-time Jewish schooling, although she remained within the Jewish orbit. In addition to going to synagogue, she joined U.S.Y., the Conservative youth movement. Later, she became active in Young Judea, a national Zionist youth movement, and became chapter president.

For all this, her Jewish involvement in college was minimal: "None that I can recall." She would, however, come home for the High Holidays and Passover, and light Hanukkah candles in her room. Then she went to law school, and, in telling me her story, she says, "This is where it gets more interesting."

"I had never dated out of my religion; all my boyfriends were Jewish," she explained. "Most of my friends were Jewish, growing up. I . . . didn't have a lot of interaction with people who weren't Jewish."

But in law school she met someone who was not Jewish and married him. Although he eventually converted to Judaism, his conversion was through the Reform rather than the Conservative movement, with which Mimi identified and still considered herself affiliated. She knew that this made her husband's conversion suspect in the eyes of some.

In time, Mimi and her husband bought a house in the suburb where her mother and father lived. "When we first moved, we did not join [Kehillath Achim] but I would attend services with my parents." And why was that? "It made me feel comfortable, warm and good to be among Jews and doing things that are familiar, and putting aside the outside world and sort of one-on-one with God, with my soul."

After her children were born, she became a member of the synagogue in her own right. The choice was simple: "I identify as a Conservative Jew, as opposed to a Reform or Orthodox. I would *not* join an Orthodox synagogue. I would not choose to go to a Reform synagogue because personally it is not my style."

In truth, however, in spite of her formal membership, Mimi's synagogue involvement was currently at a very low level; her husband's was even lower. Their home was not kosher, though they did light Hanukkah candles. When Mimi went to the synagogue, it was generally alone. And on the high holidays, her husband came only to the close of Yom Kippur services or to the first night of Rosh Hashanah. She would take her son to services on Sukkot and Simchat Torah, but again without her husband.

Ironically, though a member at Kehillath Achim, Mimi finds herself again surrounded by the many Orthodox people from the neighborhood who send their children to the nonsectarian Kehillath Achim nursery school. In turn, quite a few of them have become a part of her school-based social circle. But of course, they will likely look at her children in much the way that Mimi was treated when she was young, for many of those young Orthodox couples moving into the neighborhood will later send their youngsters to day schools, while Mimi intends to send her own youngsters to the local public schools, "and they will not see their [Orthodox] friends there."

As for Kehillath Achim, she found it a comfortable place to go on occasion, but not the community to which she felt personally called just yet. "In some respects, I'd like the shul to be a smaller place, more familiar," but, as she

said, "It's not and that's fine." For the moment, she was content to remain on
its periphery. Kehillat Achim is "simply a place to observe my religion and to
teach my children their religion. I don't feel part of the congregation. It's *not* a
social place because . . . this is not where my friends are."

That did not mean she would not like the synagogue to become her princi-
pal social circle, or at least something more embracing, a place that she could
feel as close to as other members do. Actually, Mimi assumed that her Jewish
"involvement [would] increase as my children move through the grades" of the
Hebrew school. Whether this would truly happen, however, remained to be seen.

VIVIAN AND SOL K.: IN LOVE WITH THE SYNAGOGUE AND WITH AN EVOLVING JUDAISM

Now in her fifties, Vivian was born into an "Orthodox home in Brooklyn" and
had attended yeshiva. Deeply committed to Jewish life, she holds a degree in
Jewish history, works for a major national Jewish organization, and is an active
member of Kehillath Achim, a congregation she "loves." In many ways she represents the elite of the Conservative movement.

While Vivian's family was Orthodox, it was also highly intellectual, and as
Vivian recalled "always questioning," never accepting Judaism unthinkingly as
she believed most Orthodox Jews did. Her mother actually had come out of the
secular *Hashomer Hatzair* pioneer Zionist movement, which considered much
of Orthodoxy as hopelessly Old World. Only after her parents were married some
time did they become Orthodox, in part because they found that their Hebraist
aspirations for their children could best be fulfilled in a new style yeshiva that
taught modern Hebrew and encouraged Zionism. (Vivian's mother, whose own
father had written a Hebrew dictionary, became a Hebrew teacher, and passed
her love for Jewish languages and culture on to her children.) As part of her
education Vivian was required to attend junior congregation at the school. "And
we learned everything."

In college, Vivian continued to see herself as an Orthodox Jew, although
her nascent feminism and her conviction that she knew as much if not more
than the men who were running Judaism fostered a muted but growing alienation from Orthodoxy, if not from Judaism in general. Vivian also spent a year
in Israel and came back to be "very active in Hillel and the student Zionist organization." Jewish feminism and Zionism became central to her sense of who
she was.

Sol, her husband, was also a convert to the Conservative movement. A
fiftyish college professor, he was born in Europe and spent his earliest years running from the Nazis until the family managed to get into Switzerland. His parents were Yiddishists—his father a Yiddish writer. Like many if not most
Yiddishists, Sol's parents had been ardently secular, although they themselves

grew up in Orthodox families. The war, however, moved them to a greater religious commitment. Sol's father had vowed that if he and the family managed to escape the Nazis and made it into America, he would see to it that they would become religious. That day came when Sol was nine years old: his father enrolled the children in a traditional yeshiva, where Sol remained through high school. All the while his parents' home was becoming increasingly Orthodox and their kitchen kosher. They observed all the holidays. Sol then commuted to college, and after college he met and married Vivian.

In a sense while both Vivian and Sol had grown up in the Orthodox domain, neither was ever quite at home in it. Nevertheless, the event that finally propelled them out of the Jewish orbit of their youth came during the brief time that they lived in California. They were located in a place where there was no Orthodox synagogue and where the only synagogue, which was Conservative, was not within walking distance. At this time Sol and Vivian befriended two other Orthodox couples from New York, and the three couples engaged in long debates over whether to transgress the Shabbat prohibition of motorized travel and drive to the one synagogue in the area. In the end, the other two couples decided to stay home on Shabbat. "And we drove to shul," Vivian explained. "To me it was distancing myself from the community [if I stayed home], which the Haggadah calls *kofer ba'iker* [denying the essence of Judaism]." That decision signaled their transition from Orthodoxy.

Shortly afterward, in the late 1960s, they returned to the East coast, where Sol became a professor. They could find no synagogue that suited their needs, although for a time they tried to help to revitalize a moribund Orthodox congregation in the inner city. And then they moved to suburbia, where they joined Central Synagogue and sent their young children to the local Schechter school that was just getting organized. Over the next few years they came to realize that many of those involved in the new school were affiliated with Kehillath Achim. "We discovered our community was here," as Vivian put it. At the same time, the rabbi at Central Synagogue, to which they could and did walk on Shabbat, proved to be "a disappointment" to them. When their third child was born, they decided to buy a new house and move into the Kehillath Achim orbit. In Vivian's words: "We moved because the synagogue was so important."

Both Vivian and Sol felt it suited them perfectly. In his quiet and understated way, Sol said simply: "I feel much more comfortable in a Conservative shul than I ever did in an Orthodox shul, and this one is very fine." Then he added that in this congregation, "I don't think anyone would be made to feel uncomfortable, no matter what his belief." He appreciated this laissez-faire attitude, even though his own level of observance and belief was relatively high compared to most of the congregation. "We walk to shul almost every Shabbat; we no longer drive. And we have a kosher home; we observe all the holidays."

What Vivian liked most about Conservative Judaism was not its practices, but the thought processes behind the movement. "It's not fundamentalist." As opposed to Orthodoxy, which she believed was preoccupied with minutiae and colored by increasing intolerance of pluralism, Conservative Judaism, especially as practiced in Kehillath Achim, was tolerant of change, even though it tried to remain close to the tradition. As Vivian summed it up, Kehillath Achim has a "place for every one; there's a place for seeking, a place for performing. You can find your own minyan." Then she concluded: "I love the shul."

More than that, she added, "I find I have my intimate circle of friends here but I can even transcend my grouping." That is, she felt an attachment to the congregation as a whole. And she liked the fact that she could find a way to express herself Jewishly as a woman. While she wished that this was not limited to the alternative service, she acknowledged that she was given far more opportunities here than she would ever have in an Orthodox congregation, and all this without sacrificing her real attachment to Jewish traditions and liturgy. Besides, she was convinced that in time, the congregation would approve more religious change and opportunities for gender equality. Beyond all that she added, "I love the rabbi," adding, "I think he's exceptional. He's all goodness; there's no *shtiklach*," no petty concerns. A rabbi's character, she believed, pervaded the congregation. For her, the rabbi's *menschlichkeit* (humanity), benevolence and compassion pervaded the congregation. This was no small matter. If she did not like the rabbi, "I would have a problem," she replied, recalling how just that had driven her away from the other synagogue.

Not that all was perfect at Kehillath Achim. Although two out of her three grown children, all of whom had received day school educations, were committed to a high level of Jewish observance and style of life similar to her own, and she believed that the third, who had lived in Israel for a time, was on the verge of returning to greater religious commitments, she worried about Conservative continuity. "I will say we are not as successful with Jewish continuity for our children, and that's a problem." But she also understood that there was, as she put it, "a life-cycle character" to Jewish involvement. Pointing to a member with very young children who came only three days a year, Vivian argued: "Once the kids get older, she's going to want to heighten that observance." Those with children, she was convinced, "have a second chance to get involved."

She had a theory: Jewish skills led to Jewish involvement. The key, she said, was getting young people involved. "If a kid can *lein* [read torah] he will always be found and asked to participate or even lead a service." Or, alternatively, "If you have kids who get attached to the liturgy, you have them for life." Knowing how to read Hebrew or lead prayers would always lead to one's being drawn into Jewish life wherever it existed—life-cycle rhythms notwithstanding.

DANNY AND ELLA M: CONVERGING IN THE CONSERVATIVE MOVEMENT
Danny and his family fled their native Belgium at the time of the German invasion in 1940, arriving in America when he was two. The family settled in the big city, and Danny was sent to a yeshiva affiliated with a modern Orthodox synagogue: "My parents wanted me to have a Jewish education."

Danny's parents attended synagogue fairly regularly, on every holiday and sometimes also on Friday evenings. As Danny saw it, they did what they had always done, carrying on—albeit sometimes in an indolent manner—the traditions of their parents. In a sense, Danny reflected this attitude, too. By his own appraisal, he was not an outstanding or even very devoted student in the yeshiva. At the end of his primary years, he was given the choice of whether to continue or go to another school. "And I opted to continue because I was afraid to change, and all my friends were there." In the summers, Danny went to an Orthodox camp that emphasized Hebraic and Zionist elements of Judaism. This was the culture of an emerging American modern Orthodoxy, a culture in which Danny felt most at home.

Although he had looked forward to a change after high school, the death of his father during his freshman year of college propelled him back into the bosom of Jewish life and culture. Searching for a minyan in which to recite the mourner's kaddish, he discovered the Jewish Culture Foundation, a kind of Jewish enclave on campus, and ultimately became its president for a year and a half. And so, once again, Danny found himself pulled along into the stream of an Orthodox lifestyle.

But in college Danny was starting to swim against that stream, at first imperceptibly and then more vigorously. In the beginning, he would simply start the week a bit too close to the end of Shabbat. Then he would get into the car earlier and earlier, sometimes before actual nightfall. He also became lax in his observance of the dietary laws, and, "although I wouldn't eat pork or shellfish," ultimately began to eat non-kosher meat when out of the house. It was when he had wandered far beyond the banks of his Orthodoxy that he met Ella.

Ella had grown up in a totally assimilated home. She was "third-generation American, on [her] mother's side." Her paternal grandfather was Orthodox, but his Orthodoxy remained foreign and strange to her. "I used to see my grandfather lay tefillin, but it was the weirdest thing I had ever seen in my entire life." And she recalled seeing him carrying a torah to a synagogue. But while she still could visualize these Jewish scenes, they remained a distant and inchoate mystery: "No one ever explained anything to me."

At one point this Orthodoxy invaded Ella's home: her grandfather came to stay. Once, Ella remembered, "I decided to make bacon—we were not kosher. And my mother walked in the house and turned as white as a sheet and said, 'Your grandfather's coming home from synagogue'—I can still hear her voice—

and she went around the house opening the windows and taking a towel to get the aroma of the bacon out of the house. And that was my Judaism."

She did not go to Sunday school and attended a Reform temple only on Yom Kippur, a day on which she would fast except for drinking water. Her family had a Passover seder as long as her grandfather was alive, but she could not remember for sure if they continued after his death. They did not light candles on Shabbat or on Hanukkah. She did remember receiving Christmas presents. She sometimes attended the "Progressive [Reform] Synagogue" youth group and also went to its dances and on its trips and sang with its choral group.

In college in the early 1960s, Ella dated non-Jews but, like many of her generation, asserted, "I always knew I would marry someone Jewish." Then she added: "I don't know how that was absorbed to my being, but it was. It was just like an unspoken understanding." On campus, she had only Jewish friends. Here she met Danny, and six months later they were married.

At that time, his mother made a request: she asked Ella to keep a kosher home and give their children a Jewish education. Ella, who had a real rapport with her widowed mother-in-law, agreed, although she and Danny continued to eat nonkosher everywhere else.

"The kosher home was a game to me; I loved having all the dishes, and the silverware," said Ella. But there were other Jewish demands that came with Orthodoxy that Ella discovered at the time of her marriage that she was not nearly as willing to fulfill—for example, going regularly to a mikvah, a ritual bath, to mark the end of her menstrual cycle. Danny allayed her anxieties and told her these were not his expectations.

Given the gap in their Jewish backgrounds and the fact that Danny was no longer strictly observant, they chose to affiliate with a Conservative synagogue, which seemed a logical compromise. And when the death of Danny's mother propelled him again to a more intensive synagogue involvement, this time he recited the kaddish in the Conservative synagogue, where he "felt more comfortable." Ella, however, still felt alien in that environment.

When they decided to buy a house, they came to where they now live almost by accident. Danny had been given a realtor's card from this neighborhood. When he came to look at the community, he discovered that the place had a kosher butcher and deli, a Conservative synagogue, and a house that he and Ella liked. The discovery that the son of the synagogue's rabbi had gone to summer camp with him years before helped seal the decision to move here and join Kehillath Achim.

When he walked into the synagogue, he immediately felt "it was a right match." To illustrate, he offered a story. Shortly after he joined the synagogue, he was asked to chant a haftarah. Although he knew well how to do this, he felt discomfited by the prospect. Walking over to the man who had assigned him this task, he whispered, "I'm embarrassed. I can't do a haftarah; I drive to shul on Shabbat." In the Orthodox world in which he had grown, this admission of Shabbat transgression would have disqualified him from such an honor. But the man to whom he had revealed himself gave him a friendly push and replied: "Forget it, most of the people here drive on Shabbat; it's O.K." As Danny now understood, "If we disqualified everyone who drove to shul or wasn't strictly kosher, we'd have very few who would read the haftarah." Here then was a synagogue made for him, a place where "people don't look over your shoulder to see exactly what you're doing, and yet we still attempt to do as much as we can." The fact that he had the basic competence put him way ahead of many others. He could be himself; he could participate at whatever level he wished, and he could feel comfortable about it, guilt-free.

Ella also began to change. In part because she was now a mother and in part because she was becoming involved with other Kehillath Achim couples, Ella began the journey from a marginal religious existence to being a committed Jew whose life was filled with Jewish content and observance. The source of this growth, she said, was a combination of the influence of her husband, the synagogue, and its community, as well as the work environment of a Jewish museum where Ella was a docent. Ella had immersed herself in the study of Judaism, and sometimes now she even taught others, especially about Jewish art. More than that, she concluded: "I . . . feel like a whole person. I never felt affiliated to anything. The synagogue is my second home. . . . I used to eat lobster and everything out of the house, and we don't do that anymore." Indeed, as she concluded: "I am so rooted in my Judaism now. At work, they call me 'rabbi.'"

One evening she went to hear a local Orthodox rabbi, who talked "about how important it is for children to have their Jewish education. I went home and I said to Danny, 'Whatever you want, it's fine with me.'" And that was when they decided to give their children an intensive day school education at the local Solomon Schechter school.

Ella and Danny had become part of the small circle of mainstays of the synagogue. Not only were they active in the organization, they came every Shabbat morning and often on other occasions as well. It was not unusual to see them at a Shabbat afternoon mincha service, when no more than twenty-five people normally attended. On Shabbat mornings, Ella particularly appreciated the alternative services and recently became one of the regulars at the learner's service led by the educational director. This service had evolved into a service for those who thought learning about Jewish life and discussion of the weekly torah portion or other texts was the key to Shabbat worship.

All this was not to say that Ella saw her religious development as complete. There were still issues with which she was grappling. Thus, for example, she found the concept of Divine revelation difficult, and these theological difficulties troubled her: "I felt guilty about it." She looked to the rabbi for help. He told her not to feel guilty, to keep seeking. She loved the answer.

THE PICTURE THAT EMERGES

Like the people at Central Synagogue, these members of Kehillath Achim are people who have found meaning in their attachment to the synagogue. Whether it is Gloria, Harris, or Ella, members of the core community for whom the synagogue provides help and company as they climb the ladder of observance, or Vivian and Sol, for whom it is a place where they can combine the quest for community with a sense of Jewish fulfillment, the synagogue remains an important part of their lives. Even for Mark and Stella, who are looking for something more, in particular a greater empowerment for women, Kehillath Achim remains an anchor in their lives, a place out of whose orbit they refuse to move. Still others, like Nora or Mimi, who find coming to the synagogue a bit intimidating and not always possible on a regular basis and whose involvement is therefore more peripheral, nevertheless retain positive feelings about being members. For all of these people, the story of their Jewish development—whether in its movement away from old orthodoxies or in the gradual return to Jewish interests—inevitably intersects with the life of their synagogue, and they could not conceive of it in any other way. All in some way have been shaped by their childhood Jewish experiences and find Conservative Judaism a fitting expression of that biography. And all care about how the synagogue will help them keep their children Jewish, a promise of continuity that all are committed to keep.

These Jews have not fallen into the movement by default but embraced it out of choice. In the marketplace of ideas and affiliation that modern life has become, the synagogue and its animating Judaism have proven to be powerfully attractive. In great measure this is because it provides meaning, a sense of belonging, rootedness, and continuity.

5: Passing on the Message: Children and Synagogue Life

And a little child shall lead them.

                                                        Isaiah 11:6

And you shall teach them diligently to your children.

                                                        Deuteronomy 6:7

The concern with children, and in particular their absorption of Judaism, is, as we have just concluded, one of the essentials for those who participate in Conservative synagogue life. We have seen that people often join the synagogue upon the birth of their first child or when that child is ready to begin Jewish education. That education, in turn, is often perceived and presented as a necessary prerequisite for the all-important bar or bat mitzvah rite of passage.

If the danger in this approach is that people will in one way or another come to consider going to the synagogue (and Jewish observance in general) as "kid stuff," the promise implicit in this focus is that it fosters the Jewish engagement of the adults, at least insofar as they are parents and grandparents. Being an active Jew may be a by-product of being an active parent. Even for those who remain peripherally involved in synagogue life, the anchor of that involvement is often their concern with their children.

The orientation of Judaism and synagogue life around a concern with children is further enhanced in the suburban milieu with its child-centered concerns for good schools, private homes, and open spaces. Synagogues increasingly are expected to assist in these enhancements of child development. Indeed, both Kehillath Achim and Central Synagogue use their nursery and religious schools, on which they spend large resources, as key vehicles for bringing in new members.

"We wanted to be involved in our children's nursery school," one young mother explained, accounting for her growing attachment to the synagogue. This meant attending services on nursery school Shabbat, going on a synagogue retreat, and participating in various holiday events. Yet from doing things as a parent to doing them for one's own Jewish self was a short leap. Some parents resolve that their Jewish involvement will increase as their children move up through the grades: "As my children learn and do more in their Jewish lives, I am sure I shall as well," a young mother reasoned. "I want my children to have a Jewish education, foundation, and base as does my husband, and . . . to give them this involves our coming to shul and participating," said another in the same spirit. "We're both committed shul-goers," explained a third. "We believe on Shabbat we need to be here for ourselves, and as well because we believe that we need to set an example; and we want our children to see that we need to be here."

Both synagogues have established "Torah for Tots" programs in which parents (and often grandparents as well) come (some for the first time in a long time) with their children to be introduced into synagogue life. At Central Synagogue, the rabbi regularly meets with nursery parents (commonly mothers) for a seminar in some Jewish topic. In short, Judaism and parenting are inextricably intertwined. The triumph of each is often reflected in the other. That is why the bar and bat mitzvah are often seen not only as the child's Jewish coming of age but also as a confirmation of the parents' and the synagogue's success in making that coming of age both Jewishly informed and possible. And of course, every rabbi and Jewish educator, to say nothing of parents and community members, confronts bar and bat mitzvah celebrations.

In part, of course, each family must and will make its own judgments about whether or not it has succeeded Jewishly with its children. For many, the ultimate test is in what kind of a personal Jewish life their offspring establish, whom they marry (if they do), and how in turn they act as Jewish parents and Jewishly responsible adults. Undoubtedly, many of the members of both these synagogues also evaluate their own Jewish lives by looking at whether or not their children emulate them.

Yet if each individual had ways of Jewishly evaluating his or her life and children, how is a congregation to know whether its efforts have been successful? Perhaps to provide itself with some sort of public declaration and testimony of how they are doing, both synagogues have devised special public occasions at which their children bear witness to their relationship to the synagogue, Conservative Judaism, and the Jewish people. They are what social anthropologists call "cultural performances," occasions when members of a culture community publicly enact, reflect, communicate, perpetuate, and develop the pattern of meanings and shared conceptions that define their culture. These are moments when insiders have an opportunity to make "visible, audible, and tangible beliefs, ideas, values, sentiments and psychological dispositions that [otherwise] cannot directly be perceived."[16] Or, as anthropologist Clifford Geertz has put it, these are opportunities for people to offer not only models *of* what they believe, but also models *for* the believing of it: "In these plastic dramas men attain their faith as they portray it."[17]

In what follows I present an ethnographic sketch of four such cultural performances, public occasions when some of the youth demonstrate they have received the Jewish message that the congregation seeks to pass on to them. These are moments when in one way or another, Conservative Jewish identities and beliefs particular to the congregations are publicly displayed and reinforced. The four occasions are: (1) a synagogue procession in the main sanctuary by the nursery school children on Sukkot; (2) a "Torah for Tots" service; (3) a teen Shabbat; and (4) a college homecoming Shabbat. (One might have also inserted a bar or bat mitzvah, for these ceremonies often serve much the same function.) Each of these represents a kind of religiocultural report-in-progress of where the next generation is Jewishly.

Let us begin with the following postulate: a good performance of Jewish competence and engagement in the synagogue life is a way that both the synagogue school and the children prove themselves in public. And when both prove themselves, the congregation, as well as those who have helped their enculturation, have also proved themselves.

A SYNAGOGUE PROCESSION OF THE YOUNGEST CHILDREN

The festival of Sukkot presents a challenge to Kehillath Achim. One reason is that it may seem anticlimactic, falling immediately after the High Holidays. Unlike Rosh Hashanah and Yom Kippur, when almost every member of the synagogue makes an appearance, Sukkot appeals primarily to the core congregation. But even with this group there are limits, for the festival often competes with the demands of work and weekday routines, already much disturbed during the High Holiday season. Sukkot, according to Jewish tradition, "the time of our joy," is a festival that celebrates Jewish continuity, a theme most vividly symbolized by the last day's Simchat Torah celebrations, at which the conclusion of one torah reading cycle is coupled with the commencement of another in the never-ending Jewish sequence. Parents typically bring their children to the synagogue, especially for the evening service.

Sukkot is also a time for building a sukkah, a temporary dwelling that serves as a reminder of the huts built by the Israelites in the desert. Also during Sukkot, one makes a blessing over the "four species"—the citron, palm branch, myrtle, and willow—and makes *hakafot*, circuits, around the synagogue, that symbolize the endless circle of Jewish life.

One of the veteran members at Kehillath Achim has made it his special duty to teach members how to construct their own sukkot, and over the years many have done so. Together with their children they put up their huts, and people visit one another's to compare their decorations and accomplishments. This of course serves to tie members both to the ritual and to one another, and also to enhance and connect the celebration of Sukkot to synagogue life. Indeed, this sukkah-building project has helped save the festival from the void into which it might otherwise have fallen because of its place on the calendar, as the least celebrated holiday in a busy season.

But generally, only families that are very Jewishly engaged would consider building a sukkah. Those whose involvement in synagogue life is more tentative and limited need some less demanding but still compelling activity to bring them to the synagogue. At Kehillath Achim, that something is the children's *hoshanot* procession.

The *hoshanot* procession is the part of the service when the four species are carried around the sanctuary. According to tradition, only adult men are expected to participate. But at Kehillath Achim, it is the children who lead them. On cue, from the side doors, come a line of small children, the four species in hand. With the tall palm branches waving in their hands, they appear like a moving forest of sprouts, a testimony to the growth and vitality of the congregation. All around, the adults burst into smiles—parents, grandparents, and the core members of the congregation.

The children, all between five and eight years old, sit in the front rows and on the steps of the *bimah*, the front stage, literally at the feet of the rabbi and the congregation, as the focus of the proceedings. The rabbi then poses questions that, by their tone and manner, are clearly addressed to the children.

What sorts of Jews, he asks, do each of the four species represent? And the children answer, for the most part with great enthusiasm and accuracy. In the back, the educational director of the synagogue school, for whom this display of knowledge is a demonstration of his accomplishments no less than those of his students, swells with pride.

At last, the actual *hoshanot* procession begins, led by the assistant cantor. In addition to the many children, about twenty-five adult congregants, holding the four species, also join. In this congregation, the children are expected to have more—more Jewish education, more opportunity, more enthusiasm—than their forebears. The lopsided numbers in this march demonstrate that they have. One might say that when it comes to religious ritual, the congregation has also given the children more than their parents.

They all stride smartly around the sanctuary and out into the social hall—the line too long to fit into the sanctuary alone. When the procession reenters the sanctuary, all those present have an opportunity to greet the marchers as they pass by their seats. There is a sense of security, at least for the moment, that they have passed on Kehillath Achim Judaism to the next generation. Later, when the rabbi asks them questions about the customs and traditions of the holiday, the forest of hands that shoot up and the chorus of correct answers serve as confirmation that these youngsters are really in line.

TORAH FOR TOTS

"This congregation is doing a great deal—especially through the Torah for Tots service that has brought in so many unaffiliated people. . . . This has made people become active members." So said a member who described herself and her husband as "committed shul-goers." The idea behind Torah for Tots was to provide a kind of abbreviated synagogue service and program, less than an hour, that gives youngsters (many having their first exposure to the synagogue) a taste of what goes on there. The congregation had already tried such programs on Purim and was now trying it for Simchat Torah eve, about an hour before the regular services. Like Purim, this is a religious festival when normal decorum is ignored and the entire congregation engages in merriment, but the excess is sometimes frightening for the very young, and it can last far longer than a toddler can tolerate. Hence the decision to offer this special children's service.

Standing in the main sanctuary, a wireless mike in hand, the rabbi plays the role of master of ceremonies. Though ostensibly speaking to the tots, his remarks are clearly pitched toward the parents and grandparents. He introduces some adults and older youngsters who present a skit in which they lead the tots and their parents in a series of songs, stories, and questions that take them through the Jewish holidays, beginning with Rosh Hashanah and culminating in this night's celebration. Someone dressed in a Winnie-the-Pooh outfit comes onto the podium, a subtle if not fully intended effort to integrate Jewish content with American culture. The young children are attentive, many of them clearly taken by the presence of this "celebrity" who has somehow been transformed into a Jewish symbol by his presence in the synagogue. In a way, this skit parallels the festival quiz the rabbi gave the slightly older children a few days earlier at the *hoshanot* procession. It was another chance to demonstrate Jewish learning in front of the congregation and one's parents. That, in a sense, is what all the children's programs must do, if they are to rise above mere entertainment.

Following the skit, the program moved on to more songs and circle dances. Both parents and children displayed enthusiasm and seemed swept up by the celebration. In effect, these parents who came to the services for the sake of their children and who hoped to engender the latter's enthusiasm were also stimulating their own, in a synergy between parenting and religious enthusiasm.

The Simchat Torah for Tots gathering was an occasion of Jewish parenting that laminated religion and ritual with congregation and assembly. Apples were distributed afterward, and parents lingered, chatting with one another, building a fledgling congregational social network. Mothers seemed to outnumber fathers here, and the men who were present were identifiably new to synagogue life and style. Some parents took the time afterward with their children to approach the ark to examine the torah scrolls in their white mantles and sparkling silver crowns. They communicated to each child who joined in this impromptu investigation and exploration that this was something important to see. For some youngsters, this close encounter with the hallowed scrolls and ark was even more interesting and awe-inspiring than the nearby Winnie-the-Pooh. The ark, usually so distant and untouchable in the massive sanctuary (especially to the tots and perhaps also to their parents who have not been to the ark since they were young), was now suddenly available to them. Who knows what this encounter with a palpable torah will leave? Perhaps the residual impressions will be far more lasting than memories of the skit, the bear, and the apples.

This program brought out at least a hundred and fifty parents and children. Parents came to the synagogue for the sake of their children. The fair assumption was that they would continue to do so, another sign of the congregation's and the Jewish people's capacity for continuity.

A TEEN SHABBAT

Tots and toddlers are of course important, but the greater test comes with the teens, adolescents who have passed the all-important bar and bat mitzvah and who (after their "Jewish period") are tempted to abandon their Jewish identities. With the incentive of bar/bat mitzvah over, the congregation has had a problem attracting teens. To help, the synagogue enlisted the services of a rabbinical intern, who was later hired as an assistant rabbi, following his graduation

from the Jewish Theological Seminary. He offered teens an accessible model of
what a young and totally committed Conservative Jew could be and also helped
organize the weekly services for teens in the downstairs chapel. But although
he had served notably as a counselor of teens in summer programs, he was not
altogether successful in engendering either enthusiasm or a large turnout for these
weekly Shabbat services. On average only about eighteen to twenty teens attended regularly, and those often seemed more interested in talking to one another than in participating in the service. That is, they were interested in one
another as a community, but not always ready to infuse that communion with
Jewish content or intent.

"I will say we are not as successful with continuation for our children and
that's a problem," one of the active members of the congregation admitted in a
candid moment. Bar and bat mitzvah still remain for many in both congregations a cut-off point for Jewish and synagogue involvement, rather than a commencement. Still, there are teens in Kehillath Achim who appear to display the
promise of continuity and commitments to Conservative Judaism that, as a community, the congregation wants. This became most apparent on Teen Shabbat,
when the teens were given an opportunity to run the service in the main sanctuary, instead of remaining out of sight in the downstairs chapel. It was of course
also an occasion for the educational director and his staff, including the rabbinic intern, to publicly demonstrate that they were succeeding with at least
some of the teens. The Teen Shabbat would therefore be, as the educational
director put it, "the crown of glory." Moreover, by handing the Shabbat service
in the main sanctuary over to the teens, the congregation was, as the synagogue
president put it, demonstrating that "it is the obligation of each of us to do no
less [than our predecessors] for our own children." And in their performance,
the children would in turn demonstrate to the congregation that Kehillath
Achim and its version of Jewish life do have a future, that this generation of
elders has indeed done its job. Teen Shabbat is therefore a day of no small community consequence.

On this particular Teen Shabbat the main sanctuary was full, and an additional section was opened to increase seating capacity. So important was this
event for the congregation that even the parallel service (organized because females among the teens would be on the bimah participating in ritual activity
normally prohibited by the congregation to women) was quite poorly attended.
In fact, those there had to draft a "parallel" minyan. As one of its stalwarts told
me later, while the group awaited reinforcements for the quorum and discussed
the need to have such a service, it turned out that only one man there really
demanded it. Clearly, the tide against women's greater participation in the ritual
life of the synagogue was fast turning.

As the service proceeded, there were a few absentees for torah aliyot (among the most minor of honors, for it requires almost no display of Jewish competence except a recitation of blessings), but essentially the rest of the show— and a show it was, a chance for the congregation to show itself via its teens' performances exactly who and what it was—went smoothly. Among the major ritual tasks the teens were assigned were the reading of the torah, leading of the services, and of course giving a sermon and *d'var torah* (homily). Those who carried out these assignments would be the jewels in the crown of glory.

So crucial were these performances that those parents whose offspring were not assigned a high enough honor later expressed anger at the slight. It seemed that the parents' own honor and status, no less than their children's, was at stake.

More teens participated in the service on this Shabbat than in the weekly teen minyan. Like their elders, they were more likely to come to the synagogue for a "special occasion." Given the desire to attract non-regulars, the congregational periphery, to the synagogue on Shabbat, this occasion can be defined as one of many locally generated "festivals" whose aim is to make the day special and therefore bring in those who only come on "special occasions."

For today, the teens' control over the main sanctuary created the sense that, no less than at their bar and bat mitzvah, they were crossing the bridge into Kehillath Achim adulthood. This time, however, they were veterans, not the newly initiated.

The organizers of today's service sought to make it difficult to tell the difference between the day school and Hebrew school products, in an effort to foster an image of a unified community. Indeed, this divide, sometimes a source of tension, has emerged generally in the Conservative movement since the expansion of Schechter day schools and the contraction of supplementary education. To the uninformed observer, these background differences might be hard to discern in the teens' performances. To the informed observer, who knew which honors and ritual tasks took more background and skill than others, however, the distinctions were quite clear, as the cantor admitted in a candid moment. Thus, some of the teens who were products of the synagogue school performed the more limited ritual tasks or else performed in groups, reciting prayers as part of a mini-chorus (a device used since the first grade for those who might have a harder time performing alone), while others—often (but not exclusively) the day school students—were solo acts. This mirrored the lines in the congregation, where there were also those who were equipped to tackle solo ritual acts and others for whom only a brief ritual performance was possible. As with all cultural performances, this event was a model *of* and a model *for* life at Kehillath Achim.

Although there were errors made in the torah reading and prayer pronunciation, these were not corrected as Jewish law and custom mandate; that would mar the celebratory character of the occasion. Still, some of the participants were quite nervous. One cried. And the girl who chanted the maftir, or concluding torah passage, seemed on the verge of tears. As a whole, however, the teens' achievements were overwhelmingly a cause for communal pride.

To many in the congregation the ritual acts were impressive but also somewhat recondite. More accessible were the sermons and homilies, because they were given in English. These talks were actually reports from the teens' Jewish world, a chance for the congregation to gauge what their offspring took away from their Jewish training and outlook. In a sense, the speakers became collective representations of Kehillath Achim youth. As such, they were, as Emile Durkheim put it, someone who stands for the group and "who transcends himself, both when he thinks and when he acts."[18] Today's two major speeches were given by children who represented the religious elite of the teen population. One was the daughter of the rabbi who voluntarily heads the alternative service, a major figure in the Conservative movement. The other was the son of the synagogue's educational director, a key player in the religious life of the congregation. In many ways, the speeches of these two teens articulated publicly what for them was a commonplace of their lives: the meaning of committed Conservative Jewish identity.

The first speaker was a high school junior. Her "personal prayer," as this talk was titled on the program, touched on her identity. As she stepped forward and read from her prepared remarks (a copy of which she later gave me), a hush fell over the congregation. Elisheva addressed the crowd in a soft but sure voice. She had seen her father and brother take the podium on Shabbatot past; now at last it was her turn. She began:

> Identity? A definition? To actually be someone. To maintain certain characteristics that make you a unique individual. While "identity" is not an extraordinary word in the English language, it is, I would venture to say, a word with which many adolescents my age cannot relate. The question is: Why? Why do so many youths have a problem finding their identities?
>
> High school is a time of inner struggle. Speaking from personal experience, my struggle was intensified when I was forced to begin the search for my role as a member of the Jewish society, along side the secular one. For thirteen years I had been raised in a Conservative household. I knew no other aspects of Judaism other than what I had been living. Then, in September of my freshman year, I began to attend an Orthodox yeshiva. I was faced with a new lifestyle, one that I had never before explored. The first few months of that year were strange for me. I was taught to pray differently, dress differently, and open my mind to new possibilities. And this is where my inner conflict began.
>
> Throughout that year, I was in school from 7:50 in the morning until 5:00 in the evening. I barely had time to sit and talk with my

family, let alone think about my new experiences. Yet as the months continued, I realized it was time to open my eyes. I needed to sit down and think about the dramatic changes I was going through. I remember one day I spent an entire morning in my rebbe's office, crying. I was so confused and did not know how to deal with my frustration. I felt as though I was living inconsistently. For nearly nine hours every day, I would go to school to learn and act like an Orthodox Jew. However, when I would return home at the end of the day, I had to switch gears once again and resume my usual lifestyle. As I utilized an entire box of tissues, I told my rebbe about this conflict I was facing. And the entire time I spoke, he just sat there, listening, with a subtle smile stretched across his face. Then he began to speak, and the words that followed were ones that will remain with me for the rest of my life.

"Elisheva," he said, "nothing is wrong with you. In fact this is a very good thing. You have shown me that you are thinking, something most kids your age do not know how to do."

I heard these words, yet I had no response.

I spent the next couple of weeks thinking about what my rebbe said, his voice ringing in my ears. I never did come up with any definite answers to the problems I was facing. Even now, almost three years later, I often stop to think about what I am doing.

Everyone wants to have an identity. Feeling lost can be a very scary thing. And I know that while things may be hard for me now, they do not become easier next year when I leave home. Without anyone telling me how to observe Judaism, I am not sure which path I will choose to follow. Yet throughout all of my grappling, I have learned one thing. That is, for right now, I do not need to have a label. As long as I continue the search for my identity as a Jew in society, I am well on my way. As my rebbe said to me, I have begun to think, and sometimes that is what is most important.

There are several essential themes expressed here. First, Elisheva has taken this opportunity to reveal herself publicly to her community, to share with them her personal dilemma as a young woman committed to normative and active Conservative Judaism, as expressed in Kehillath Achim, and as a dedicated student in an Orthodox yeshiva. Does this put her at odds with either or both of these identities? Can she accept inconsistency? Implicit is a question that at least some of those in her audience might also be asking themselves. In a sense Elisheva has simply articulated the essential dualism of the culture in which she was nurtured. Elisheva knows her Judaism is a matter of thoughtful choice, yet she does not know what path she "will choose to follow" when she is soon away from home.

That she should make this conflict public at Kehillath Achim's teen Shabbat service, a setting in which she assumes she will be understood, demonstrates the

communal aspect of the congregation—it is a place where the young feel comfortable in baring their souls. She is torn by her Conservative Jewish identity
and her yeshiva worldview, as she tries to sort out which of these identities is
hers. Her answer is to ponder these things. She is a serious Jew, one who does
not do what she does by rote. Her choices, she suggests, are thoughtful Jewish
choices.

For the active members of this congregation, thoughtfulness, combined with
knowledge and commitment, is the hallmark of Conservative Judaism. And so,
Elisheva seems to be affirming an ethos she at least partially gained from the
very congregation she addresses: the key is to think, not just to do. And though
she is a Conservative Jew (albeit one who is not yet certain "which path I will
choose to follow"), her teacher's assurance that "there is nothing wrong with
you" may be for her (and her audience) a kind of legitimization (even by the
Orthodox) of her "usual lifestyle," the Conservative one.

One might argue that Elisheva's concerns were atypical. Obviously, the fact
that she went to an Orthodox yeshiva high school (at the time, there was no
Conservative high school in the county) played a key role in her identity consciousness. But she was also a product of Conservative Jewry's elite. The *d'var
torah* that followed a few minutes later suggests that Elisheva was not alone.

Yona, youngest son of the synagogue educational director and likewise a
graduate of the Schechter school and now a senior in the same yeshiva high
school, was to deliver today's talk in place of the rabbi's sermon. He also gave
me a copy of his remarks. Yona too presented his understanding of the special
contribution that Kehillath Achim had made to his life, and presumably as well
to the other teens whom in some way he represented this morning.

> Our parsha [the week's torah reading] begins with God revealing himself
> to Moshe with a new name. In doing so He says that He revealed
> himself in a different way to each of our forefathers: Abraham, Isaac,
> and Jacob. The verse reads:
> "And God revealed himself to Abraham, to Isaac, and to Jacob."
> Our commentators on the Bible were bothered by the additional
> use of the words "*To* Abraham, *to* Isaac, and *to* Jacob," when it could
> have simply said, "To Abraham, Isaac, and Jacob."
> One of the ways they reconcile this problem is to say that the
> seemingly extra words come to illustrate the special and personally
> unique relationship that God maintained with each of the forefathers.
> He revealed himself to Abraham in one way, to Isaac in another way,
> and to Jacob in yet another way.
> In many respects this understanding represents what Kehillath
> Achim has done for me. The Kehillath Achim community has given me
> the tools with which I can forge my own unique relationship with God.
> There are three specific tools that I would like to share with you today.

First, the practical tool. Learning how to read torah for my bar mitzvah with Cantor A. was an extremely valuable quality to learn. Through being able to read torah I have come to understand and comprehend better the beauty of Judaism's most sacred entity. Kehillath Achim has also given me the chance to use this tool. Reading torah every Shabbat, whether it be in junior congregation or teen service, is something that I cherish and enjoy.

Second, the tools of ideology. Kehillath Achim and especially the teen service have given me the ideological basis I have needed to form my own opinion about God and about Judaism. Two years ago when Rabbi S. informed us downstairs about the new policy of female participation, I was not pleased with it. And that is putting it mildly. Being that I attend an Orthodox yeshiva I was used to davening without female participation. Over the years, however, I have begun to realize the importance of *kahal*—congregation. I now know that no matter who is doing the davening, if the voice and prayers are from the heart, Hashem will hear.

The third, and probably most valuable, are the spiritual tools. Kehillath Achim has given me the opportunity to grow as a Conservative Jew and to give back that which I haven gotten. One of my favorite activities at Kehillath Achim is when I teach. (With two Jewish educators as parents, it's probably in the genes.) Whether it be a *d'var torah* such as this one or leading junior congregation, there is nothing more satisfying than knowing that you made someone think. I don't know how many people here have experienced this, but the look, the expression, on the face of the child when they have just learned something for the first time that you taught them is one of the most incredibly moving experiences of a lifetime. Kehillath Achim has given me that opportunity.

Like Abraham, Isaac, Jacob, and in this week's parsha, Moshe, I feel that I truly have the tools to begin to forge my own relationship with God. I will continue to collect tools throughout my life; still, I am thankful to the Kehillath Achim community for giving me the tools I have, and for affording me the ability to understand my relationship with Hashem beyond the walls of my house on Webster Avenue and past the doorways of my home at Kehillath Achim.

Before I conclude, I would like to recognize one person who has had an incredible effect on the youth of Kehillath Achim, and especially on me. Many of the tools that we, the youth of Kehillath Achim have, we attribute to him and his work. He has been an inspiration, not only because he gives me the keys to the soda machine, but because he gives me the keys to learn, to know, and to teach. He tells everyone that they have the right to call him Jim, but I have the honor to call him Abba [Dad].

Yona presents himself as a product of the congregation and community. His explications and interpretations of tradition—specifically, a midrashic and homiletic explanation of a biblical text, a skill beyond what most of those in the room listening to him could probably muster—at once reveal his impressive knowledge of Jewish sources and serve as a testament to the capacity of the Conservative movement to educate its children. He reminds them how these skills are tools for a relationship to his faith and his God, an educational lesson no less relevant to the adults and parents.

The knowledge he displays comes not only from his yeshiva education. It has, he reminds his listeners, come from their synagogue, from their cantor. To be sure, as a son of their educational director, he is probably considered someone a cut above the rank and file. Yet Yona is someone who has been nurtured by the Kehillath Achim community and feels at home there. Thus, as Yona demonstrates, people do not forfeit their Jewish heritage or continuity by being Conservative.

Like Elisheva, Yona experiences conflict, pressures from the right and the left, from the world of the yeshiva and a world struggling with issues of women's participation. The question of egalitarianism serves as a kind of subtext to part of Yona's remarks, reflecting more generally a communal fixation that pervades the congregation's religious and communal agenda. It comes up at almost every public gathering. It is also a subtext of this morning's service, where, after all, the girls are treated more equally than their mothers are on a regular Shabbat. Their participation in the services is, as already noted, the reason that there is a parallel service today (though one that is very poorly attended).

Yona's remarks, like Elisheva's, also resonate with the language and syntax of the yeshiva. Surely some of the members of this congregation must wonder if he is truly still one of them, but with each paragraph he reassures them that while he may sound as if he is in the yeshiva, he is here among them to celebrate Conservative Judaism and its institutions. Like Elisheva, he tells the congregation that as a Conservative Jew he has been taught to think, to form his own opinions. That independence, he implies, is also a hallmark of the movement, its essential core and most important contribution to his Jewish identity. Finally, Yona reveals that this sort of Judaism and what it provides has brought him closer to his parents and their way of life.

Given all this, it is no wonder that at the end of the service both Yona and Elisheva receive the congregation's highest prizes, which is given to "strengthen the commitment to the ideals and values of Judaism, so important to" the donor family, longtime members. In a sense by honoring these young people, the congregation was honoring itself for bringing them to this point.

When the service was over, the audience seemed touched. For the parents and relatives of the teens, but also for others in the congregation, the morning was a tribute to what the synagogue could hope to achieve. As Elisheva's mother said: "Today, I got my money's worth," meaning, I suppose, that in her daughter's presentation she saw what all her expenditure of money and effort on Jewish education and life had produced. This was a day on which she felt she saw the result of her parental, Jewish labors. In a sense, the congregation might have echoed these sentiments.

COLLEGE HOMECOMING

In addition to the range of youngsters currently in the congregation, there are also its graduates. What of them? To keep them in the fold, the congregation instituted College Homecoming Shabbat, which occurs on Thanksgiving weekend, the first college holiday of the school year. On this Shabbat the returning students are invited to play an active role in the services. Furthermore, there are no competing alternative or teen services, so all can gather in the main sanctuary to see how the fruits of congregational upbringing have fared in the outside world.

The main sanctuary was filled to overflowing. In addition to the returning college students and their relatives, there was also a bar mitzvah being celebrated this day. Finally, the crisp late autumn sunshine brought out some who might not otherwise have come. Indeed, there were so many in attendance that some of the removable walls were taken down to make the room larger. The congregation hummed with excitement: the bigger the crowd, the bigger the smiles. The festive nature of the occasion was also marked by some special additions to the service. The rabbinic intern who normally led the teen service today sat on the bimah. Young college men from the congregation took over the tasks of the regular torah reader, and their peers were called up for aliyot. (The selection of men—more precisely the exclusion of women—from these ritual tasks was a strategy to obviate the need for a parallel service, thus enabling everyone in the congregation to attend the service in the main sanctuary.) Women led selected readings in English or Hebrew. And perhaps to compensate for the fact that women were not carrying out the traditional ritual tasks, those chosen to deliver the sermons were two young women.

In all this, the bar mitzvah boy also had his moment in the sun. He read the maftir section from the torah and chanted the haftarah. The rabbi addressed him, and his parents were called up to make an obligatory blessing. Moreover, his many guests and family helped fill out the congregation. In his remarks to the boy, the rabbi played on the fact that the youngster was a soccer goalie, whose job was "to protect something precious." But even as he addressed the bar mitzvah, his message was not lost on those present for the homecoming—that the responsibility of the Jew was to protect and preserve something precious and sacred, our holy torah and way of life.

Following these remarks, the rabbi called upon three female college students to do something of communal and religious importance. The first recited the prayer for the government of the United States; the second said the prayer for Israel; and the third led a responsive reading of the *Ashrei* prayer. There was no apparent distinction being made between the traditional ritual tasks and these "new" ones. Each woman, after her performance, was given a full measure of approbation from relatives and friends, including handshakes and kisses.

Next, two women students came forward to give brief talks about Jewish life and their experience as Jews on their campus. The first woman spoke about life at Cornell. The theme of her talk was that her connection to the Jewish community gave her a special feeling of belonging that she did not share with the rest of the campus community. She spoke of attending High Holiday ser- vices in an Ithaca synagogue, and how that gave her a feeling of being connected to something beyond the campus.

Her talk climaxed with an account of an anti-Semitic incident on campus— her first real encounter with anti-Semitism—and how it made her feel apart from the rest of those around her on campus, a feeling that was more subtly reinforced when her non-Jewish roommate told her she could pick out all the Jews from a picture. This notion of us-versus-them was perfectly at home in the synagogue. It was a reminder to the listeners that a Jewish congregation was a protected (and protecting) enclave in a hostile world. In a sense, this woman was bearing witness that even in her outpost on campus she was once again in the arms of the Jewish community.

The second speaker, from the University of Maryland, described the oppor- tunities for the serious study of Judaism on her campus. She bemoaned the fact that more of her fellow Jews did not take advantage of the study opportunities or the rich Jewish life on her campus. This was a kind of echo of the lament that many active congregation members, her parents among them, might make about what they do and what others among their Jewish neighbors do not.

In a sense these two college women focused on two essential elements of Jewish life: the sheltering community and the circle of study. In effect, these young people had indicated that at least for them, Jewish life extended beyond the boundaries of the Kehillath Achim community. Finally, I overheard a third college student who greeted a friend in the pews not far from me. "How's Jew- ish life on campus?" she whispered to her friend. Off the bimah, her friend spoke more directly: "Jewish life on campus shits," she said. Yet this comment too could be seen as good news for the community, for it not only marked her as someone willing to tell it like it is, but also indicated that the two friends cared about that Jewish life on campus. So even this off-bimah conversation was in a sense a testament to the congregation's success in engendering a feeling of closeness to Jewish life.

The cumulative effect of all these performances by the congregation's off-spring offers reason for collective hope. Even though these youngsters may represent a minority, perhaps an elite few, they still can be the repository of the synagogue community's confidence in its continuity. In these cultural performances they serve as the embodiment of the best that the congregation—and through it the Conservative movement—can reproduce. They bear witness to the future.

6: *Marking the Completion of Kaddish*

If the performance of the children connects the congregation to its future, the recitation of mourners' kaddish is its homage to the past. Both play a part in the theme of continuity. Indeed, in the Conservative movement, the recitation of kaddish, the memorial prayer, has probably brought more people to the synagogue for more years than any other single ritual. Ironically, it is often the same parent who during his or her lifetime could barely get a son or daughter to come to congregational prayers who achieves in death the goal that remained elusive in life.

According to the dictates of Jewish law, kaddish is to be recited daily as part of congregational worship during the first eleven months following the passing of a parent or a child, for thirty days for other family members (siblings and spouse), and for all of the above each year on the *yahrzeit*, the anniversary of the death. In addition, there are those who recite kaddish whenever they are in the synagogue. This is not a halakhic requirement, but for some the fact is that they commonly come to the synagogue for recitations of kaddish only. Hence if they find themselves at services on another occasion, they may make this recitation out of habit or the assumption that they should always recite it. The attachment to traditions so ubiquitous in the Conservative movement is not always accompanied by a complete knowledge of their requirements.

Those who choose to recite kaddish regularly following bereavement find themselves coming to synagogue far more frequently than ever before in their lives, not only on Shabbatot and holidays but also as part of the daily minyan, a far smaller and in many ways more intimate circle of people. For some, this new synagogue experience may be the first step in a personal Jewish renaissance that leads to their becoming more active members of the core congregation. Certainly, those in the synagogue who seek to build up the ancillary Jewish commitments of the kaddish reciters see this as a real possibility. In all events, the combination of the repeated routine of coming to prayers, as well as the natural ties that are forged among the few who count on one another's daily presence, creates a special bond among the members of this smaller congregation, the daily minyan within the larger one.

In a sense, the recitation of kaddish serves not only to bring those reciting it into the synagogue but also to make them realize how dependent the solitary Jew is on other Jews, how crucial the community is. This is because in traditional Jewish practice recitation of the kaddish requires the presence of a minyan, a sustaining community of Jews who will answer "amen" to the mourner's prayer. Thus kaddish is not just a sign of mourning; it is a means to knit the individual into the community of the living, to overcome existential loneliness. Some seek this communion well past the end of the kaddish period.

One regular attendee at Kehillath Achim who began coming to the synagogue to recite kaddish, for example, stayed on long after his year of bereavement was completed. Coming each morning, he said, "helps set my day; it gives me a chance to shoot the breeze with a bunch of guys I see every day and feel close to, like family; it sets me straight, gives me a sense of rootedness."

Recognizing this reality, Kehillath Achim, like many congregations that have built upon the special ties fostered by mourning, kaddish recitation, and the routine of quotidian synagogue attendance, has tried to make the most of the year-long experience by cementing the ties of individual member mourners to the synagogue and of arousing in them an enlarged and enhanced feeling of Jewish obligation and congregational belonging. (Actually, not all mourners start out as members. Some may come to the synagogue simply because they find the services convenient; the challenge for the congregation is to transform such a liaison of convenience into one that leads to formal membership and involvement in Jewish life beyond the minyan.) This process is vividly illustrated by a ceremony held annually at the synagogue: a Sunday breakfast in recognition of all those who during the preceding year completed reciting kaddish and attended services "regularly," with "regularly" defined very liberally, to be as inclusive as possible. The rabbi explained to me in confidence that his elastic definition of "regularly" was a part of his need to find ways of including as many people as possible among the honorees.

The celebratory breakfast, larger and more elaborate than on a regular Sunday, offered all the trimmings of an American Jewish stylized brunch: bagels, lox, smoked fish, herring, juices, coffee. As Kehillath Achim gatherings go, the event was small—only about thirty-five people, including honorees and those who were (or had become) regular minyan people. It is held in one of the synagogue's social halls and concludes with a ceremony at which those who have completed saying kaddish receive a personally inscribed weekday prayer book signed by all the regular minyan attendees and presented by the rabbi.

But of course this breakfast was more than just a chance to mark the end of a year of kaddish. It was a community celebration, a kind of cultural performance affirming and confirming the fact that these people were knit into the community and tradition, affording them a chance to give testimony to what the syna-

gogue and the regular members of the minyan meant to them. Such is the nature of a cultural performance: it makes manifest and repeats truths about the
group that other times remain implicit.

As the eating neared its end, the rabbi, who was not just the spiritual leader
but also one of the regular members of the daily minyan, stood up to speak as
master of this ceremony. He took the microphone and began first by celebrating the meal itself: "This beautiful breakfast . . . prepared . . . in the wee hours
of this morning. . . . " His remarks resonated with a sense of intimacy and caring. His notes, as all could see, were scribbled on a napkin. No formal speech
this; he was speaking from the heart, as he reviewed each person and how he or
she was connected to the rest and the congregation. For the assembled around
the table, this was, to paraphrase Walt Whitman, "a song of us." Words of appreciation at such an affair are public indicators that a person counts. Following grace, the rabbi again took the microphone. Quoting his rabbinic predecessor
"of blessed memory" (a key and oft-repeated phrase this morning), he compared
the daily minyan to the eternal light, a flame that stands out among all the lights
in the holy places because of its constancy. It might not be considered among
the big news events at the synagogue, but it was an activity of profound importance.

The minyan was, he continued, a place where people came "for comfort,
for strength, for solace, for the encouragement the community is able to
offer. . . . Often in certain occasions, and I've been humbled by that, I've found
that the greatest gift we can give to another human being is simply our presence, simply being there." What could better articulate one of the most important subtexts of any synagogue congregation? The rabbi was telling the people
around the tables that they were the ones who offered this "greatest gift," even
if it was "not something that's *featured* in the bulletin."

And he underscored the point with a biblical analogy: "The rabbis point
out in the torah reading we read yesterday that when our ancestors stood at
Mount Sinai—many say it was intentionally not the most powerful, or largest,
or most glamorous or even the most beautiful mountain chosen by God but rather
a more humble and modest one. . . . We're reminded, as was true at Mount Sinai,
that often the most powerful and enduring events are those that may not grab
public attention either. . . . I cannot think of any [program at Kehillath Achim]
that is more the core of what we revolve about than our daily minyan." Beyond
expressing how important prayer was, the rabbi also celebrated the idea of continuity and constancy. The attentive silence of the assembled was eloquent testimony to the extent to which they associated themselves with these remarks.

The rabbi continued by pointing out that the daily minyan included members from other towns and with affiliations in neighboring synagogues. The fact
to be acclaimed here was that people of all sorts, from all kinds of other synagogues, could with confidence assert: "I know that there will be a minyan at

Kehillath Achim." And, as the rabbi concluded: "No one individual could make it possible. It is by definition a community event."

This Kehillath Achim minyan was, as the rabbi characterized it, a living social organism with its own life and its own evolving traditions that had become grafted onto the fundamental tradition and constancy of the daily service. Today, however, was a *special occasion*, a time that went beyond the quotidian. This was that one day a year "to sort of publicly say what I think we all know, and that is the importance of the daily minyan to all of us." What was ostensibly a chance to honor individuals was really an opportunity to celebrate a congregational institution that exuded intimacy and constancy as well as interdependence.

To be sure, it was "also to have an opportunity to present a gift to men and women who have completed—some a few weeks and some it could have been almost a year ago—who have completed saying kaddish in memory of those whom they loved and cherished in life."

7: The Board Meeting

While synagogues are commonly considered religious institutions, they are also fairly complex organizations that engage in a variety of tasks aimed essentially at perpetuating themselves. The character and much of the structure of the synagogue community, the way decisions are made and values maintained, is often decipherable in the meetings of these organizations. To demonstrate this and to give a sense of Central Synagogue, a look at a board meeting proves useful.

As already noted, Central Synagogue has been engaged in congregational rebuilding. They seem to be having success. For example, as if to confirm its growth and new lease on life, the synagogue's nursery school enrollment, an important conduit for new members, has grown to near capacity, and in terms of enrollment the religious school is also doing well. Reflecting this new lease on life, and as part of its ongoing efforts to renew and revitalize itself following a period of decline and ferment, when significant numbers of congregation members left to join other synagogues, the synagogue has become deeply immersed in its building campaign. What follows is a brief review of a board meeting at which the plans for the new design were first presented to the board by the subcommittee that had prepared them. But it is more than just a planning meeting; it is a cultural performance. One can discern in it some of the underlying concerns of the membership as well as clues to their self-image as a congregation, in their struggle to find the physical representation that best suits who they are.

THE MEETING

Much work and planning went into the evening's board meeting: drawings and displays were made and there was much politicking. As in all informal organizations, the goal had been to reach consensus before the public meeting to avoid surprise disputes and dissension. Everybody wanted to avoid the acrimony of the preceding years, when disputes were a regular part of the public discourse. The whole point of the rebuilding was to put all that into the past.

Although this was a business meeting, it began with a brief *d'var torah*, a word from the rabbi. He drew from the Jewish textual treasury in *Pirkei Avot*, a book replete with rabbinic homily and moral instruction. The members were thereby reminded that they were engaged in a religious endeavor whose physical efforts were inextricably intertwined with spiritual ones.

The rabbi began by quoting from the sage Shammai, the classic disputant of the more famous and popular Hillel. Shammai had urged that people "make [their] study of torah a regular practice, say little and do much, and receive all people with a cheerful countenance." This was, the rabbi explained, a lesson in the importance of being constant in study, of doing rather than just talking about it, and of practicing hospitality. His advice was particularly apt for a group of people—some of whom had perhaps once been perceived as part of a congregation not always considered hospitable—who were about to discuss the building of a site for torah study. The message was unmistakable. First, they should study Jewish sources. Second, they should be doers, not just talkers. Finally, they needed to construct a place that would be welcoming of strangers and outsiders.

"I want to look at this whole triad of Shammai," the rabbi said, "because it seems to me at some point, Shammai had something to do with a capital campaign." This brought a big laugh from the assembled, but it also subtly informed them that the rabbis have something to say to them about the task at hand. The congregation was not just redesigning Central Synagogue but was also a link in a long tradition. And with this the rabbi developed his message from Shammai's three points. Here was a chance to define the spiritual parameters of the organization and its rebuilding campaign, a chance to place it in the context of Jewish tradition.

Following the rabbi's brief remarks, elections were held to fill some board vacancies. Uncontested and predictable, the election was a clear sign that the organization was working well.

At last the real work of the night began: a discussion of the proposed building design and of how to raise the necessary financial endowment. The former president led this part of the meeting and, apologizing for his hoarse voice, reported that he was sick and had stayed home from work, though he came to the synagogue meeting nevertheless. His implicit message was unmistakable: the synagogue and community were more important to him than his regular job.

The rest of his presentation would underscore this need for all to express their own commitment.

Next, he took time to list all those synagogue members who worked with him on the building project. By implication, this was not just *his* plan but one that reflected the contributions of many others; it thus spread the responsibility (and possible blame) for the projected design changes.

Next he gave the rationale for the project: "We are growing, and growing very rapidly." This was a synagogue on the ascendant. "Those of you who come on Shabbat know how busy we are." A big turnout on this day was the congregational barometer. And in case anyone missed point, he noted, "We're going to have trouble [fitting in everyone] with more bar and bat mitzvahs next year." The members here were not the aged grandfathers like him, but people who were in the acme of their family-building years, parents with children who were just coming of age.

But growth also confronted them with a dilemma, what he called the "biggest problem" confronting the planners and architects. As he put it: "You want an intimate, warm, caring space for Shabbat [for the two to three hundred who come regularly] and that space has to go *poof* to accommodate fifteen hundred people on the high holidays." They needed a design that could feel small but could easily become large.

The chairman reviewed the details, explaining how the planning process had made "us look at our own building and realize how many choices *we* had to make." The physical dilemma, of course, mirrored the social and spiritual one of the congregation, that only a minority of their membership was involved in an ongoing and regular way. But those who did not come regularly also had a legitimate right to expect that they would always have room in the congregation. Tonight's meeting was called to "talk about a concept" and not about details, he added.

Finally the chairman reported that he, the rabbi, and the president had had lunch with one of the member families who were potentially large donors. The implication was that there were some significant donations in the works, people had "put their money where the mouth was," and were willing to "kick start" the campaign. He hoped that this news would discourage those who might object to the plan as being too ambitious or economically daunting. He concluded his small drama emphatically: "We need your help. We need your support, and we want you to feel the same sense of being involved as we do."

In this small drama, the former president portrayed his faith in the synagogue community and its growth and new life, while he helped others attain this same faith that the congregation could and would remake itself.

He then introduced the three architects. They led the assembled congregants through the plans, which were prominently displayed on color-coded boards on easels at the front of the room. At the end of the presentation, there were questions from the floor about size and space. These were people used to working with plans, architects, and designers. Many had redesigned their own well-appointed homes. Quite a few made suggestions and amendments. Yet for the most part, the comments implied a tacit acceptance of the fundamental commitment to rebuild and redesign the synagogue and a confidence in the congregation's future. Perhaps the statement most reflective of this commitment and confidence came in the following question from a member of the board: "What are the projections of increase in membership? I'd hate to see this as another 'Bronx River Parkway'—I mean that after it was built, it was already obsolete, too small, whatever."

Here, in the guise of information gathering, was public affirmation of the assumption that this was a community on an upward trajectory. And as if to validate the point, the chairman replied, "That's a very good question." It was good because it required reflection about the synagogue's future and because it affirmed faith in growth. Other members tacitly endorsing these assumptions started suggesting other directions for expansion—even the possibility of selling the building and buying a new property. But this was beyond their projections and imagination. "We have to live within the confines of what we have," the chairman concluded. The meeting ended with the board unanimously approving the plan and giving the go-ahead for a "feasibility study," to see if they could raise the needed funds. Many said that they were excited by the plan, impressed by the amount of work the planners had done, and hopeful about the future.

Now came a brief coda, a report about the synagogue retreat, which served as a reminder of why people felt so upbeat about the synagogue. Stella, a board member who had been at the retreat, offered her summary. She began by noting how many services there had been at the retreat: Friday night, Saturday morning, Saturday afternoon and evening, and of course at each of the meals. "And yet, everybody came over to me throughout the weekend to tell me how much *fun* they were having." The remark elicited much laughter—services could be "fun"?!! The unexpected becomes true. It also reveals the common assumption: services were typically *not* fun. The retreat had shown that other aspects of Judaism that seemed forbidding could in fact be engaging, that what seemed out of date could be attached meaningfully to one's life, could in fact be fun.

The retreat, Stella reported, had been oversubscribed, attended by an even representation of the major segments of the community: "a third religious school families, a third Schechter families, and a third older couples with grown children, and interspersed in those three were five or six new families." The message of the report was that while there are distinctions in the congregation, they are not divisions that will lead to disintegration, as once they might have. On the contrary, these different people had come together and found it possible to share the retreat and Shabbat. "People were very enthusiastic, in a very good frame of mind; people got to know people that they didn't know before." That was a sense of community, as new ties were created.

The retreat also served to motivate the next generation: "Just to look at the kids, to keep the teenagers interacting, to keep the little kids engaged in activity; it was very, very special." "That was really one of the most extraordinary parts; the interaction between the children . . . because they cared about each other." And the testimonials went on.

All these comments, presented as a report to the board, were in fact a way for the speakers to remind everyone how far the congregation had come from the days of divisiveness and polarization. The animosities were no more and the community had a future. Hence, the congregation could invest in rebuilding. Stella added that while this was the first such retreat, there was now hope to schedule two a year so that the good feelings it engendered could be spread throughout the congregation.

Having opened the evening, the rabbi now concluded it. As he explained, "Part of a retreat is getting away from where you commonly are." It was a metaphor for religion, which likewise offers another world into which to go. A brief videotape was shown of some of those on retreat singing. It was a scene of coming together, expressing solidarity.

Everyone seemed to be beaming; for such a reshaped congregation, a newly designed sanctuary and building were certainly in order. Yet there would be more to do in the days ahead. As the congregation would decide, this plan was not radical enough. They wanted an even greater break with the past, an even more comprehensive rebuilding.

8: Conclusions

What I have learned about Conservative Judaism is naturally skewed by the fact that the source of my knowledge was synagogue *members*, however varied their level of synagogue involvement. Hence, these conclusions do not reflect what there is to learn about Conservative Judaism from those who are not members of a Conservative synagogue, a significantly large segment of the population who call themselves "Conservative Jews." In addition, my information is neither random nor necessarily comprehensive. Rather, it comes from those informants who opened their lives to my eyes and my inquiries during the time I spent as a participant-observer in their synagogues.

There is no simple way to sum up the multiple realities that constitute the character of the synagogue life of Conservative Judaism, nor can one suppose that even an ethnographic biopsy of the blood and tissue of two relatively large and successful synagogues can reveal all of that life. Moreover, each congregation has its own special history, one that grows and changes with the biographies of those who come into and out of its life. Nevertheless, certain general aspects of the Conservative synagogue species can be discovered from an examination such as I have offered in the preceding pages. I discuss some of these aspects below.

CORE VERSUS PERIPHERY

Just as the people who identify themselves as Conservative Jews may be divided into those who are members of Conservative synagogues and those who are not, so among members, at least in the two large congregations considered in these pages, the population may essentially be divided into core and peripheral elements. Moreover, as one would expect, the core group—by and large those who come regularly, who participate most actively, and who determine the direction and character of the congregation—is significantly smaller than the periphery, whose affiliation is more intermittent. Increasingly, this small core is made up of Jews who not only are active synagogue members but who also take an activist stance in their practice of Judaism and make Judaism a living reality in their personal lives. These are people who feel that "they want more" or at the very least that the synagogue fills important voids in their lives, yet they want their attachments to remain voluntary, to be "held firmly with an open hand," a phrase I believe captures the character of the Conservative Jewish commitment.

It is also a given that in a Conservative synagogue, people may at various points in their lives move from being part of the core to being in the minimally affiliated periphery, and vice versa. As one of the members of Central Synagogue, quoted earlier, put it, "In different stages of your life, you need the synagogue in different ways."

Moreover, while the core group is in principle committed to reaching out to the periphery and often expresses the desire to bring more people into the synagogue, it is also often quite accepting of the fact that a large number (perhaps a majority) of the membership will show up very seldom and remain in a relatively quiescent relationship with the synagogue and Judaism.

This abiding tolerance may reflect the fact that quite often members of the core have themselves once been in the periphery or can imagine circumstances under which they would once again. Or perhaps members of the core understand that those in the periphery, though not active in the synagogue, may nevertheless feel a genuine allegiance to it and Conservative Judaism. In any event, the core members of these synagogues tend to be far more tolerant of those on the periphery than are their Orthodox counterparts, who are inclined to be far more dismissive and contemptuous of those whose Jewish commitments and synagogue involvement are not as powerful or unwavering. As one member of

Central Synagogue put it, in terms that are probably equally true for members of Kehillath Achim as well many other similar synagogues, "You flow in and flow out."

There is of course also an economic aspect to this divide between the core and the periphery. One might even call it a "division of labor." In effect, the large majority pays the dues that help to pay for the services, staff, and plant that the minority core group uses most of the time. In effect, those who come only rarely subsidize the synagogue. This is something that members of the active core do not like to recall, although when pressed some admit the reality. In a way, the economy of the synagogue is a bit like insurance: everyone pays and only a few collect more than they pay in premiums. For many in these congregations, however, that reality is fine: the synagogue is important to have, is a good investment, assures some level of continuity, is available in a crisis, and is renewable each year. As Claire of Central Synagogue said, "I will support it whether I come three times a year or fifty-two times a year."

For the most part, those who make up the core write the story lines of these synagogues. They shape their character. They are therefore very much at the focus of this ethnography. These are people ready to make religious and communal commitments, albeit sometimes more loosely than their rabbis might wish. They do not want those commitments to make them feel awkward or ignorant, nor do they want to feel guilty when they do not always fulfill them to the letter. As Eliot, an extraordinarily active member and former president of Central Synagogue said, "No one ever said to me, you can't join if you won't do this or you won't do that."

While proud of the commitments that they believe Conservative Judaism has made to the tradition and ritual, even the core members may not always consistently practice Judaism in a way that conforms with the movement's ideological commitments. Reflecting on this indulgent way of practicing Conservative Judaism, Eliot added, perhaps speaking for many others like him, "I know it's inconsistent, but every Jew has to find out where they are and who they are." That attitude, expressing more of the outlook of do-it-yourself Americanism than a religious conservatism, often acts as the dynamic behind the striving for Jewish empowerment. For many a rabbi, who is often committed to enhancing the Jewish practices and sense of religious obligation of his or her congregants, this relaxed attitude toward inconsistency even among their dedicated core can often prove enormously frustrating.

These are Jews who are convinced that, whether part of the regularly active core or the intermittently active periphery, they nevertheless have made a significantly greater commitment to their Judaism than their counterparts on the Reform Jewish left. While this impression may not always be substantiated—particularly on the part of those on the periphery—by either their Jewish knowledge or level of involvement, or even by their permissive attitude toward such extreme matters as "who is a Jew" (many Conservative Jews are ready in practice if not in principle to disattend halakhic strictures on this point), it seems an important feature of Conservative Jewish identity. That is, these are Jews who by their own definitions are neither so intolerant of Jewish variations as the Orthodox nor so liberal toward Jewish practices as they consider Reform. And that is one reason they believe they have chosen to be Conservative. To be sure, some, like Evelyn of Central Synagogue, recognize that by staking out a place in the center, they sometimes "tend to define ourselves by what we're *not*. 'The Reform do this; the Orthodox do that. We don't like that so we're Conservative.' We don't seem to articulate what we truly stand for." But, most of the core congregation have evolved a fairly clear idea of what the character of their Judaism is, both in terms of ideals and in terms of practices. And if it is inconsistent, then so be it.

Many of them also believe themselves to be part of the Jewish majority in America. And they are at ease with that Jewish identity choice. As Conservative Jews, they do not expect "to do it all" nor do they think that Conservative Judaism requires that of them, at least not in practice. Many hold that they can personally (albeit with some occasional but not imperative guidance from the rabbis of the Conservative movement) choose the parts of Judaism they find meaningful. That is the "open hand" they so much appreciate.

THE COMMITMENT AND LOYALTY OF SYNAGOGUE MEMBERS TO CONSERVATIVE JUDAISM

Overall among the synagogue members I observed and interviewed, whether they were active or not, their commitments and loyalties are formally expressed as first and foremost to Judaism as a whole, then to the synagogue and its community in particular, and lastly to Conservative Judaism as a movement. In practice, however, they tended to define both the demands of Judaism and the expectations of their Conservative affiliation largely through the prism of their experience in their particular synagogue. Often they admitted to a greater loyalty to their particular synagogue, rabbi, and fellow members than to the movement as a whole. In many cases, however, the relationship was synergistic. As people became engaged in their synagogue life, they often "discovered" that they were indeed able to identify as Conservative Jews, and that ideological commitment consequently became more powerful.

Whatever their involvement in synagogue life, they were largely convinced that Conservative Judaism, while holding fast to certain standards of tradition, allowed them a great deal of freedom to interpret the nature of these attachments and commitments. This identity was subject to a sort of improvised and personalized reinterpretation. Moreover, it expanded or contracted throughout the life cycle. Frequently, the people I observed understood their decision to be part of Conservative Judaism as a rejection both of Reform, which they found too indefinite and vague in its demands, and of Orthodoxy, which they saw as rigidly narrow and hostile to women. In contrast to these extremes, Conservative Judaism provided them with a middle ground, a niche that granted freedom and flexibility along with some level of commitment and tradition.

In this niche, they expected to feel "comfortable" about the way they practiced (or did not practice) being Jewish, even if that did not quite square with the formal ideological or behavioral demands of the movement or even if it was at odds with their rabbi's interpretation of it. Concretely, they believed this meant in practice that Conservative Judaism allowed them to be inconsistent in their Jewish lives. And it imposed no guilt about those things they did not do while encouraging them in whatever they did choose to do.

THE SYNAGOGUE AS A COMMUNITY

For some members of both these congregations, synagogue life is most importantly an expression of community. "Community," as sociologist Herman Schmalenbach long ago noted, "develops on the basis of natural interdependence."[19] Thus, members of the core seek, at least in principle, to draw those on the periphery into a more active dependence on synagogue life, and some on the periphery can still experience moments of connection despite their limited involvement in the life of the synagogue.

This interdependence is expressed in a variety of contexts. People may, for example, be drawn in to the congregational rebuilding effort and may consequently become increasingly engaged by the campaign, leading to their considering the synagogue in the way some claim to do, as "a second home," with the congregational community as an "extension of the family." At a somewhat lower level of involvement, others may consider the synagogue community as a place where the holidays are observed and where important family passages from birth, through coming of age, marriage, and death are solemnized and publicly marked. This too is attachment. As Charlotte of Central Synagogue put it, "You might not always be in touch or visit, but it was always there when you were ready to return."

These feelings of community can be nurtured only when the core group, which in essence holds things together on a regular basis, makes the synagogue feel not like a closed clique but open to all who wish to affirm their Jewishness and share common concerns, values, goals, and lifestyles. This was what Kehillath Achim tried to do, especially with its sit-down kiddush and variety of service options, and what Central Synagogue aimed for with its retreat, special Friday night dinners, and plans for rebuilding. Both rabbis strongly affirmed this approach in their willingness to accept people "where they are," as one of them put it. Moreover, the willingness to tolerate varying levels of commitment and involvement—"holding firmly with an open hand"—is paradoxically the affirmation of the strength of these communities.

What moves people to become part of the synagogue community, or at least part of its extended family? It happens when people decide that they have a contribution to make to the synagogue and that the synagogue has a contribution to make to them and their lives. This frequently occurs when people have their first child or, more specifically, a bit later when parents want the "kids to see more" and "understand what it means to be Jewish." As Joan of Central Synagogue phrased it: "Somehow you become a parent and you feel like you need to join somewhere." Life-cycle events awaken these dormant feelings.

From these feelings, events and emergent attachments can take on a life of their own, at least during the years of parenting. That is, what was initiated for the sake of the children can become something parents do for themselves, as so many of the biographies presented here demonstrate. As Joan noted, at a certain point you may realize that "your tennis cannot be more important than your synagogue life." Finally, if the momentum of engagement is maintained, these people may come to feel that when they are in the synagogue, whether for a service or education or some other community event (even some sort of committee meeting), "I belong there." When that happens, they have made a transition to a personal connection to the synagogue that is crucial for continuity.

In the open, highly mobile society of late twentieth-century America, however, continuity has not always the norm: in the Conservative movement 763,000 have left even as 650,000 have come in.[20]

Not surprisingly, therefore, many members in both congregations are currently living a Jewish life that is significantly different from one they used to lead. They are people who as adults redefined their connection to the community and Conservative Jewish life. Some have moved increasingly toward the periphery and Jewish passivity. Others, whose sense of belonging began with a minimal or marginal affiliation, shifted toward an increasingly ardent attachment to Judaism, synagogue life, and the community. And the congregation that finds a way to elicit or sustain such feelings succeeds in sustaining itself and its membership.

Still others may have dropped out of the Orthodox world and then found in Conservative synagogue life a way back to Judaism and a more comfortable connection to the traditions that once held them firmly with a closed hand. They find a new way to fall "in love with the shul." To be sure, in quite a few instances members are drawn because someone in their nuclear family has been so drawn in. And in a sense, everyone's emphasis on the education of children, the preparation for bar and bat mitzvah, has this sort of dynamic as an ulterior or at least latent motive. One might even suggest that, as often as not, adults may be drawn into the synagogue and the core community inside either because they seek to be better parents or because (mostly via the recitation of kaddish) they aim to be better children.

Paradoxically, even as the inner circle seeks at least in principle to draw others into the core and its activities, they are also likely to react to the presence of too many outsiders in the synagogue with ambivalence at best and disdain at worst. Yes, they like a big turnout for services, but they also (at Kehillath Achim) support the smaller alternative services and or (at Central Synagogue) desire a small retreat-style setting or an intensive learners' service that will also "make greater demands" on the participants. In a sense, some wish to separate themselves from those who are less engaged and involved, to present themselves as a more dedicated class of Conservative Jew. As the rabbi at Central Synagogue articulated it, the synagogue stands somewhere between the two.

The synagogue is sometimes a closed club to those overwhelmed by how much they do not know about Judaism and the mechanics of synagogue ritual. Sensitive to these feelings, the synagogues have tried in a variety of ways to make Judaism and thus also the community more accessible and "user friendly." They have done that with ambitious instructional programs (from partnered study to special "torathons," when all manner of Jewish education is offered), learners' services, congregational retreats, and of course the constant and repeated conversations with the rabbis. Yet here, too, the more the core group seems to know about the lessons of Judaism and Jewish practices, the more complex the social process by which those outside the core can get inside. Often the opportunities for learning more about being Jewish is a case of preaching to the converted rather than to those who already feel marginalized. Hence, the need to make people feel Jewishly competent is ineluctably wrapped up with the process of creating or nurturing communal attachments to synagogue life.

A PLACE TO MARK LIFE'S PASSAGES

The community aspects of synagogue life are especially appealing in bedroom suburbs, the antiseptic suburban frontier, perhaps because they serve as an antidote to the quiet desperation and loneliness of individuals who live in nuclear family isolation from their extended relations. People often seek a synagogue in which there will be, as one woman put it, "more participation, and opportunities for families to get to know one another, and different congregants to talk to one another." They want more than study and meetings. They want a place to take their young children and find someone who knows who they are, who will greet them and remind them how much they are missed when they are not there. They want a group of people with whom to share their joys, who will comfort them in their sorrows, who will care that they have completed reciting kaddish or named a new baby daughter, who will be proud of their bar and bat mitzvah celebration as well as of returning college students, and who will dance at their children's weddings. These are the occasions that cement the ties between the family and the congregation. In short, when the synagogue becomes the canvas on which life's passages are marked, it becomes an inalienable part of life.

In some cases elements of synagogue life become redefined as passages in family life. Thus, for example, at Kehillath Achim and Central Synagogue there are the special Shabbatot for each of the grades of Hebrew school, days on which families come to a singular service to witness their children or grandchildren perform as synagogue Jews. In a sense, the Shabbat on which a bar or bat mitzvah is celebrated actually may be perceived as the culmination of these special annual Shabbat performances of childhood. As it was so in the beginning, so it is at the end: children are given a chance to perform, to demonstrate they have some synagogue skills, to give their parents and loved ones a good feeling about their efforts in educating them, and ultimately to sustain the synagogue staff and congregational community with optimism about the Jewish future. Children and their families grow up as Jews and people in front of their congregation.

This sort of public display goes on throughout life. As the rabbinic sage Yehuda ben Tema outlined it: At age five one begins to learn Scripture, at ten Mishnah; at thirteen one takes on the obligation to observe the mitzvot, and at fifteen one begins to learn Talmud; at eighteen one is married, at twenty, one pursues a living, and so on throughout life.[21] This principle, one might suggest, is still at work in the synagogue. Many have come to measure themselves and their own progress through life in terms of what they can or have decided to do in the synagogue as Jews. Sometimes this is a matter of personal accomplishments, such as learning to lead a service or chanting a haftarah in the synagogue, or even being elected to some high status synagogue office or being given a congregational testimonial.

But Jewish empowerment is marked not only by individual performance, it is also marked by congregational accomplishments—as when the members of Central Synagogue succeeded in organizing a successful retreat, or Kehillath Achim introduced a successful "torathon." Or when Central Synagogue launches its rebuilding campaign, or when the worshipers at Kehillath Achim marked the completion of their kaddish recitations as a group—the personal and the communal become conflated. This integration of the singular and the congregational experience not only serves to bond individuals and families to the synagogue but may also mark the beginning of a religious renaissance. Indeed, members are more likely to feel drawn to Jewish life and observance out of these feelings for community than out of a feeling of being commanded to do so by God or Jewish law or even Conservative Jewish ideology.

To be sure, the maximalist prospect is still relatively rare. Most Conservative Jews are comfortable doing relatively little. Attending Shabbat services a few times a year, some Jewish education, performing the main rites of passage in a Jewish way, and so on are often Jewish activities isolated from the rest of their lives. Nevertheless the very possibility that they might decide to do more and be more as Jews and that the synagogue will be there for them when they decide to do so is what stands behind the promise of Conservative Jewish synagogue life.

CONTINUITY

Perpetuation, the capacity to pass on Judaism and Jewish affiliation to the future, inevitably raises the matter of children, who represent the promise of the continuing vitality of Conservative Judaism. That of course is why so much of what draws people to the Conservative synagogue is somehow related to children: birth, school, bar/bat mitzvah. Their continuing involvement with Jewish life when they are away at college and their return to the synagogue when they visit home and family offer vital encouragement for their parents and signs to the congregation that something is right in the way they are transmitting Judaism. Their marriage to other Jews and their own decisions to join a Conservative synagogue, once again repeating the cycle, are the sure sign of perpetuation of the kind of Jewish life and affiliation in which they have been raised.

While the nursery and supplementary schools at both synagogues are filled, most of the young, not unlike their parents, remain at a distance from regular voluntary participation in synagogue life. This is not for want of congregational efforts. Nursery and Hebrew school services, Torah for Tots programs, and junior congregations are ubiquitous. And of course much is made of those special Shabbatot centered on the youth. A good deal of the education is geared to seeing to it that the youngsters know how to perform well at Shabbat and other worship services.

One might conclude, nevertheless, that in some subtle way the children have gotten the message that synagogue life, at least in the main arena, is not really for them. Consider the following illustration from Kehillath Achim. One Shabbat when the rabbi went to address those at the children's service, he was, as usual, introduced by the educational director, a devoted Conservative Jew and in many ways one of the most inspiring figures in the congregation for both the children and their parents. Speaking to the youngsters of the *aleph* class, he introduced the rabbi as follows: "And look who's here from way across the hall in the main sanctuary, where I guarantee that they're not having nearly as good a time as *we* are."

Although he regretted this slip when I later pointed it out to him (and asked me not to quote him in "the book"), there was no mistaking the subliminal thrust of his remark—that kiddie services like these were far more fun and engaging than what happens in the main sanctuary, that even the rabbi was glad to be here rather than there, and that those here would not enjoy coming to the synagogue as much when they were forced to be in the main sanctuary, the place for regular adults. As if to confirm this message the rabbi, in a nod to the feel-good Judaism pitched to the children and the accompanying adults, offered his own comments about the extraordinary joy and light that he discerned here at this service.

To be fair here, most *aleph* parents are new to the synagogue process, as many are affiliating for the first time with the start of their children's Jewish education. Furthermore, those parents who have a stronger commitment to Jewish education have probably chosen to send their children to a Conservative day school. This means that an *aleph* service is made up of the weakest of the affiliated in the congregation, people in need of the most nurturing. So both the educational director and the rabbi were probably simply trying to make the young participants and the accompanying adults feel good about what they were doing in the synagogue, and their words probably had that effect.

Yet there are disconcerting signs that, following the years of these special Shabbatot and the bar and bat mitzvah, the young are not finding their way back to the synagogue. This is the case at both Kehillath Achim and Central Synagogue, where the services geared to the young are poorly attended. For the most part, Conservative Jewish youth remain more represented in the congregational periphery than in the core, or in the school or youth groups.

And of those who have responded to the message of continuity and heritage and whose commitments to Jewish life are most powerful, one often finds moving to the religious right. In part this happens because their day school educations often lead them to institutions sponsored and guided by the Orthodox. And their ritual skills, their competence with Hebrew, their love of Zion, and the time they spend in Israel—all highly valued within the Conservative movement—ultimately make it easier for these young people to find a place in more traditionalist circles. But precisely the openness, tolerance, and pluralism (including a tendency toward religious egalitarianism) they have grown up with in their synagogue and family life are not easily integrated with the values of more traditionalist circles. The result is sometimes a kind of ambivalence toward Conservative Judaism, though one that can be healthy, for it forces each young person to make conscious choices about the direction of his or her Jewish future. These sorts of engaged and religiously struggling young Conservative Jews are the hope and the promise of the movement. One is not surprised to learn, for example, that among the Kehillath Achim "graduates" one young woman is head of a Jewish campus organization, another young man has become a teacher in a Schechter day school, several have moved to Israel, and more than one is considering the rabbinate. Similar tales could be told about Central Synagogue youths. Yet these sorts of youngsters remain part of a very small core, at least at the two synagogues examined here.

THE COMMITMENT AND LOYALTY TO THE LARGER JEWISH COMMUNITY
For many, the synagogue serves as the nexus point with the larger Jewish community. It is here, for example, they might assemble to mark some occasion that
affects Jewry in general. Obviously, the universal Jewish calendar of holidays is
marked in the particularities of synagogue life. Additionally, when world Jewry
mourned the assassination of Prime Minister Yitzhak Rabin, an event that took
place during the period of this study, members expressed their solidarity with
the mourners in a variety of venues, but primarily through gatherings in their
synagogues.

Often people conceive of their attachment to their particular synagogue as
tantamount to an association with Jewry in general. Correspondingly, the creation of "good Jews," a resource for Jewry in general, is one of the tacit educational goals of the synagogues. Thus, the local and specific goals of the synagogue
often coincide with the more extensive and universal aims of the Jewish community in which that synagogue and its members locate themselves.

Finally, the biographies demonstrate that as synagogue members experience
a Jewish religious or cultural awakening, they develop a commitment and loyalty not only to their congregation but also to the Congregation of Israel, the
Jewish People.

THE IMPACT OF EGALITARIANISM
At both Kehillath Achim and Central Synagogue, the dilemma of being simultaneously open and closed has also become intertwined with the issue of women's
Jewish empowerment, or "the egalitarian question," as it is commonly called. It
is an issue that is at the heart of the dynamic tension of who will be able to
participate fully in synagogue community life. Women often felt relegated to the
Jewish periphery, even when in other respects, unconnected to the ritual life of
the synagogue, they were part of the core synagogue community. By giving
women who wanted it the same access as men to all ritual and religious roles,
Central Synagogue empowered them and brought them fully into the core. As
of this writing Kehillath Achim was also trying, although more gradually, to bring
women in.

In effect, egalitarianism may be defined most simply as a willingness to afford equal rites and Jewish obligations to men and women in the synagogue.
For many people in the synagogues studied, an acceptance of an enhanced role
for women in synagogue life that egalitarianism allows is perhaps the single most
important symbol of a congregation's openness. Conversely, those congregations
and movements that do not accept the principle and practice of egalitarianism
are, in words heard repeatedly, considered "hostile to women."

When individuals and congregations embrace egalitarianism, they are seeking to expand the private responsibilities incumbent upon the Jewish woman

by endowing her with some of the public honors that may be associated with these responsibilities. Thus, the women who are most supportive of egalitarianism tend to be among the synagogue members who seek to increase rather than diminish their involvement in matters Jewish. Furthermore, those who embrace this sort of change do not necessarily advocate a decline in other commitments to tradition. In fact, within the congregations observed, many of those who were committed to the highest levels of Jewish observance also supported egalitarianism.

Those who claim, therefore, that women's full participation in Judaism is religiously threatening do not understand that these women were, as one man who supported egalitarianism explained, "still doing mitzvot," still accepting the obligations of Judaism. "So long as the movement is saying there is more that is allowable," he concluded, "let's get there. Why deprive a woman from learning more or caring more about her Judaism? What have we accomplished by limiting women?" The enhanced Jewish engagement that egalitarianism brings about among women as prayer leaders or torah readers allows women to display their empowerment and competence in a most public way. It may, furthermore, stimulate others in the family to likewise intensify their religious, ritual, and synagogue involvement. Thus, for example, the wife and mother who chants the haftarah brings her husband and children to the synagogue to hear her and may by example encourage them to do what she has done.

The fact that the Conservative movement has a formal commitment to egalitarianism has also made women, and those who care about them, feel a more powerful affinity with this movement, which they believe now welcomes them as full-fledged members. In congregations that reject egalitarianism, women may seem to be second-class citizens, peripheral to the proceedings, while in the egalitarian Conservative synagogue they can be fully part of the active core.

THE IMPACT OF INTERMARRIAGE ON THE CONSERVATIVE SYNAGOGUE

Intermarriage between Jews and non-Jews is a fact of American life. Yet whereas in generations past, an intermarriage was assumed to lead to a complete or near-complete breach from the Jewish community and way of life, if not the Jewish family—especially when the non-Jewish partner did not convert—this is no longer inevitable. Today, as these pages document, the intermarried may continue some sort of affiliation with the synagogue and Jewish community. This has led to the presence of both converts and non-Jewish spouses within the congregation.

To understand this dynamic, one must first realize that religion is today perceived less as a matter of fate and more a matter of personal choice. Non-Jews who choose to marry Jews are often estranged from their own religious backgrounds. At the same time, their willingness to date and then marry a Jew often reflects an openness to Judaism and Jewish people. When and if they convert, they may become more engaged by Judaism than are their Jewish spouses. In part this is explained by the fact that their Jewish spouse is often someone who has become estranged from or is at the very least indifferent to Judaism and detached from the Jewish people—commonly a precondition to interdating and intermarriage.

Ironically, sometimes the Jewish involvement of the convert acts as a stimulus for the spouse to become more involved. Other times the desire to explain Judaism and Jewish life to a non-Jewish spouse serves as a trigger for greater Jewish involvement. But all of this becomes possible because of the Jewish community's greater openness to non-Jews and converts within its midst. It is a tolerance bolstered by the increasing numbers of such individuals in and around congregations.

While by no means always the case, intermarriage may in some family situations become an occasion for Jewish renaissance. This is more likely to occur when the non-Jewish partner converts, as several of the biographies in these pages demonstrate. To be sure, this requires an enormous educational effort and community outreach. The convert needs to learn sufficient Hebrew to use the prayer book; he or she may desire to gain competence in the laws of kashrut (particularly daunting when the convert is the primary cook); and sometimes there is even a commitment to giving the children an intensive Jewish education. For this renaissance to occur, moreover, the congregational community and its religious and lay leadership must be more than tolerant; it must be welcoming.

While the Conservative movement and the synagogue may demand conversion as the price of tolerance and welcome, the rank-and-file membership will often settle for a mild interest in matters Jewish or even the absence of estrangement. This is exhibited in the fact that non-Jewish family members who have not converted often make their way into the congregation's social network and occasionally appear at services (most commonly on the High Holidays or Passover). On the occasion of their children's bar or bat mitzvah or even on some other synagogue performance, these non-Jewish parents are routinely expected to join in the celebration. Thus, while formal boundaries remain between the non-Jewish members of Jewish families and the Jewish community, these have become increasingly tenuous in practice.

THE ROLE OF INFORMAL JEWISH EDUCATION IN THE CONSERVATIVE SYNAGOGUE

By and large, today's Conservative Jews—particularly those with college degrees—recognize Jewish education as an important element in their synagogue lives. While they come to worship, they come no less to be intellectually stimulated and Jewishly informed. A successful rabbi therefore must also be an educator, using many encounters with congregants as opportunities to instruct them. Even the sermon—for generations the single most important speech event in a rabbi's role—is now frequently transformed into an occasion for teaching, for give-and-take with the congregation, for a joint review of a written text.

While the rabbi remains the primary educator in the congregations observed, this role is increasingly shared with lay members who often regard their Jewish commitments and involvements as including a capacity to study and teach some Jewish sources. Many rabbis thus see a part of their role as educators empowering their congregants to share in the educational role. Occasions such as a *seudah shlishit* (the third Shabbat meal), or the commemoration of a *yahrzeit*, or a child's coming of age are now frequently opportunities for laity to offer remarks instead of the rabbi.

Thanks to day schools and Camp Ramah, there are congregants who are capable of handling Jewish sources on their own. These are people with high levels of secular education—the proportion of college graduates in the synagogues approaches 80 percent—who not only value learning but also assume that one should be able to study on one's own.

Thus, even though large sectors of Conservative congregations remain undereducated Jewishly, there is a growing consensus among those in the active core that Jewish knowledge is essential to being active in synagogue life. In one of the synagogues I observed, for example, board meetings always begin with a brief but intensive *d'var torah*. The lay leader who is satisfied with activity limited to social or financial affairs—a common figure in Conservative synagogues of generations past—has largely disappeared.

There are many opportunities for informal study in the synagogue: the "Shabbat retreat," the so-called *havurah* services, and the learner's services. Special Shabbatot on which children in the synagogue perform or lead the services are also often presented as opportunities not only to display what they have been taught but also to teach and inspire parents to improve their own Jewish skills. This even includes the bar and bat mitzvah, which is no longer limited to the adolescent. Adults who either missed their own such celebrations or else have acquired new Jewish skills like chanting the haftarah or reading torah may display this learning in an "adult bar or bat mitzvah."

In sum, the synagogue is expected to extend Jewish knowledge and empower its members educationally. If it does not succeed in this task, the membership will see it as having failed institutionally.

THE SOURCES OF VITALITY IN THE CONSERVATIVE SYNAGOGUE
When it works best, the synagogue gives its members a sense of empowerment, a feeling of competence, an experience of community, and opportunities for spirituality. The degree to which these are enhanced is often a direct consequence

of being part of the active core of congregational life; those who do more in the synagogue get more out of it. Moreover, each of these is linked to the others. Thus a sense of empowerment grows out of a feeling of competence; people who know their way around the synagogue, who are proficient in their ritual behavior, who know "how things work in this place" not only feel Jewishly empowered. They also feel communally empowered, feel as if they are part of a living and breathing community. And spiritual exaltation, the "raising of the individual above himself," as well as the activation of religious beliefs and energies, occurs "only when they are partaken by many," shared with the community: no one can "retain them any length of time by a purely personal effort."[22] Moreover, because for such engaged people the synagogue generally plays an important part in family life, many of these positive feelings reverberate in their feelings about their own family.

Epilogue

"In telling the story of the congregation, we unravel its plot," wrote the late James Hopewell, and then he added: "Perhaps our version is less authentic than others yet to be told, but only in relating it does the congregation come to terms with its symbolization of the way things have been for it."[23] These words are no less appropriate for this account. No single account of a congregation's life can follow all the strands of its existence, even less an account that seeks to document two congregations at once. Rather, these pages have been intended to offer one man's glimpse into Conservative synagogue life and to allow those whose congregations are here presented to have an opportunity to come to terms with that vision. To borrow from another study of religion in America, *Habits of the Heart*, upon which some of what I have done here is modeled, I have aimed "to open a larger conversation," to give the readers and especially those who are affiliated with Conservative Judaism an opportunity to compare my vision with their own experiences, and to join the discussion about what Conservative synagogue life is.[24] Religious awakening and continuity are, after all, assured when people engage in such conversations.

Notes

1. Clifford Geertz, *The Interpretation of Cultures* (New York: Basic Books, 1973), 12.
2. Robert Redfield, *The Little Community* (Chicago: University of Chicago Press, 1956), 11, 1.
3. Ibid., 52.
4. Ibid.
5. Ibid., 91.
6. Renato Rosaldo, *Culture and Truth: The Remaking of Social Analysis* (Boston: Beacon Press, 1989), 129.
7. Redfield, *Little Community*, 59.

8. Ibid., 81.
9. Ibid., 93–94.
10. James P. Wind and James W. Lewis, eds., *American Congregations* (Chicago: University of Chicago Press, 1994), 2:6.
11. R. Stephen Warner, "The Place of the Congregation in the Contemporary American Religious Configuration," in ibid., 2:600.
12. Redfield, *Little Community*, 85.
13. Rosaldo, *Culture and Truth*, 132.
14. For a discussion of this dynamic, see Samuel Heilman, "Inside the Jewish School," in Stuart L. Kelman, ed., *What We Know about Jewish Education* (Los Angeles: Torah Aura, 1992), 303–330.
15. Robert Bellah et al., *Habits of the Heart* (Berkeley: University of California Press, 1985), 137.
16. Victor Turner, *The Forest of Symbols: Aspects of Ndembu Ritual* (Ithaca, N.Y.: Cornell University Press, 1967), 450.
17. Geertz, *Interpretation of Cultures*, 114.
18. Emile Durkheim, *The Elementary Forms of the Religious Life*, trans. J. W. Swain (New York: Free Press, 1965), 29.
19. Hermann Schmalenbach, "The Sociological Category of Communion," trans. K. D. Naegele and G. P. Stone. In T. Parsons et al., *Theories of Society* (New York: Free Press, 1961), 331.
20. Jack Wertheimer, ed., *Conservative Synagogues and Their Members: Highlights of the North American Survey of 1995–96* (New York: Jewish Theological Seminary, 1996), 10.
21. Mishnah Avot 5:21.
22. Durkheim, *Elementary Forms*, 473.
23. James F. Hopewell, *Congregation*, ed. Barbara G. Wheeler (Philadelphia: Fortress Press, 1987), 197.
24. Bellah et al., *Habits of the Heart*, 307.

Part II

The Congregation

Chapter 4

PAUL RITTERBAND

Public Worship

The Partnership between Families and Synagogues

Introduction

The typical synagogue building is divided into wings or sections, each dedicated to some aspect of congregational life. Typically, there is a school wing that houses the supplemental religious school that meets in the afternoons and on Sunday mornings and, in more recent years, perhaps the day school as well. There is another wing in which the professional staff of the synagogue, led by the rabbi, has its offices. Then there will be the core of the synagogue, centered on what is now called the "sanctuary," a term invented in post-traditional times for a post-traditional institution. The sanctuary itself, in a Conservative synagogue, is likely to be oriented toward the ark containing the torah scrolls situated at the far end of a stagelike platform (*bimah* in Hebrew) from which the services are led by rabbi, cantor, and Scripture lectors.

The spatial arrangements of the synagogue and the sanctuary within it bespeak a religious perspective that has come under question within the Conservative movement. As a consequence of the vast differences in attendance on Shabbatot and the High Holidays, the sanctuary is likely to be partitioned off from a large multipurpose space by means of accordion doors that are folded back for the increased attendance on Rosh Hashanah and Yom Kippur. The seats in the synagogue are arranged theater style, in rows facing the ark. In the center of the platform there is likely to be a table on which the torah scrolls will be unrolled and read to the congregation. Near the table stands a lectern from which the rabbi and cantor conduct the service from "up above," from the raised stage. The lectern is usually placed so that the cantor faces the congregation while chanting the service.

What I have described briefly here represents the accommodation of traditional

Judaism to Western ways in the modern period. It is consistent with the idea of service and liturgy as performance, with an active professional leadership and a passive laity. It reflects a community of worshipers far smaller than the community of affiliates. On the walls of the sanctuary one typically finds plaques with brass strips containing the names of deceased members or relatives of members of the congregation with small light bulbs next to each name. The bulbs are illumined on the *yahrzeit* (anniversary) of the person's death, as the survivors link their family with the larger synagogue community.

The sanctuary is the architecturally most impressive and interesting part of the building. At the same time, it is probably the congregation's least rational "investment," as dollar for dollar more is spent here per person per hour of use there than on any other part of the synagogue complex. That is true of both the capital expenditure and the operating budget. Back in the 1950s the executive director of the Conservative movement's United Synagogue commented upon a recent study of the movement leadership, noting how the hard facts of the report turned "the spotlight on stately synagogues filled often with the heavy emptiness of empty pews."[1] Neither the 1953 report nor the later report of the 1970s brought much joy to the movement.[2]

This chapter focuses on that least rational yet undeniably central element in the life of the community, namely, synagogue services. Using a sample survey described elsewhere in this volume, we seek to understand why members of Conservative congregations do and do not attend services regularly. We shall look to determine what sets the community of worshipers within the synagogue apart from their fellows who are absent from services. We shall examine their upbringing, the reports of their lives from childhood onward, and their current beliefs and practices.

In the last part of this chapter, we shall look at some of the implications of the orientation of Conservative synagogue members to worship services for an understanding of the larger Jewish and religious orientations. This last part is admittedly less scientific, based as it is on less statistical evidence; rather, it is more interpretative and even speculative.

The Context

Of all the major religious groups in the United States, Jews stand at the bottom or near the bottom in their frequency of attendance at religious services. In this regard Jews are just about equal to those who identify themselves without religious affiliation and to those who identify as Universalists or Unitarians, the most liberal Protestant churches.[3] A large fraction of North American Jews never attend synagogue services at all except for the wedding or bar mitzvah service of a relative or friend.

At the beginning of the twentieth century, when immigration from Eastern Europe was at its height, Jewish absence from Shabbat services was already well established. Surveys taken in 1899 in two New York City neighborhoods reported that about one in ten Jews claimed regular attendance at services as compared with about half of the Protestants and eight in ten Roman Catholics.[4]

Jewish communal leaders of various persuasions expressed great concern over the disconnection between American-reared youth and Jewish public worship. The immigrants organized their synagogues around town or region of origin in Europe and so maintained the style of worship of the old country. But for the partially acculturated youth, the parents' nostalgia had little meaning and even less significance. The absence of youngsters engendered attempts to create services and synagogues that would appeal to those to whom the liturgy and manners of the old country were alien and frequently off-putting; these efforts, too, were largely unsuccessful.[5]

By the time of the First World War, there were only enough synagogue seats in New York City to accommodate less than half the adult Jewish population of the city.[6] In the 1920s another investigator estimated that fewer than 20 percent of Jews living in small Jewish communities attended services on a regular Shabbat.[7] In the mid-1930s a survey of New York's youth reported the rates of attendance at church or synagogue services during the week prior to the survey: Protestants, 40 percent; Catholics, 65 percent; Jews, 9 percent.[8] The picture is one of almost total breakdown of regular Shabbat public worship among American Jews.

At the same time, Jewish religious observance was declining in Eastern Europe, particularly among the communities from which the immigrants came. The forces of tradition were still strong in Eastern Europe, but they were increasingly challenged by powerful forces of secularism. A secular intelligentsia had arisen to challenge the authority of the rabbis. In the larger cities, some Jews kept their shops open on Shabbat and others smoked Russian cigarettes on Shabbat while strolling down the main street of the city. But there is little doubt that the erosion in Jewish religious behavior was more pervasive and rapid in America. As one Eastern European rabbi expressed it, "In America, even the stones are unkosher." Within a generation or less, then, regular attendance at services had become the province of a small and declining minority.[9]

For its part, the Reform movement, with few exceptions, could not reach the immigrants or their children; by the end of the nineteenth century it had initiated such radical liturgical changes as to make its services seem foreign and even churchlike to the immigrant community. Moreover, having its own problems attracting people to Shabbat services on Saturday mornings, many Reform temples moved their major weekly liturgy to Sunday mornings. This, too, alienated rather than attracted the newcomers. The Conservative movement, with its moderate reforms in liturgy and synagogue manners, was created in part to deal with the growing alienation from the synagogue of the newly American-ized first and second generation. The new Conservative movement did not see itself as being in opposition to or in competition with Orthodoxy. Indeed, it at-tempted to weld a coalition of traditionalists who would offer a westernized though traditionalist service and community to the rapidly acculturating immi-grants and their families.

The conservative innovators, including those who would become denomi-nationally Conservative and many of those who were to establish Modern Or-thodoxy, were an embattled minority in the traditionalist camp. They were often opposed by Orthodox immigrant rabbis, who saw the slightest deviation from the *Yiddishkeit* they had brought with them from Eastern Europe as heresy.

In the years following the Second World War, Jews showed an anomalous pattern. Jewish structural assimilation was low compared with that of other Americans, but acculturation and secularism were high. Using the intermarriage rate as an indicator of structural assimilation, we find that by 1957 only 7.2 per-cent of marriages involving a Jew was an intermarriage, compared to 8.6 per-cent of Protestants and 21.5 percent of Catholics. This low Jewish rate of intermarriage was not a random occurrence: it must be seen in light of the very small Jewish population, which would have meant that the random probability of a Jew marrying a non-Jew was very high. (By contrast, Protestants, the most numerous group, but with an intermarriage rate only slightly higher than that of Jews, were statistically likely to show a high rate of endogamous marriage sim-ply by being such a large portion of the total population.)

Although Jews were structurally "whole," they had nevertheless undergone a very rapid and extensive process of acculturation and secularization. This was part of the social context in which suburban Conservative hegemony emerged. Jews associated with Jews at work and even more in their leisure hours. They wanted to continue associating with Jews, a desire that was supported by the unwillingness of some gentiles to associate intimately with Jews. They had moved from the densely Jewish neighborhoods of the cities to the newly opened sub-urbs. Frequently the products of no Jewish education, or an unhappily remem-bered Jewish education in the basement room of the local Orthodox shul at the hands of an untrained teacher, they wanted something better for their children. They wanted a Jewishness that would give them a sense of continuity with the Jewish past (as they understood it) while not seeming fanatical. As one congre-gation put it, "The community needs a place for our children and we adults need some place to carry on our social lives. What better place can there be than our synagogue."[10]

And what sort of synagogue shall it be?

"We figured that the Conservative was 'middle of the road' and would not offend any group in the community. So we called it Conservative."[11] The Conservative synagogue then became the modal Jewish institution of the new suburban Jews. Children were registered for Hebrew school or Sunday school. High holiday services were packed. Men's clubs and sisterhoods and newly married groups were formed and offered a wide variety of cultural and social activities. But the Shabbat service? By the time these second- and third-generation American Jews established and operated their new suburban synagogues, public worship on Shabbat had become a lost art to the majority of the members. As will be demonstrated, synagogue service attendance is something initially learned from one's parents, and few Conservative Jews had parents who attended services regularly. In our sample of current Conservative synagogue members, 22 percent reported that their fathers attended services regularly (that is, twice a month or more) and 15 percent reported that their mothers attended services regularly.

So here we have the Conservative synagogue, an institution committed to fostering the continuity of Jewish tradition, with a rank and file for whom the Shabbat service, a central element in that tradition, was not part of personal patrimony. In the main, these Conservative Jews did not lose the habit of Shabbat service attendance. They never had it! Enter the late Friday evening service and the bar mitzvah. The late Friday evening service, introduced in the nineteenth century by the Reform movement as its primary Shabbat service (as a response to the Saturday workday schedule of its constituency), was emulated by traditionalist congregations that would tolerate moderate reform. By 1933, 95 percent of Conservative congregations offered late Friday evening services.[12] The Shabbat morning service became the province of women and children. The late Friday evening service had less competition from the world of work, but it too had attendance problems. However, rabbis discovered that they could deal with their congregations in segmented fashion.

As one Conservative rabbi summed it up: "To assure a consistently large Friday evening attendance, we have discovered that all that is necessary is to invite a different local organization or group to sponsor the service."[13] But it was a solution that created its own problems. It was as if the synagogue sanctuary had become a hall for hire in which to celebrate the glories of the men's club or Hadassah or the Jewish War Veterans. If it was not your group's turn, in other words, why go to services? This was no way to make public prayer a habit of the heart.

The bar mitzvah, later joined by the bat mitzvah, became the focal point of the Shabbat morning service and served a dual purpose. First, it gave Jewish education a goal and thus no doubt motivated attendance at the Congregational Hebrew school, first for boys and then, with the introduction and diffusion of bat mitzvah, for girls as well. It became a "sacrament" to which one could aspire if one met the requirements of worthiness, usually translated into instruction for a certain number of hours per week for a certain number of years. Second, it supplied the "audience" for the bar/bat mitzvah performance, again a floating population of friends and relatives, some from the congregation, many not; some able to participate in the liturgy, many not. What was missing from both the late Friday evening service and the bar mitzvah-dominated Shabbat morning service was a significantly large group of regulars, members of the congregation, who were there at Shabbat services because they wanted to pray, to study torah, to celebrate Shabbat.

Changes are under way. As compared with the near universality of late Friday evening services during the 1930s, now fewer than two-thirds of Conservative congregations hold late Friday evening services and one-fourth of the congregations have curtailed them during the past five years. Large congregations that are able to hold more than one service at a time now report the establishment of alternative services for different constituencies: a learners' service for those without a synagogue background, a traditional, or *daveners*, service for those who want to avoid the bar mitzvah celebrations and/or want an informal "low church," lay-dominated liturgy rather than the formal service characteristic of the large "cathedral" Conservative synagogue.

This, then, is the context in which we will study contemporary Conservative synagogue attendance. It is a context in flux, characterized by a quest to link modernist (or postmodernist?) Jews who have attenuated personal links to a living Jewish past to traditional modes of piety that are consonant with other parts of their lives.

The Pattern of Synagogue Attendance

THE BEHAVIORAL ANTECEDENTS OF REGULAR SERVICE ATTENDANCE

In our sample of Conservative congregation members, 29 percent claim to attend services twice a month or more. This frequency of attendance claimed by the members of our sample is consistent with reports from other surveys.[14] However, it has been established that Protestants and Catholics exaggerate the frequency of their attendance at church services, and there is every reason to believe that Jews do the same.[15] Although we do not assert that the rate of attendance is what is actually reported, we can identify the "maximalists," or "regulars." In this chapter we shall consider why the regulars are in fact regular attenders, even if not necessarily at the level that they claim.[16]

The practice of attending religious services begins at home. The probability of attending services as an adult householder is lowest when the individual did not attend services regularly as a child. The probability of current attendance increases when the individual himself or herself attended regularly in childhood but neither parent attended regularly. Current attendance increases further when one parent attended as well as the respondent, and it increases further still when both parents attended along with the respondent. The tendency to continue childhood behavior can be attributed to habit. However, the effect of parental behavior, in the way we have reported here, suggests that something more than habit is operating. As a general proposition, we can state that the more the household is involved in attending services, the greater the probability that the habit will take hold. When the parents as well as the children, particularly both parents, attend services on Shabbat, the life of the entire household is organized around service attendance. In addition to habit, the children receive an unambiguous message telling them that services are important and attendance is to be taken seriously. The children internalize that message and continue the behavior into maturity.[17]

In addition to current reports of service attendance, attendance of children, and attendance of parents, we have reports of attendance in the college years, often a period of reduced religious involvement.[18] Thus for the college period, we have defined regular attendance as one Shabbat service per month. In all, only 17 percent of the sample were regulars during their college years. While the propensity to attend is diminished, the family pattern of attendance still predicts the pattern of attendance during the college years (see table 4.1).[19]

The message transmitted through family participation in Shabbat services during childhood is broad and pervasive. Childhood service attendance predicts participation in Hillel activities in college, as well as taking courses in Jewish studies while in college. The message influences the outcomes of intermarriage, such that if those who attended services with both parents intermarry, they are far more likely to have their spouse convert to Judaism. Childhood service attendance patterns carry with them a broad message concerning the importance of religion in a wide variety of manifestations throughout the life course. This is a theme to which we shall return later in this chapter.

It should also be noted what the childhood service attendance does not predict or predicts only weakly, namely, synagogue skills as indicated by having read the torah or having led services during the year prior to the administration of the questionnaire. With respect to skills, attendance at services predicts competence whether or not the rest of the family participated in services. Family involvement in synagogue services during childhood speaks to the question of motivation to attend services regularly far more than it does to competence in synagogue skills. Basic religious identity and behavior are products of the home environment to a far greater extent than they are the result of formal schooling, youth groups, or religious camps. Our sample is no exception to this general pattern. The varieties of Jewish educational experiences, youth groups, and summer camps, including Camp Ramah, show little or no effect on the frequency

Table 4.1
The Effects of Childhood Service Attendance on Adult Attendance and Other Jewish Activities and Values

	Did not attend services regularly as a child	*Attended services regularly as a child but parents did not attend*	*Attended services regularly as a child and one parent also attended*	*Attended services regularly as a child and both parents also attended*
% attended services regularly in college	9	22	36	45
% attend services regularly now	25	33	37	46
% attended Hillel in college	26	37	50	53
% took a course in Jewish Studies in college	14	22	27	31
Of those whose spouses were not raised as Jews, % who are now Jews	54	54	70	79
% believe that being Jewish is very important	76	80	83	84
% believe that religion is very important	38	45	51	54
% chanted the torah	6	11	11	11
% lead services	6	11	11	11

of adult religious service attendance, although they do show an effect in the short term.[20] That is, both Camp Ramah attendance and USY or LTF (Leaders Training Fellowship) involvement affect service attendance in college but not later on. The childhood family experience sends a more enduring motivational message.[21]

However, Jewish education—particularly day school training, Camp Ramah, and to a lesser extent youth group involvement—does show an effect on synagogue competence. Thus, those who received a more comprehensive Jewish education or attended Camp Ramah were more likely to report that they had served as torah readers or had led services *when they attended services.* However, they were not significantly more likely to have attended services (see table 4.2).

While school and home may share ultimate goals, they perform different functions. Schools and their informal analogue, educational camps, impart knowledge and skills. For the most part they do not impart basic values and moral commitments. The latter come from the home and family. They are almost inherited in a biological sense from significant others, particularly parents. It is the rare formal or explicitly didactic organization that can reach the soul of a child or even an adult, for that matter. We shall return to this distinction later in this chapter.

Table 4.2
The Relationship of School, Youth Groups, and Camps to Service Attendance
and Service Competence

a. Formal Jewish schooling

	No Jewish education	Sunday School	Supplemental school	Day school
% attended services regularly in college	14	14	20	28
% attend services regularly now	27	24	31	30
% chanted the Torah	6	5	8	15
% lead services	4	3	8	15

b. Jewish training through camps and youth group

	Attended Camp Ramah	Did not attend Camp Ramah	Member USY or LTF	Not member USY or LTF
% attended services regularly in college	37	16	28	14
% attend services regularly now	29	29	29	29
% chanted the torah	22	7	10	7
% lead services	14	6	8	5

A PRELIMINARY SUMMARY

In the next section, we shall examine some of the subjective predictors of Jewish religious behavior. Before entering into that complex issue, let us summarize some of what we now know. Some basic summary statistics are presented in table 4.3. In the introductory section of this chapter, we discussed the rapid and extensive secularization of American Jews and its implications for the religious behavior of members of Conservative synagogues. In part a of table 4.3 we see the results of the historical process as reflected in the service attendance history of Conservative Jews. Almost half (48 percent) of the current members of Conservative synagogues were not regular synagogue service attenders during any of the three periods for which we have information. At the other extreme, only 6 percent were regular synagogue service attenders in all three periods. These two numbers give one a sense of the enormity of the task facing the Conservative movement as it tries to bring its membership to Jewish traditional practice. The disparity between aspiration for the future and current reality is far greater for the Conservative movement than it is for the other Jewish movements. Orthodoxy has closed the gap between the aspirations of the leadership and the reality of the rank and file by turning within and demanding an a priori commitment to Orthodox standards. Reform by contrast has adjusted its aspirations to fit reality.

Part b of table 4.3 gives us another perspective on these trends. It presents the probability of being a regular service attender given various life history configurations. As expected, the greatest probability of being a current regular attender is to be found among those who were regulars in childhood and during college years. As we noted at the outset, personal history is powerful. However, personal history is not all powerful, in that almost half of those with a consistent pattern of early regular service attendance are not current regulars. Something happens during college years that markedly affects the propensity to be a regular. The probability of being an adult regular given regular attendance in childhood is reduced markedly when not followed up during the college years. The net loss in Jewish commitment that occurs during the college years is common knowledge. However, when regular service attendance is begun in the college years, the probability of being an adult regular is raised markedly. While we note the decline in Jewish involvement during the college years, when college can become a period of Jewish discovery, there is a good chance that the process will continue into maturity. At the other extreme, among those without a history of regular attendance in childhood, almost a fourth (23 percent) are current regulars. These people are Conservative *ba'alei teshuvah*, or what some call "newly religious." While a history of regular service attendance predisposes one to continue in that path, there are those who stray. On the other hand, the Conservative movement is the locus of return to tradition for a significant proportion.

We found three points in life where people are most likely to experience a change in the degree or intensity of their Jewishness. These are their teen years, their college years, and when they first get married. Teenagers frequently search for themselves. They put on and take off personae like a loose fitting jacket. Children from a secular background will suddenly become pious while children from religious homes taste forbidden fruit. The odd thing about teen changes is that they usually last but a short time before the teenagers move back to near whence they came. In other words, the conversion or apostasy of teenagers is evanescent.

For most young Jews, the college period is probably the first time that they really feel on their own. They have to define themselves anew in a context that is unlike the homes in which they were raised. These years show more self-defined alienation from Jewishness in its various forms. The longer they remain in the world of the university, the more likely they are to report that they have experienced a decline in their Jewish commitment—so much so that their probability of attending services again after leaving university is diminished as a function of the number of years they spend in the university.

The third important period of self definition is the period when they first get married. It is at this time that they seek to reclaim the experiences they re-

Table 4.3
Summary of Trends across the Life Course

a. Distribution of regular service attendance at three points in time: percent attended regularly

Did not attend services regularly at any of the three points in time	48%
Attended regularly one of the three points in time	32%
Attended regularly two of the three points in time	13%
Attended regularly at all three points in time	6%

b. Probabilities of attending services regularly given the personal history of service attendance

On condition that respondent attended regularly at ages 11–12 and during college	.51
On condition that respondent did not attend regularly at ages 11–12 but did so during college	.40
On condition that respondent attended regularly at ages 11–12 but did not do so during college	.30
On condition that respondent did not attend regularly at ages 11–12 or during college	.23

jected in the university. This, and the time when they first have children, is the time when they return to the community, though they are significantly changed by their university experience.

SUBJECTIVE PREDICTORS OF REGULAR SERVICE ATTENDANCE

ETHNIC AND RELIGIOUS IDENTITY. The discussion has dealt so far with objective conditions and their impact on service attendance. We imputed states of mind without direct evidence. In this section, we shall examine subjective states and their relationship to service attendance. We shall examine states of mind from two perspectives: identity and ideology.

The Jewish condition is unique in the Western world in its being a fusion of ethnicity and religion. In traditional language, the Jews constitute *Am Yisrael* and *Knesset Yisrael*, the Jewish people and the Jewish *ecclesia*. The joining of the two elements is epitomized by Ruth's declaration to Naomi in the Book of Ruth: "Whither thou goest, I shall go. . . . Your people shall be my people and your God shall be my God."

With the rise of secularism during the last two centuries, Jews began distinguishing between Jewish religion and Jewish peoplehood. That separated religious identity from ethnic or national identity. In parallel, classical Reform Judaism in Western Europe and the United States affirmed Jewish religion but denied Jewish nationality. Secularists therefore asserted the continuation of Jewish peoplehood independent of Jewish religion, while reformers asserted the continuity of Jewish religion independent of Jewish ethnicity.

Jews in the United States and Canada show the highest level of secularity of any European-origin ethnic or religious-ethnic group. Jews are the least likely to attend religious services, to express belief in God and miracles, to believe in divine revelation. At the same time Jews show an incredibly high level of communal solidarity. Jews are far more likely to befriend coreligionists than are Protestants and Catholics and are more likely to live among fellow Jews, thus forming Jewish neighborhoods, while Protestants and Catholics are distributed across the cities and towns without reference to religious identification. As an example of Jewish solidarity, the struggle for the emancipation of Soviet Jews galvanized tens of thousands of North American Jews to protest, attend rallies, and contribute funds.

A few years ago, the Gallup poll asked a sample of North Americans, "How important would you say that religion is in your life?" In all, 56 percent of Roman Catholics, 37 percent of Episcopalians, 55 percent of Presbyterians, 72 percent of Southern Baptists, and 25 percent of Jews replied that religion was very important to them.[22] The same question was posed to members of Conservative synagogues, and 41 percent said religion was very important. Thus as one would expect, a much larger proportion of members of Conservative congregations expressed the view that religion was very important to them than was true of Jews generally. Yet it is surprising that the majority of the members of a religious organization report that religion is not very important to them. Would the majority of the subscribers to the local orchestra report that music was not very important to them?

Many Jews consider themselves, and are considered by their fellow Jews, to be good and loyal Jews without being terribly religious. Indeed, over the past 150 years there have been many important Jewish movements that were not religious. So too were there many Jewish leaders and heroes who were not religious. It would be fair to say that most of the key events in modern Jewish history took place outside of the orbit of the synagogue. To get at what we might call the "tribal" element in the Jewish experience we asked the question, "How important would you say that being Jewish is in your life?" We found that 78 percent of the members of Conservative synagogues felt that being Jewish was very important to them. This fraction is far greater than among the Jewish population as a whole, where only 55 percent say that being Jewish is very important to them.[23] Jewish peoplehood is important to a higher proportion of Conservative Jews than is Jewish religion.

By cross-tabulating the question of the importance of religion and the importance of being Jewish, we find some interesting patterns. In all, 40 percent of the sample reports that both religion and Jewishness are very important; 37 percent report that being Jewish is very important while religion is not very important; 21 percent report that neither being Jewish nor religion is very important; 1 percent tell us that being Jewish is not very important while religion is very important. We shall call the group that is committed to both religion and to Jewishness the "core"; the group that is committed to Jewishness and not to religion, "secular"; and the group that is not committed to either Jewishness or religion, the "periphery."[24]

The cross-tabulation tells us that in order to give priority to Jewish religion in one's life, one must give priority to being Jewish. That is, only a tiny minority of the sample of Conservative synagogue members (1 percent) tell us that religion is very important but that being Jewish is not. Though logically possible, it is extremely unusual for a person to express strong attachment to religion without strong attachment to the Jewish people. For Conservative Jews, religion is not embraced in the abstract but in the particularity of Jewish experience. Judaism without particularity floats in the air much like figures in a Chagall painting.

Until modern times, Jewishness and Judaism were linked together such that it was impossible to affirm one without affirming the other. The religion of the Jewish people is predicated on the history of the Jewish people. The Book of Genesis is the tale of a Bedouin family wandering in and about the land of Canaan some 3,500 years ago. The Book of Exodus is an epic saga of the children of the Bedouins of Genesis and their families after their descent into Egypt, their enslavement, and their redemption from bondage. They entered Egypt as a clan and emerged as a nation.

In traditional Jewish imagination, the Jews live on two levels that exist easily side by side. Jews gave their children the names of heroes and heroines from the Hebrew Bible. Thus, there was Avraham Avinu (our father Abraham) and Avremele (little Abraham) who lived down the street. They were equally real. Somewhere along the way to westernization and modernization, a large fraction of the Jewish people lost touch with their ancestors and the ancient family saga, though they maintained contact and concern for and with the Jews of their own time. In their turning away from the past, many Jews became secular and some became peripheral.

There are two fundamental parts to Jewish consciousness. These are Jewishness, the sense of solidarity with other Jews wherever they are, and Jewish religion or Judaism, a sense of cosmic order and the place of the Jewish people in that order as filtered through Jewish historic experience. Jewishness is threatened by assimilation and Jewish religion by secularization. Both processes have been going on for the past 150 to 250 years, and they have wreaked havoc on Jews and Judaism.

Secularization worked much more rapidly and pervasively among the Jews of Europe than did assimilation. Jews remained Jews long after they stopped believing and practicing as Jews. While some Jews sought to disappear as Jews through conversion, the vast majority remained identified as Jews, though frequently with few of the markers of traditional Jews, whether the markers were religious (maintaining kashrut, observing Shabbat) or national (switching from Yiddish to German or Russian).

In light of their new circumstances, the response of the Jews of the West was to denude Judaism of its particularistic ideas and practices and to make Judaism "universal," yet part of the culture of the host country rather than the historic culture of the Jews. The response of the Jews of the East was to create Jewish ideologies that dealt with the here and now, without reference to what they perceived as pie-in-the-sky religion. Both problems were solved in the short run, but the solutions ultimately failed (classical Reform or Jewish socialism) or were successful and then had to work out where to go from there (Zionism).

So much for historical context and analysis. What does all this have to do with Conservative congregations and their members? How did it come to pass that people with little interest in religion became affiliated with the synagogue? The answer lies in the fact that the synagogue became the major address of the Jews in the diaspora. It is a Jewish response to the West, where the reality is that institutionalized ethnicity is weak while institutionalized religion is strong.

By the time that North American Jews moved in large numbers to the suburbs, where the Conservative congregation flourished, religion had almost entirely displaced ethnicity or nationality as a focus of *communal* organization, while for the *individual* member of the congregation, the Jewish people was the anchor of his Jewish life. The immigrant generation and their children could lead rich Jewish lives through their commitment to Yiddishism, socialism, and a host of other Jewish secular "isms." This is no longer possible. For the most part, secular Jews are now homeless except for the synagogue. To meet the needs of seculars, the synagogue has taken on a wide variety of functions that are apparently secular. These include sports and social gatherings. To some extent the synagogue's movement into nonreligious areas has come about because of self-interest on the part of synagogue leadership. They do not want to lose the involvement of the less religiously inclined Jews. Some thought that as long as the organized Jewish community maintained contact with the secularized or peripheral Jew, all was not lost. Thus was created "the shul with the pool."

Here then we have three groups of congregants (core, seculars, and peripherals) who differ in their Jewish identity. Their differences have practical consequences for the nature and kind of congregational activities in which they engage. Taking Shabbat service attendance as our first concern, we find that there is a vast difference between the core members on the one hand and the seculars and peripherals on the other, while the difference between seculars and peripherals is relatively small (see table 4.4). This finding is almost embarrassingly obvious but its implications are not. In the absence of religious commitment, congregations have substituted "special occasions" as pretexts for conducting services. While this may work for any given Shabbat, it will not create a Shabbat community around which a Jewish community can be built.

Table 4.4
Percentage Participating Regularly in Congregational Life among Sectors of
Conservative Congregational Membership

	Core	Secular	Peripheral
Shabbat services	42	19	13
Family Shabbat	56	42	42
Board meeting	19	14	8
Committee meeting	32	19	17
Lecture	61	47	34
Class	30	15	10
Men's club	43	31	30
Personal celebration	75	63	35
Family program	46	36	30
Social action	22	14	13
Average number of activities attended regularly	4.45	3.29	2.82

Shabbat services aside, we have a list of nine congregational activities and the fraction of each of the three groups (core, seculars, and peripherals) that participates frequently in each of the activities. In every instance, the members of the core are more involved in the life of the congregation than either the seculars or the peripherals. This pattern shows up in the detailed list and in the summary figure at the bottom of the table. The detail makes it clear that differences among the three groups are not restricted to religious activities but are reflected strongly in intellectual activities such as classes and lectures as well. The probability of participating in Jewish learning is enhanced by commitment to the Jewish people and to Jewish religion. Committee and board meetings, which are heavily involved in administration and finance, are also the beneficiaries of Jewish and religious commitments. These commitments make it possible for the congregation to carry on its work.

If the members of the congregation went to services regularly as children, they are far more likely to become core members of their congregations than if they had not. If they went to services with a parent, rather than being sent, their probability of being a core member is enhanced. It is enhanced further if they went to services with both parents. Childhood service attendance shapes the nature and extent of adult participation in the life of the Jewish community (see table 4.5).

Going to services is not magic. While we should take the service attendance pattern in childhood literally, we should also understand that it stands for something beyond itself. What it stands for is the pattern of family life that makes clear to the child the family's commitment to Judaism and the Jewish people. Interestingly enough, while formal Jewish schooling has some effect, it has much less effect. Again we find that the Jewish community cannot place its bet on schools (or camps and youth groups) alone. The households that constitute the community have to assume much of the responsibility for raising Jews who are

Table 4.5
Childhood Service Attendance as a Predictor of Membership in the Congregational Core

	Did not attend	Attended without parents	Attended with one parent	Attended with both parents
% members of the core	36	44	50	54

committed to the Jewish people and to Jewish religion. Schools teach facts and skills. These are their tasks. It is unrealistic to expect them to do much more.

COMMUNITY AND IDEOLOGY

In many communities, particularly where it was possible to organize only one congregation, the Conservative label was sought in order to represent the "middle of the road," the label that "would not offend any groups." There was no mention of religious standards, and no one would be expelled for violating Shabbat or for not attending services. People were encouraged to join the synagogue for Jewish togetherness and to give their children the Jewish education that they themselves did not have. No wonder the new synagogue is perceived and characterized as an ethnic shelter.

Early in its career in the United States, in 1885, the Reform movement issued a manifesto, the Pittsburgh Platform, that delineated the radical changes it was making in Jewish belief and practice. As Orthodoxy shifted from being the nominal modal position of the Jewish community to becoming a section of the larger Jewish community, it too began to define itself more sharply, using such self-applied terms as "torah-true Judaism." The Conservative movement had and still has a more difficult time in establishing an ideological position. Committed as it is to Jewish tradition yet willing to "negotiate with the tradition," Conservatism is necessarily pragmatic and less willing and able to assert a coherent ideology.[25] Over the years, however, issues have arisen that have occasioned debate within the movement. The positions taken on these issues can be classified along a continuum from liberal to conservative (with a small "c"). Some of the issues that currently engage the Conservative leadership and membership were put to the Conservative laity included in the study sample. In all, eight questions were chosen to represent the range of Conservative ideological issues and to represent the location of the individual along the array of Orthodox, Conservative, and Reform. Another three items were constructed to develop an understanding of the individual's sense of integration into the congregational community. The wording of the questions and the responses are presented in table 4.6.

Table 4.6
The Construction and Utilization of Ideology and Communal Integration
Scales

a. Ideology: questions and distributions of responses (percentage agree)

	% agree or agree strongly
1. Anyone who was raised Jewish—even if their mother was Gentile and their father was Jewish—I would personally regard as a Jew	68
2. Conservative Judaism lets you choose those parts of Judaism you find meaningful	74
3. Reform is "more relevant" than Conservatism	9
4. Orthodoxy is too shut off from modern life	54
5. I don't think I could ever be Orthodox	70
6. I don't think I could ever be Reform*	61
7. Conservative Jews are obligated to obey Halakha*	61
8. My rabbi should be willing to perform intermarriages	27

* The scoring is based upon disagreement: the higher the positive summary score, the more liberal the ideology of the respondent.

b. Communal integration: questions and distributions of responses (percentage agree)

	% agree or agree strongly
9. Members of my congregation are friendly to newcomers	74
10. I feel included in the life of my congregation	67
11. There's a group in my congregation with whom I feel very close	64

Items 3–6 in table 4.6 give a sense of the commitment to Conservatism as a real choice and help individuals to locate themselves along the continuum of Orthodox, Conservative, and Reform. The majority of the sample has evaluated the religious choices available to American Jews and has opted to be Conservative. They agree overwhelmingly that they could never be either Orthodox or Reform (items 5–6); they overwhelmingly withhold agreement from the assertion that Reform is more relevant and by a small margin accept the notion that Orthodoxy is too shut off from modern life. Conservatism is not therefore a default position but a conscious choice made in the context of the available interpretations of Judaism.

Those who affirm that Orthodoxy is "too shut off from the world" and that Reform is "more relevant" tend to locate themselves in the liberal wing of the Conservative movement. Those who affirm that they could never be Reform, or disagree with the statement that they don't think that they could ever be Orthodox, are locating themselves in the more traditional wing of the Conservative movement.

Items 1, 2, 7, and 8 were put to the sample to determine their agreement with Conservative religious principles as articulated by the Jewish Theological Seminary and the Rabbinical Assembly, which is the rabbinic arm of Conservative Judaism. The items were chosen to comprise two pairs, both with expressions of the more and the less traditional point of view. Item 1 refers to the principle of patrilineality, that is, whether Jewish identity is carried by the mother or father or both; this item was paired with item 8, which refers to Conservative rabbis performing intermarriages.

Jewish law, halakha, clearly supports the position that identity comes through the maternal line. Thus the majority of Conservative Jews reject the legal position of their own rabbis, accepting instead the position of the Reform and Reconstructionist movements. By contrast, they reject the notion that their rabbi should perform interfaith marriages, thus agreeing with the rabbis of the Conservative movement. By a clear majority, they want the line held on intermarriage. As one would expect, those whose spouse was not raised as a Jew and is currently not a Jew, as well as those whose eldest child is married to a non-Jew, are more likely to be in favor of their rabbi officiating at a mixed marriage. However, it is striking that among those married to non-Jews or those whose son- or daughter-in-law is not Jewish, there is not a majority in support of rabbis officiating at interfaith weddings. In the main, the source for the position seems to be principle rather than reflexive self-interest.

What, then, is the principled stand of those who affirm what appears to be a self-contradictory position? They are stating that there should be a boundary around the Jewish people. They are more than willing to welcome Jews by choice, but they do not want their rabbis to weaken the boundary by seeming to support intermarriage. However, after the fact, if a child raised as a Jew though his/her mother is neither a Jew by birth or by choice, they would accept that child into the community as a full-fledged member. Though traditionalists would reject the compromise position in this case, the principle of distinguishing between issues before and after the fact is well accepted in Jewish law. A significant fraction of the laity exercises the option of that distinction and comes up with what appears to be a compromise position that is not consistent with the position taken by legal decisors of the Conservative movement.

Items 2 and 7 were also paired. The sample was asked whether Conservative Jews are bound by halakha and whether Conservative Judaism allows one to choose those parts of Judaism that one finds meaningful. The pattern of responses that one finds in the ideological questions shows an inconsistency that would be incomprehensible to an Orthodox or Reform Jew. The majority of Conservative Jews (over 60 percent on each item) agree that "Conservative Jews are obligated to obey Halakha" and "Conservative Judaism lets you choose those parts of Judaism you find meaningful."

The correlation between these two questions is negative, as one would expect, but only weakly so (Spearman R=.088). Thus a significant minority, 47 percent, hold to both propositions simultaneously, despite obvious internal contradiction. To a Reform Jew, the obligation to halakha does not hold, while to an Orthodox Jew, the notion that one can choose makes no sense.[26] On the face of it, one position or the other must be correct, so one should not be able to affirm these contradictory positions. Does this frequent Conservative contradiction simply bespeak illogic or muddy thinking, or does it signify something intentional and positive? There is more here than an attempt to square a metaphysical circle. A careful reading of the two ethnographic chapters in this volume (chapters 3 and 6) gives us a sense of the possible meaning and significance of the self-contradictory position held by almost half of Conservative Jews.

In two of the congregations dealt with in detail in this volume, the rabbis began the liturgical year with programs to enhance Jewish observance. The rationale given in both cases was not the need to observe per se but rather the function that the observance would play in the life of the Jew. It was not so much that God commanded and you must do; rather, it was that God is offering you a chance to choose to bring sanctity into your life. From what will you choose? From what list of possibilities will you take the elements to construct holiness in your life? You will choose from that list offered by the tradition, through the halakha. In both congregations, the message of observance implied *mitzvah goreret mitzvah*: the observance of a commandment brings one to the observance of further commandments.

The use of the words "commandment" and "mitzvah" requires exploration. Consider the comment of Charles S. in chapter 3. He saw in the two synagogues in question an ability to "hold firm . . . with an open hand." What Heilman has to say of the two Conservative congregations he studied can be generalized to the movement and in particular to those who wish to choose and to be bound by halakha as Conservative Jews. And consider the comments of one of the founders of Beth Jacob reported in the chapter 6: "We come together around torah. . . . We consult halakhic sources and apply them appropriately to solutions that are workable." A commandment becomes a commandment upon its being accepted as such. In the words of one of the people interviewed by Heilman, "It [Conservative Judaism] wrestles with tradition, and I like that wrestling."

"Blessed art thou O Lord our God, King of the Universe, who has sanctified us by His commandments and has commanded us to. . . . " Thus begin many of the blessings that a Jew recites prior to performing a mitzvah, a commandment. Many of these Conservative Jews assert God's kingship, even as they seem to be saying that God is not an absolute king but rather a constitutional monarch. God's command stands as a challenge to these Conservative Jews and

Table 4.7
The Sources of Ideology and Communal Integration

a. Percentage liberal ideology by service attendance in childhood

Did not attend	Attended alone	Attended with one parent	Attended with two parents
31	22	18	10

Percentage liberal ideology by denomination raised

Conservative	Orthodox	Reform	Other	not Jewish
26	18	57	35	29

b. Percentage highly integrated in congregation

friends in congregation	none	a few	some	most	all or almost all
	8	14	25	41	48

number of activities in which participates	none	few	many	most
	10	14	29	44

becomes a mitzvah when they accept it as such. Nevertheless, while one could adduce prooftexts from the vast body of Jewish religious literature that would seem to justify this position, it would be disingenuous to say that this perspective is the main thrust of rabbinic tradition. These Conservative Jews who assert their loyalty to halakha while reserving the right to choose, if they are serious, resonate with the formulations of several modern Jewish thinkers, including some of the leading figures in Conservative Judaism. The difference between the laity in our survey and the rabbis and scholars who articulate similar notions of two sources of Jewish practice is a simple but crucial one. The laymen are asserting that they will make the choice, while the rabbis and other learned Jews would, in effect, require licensure by the learned.

The sources of the ideology scale are to be found in the experiences of childhood and adolescence (see table 4.7). The most significant of these are the childhood patterns of service attendance and the denomination in which one was raised. The more the family of one's childhood was involved in regular Shabbat service attendance, the more likely one is to reject the liberal religious stance. Conservative and Reform upbringing, particularly the latter, lead to a liberal religious position. Formal Jewish schooling, Camp Ramah, and USY show similar relationships, though for the latter two it is rather weak.

Table 4.8
The Relationship of the Ideology Scale to Other Variables

a. Percentage for whom being Jewish is very important, by ideology

liberal	moderate	conservative
64	78	95

b. Percentage for whom religion is very important, by ideology

liberal	moderate	conservative
24	42	66

The items that represent communal integration (9–11) are more straight-forward and easily understood; they form a coherent cluster. The communal integration scale is *not* predicted by early life experiences in the same way. High communal integration is predicted by having a congregational friendship circle and participation in congregational activities.[27]

If the ideology scale reflects basic values and attitudes, then it should relate well to other questions probing similar complexes of values and attitudes. Table 4.8 shows the relationship of the ideology scale to the questions of the importance of being Jewish and the importance of religion in the respondents' lives. Those whom we classify as being conservative on the ideology scale are more likely to acknowledge the importance of being Jewish and of religion than are the religious liberals.

The relationships in this table give us a more refined sense of the meaning of the ideology scale. Of greatest interest is the finding that the religious liberals are less committed to *both* the importance of being Jewish and the importance of religion. That liberals find being Jewish less important can be understood as part of their more universalistic orientation to the world. It is a relationship that makes intuitive sense. But why should the liberals report that they are less committed to religion? The liberal religious stance is not only a different religious orientation, it is *less likely to be a* religious orientation at all. In other words, the liberals are more secular than the conservatives.

In table 4.9, we present the effects of the ideology and communal integration scales independently and their joint effect on regular service attendance. Looking first at religious ideology, the conservatives are more than three times as likely to attend services regularly as the liberals (56 percent as compared with 15 percent).[28] In the communal integration scale, those who are highly committed are more than four times as likely to attend as those who show low integration (47 percent compared with 11 percent).[29] Taking into account both

Table 4.9
The Separate and Joint Effects of the Communal Integration and Ideology
Scales on Regular Service Attendance

a. Service Attendance by Ideology
Percentage attend regularly

liberal	moderate	conservative
15	27	56

b. Service attendance by community integration
Percentage attend regularly

not integrated	moderately integrated	highly integrated
11	28	47

c. Service attendance by ideology and communal integration
percentage attend regularly
ideology = liberal
communal integration =

not integrated	moderately integrated	highly integrated
7	15	23

ideology = moderate
communal integration =

not integrated	moderately integrated	highly integrated
10	26	43

ideology = conservative
communal integration =

not integrated	moderately integrated	highly integrated
26	51	76

ideology and communal integration, those who are conservative ideologically and show high integration into the community are almost *eleven times* more likely to attend regularly than are those who are religious liberals and show low communal integration (76 percent to 7 percent).

The ideological conservatives who are also communally integrated are 8 percent of the population but 19 percent of the regular attenders. The moderate ideologues who show middling communal integration are 30 percent of the regular attenders and 28 percent of the population. That is, their proportion in the population as a whole is approximately equal to their proportion among the regular attenders. The ideological liberals with low communal integration are 5 percent of the total population and only 1 percent of the regular attenders.

Communal integration and ideology compensate for one another. Let us look at two examples. Moderate believers who score high on communal integration have about the same rate of regular attendance (45 percent) as conservative believers who score medium on communal integration (46 percent). Conservative believers who are low on communal integration have about the same rate of attendance (23 percent) as liberal believers who are high on communal integration (21 percent). This pattern has both practical and theoretical implications. On the practical level, it is probably more difficult to change ideological orientation than it is to change communal integration. The roots of religious ideology go back to childhood and are reinforced by a more general social value orientation; that is, religious values are part of a more general value system, such that conservative religionists are likely to be conservative in their general worldview. By virtue of their embeddedness, the religious values are relatively stable. By contrast, the degree of communal involvement is subject to influence by external forces. I should think that the uninvolved members of the congregation can be invited to participate in communal activities that are close to their interests, thus increasing their communal integration score with a reasonable chance of getting them to services more regularly.

On another level, the presence of "believers" can create an atmosphere of belief that serves to carry others who have doubts. A sense of holiness or religious fervor is contagious, permitting the skeptic to suspend disbelief, at least for the moment. The "private capital" of the believer becomes part of the "social capital" of the community, including those who are less convinced.

So far, we have discussed religious ideology and service attendance without mention of God. Table 4.10 presents the effects of belief in God on attendance at synagogue services. We posed three questions dealing with belief in God. These are the belief that (a) there is a God, that (b) God rewards good deeds, and that (c) God answers prayer. The relationships of the three belief items with service attendance are presented in table 4.10. The denial of God's existence, His answering prayer, or His rewarding good deeds lead to significantly reduced participation in services. However, the affirmation of belief does not lead to much higher level of synagogue service attendance than the average level of attendance of the population as a whole. Thus, firm commitment to belief in the existence of God raises synagogue service attendance at the level of twice a month or more by a mere 5 percentage points; belief in God answering prayers by 6 percentage points; and belief in God rewarding good deeds has no effect on regular attendance at all (see part c).[30] Belief by itself shows a small effect, but that effect disappears when the ideology and communal commitment scales are entered along with the belief items.

What, then, are we to conclude about the significance of belief in God and his powers? Belief seems to be a necessary but not sufficient condition for

Table 4.10
Regular Attendance, by Belief in God

Percentage attend regularly who

	definitely no	probably no	not sure	probably yes	definitely yes
a. Believe that there is a God	8	9	24	25	35
b. Believe that God will reward you for your good deeds	18	22	32	32	32
c. Believe that God answers your prayers	16	25	29	31	38

attending services. Ideological conservatism incorporates the predictive power of belief. A conservative religious ideology contains within it an implied belief in God to a far greater extent than a liberal religious ideology.

SERVICE ATTENDANCE AND ITS PROXIMATE CAUSES

We have examined the long-term effects of childhood experiences (home, school, camp, youth group), the individual's service attendance history, broad ideological orientations, communal integration, and belief in God as factors that influence the adult householder's current attendance. We now shift our attention from factors that are at some remove from attendance to factors that are more proximate. We shall look particularly at two factors, one motivational and the other skill-related. The motivational factor is the degree of agreement with the statement, "I don't find synagogue prayers especially moving or meaningful." The skill question is "Are you able to read the prayerbook in Hebrew (not necessarily understanding the prayers)?"

Almost one-third of the sample responded that they agree or agree strongly that synagogue prayers are not moving or meaningful (see table 4.11). About one-fourth of the sample reported that they cannot read the Hebrew prayerbook. As one would expect, those who do not find the services moving or meaningful are far less likely to attend, and those who cannot read the prayerbook in Hebrew are also less likely to attend. Let us examine the context of each of these factors.

Neither factor comes out of the blue. Those who do not find services moving or meaningful are far less likely to report that being Jewish and religion are very important to them. They are less likely to have attended services as children, and their parents did not attend. They tend to feel unintegrated into the life of the congregation and in fact are not, as measured by the number of friendships they maintain within the congregation. Consistent with the findings reported earlier, Jewish education and experience at Camp Ramah and/or USY that have had no effect on service attendance also show no relationship with

Table 4.11
The Relationship of Skill and Motivation to Service Attendance

a. Motivation

Percent who attend regularly, by their level of agreement or disagreement with the following statement:
"I don't find synagogue prayer especially moving or meaningful."

	agree strongly	agree	not sure	disagree	disagree strongly
no controls	18	18	18	31	53
control for ideology and communal integration	28	24	21	24	42

b. Skill

Percent who attend regularly, by response to the following question:
"Are you able to read the prayer book in Hebrew (not necessarily understanding the prayers)?"

	yes	no
no controls	35	12
controlling for ideology and communal integration	32	20

finding services meaningful or moving. When the relationship between finding the services not moving or meaningful and attendance is statistically controlled for religious ideology and communal integration, the initial relationship is reduced very sharply. The percentage difference between the extremes is initially 35 percentage points. When controlled for ideology and communal integration, the percentage difference between the extremes is reduced to 14 points. The reduction in percentage difference signifies a reduction in the power of the variable in question (finding prayer meaningful) to influence the dependent variable, here regular attendance at synagogue services.

Reporting inability to read the Hebrew prayerbook is related to Jewish education. Those who report having had a Sunday school education or no Jewish education at all are about equally likely to tell us that they cannot read the prayerbook. Those who attended a supplementary school or day school are more likely to be able to read the prayerbook. But here, too, the problem lies in part in the orientation of the would-be worshiper. Those who report that they cannot read the prayerbook in Hebrew and thus attend services less frequently tend to be individuals with a liberal religious ideology and tend to feel unintegrated into the life of the congregation. Those who can read the prayerbook are 23 percentage points more likely to be service regulars. However, when controls are introduced for ideology and communal integration, the percentage difference is reduced to 12 points.

For those whose lack of competence in reading the Hebrew prayerbook is a consequence of lack of training and nothing more, making such training available will likely solve their problem. Insofar as the lack of Hebrew competence is motivated by ideology or marginality, however, it is unlikely that the approach will be successful.

We should note at this point that differences among Conservative congregations in the way they conducted services and in the prayerbook that they used had no effect on the attendance patterns of their membership. When congregation members ask themselves whether or not they will be attending services they clearly do not take into account the characteristics of the services or even of the cantor or rabbi. They are responding to their values and their commitment to their community.

SERVICES ARE DIFFERENT—WHAT DOES THE DIFFERENCE MEAN?

We have located some of the key factors that distinguish regular service attenders from those who attend less frequently or not at all. Now that we have some understanding of the place of attendance at services in the lives of Conservative Jews and Conservative Jewish congregations, we will try to extend that understanding by comparing Shabbat service attendance with other synagogue activities and with home observance. To this end, we shall look at the relationship between each of the activities and rituals and the two primary scales, namely, religious ideology and communal integration. These relationships, expressed in correlations, can be understood as hurdles or obstacles to be vaulted. The higher the correlation, the more dependent the performance of the act in question on the scale with which it is being correlated.

There are three classes of activities listed in table 4.12: service attendance, other synagogue activities, and private or home rituals. The class of behaviors that we have termed "other synagogue activities" tends to be weakly correlated with conservative (i.e., traditional) ideology and relatively strongly correlated with communal integration. The opposite is true of the class of behaviors labeled "private rituals." Private ritual observance is strongly correlated with traditional ideology but weakly correlated with communal integration. Service attendance is highly correlated with *both* scales. In this, service attendance is unique. In each column, there is at least one correlation that is greater than service attendance (for example, social program with communal integration and two sets of dishes with conservative ideology), but in no case is the sum of the two correlations greater than or even equal to the correlations with service attendance.

Service attendance stands at the intersection of the community in which one lives one's life and the historic community of memory and tradition. Services demand participation in the life of the living community and in the com-

Table 4.12

Synagogue and Private Jewish Activity, by Ideology and Communal Integration (expressed in correlation coefficients)

activity	Correlated with communal integration	Correlated with ideology
attend services regularly	.267	.329
Other public activity		
celebration (such as baby-naming)	.270	.145
Class	.156	.135
Family Shabbat	.233	.114
Lecture	.249	.161
Men's club, etc.	.254	.092
Family program	.211	.121
Social action	.153	.043
Social program	.319	.122
Home or private activity		
Light Sabbath candles	.162	.230
Two sets of dishes	.137	.391
Don't eat meat in non-kosher restaurant	.082	.330
Fast on Yom Kippur	.078	.233

munity of history. As we have shown, services prepare the ground for the community of future generations.

The cycle of prayer and scriptural reading confronts the Jews with questions of ultimate value. Public worship, more than any other collective event in the life of the Jew, confronts the individual with the historic myths and memories of his or her people. The prayerbook makes claims about right and wrong, about human limitation, about an unseen world that it asserts is real. Services make these historical and mythic connections in a communal context, with at least nine other adult Jews. Participation in public worship requires knowledge and skills, but these are not the problem. Rote reading of the Hebrew prayerbook can be learned easily, and even understanding the text is not beyond the capacity of the typical Conservative Jew.

REFLECTIONS ON SERVICES: MEANING AND CONTINUITY

"The suburban synagogue is not a shul, and it has become a service center for its affiliate members rather than a communal center." [31]

"The laity construes Conservative Judaism as primarily a sociological tool and not a structure of belief and practice which is true, authentic and good in its own right."[32]

These are the judgments of two prominent Conservative rabbis: the first, the leader of one of the major Conservative congregations in the United States and the second, an academic. Without searching very hard, one can easily find even more severe criticisms of the Conservative movement from its leadership.

Indeed, self-criticism is one of the favorite activities of Conservative Jewish leadership. One historian of American Jewry has tried to capture the mood of the leadership of the movement in the title of a published paper, "The Conservative Rabbi: Dissatisfied but Not Unhappy."[33]

With the passing of generations, Jews are more likely to identify and/or affiliate with one of the more liberal branches of Judaism. The Conservative movement, once the net beneficiary of the shift, is now threatened by it, as many Jews raised in the Conservative movement have shifted to Reform or nonaffiliation, just as their parents or grandparents once shifted from Orthodoxy to Conservatism. With each passing generation, Conservative Jewry increasingly recruits Jews who grew up in Conservative homes. For better or worse, the Conservative movement recruits a smaller and smaller fraction of its membership from Orthodoxy, as Orthodoxy has been able to motivate its adherents to pass the tradition along from generation to generation.

We have found that a large fraction of Conservative homes and formal institutions are unable to pass along a vision of Jewish life that includes regular participation in public worship. The result of these social processes is a steady decline in service attendance among Conservative Jews by generation in the United States and Canada. In the first generation 38 percent report attending services twice a month or more. That proportion is reduced to 29 percent in the second generation, 27 percent in the third generation, and 22 percent in the fourth or later generation.

The practice of Judaism is an art form, an acquired taste. Though formal Jewish identity is usually given by descent, acting on that formal identity requires effort, first on the part of the parents, then on the part of teachers, and then on the part of the actor and his/her community. We cannot overestimate the power of the home. The home prepares and motivates the individual to live within a Jewish community. However, the major investments of the Conservative movement have been in educational institutions, the supplementary school, the day school (Solomon Schechter schools), and Ramah camps. The home has been largely off-limits as a target of Jewish religious renewal, yet it is within the home that the battle is won or lost. The educational institutions supported by the Conservative movement have been very successful in *training* but significantly less so in *indoctrinating*. To a considerable degree, the failure to indoctrinate or socialize youngsters is not the fault of the formal institutions themselves. We are asking too much of them. In a more traditionalist period, the Jewish school—whether *heder*, Talmud Torah, or yeshiva—was not expected to "make Jews" but to train them in the skills of reading Scripture and Talmud. Now, with fewer hours, and the need to present a state-mandated (and parent-supported) secular curriculum, the schools are being asked to create Jews.

One of the problems of mainstream, liberal religion is that it tends to demand too little. Liberal religion may well be a contradiction in terms. Liberal religion does not lead to the sense of obligation that is essential if community and holiness are to make sense. The critical question then is, can there be a Judaism that is not fundamentalist yet is compelling? Constructing such a religious stance is the task that Conservative Judaism has set for itself.

Jews need other Jews in order to be Jews. On the simplest level, public prayer needs a minyan. On a deeper level, after the family, the community is the guardian of the tradition, the spring from which the individual draws the strength to continue as a Jew. We must be clear in our terms here. Community does *not* mean hangout, a place where we happen to coexist. Community means shared experience, shared ideals, shared lives, shared values that are embedded in the life of the community but whose authority comes from beyond the community. The synagogue community of the first and perhaps second generations in North America could be viewed as an inertial institution. Its motive force was nostalgia for a lost world. In its place, the Conservative movement must create a willed community with a shared, articulated vision of what might be achieved and the necessary resources for giving reality to the vision.

We can expect some kinds of Jewish communities, holy congregations, to be more successful than others. To cite one study of religious communities, a successful congregation is one "in which the membership is strongly 'engaged'; not warm and fuzzy but warm and focused."[34] A strong religious community is one that makes demands of its members. As a general rule, strict denominations/ religious communities generate greater loyalty and participation. As one scholar has put it, "A certain amount of tension with secular society is essential to success—the trick is finding and maintaining the right amount."[35] This is a particular dilemma for the Conservative movement by virtue of its commitment both to the strictures of tradition and to pluralism, the big tent and religious standards. But what is the boundary between pluralism and chaos, tradition and immobilization?

The rabbis of the Talmud declared, "One cannot make a ruling for the community unless the majority can live with it."[36] If the demand is too rigorous, the community will ignore it and the tradition will lose its authority. If demands are not made, however, the religious community loses its distinctiveness and its members will not maintain their commitment. Given the wide gap between practice and expectation, finding the right tension calibrating demands—such that the people will be able to live with them and at the same time will be stretched to achieve more as Jews than they thought they could—calls for refined judgment.

The contradiction between the values of many Conservative Jews and the demands of the tradition makes the task of the Conservative movement particularly difficult. The Jewish tradition makes claims that can make Jews uncomfortable.

In reciting the Shabbat kiddush, one affirms a belief in the Jewish people as God's chosen instrument in history. To make that claim plausible, the Jew needs a believing community that supports the plausibility of the claim. Without reinforcement from a community, Jewish beliefs (and practices) become eroded. Believers need to be able to withdraw from secular society so that they sustain their belief. The problem of the Conservative movement is how much withdrawal it can mandate. Success for the Conservative movement need not be measured in degrees of observance; rather, it should be measured in the extent to which Conservative Jews take seriously a mandate to wrestle with the tradition of historic Judaism. If they are to engage the tradition, they would need to understand it in its historic context. However it defines success for itself, the Conservative movement must take a course that moves it against the currents. Given the individualism and secularity of contemporary Jews, these will be difficult tasks.

Notes

1. See report of Emil Lehman commenting on the *National Survey on Synagogue Leadership* (1953), in *Biennial Convention Report* (1953): 6–37, cited in Jack Wertheimer, "The Conservative Synagogue," in Jack Wertheimer, ed., *The American Synagogue: A Sanctuary Transformed* (New York: Cambridge University Press, 1987), 111–149.
2. Charles S. Liebman and Saul Shapiro, "A Survey of the Conservative Movement and Some of Its Religious Attitudes" unpublished paper, Bar-Ilan University, 1979.
3. Wade Clark Roof and William McKinney, *American Mainline Religion* (New Brunswick, N.J.: Rutgers University Press, 1988), 84.
4. "Summary Religious Statistics," *The Federation of Churches and Christian Workers in New York City, Fourth Annual Report, 1899–1900*, 48–49. The neighborhoods in which the surveys were conducted were the 14th Assembly District in Manhattan and the 17th Ward in Brooklyn. See Jon Butler, "Protestant Success in the New American City, 1870–1920: The Anxious Secrets of Rev. Walter Laidlaw, Ph.D.," in Harry S. Stout and D. G. Hart, eds., *New Directions in American Religious History* (New York: Oxford University Press, 1997), 296–333. My colleague Mechal Sobel brought Jon Butler's article to my attention.
5. On the attempts within Orthodoxy to reach the youth and the reactions of the Orthodox leadership, see Jeffrey Gurock, "The Orthodox Synagogue," in Wertheimer, *The American Synagogue*, 37–84.
6. Mordechai M. Kaplan, "Affiliation with the Synagogue," *Jewish Communal Register of New York*, 2d ed. (New York: 1919). A wide variety of indicators point to the massive erosion of Shabbat observance on the part of immigrant Jews in New York City before the First World War. In 1912 it was estimated that no more than 25 percent of Jewish workmen observed Shabbat. A survey made on the Lower East Side in 1913 reported that almost 60 percent of the stores were open on Shabbat. See Moses Rischin, *The Promised City* (1962; reprint, New York: Harper Torchbooks, 1970), 146–147.
7. Wertheimer, "The Conservative Synagogue," in Wertheimer, *The American Synagogue*, 120.
8. Nettie P. McGill and Ellen N. Matthews, *The Youth of New York City* (New York: Macmillan, 1940), 241. I have recomputed so as to report by religion without reference to gender.
9. Concurrently, there was a marked decline in the observance of kashrut. Between 1914

and 1924, a period of significant growth in the Jewish population of New York and a period of great prosperity as well, kosher meat consumption fell by 25 to 30 percent. See Harold Gastwirt, *Fraud, Corruption and Holiness* (New York: Kennikat Press, 1974), 7, cited in Jenna Weissman Josselit, "Jewish in Dishes," in Robert M. Seltzer and Norman J. Cohen, eds., *The Americanization of the Jews* (New York: New York University Press, 1995), 247–264.

10. Quoted from a promotional leaflet for a new Conservative congregation. See Wertheimer, "The Conservative Synagogue," 126.

11. Comment of a synagogue organizer reported in Albert Gordon, *Jews in Suburbia* (Boston: Beacon Press, 1959), 197, cited in Wertheimer, "The Conservative Synagogue," 124.

12. Morris Silverman, "Report of Survey on Ritual," *Proceedings of the Rabbinical Assembly of America* (1933): 328–335, cited in Wertheimer, "The Conservative Synagogue," 111–149.

13. Elliot Burstein, *Proceedings of the Rabbinical Assembly of America* (1949), cited in Abraham Karp, "The Conservative Rabbi: Dissatisfied but Not Unhappy," *American Jewish Archives* 35, no. 2 (1983).

14. The New York survey of 1981 reports that 18 percent of the Conservative men and 12 percent of the Conservative women claim to attend services at least once a week. This compares with 80 percent of the Orthodox men and 43 percent of the Orthodox women, while 4 percent of the Reform men and women claim attendance weekly or more frequently. See Paul Ritterband, "Orthodox Jews in Community Context," unpublished paper, City University of New York, 1987.

15. C. Kirk Hadaway, Penny Long Marler, and Mark Chaves, "What the Polls Don't Show: A Closer Look at U.S. Church Attendance," paper delivered at the annual meeting of the American Sociological Association, Louisville, September 1993.

16. The rates of attendance reported by Wertheimer based upon data supplied by rabbis of Conservative congregations are sharply discrepant. Though I believe that the laity exaggerates its attendance, the individual is in a better position to know his/her habits than the involved observer in this instance; thus I side with the congregants' reports of their individual behavior.

17. In Jewish tradition, public prayer is a man's obligation that does not devolve on women. However, in recent years, Conservative and Reform women have come to attend services almost as frequently as men. Thus, we take into account mother's attendance as well as father's attendance.

18. Gary E. Madsen and Glenn M. Vernon, "Maintaining the Faith during College: A Study of Campus Religious Group Participation," *Review of Religious Research* 25, no. 2 (1983).

19. Most of the sample attended college. For the sake of simplicity and comparability, the table reports college years attendance for the entire sample. The same pattern is produced when those who did not attend college are excluded from the sample.

20. Harold Himmelfarb, "The Non-Linear Impact of Schooling: Comparing Different Types and Amounts of Jewish Education," *Sociology of Education* 50, no. 2 (1977); Cohen, "The Interaction Effects of Parents, Spouse and Schooling: Comparing the Impact of Jewish and Catholic Schools," *Sociological Quarterly* 18, no. 4 (1977).

21. It is clear that Jews, particularly non-Orthodox Jews, join congregations most frequently when they become parents. Joining and participating in synagogue life is part of growing up and having a family of one's own. However, there are limits to how fruitful it is to "do Jewish" for the sake of the children. For example, those who say that they attend services to serve as an example for their children in fact are not likely to be regular attenders. This comment is based upon my unpublished analysis of our survey data. Synagogue service attendance is most likely to be part of an individual's life if he/she is convinced of its value for him/herself.

22. See the responses to the question on the importance of religion found by the Gallup Poll in 1983 as reported in Roof and McKinney (1988), 103. The difference between our sample and the Gallup sample is consistent with the notion that Conservative Jews are somewhat more religion-minded than the rank and file of Jews, but as a group they are more secular than the rank and file of the American population.

23. In a national opinion survey of American Jews, of those who identified as Orthodox, 97 percent agreed that being Jewish is very important in their own lives, as compared to 73 percent of those who identified as Conservative and 53 percent of those who identified as Reform. See *1997 Annual Survey of American Jewish Opinion* (New York: American Jewish Committee, 1997), 81.

24. There are many dimensions of Jewishness/Judaism. Referring back to the national opinion survey cited above, we find that when asked for the most important element in the constellation of modes of Jewishness, Conservative Jews were most likely to say that being part of the Jewish people is most important, while Orthodox Jews are most likely to say that religious observance is most important. The stress on peoplehood has characterized the Conservative movement since its beginning. However, the movement has also stressed religious observance. Clearly one message resonated with the rank and file far more than the other did. Ibid., 82.

25. On negotiating with tradition as an approach to Judaism, see Charles S. Liebman, "Jewish Survival, Antisemitism, and Negotiation with the Tradition," in Robert M. Seltzer and Norman J. Cohen, eds., *The Americanization of the Jews* (New York: New York University Press, 1995), 436–450. On Conservatism's ideological inhibitions, see Herbert Rosenblum, "Ideology and Compromise: The Evolution of the United Synagogue Preamble," *Jewish Social Studies* 35 (1973): 18–31. Rosenblum shows how the drafts of the formative document of the Conservative movement became less and less ideological, as the founders worked at being inclusive and broad. Ideological clarity would have left some faction out of the big tent.

26. Obviously Orthodox Jews do in fact make choices, leading to, among other things, a spectrum of Orthodoxy, from the left of the modernists to the right of the ultra-Orthodox, with many refinements within those categories. Part of what makes them all "Orthodox" is the principle, no matter how much violated in practice, that halakha is binding upon all Jews and covers all of life.

27. On the relationship between service attendance and friends in the congregation, see, for example, Daniel V. Olson, "Church Friendships: Boon or Barrier to Church Growth," *Journal for the Scientific Study of Religion*, 28, no. 4 (1989): 432–447. Friends in the congregation and participation in activities are not temporally prior to integration into the community. I take the relationships in table 4.7b as showing consistency rather than causality.

28. A common theme throughout the literature is the strong relationship between theological conservatism and religious behavior, including attendance at services. See, for example, Alan W. Black, "The Impact of Theological Orientation and of Breadth of Perspective on Church Members' Attitudes and Behaviors," *Journal for the Scientific Study of Religion* 24, no. 1 (1985): 87–100. Black asserts that "theological conservatism is the best predictor of church attendance."

29. A study of Catholics reports that "loyalty to the community and communal values is the factor that separates the active from the lapsed Catholics in the 1980s." See Michael Hout and Andrew M. Greeley, "The Center Doesn't Hold: Church Attendance in the United States, 1940–1984," *American Sociological Review* 52 (1987).

30. The very weak relationship between religious belief and religious attendance has been noted by others as well. See Michael Winter and Christopher Short, "Believing and Belonging: Religion in Rural England," *British Journal of Sociology* 44, no. 4 (1993): 635–651.

31. Stanley Rabinowitz, "Where Do We Stand Now?" *Judaism* 26, no. 3 (1977).

32. Elliot N. Dorf, "The Ideology of Conservative Judaism: Sklare after Thirty Years," *American Jewish History* 74, no. 2 (1984).
33. See Karp, "The Conservative Rabbi."
34. David A. Roozen and C. Kirk Hadaway, *Church and Denominational Growth* (Nashville: Abingdon, 1993), 232.
35. Laurence R. Iannaccone, "Why Strict Churches Are Strong," *American Journal of Sociology* 99, no. 5 (1994): 1203.
36. Baba Kama 79b.

Coming of Age in the Conservative Synagogue

Chapter 5

BARRY A. KOSMIN

The Bar/Bat Mitzvah Class of 5755

CONSERVATIVE JUDAISM evolved in America during the early part of this century in the face of strong evidence that traditional normative Judaism was failing to adapt to the New World. Orthodoxy and an Orthodox Jewish lifestyle were rejected, particularly by the masses of the U.S.-born second generation. Yet two generations later, when the Council of Jewish Federations 1990 National Jewish Population Survey (NJPS) findings came out, the report card on the liberal Judaism of post–World War II America was also negative. The liberal alternatives to Orthodoxy, it seemed, were unable to stem the erosion of the religious and ethnic loyalties of younger American Jews.

The failure of Jewish continuity, or the process of the intergenerational transmission of Jewish culture rather than hostile external forces, is now recognized as the real threat to Judaism in contemporary North America. We are thus at a stage where the insights from social science, particularly in the area of the socialization of the younger generation, should be a central focus of concern for Jewish religious organizations.[1] This essay considers what socialization theory can contribute to our understanding of the processes involved in the religious education of young people, as well as what other cultural and historical driving forces are having an impact on the younger generation of Conservative Jews. Bar/bat mitzvah provides a particularly useful insight into these processes because it deals with an event that is widely believed to be central to the exit process from organized Jewish life. In this version, bar or bat mitzvah is the proverbial Pied Piper of Jewish life: a seductive but essentially destructive occasion that leads children away from the synagogue. Even were this the reality in the past, however, it need not be predictive of future trends. Bar/bat mitzvah is also an important issue because it allows us to assess the effects of egalitarianism on the first generation of young people to be largely socialized within a new, gender-free synagogue environment.

There has been surprisingly little research on the meaning and consequences of life-cycle events for contemporary Jews or their synagogues. This lacuna is particularly striking among Jews affiliated with the United Synagogue of Conservative Judaism. The decline in participation rates for certain life-cycle events such as synagogue weddings and death-related rituals over recent decades is generally noted and accepted. Kashrut and Shabbat observance have also declined. By contrast, the coming-of-age ceremony of bar and bat mitzvah has withstood this general erosion of tradition. Moreover, the extension of the rite to Jewish girls, who constituted 45.3 percent of the class of 5755 (1994–95), has occurred without any diminution in male participation rates or any lowering of the legitimacy and the enthusiasm for this *simcha* (joyous event). The essential popularity of this rite of passage and its essential contemporaneity and "Americaness" was first revealed to the author when studying the acculturation of the new Americans from the Soviet refugee population. Ten years after their arrival in the United States, this largely unaffiliated and secularized population reported that over 75 percent of their twelve-year-old children were being prepared for bar/bat mitzvah.[2] The content and meaning of these particular ceremonies notwithstanding, the fact is that these newcomers learned very quickly that bar mitzvah is a normative event for contemporary North American Jews.

Anecdotal evidence suggests that the bar/bat mitzvah has become a quintessential and acceptable American ritual, one worthy of the attention of Hallmark greeting cards. This uniquely Jewish rite has reached the public square, such that many American gentiles are now aware of, even familiar with, this rite of passage, not least by being invited to both the religious service and the social celebrations that mark it.[3] Obviously this is an acceptable part of Jewish identity and continuity, as well as a matter of pride for most of today's North American Jews. It is also a core part of the life, purpose, and worship service of the Conservative synagogue. Calculations, based upon the CJF 1990 National Jewish Population Survey and confirmed by this research, suggest that currently the Conservative movement has 17,000 to 18,000 b'nai mitzvah students annually. Of the 112 Conservative synagogues from which the b'nai mitzvah sample was drawn, only 21 percent had fewer than ten bar/bat mitzvah ceremonies in the Jewish year 5755. (See appendix for details of sample and methodology.) Thirty percent had eleven to twenty-five ceremonies; 37 percent had twenty-five to fifty; and 13 percent had an average of one every week throughout the year. Six synagogues reported having more than eighty ceremonies that year. The harsh reality of synagogue life for rabbis and regular Shabbat worshipers is that it is the bar/bat mitzvah that accounts for most of the attendance at otherwise sparsely attended Shabbat services. Yet in the parallel universe of synagogue life that has emerged in every congregation, this is not a problem for the average bar/bat mitzvah family, for whom regular Shabbat attendance is often only a one-year reality. They perceive neither their presence nor their limited agenda as a challenge to the synagogue's religious integrity.

In theory, becoming a bar mitzvah (a "son of the commandment"), with the right to be part of a minyan, does not require a special ceremony. It merely marks the traditional Jewish age of obligation—thirteen (for boys). It was only in the fourteenth century that the custom arose of calling boys to the torah for an aliya on Shabbat following their thirteenth birthday according to the Jewish calendar. This late development in the history of Judaism involved the innovation of a final *maftir* aliya, the addition of an aliya to the prescribed seven Torah segments in the morning service. The youngster being honored usually recited the torah blessings and then chanted the *haftarah*, the weekly portion selected from the Prophets (*Nevi'im*). Following this the parents hosted a celebration. In theory the ceremony can take place any time the Torah is read, not only on Shabbatot but also on a Monday, Thursday, *Rosh Chodesh* (new moon), or a festival. And for families that are Shabbat observers, a weekday might even be preferable, since relatives and friends can travel on those days. In fact, however, only 4 percent of the ceremonies in Conservative synagogues in 5755 (1994–95) occurred on a weekday. Moreover, the survey of rabbis and congregational practice showed that weekdays were reserved for nonmembers, new Americans, and "problem" and "hardship" cases—in the small number of congregations (6 percent) that allow ceremonies for those young Jews who do not meet the synagogue's regular educational or financial requirements.

As stated, the bar/bat mitzvah became more popular with Americanization. In Philadelphia in the early 1980s, it was found that the variable "generation in the U.S. is strongly related to being bar/bat mitzvah. . . . There is an increasing tendency for the younger cohorts to have been bar or bat mitzvah."[4] The bar/bat mitzvah now serves as "the most important token of children's entry into the Jewish community."[5] If one is looking for ways to engage Jewish families in the synagogue, this is one that obviously works. Moreover, it is an unambiguously Jewish event on Jewish religious turf. Regardless of a parent's religious inclinations, the bar/bat mitzvah has religious ramifications: it is ritual requiring extended instruction, usually from the religious institution that will be the setting for the event and where the parents must be or become members. The bar/bat mitzvah ceremony is essentially congregation-based, and as such its well-being speaks to the viability, potential, and future of the synagogue as well. Even more, it is the cultural event that teaches and demonstrates what it means to be a Conservative Jew, as will be demonstrated below.

This research hypothesizes that the bar/bat mitzvah is one of the most significant ways parents can publicly affirm their identity as Jews at this life stage. A bar/bat mitzvah is

> a powerful moment in the life of the family, assuming for many almost gigantic proportions. Families use that occasion as a focus for many issues: loved ones on the verge of breaking up decide to wait until after that day; long-neglected and distant relatives are once again invited back into the family arena. [An enormous] investment of emotions, thought, and money . . . are made for this day.[6]

The significance of this event in the life of a young person is notable, too. The pressure placed upon the child is obvious: at a vulnerable age he or she must train to show competence in a variety of social skills, ritual, ceremony, and memory. The teenager undergoes a public initiation in a synagogue by singing in a foreign language before an audience containing many strangers. Moreover, the event cannot be postponed, since one prepares for a specific Shabbat in the annual or triennial torah cycle: there is only one chance to perform that particular week's portion. The experience can be nerve-racking. It is also time consuming, with 94 percent of the students reporting over nine months of preparation. Interruptions in their normal routine were reported by 81 percent, and 48 percent had to give up sports and social activities to accommodate their training. But the rewards are also great. The student is surrounded by the good will of supportive family and friends. Where else in our society can a seventh grader gain the attention, admiration, respect, and applause of several hundred peers and adults? Perhaps only the experience of the high school athlete can compare with it. Pushed to perform beyond anything he or she has done previously, the child, like the athlete, emerges from the ordeal with a sense of great pride. When asked, "Was your bar/bat mitzvah worth the time it took, or was it not worth the time it took," fully 99 percent said it was worth it.

These young people did in fact accomplish a great deal. Presumably in response to local congregational norms or standards, the majority participated in the service far beyond the minimal requirements, with 47 percent reading an additional torah portion beyond the *maftir* and 23 percent reading the whole *sedra* (weekly portion). To do this, 69 percent learned both musical cantillations. In addition 37 percent led the *musaf* (additional service), 12 percent led the *shacharit* (morning service), and a further 13 percent led the torah service. A speech or *d'var torah* was given from the *bimah* by 85 percent of the young people.

The survey revealed that for the parents, too, the event involves extensive psychic, temporal, and economic investment. Fifty-one percent of parents reported that the bar/bat mitzvah dominated life of the family during the year of preparation. Among these parents, apparently the child's preparations (54 percent) were more time-consuming than organizing the party (31 percent). In addition, 42 percent participated more in the activities of the synagogue during the bar mitzvah year. Despite these pressures and the fact that 29 percent of families felt the celebration imposed a financial burden on them, 97 percent of the parents felt the bar/bat mitzvah "was worth the time and trouble involved." Thus we can visualize this rite as a one-day event that takes place over the course of an entire year and for which the whole family prepares. It becomes the "bar mitzvah family" and enters a kind of "sacred space." The preparations are part of the ritual itself. If ritual is therapeutic, then bar/bat mitzvah is both necessary and successful in helping Jewish families cope with the normal crisis of adolescent transition. It is a ritual that bonds the child to the family and its heritage while paradoxically enabling and celebrating separation.[7]

According to Davis, the essence of the appeal of the bar mitzvah to the adult population is that it links the generations and provides communal testimony that the chain of transmission remains unbroken. A first child's bar/bat mitzvah is a developmental milestone for the parents, who in a way also come of age during this event. For many couples it is the first major family and social event since their own wedding. The logistics to be managed are complicated and more expensive and more emotionally laden than any in the nuclear family's previous experience. And the parents, too, must present themselves publicly in relation to their religious tradition to the most significant people in their lives—their family, colleagues, and social network.

Religious Socialization

This study was designed to analyze the triadic relationship of three sets of actors in the contemporary Jewish drama around this life-cycle event—the young persons or celebrants, the parents and home environment, and the community or congregation. This work is thus a study of socialization: the process whereby an individual acquires the skills, motives, standards, and behavior style that will enable him/her to conform to the expectations of his/her present and future social environment.[8] The continuity, even the mere existence, of any religious or cultural group is dependent upon socializing its members and its children, for if individuals are not socialized according to community norms and values, the community will eventually disintegrate. Socialization takes place in numerous settings at home, in the playground, in youth groups, in camps, at school, in the synagogue. Adults, by their behavior, define for the children the social reality to which they in turn respond.

The process of socialization itself entails specialized learning components, such as psychoemotional identification with significant others (for example, parents and siblings), acquisition of norms, roles, and values, and the adaptation of the self to social boundary definition.[9] The members of each society become socialized beings by acquiring the specifics of its culture—its body of knowledge, beliefs, art, morals, law, custom, and habits. Transmission of cultural practices occurs in different ways at different stages of the socialization process. Children come to understand their cultural group first in terms of external manifestations such as costumes, holiday celebrations, and rituals; as they grow older they internalize the substantive aspect of their culture, such as its belief system and the norms and values that are related to it.

Another important stage in socialization to a subculture is the one in which the child learns cultural identification by distinguishing between his or her cultural group and others, and learning to identify the borders between "us" and "them." In this stage the child feels that he or she belongs to a particular collectivity and internalizes the collective identity. This process can be reinforced by participation in activities that are unique to the culture, such as holiday celebrations, learning a special language, participating in ceremonies, and learning values, legends, stories, and so on. The child develops what Gordon Allport named "ego extension," the identification of the collective as "mine." An example of this would be the interest of American Jews in Israel.[10]

Religious socialization is the teaching of religious roles and their supporting values, such that individuals make them a part of their own personality patterns. As young people deepen their involvement in religious institutions, they learn those specific skills of particular value to their religious group, such as language, prayers, and music. Religious value systems attempt to channel personal responses to religious ends. Generally religious socialization, but particularly normative Conservative Judaism with its strong behavioral emphasis, attempts to develop a basic sense of discipline by which one learns to postpone, modify, or even forgo gratification in order to reach some religiously sanctioned future goal. Strong institutional socialization results in a tendency toward membership conformity; and weak institutional socialization leads to assimilation.

Social science literature asserts that of the many forces involved in the formation of children's identity, parents are the primary agents for transferring cultural and religious elements across generations by transmitting values, norms, and knowledge. Though not the sole socialization agent, the family is the one that places the child in a certain social position, in terms of class, status, culture, and even geographic area. All these elements prescribe specific values and even assign the type of interactions the child will have with others. Awareness of this process influences which particular techniques parents and other child-rearing agents use in raising their children. "Unless children learn and experience their basic ethnic identity within the family or other primary groups, it is unlikely that they will ever strongly feel it thereafter."[11]

Erickson developed a model that is particularly relevant to the study of

Conservative Judaism.[12] He argued that adolescent religious development is triggered by home religious habits and education. Following Cornwall's concept of "channeling,"[13] which is the indirect social influence parents have over their children, Erickson holds that "parents direct their children to other social influences, and it is these influences which are more salient. Of particular interest is the strength of the religious education variable."[14] This approach recognizes that the growing trend in contemporary society is for formal institutions to take over the responsibility for socialization of children and adolescents from the family.

Though Jewish tradition regards the b'nai mitzvah as moving from childhood to adulthood in terms of religious obligations, today's social and psychological reality is that it marks a transition from childhood to adolescence, the entry into puberty and acceptance as a "teenager." This is an interesting time to study these young people, since a crucial aspect of the transition is the transformation of the relationship between parent and child, as they renegotiate the terms of control, responsibility, and autonomy. In this search for self-definition, the adolescent interacts with his or her environment and seeks out new connections, and it is the peer group, as opposed to the family, that comes to dominate the adolescent's thinking and behavior and to serve as a catalyst for identity development. Martin and Stendler noted the particular influence of the peer group as another agent of socialization that grows ever stronger in our fashion-conscious consumer society as the child advances in age:

> In the American society the child's own contemporaries have great
> importance. The child learns to give great weight to what other children
> think of his behavior, to want to gain their approval and avoid their
> disapproval. In societies in which the peer group is an important
> socializing agent, there may be greater conformity to age group
> standards. . . . Undoubtedly the use of peer group as a socializing agent
> by Americans produces a different sense of self, a person who always
> pays attention to what others are doing in order to get a signal for what
> he himself should do.[15]

This need not necessarily be a negative development. Peers have also been used as agents of reinforcement for approved social behavior.[16]

Stated positively, one can say that the adolescent's attitude toward his or her ethnic or religious background in relation to the peer group is fashioned by a number of factors, including "his sense of personal security, the warmth and constructiveness of the family constellation in infancy and childhood, the attitudes prevailing in the immediate neighborhood and how they are fostered in the schools and religious institutions . . . and the strength and nature of the individual's feelings of belonging to his minority group."[17]

The formation of a specifically Jewish identity has its roots in the home and the tradition of the individual. It depends on whether the parents provide the child with a clear and positive feeling of belonging to Judaism, and whether that feeling extends to peer group interactions and is reinforced by a support system like a synagogue community with institutions such as a Jewish youth group. This is because youth perceive other people around them as models for behavior, and role models play an important part in development of the self and the child's behavior.

The research design of this study was posited on the hypothesis that the primary agent in the child's socialization process is the home environment and the immediate family. Another, increasingly important agent as the young person grows up is the synagogue community at a number of levels: as an institution of religious education, as a supplier of a peer group network, and as a purveyor of adult role models (e.g., teacher, rabbi, cantor). For the religious identity of a Jewish child is ultimately derived from the collective in which s/he is a member. From the child's point of view, being a Jew is his or her religious and cultural identity, but the social and geographical location where this is played out (outside the home) for this age group is almost entirely the local synagogue.

Thus in the contemporary United States the synagogue provides the emotional content, the religious and experiential dimensions of Jewish education that in Europe was provided by the *yiddisher gass* (the Jewish street). It is where children learn to behave as Jews to pray, to observe Shabbat by emulating the adult models around them. Here they absorb their values and learn how to practice Judaism by example. Moreover, for the non-day school students, it is the synagogue, through its school, that also provides the cognitive experience. Jewish knowledge is largely transmitted through the self-contained classroom using a methodology largely influenced by American education.

Elite Concern over B'nai Mitzvah

One possible outcome of socialization is that it will be negative and fail, or that individuals will be socialized into dysfunctional behaviors or deviant subcultures. Degeneration into a "folk religion" has long been the fear of Jewish elites, particularly as it concerns bar mitzvah.[18] Novelists as well as educators and rabbis have mocked the conspicuous consumption and vulgar parties of the "bourgeois bar mitzvah." In fact, already in the *shtetl* (small town) of nineteenth-century Eastern Europe there was criticism of the "elaborate gifts and parties associated with a less 'religious' observance."[19] In North America the commercial bar mitzvah ceremony evolved its own ritual. The catered meal and the band "affair" with the proverbial gift of a fountain pen were commonplace by the 1930s and the "theme" bar mitzvah had emerged by the 1950s. It may be that the well-educated, affluent baby boomer generation of Jews is no longer nouveau riche requiring displays of parental wealth, or that there are now mechanisms besides the bar mitzvah that are better candidates for ostentation, but this theme did not emerge much in this research. Indeed, when asked what the most important part of the event was for themselves, only 2 percent of the teenagers mentioned the gifts and only 8 percent the party, whereas 90 percent cited the ceremony. In fact 58 percent of the youngsters used the occasion to make a personal donation to a charity.

Another area of concern regarding celebrations for the synagogue elite is desecration of Shabbat and failure to observe the laws of kashrut. Only 42 percent of the celebrations took place following the service on the Sabbath, when there was a likelihood of violating Shabbat restrictions. Eighteen percent of parents reported that the rabbi made suggestions regarding the format of the party. In addition the congregational survey reveals that 29 percent of synagogues allow parties with musical instruments on Shabbat but require that only Jewish and Israeli music be played; they also limit the range of instruments.

Kashrut observance at celebrations has to be seen in the context of both home practice and access to local facilities. Only 29 percent of the parental homes fully observe the laws of kashrut although 83 percent retain some elements of traditional Jewish food taboos. Moreover, only 69 percent of the synagogues report that there is kosher catering available locally. Yet only about half the parties were kosher (48 percent), with 35 percent of respondents reporting this was their personal preference, 3 percent reporting that they were influenced by pressure from family and friends, and 10 percent reporting that it was the rule of the synagogue. This finding on kashrut suggests that there is a growing similarity between home and public observance and there are fewer ambivalent "kosher in the home but not outside" families than there were earlier in the century. Yet the overall finding is emblematic of the tensions in Conservative synagogues, whereby rabbis have to learn to live with the fact that half the functions celebrating a religious event in their synagogue ignore the dietary laws.

The question of imposing rules and demanding standards from members is fraught with difficulty for a congregation because it is a voluntaristic organization. Moreover, most Conservative congregations exist in a competitive environment: 92 percent report that their congregants have the choice of another synagogue in the area, and for 63 percent there is direct competition from another Conservative congregation in the vicinity.

The same concern arises in the areas of Jewish education and religious services, where elites have more unambiguous authority and direct control. For the rabbi and the *shomrei mitzvot* (observant) elite, the bar mitzvah is not the primary element of Jewish identity, since they are committed to a Jewish way of life rather than episodic and life-cycle events. Elites are disappointed by and critical of obvious messages that a family is concerned solely about coaching for the performance; for elites, this signals inevitable discontinuity, as the child ends his or her religious education. "While the bar mitzvah is intended to mark the beginning of a Jewish boy's adulthood, for non-Orthodox Jews it frequently signifies the end of his Jewish education."[20] However, this is not a new trend among the less religious and academic elements of the Jewish community. In the *shtetl* it was reported that "many leave the *kheyder* on their thirteenth birthday, and some are apprenticed to a trade."[21] In part the cynicism associated with this event among committed Jewish leaders and educators arises because this occasion evidences both success and crisis for the synagogue and Jewish education. The bar/bat mitzvah is blamed for the fact that America's Jews have on average a seventh-grade religious education, even though they have attained the highest level of general education among the nation's religious and ethnic groups. Thus the supposedly limited vocabularies and widespread Judaic illiteracy of Conservative Jews is directly blamed on the "folk version" of the bar and bat mitzvah. We will now examine whether this indictment is indeed correct.

Jewish Education

A brief introduction describing the historical relationship between the synagogue and Jewish schooling is in order. During the synagogue's formative stages, synagogue liturgy developed around the instruction of the Pentateuch and the Prophets. Indeed, "the scriptural readings supplied the content and form of the instruction." An example of this is the early synagogue practice in Eretz Yisrael (around 100 C.E.) of weekly readings in which the Torah was first completed in seven years, then in three years, and later still, in Babylon (400 C.E.), in an annual cycle. As early as the second century of the Common Era, Jewish schooling for the young became identified with the synagogue. In addition to physically housing the Jewish school, the synagogue of the Babylonian, pre-Geonic, and Geonic periods was directly involved in the organization and curriculum of the Jewish school. It also had a significant indirect impact upon the education of the children through their participation in worship-related activities. And in the Middle Ages the chief aim of Jewish elementary schooling was to prepare young boys for participation in synagogue service.

For the Sephardi and German immigration to the United States in the nineteenth century, Jewish schooling was congregationally based. However, for the East Europeans in the U.S. environment, this link with the synagogue was at first broken, as American Jewish education in the immigrant period took place outside the synagogue in the independent Talmud Torah. This changed in the 1940s and 1950s, with the growth of large one-day-a-week and three-day-a-week congregational schools. Concomitant with this development was the almost total eclipse of the communal Talmud Torah, which, with rare exception, ceased to exist by the mid-1960s. It was demographic changes that hastened this disintegration of the Talmud Torah, as the suburban congregational school grew by leaps and bounds.

In addition to its sponsorship, the main difference between the communal Talmud Torah and its synagogue counterpart was the schedule of instruction. Whereas the students in the Talmud Torah studied five days a week, two hours each day, for forty-six to forty-eight weeks per year, the synagogues conducted either three-day-a-week schools, one and a half to two hours each day, for thirty-six weeks, or one-day-a-week schools, two hours each session for thirty-two weeks. Concern that too many children were in the last category led the Conservative movement to impose standards in 1946. These stipulated three years of enrollment with classes three times a week for six hours of instruction. This decision largely eliminated the Sunday-only schools by 1960.[22]

Despite this coerced enrollment, by the 1970s rising rates of acculturation and assimilation were evident. So many academicians and practitioners bemoaned the failure of the synagogue school: the continuing shift away from Hebrew language instruction and its correlative subject matter, the lowering of curricular standards, the emphasis on bar/bat mitzvah preparation instead of "serious study," the inability of the school to overcome the negative impact of the home, the lack of new initiatives to meet new needs, the increasing part-timeness and ineptness of supervisory and instructional personnel. The supposed erosion of the Jewish schooling provided by the synagogue religious school led to a reaction and a solution. This was the development of the Jewish day school with intense Judaic programs successfully modeled on the Orthodox yeshivas. The rise of the Conservative day school, usually a Solomon Schechter school, has led once again to a distancing of the synagogue from the Jewish education of a growing number of children, ironically in this case, of those raised in the most committed households.

Day school parents are now often contrasted with the religious school parents. The former make a considerable financial sacrifice and are supposedly very "serious" Jews. In contrast, according to Alvin Schiff: "Parental involvement in the [supplementary] school is virtually nonexistent. Most feel that they have neither the time nor the desire to become involved in the school. For those parents who do express an ongoing commitment to the school, most of their involvement is related to bar/bat mitzvah preparations."[23]

Undoubtedly the overwhelming majority of parents enroll their children in a Jewish supplementary school for that preparation, and they feel that the supplementary school is the right place for their children until bar/bat mitzvah. Thus, in the Conservative movement one now finds two classes of families and children—an elite associated with the day school and a mass associated with the supplementary school. The problem with this model is that beyond the question of quality, it ignores the question of access: location and financial wherewithal probably limit entry to the "elite" of many committed families. Moreover, the day school is a new development and in many areas is unavailable past grade six, since high schools are rare. This survey provides the opportunity to test out Erickson's model and some assumptions about the relationship of a day school elite to the supplementary school majority on a number of behavioral and attitudinal indicators.

Setting Synagogue Standards

How successful is the desire to assure educational standards in Conservative synagogues today? The stipulation that the bar mitzvah not be a short-term commitment seems to be successful, with 82 percent of synagogues requiring at least five years of Hebrew or religious school. Eighty-two percent of the congregations also have six or more hours of classes per week. Half the supplementary schools operate three days a week, 26 percent meet two days, 17 percent have a variable schedule, and only 3 percent have once-a-week classes. Most schools insist that training for the actual bar/bat mitzvah ceremony be done outside the regular school curriculum in the form of additional study with the cantor, the rabbi, or a tutor. There is also a religious requirement in terms of Shabbat services. Two years of attendance, usually at a junior congregation service and for a minimum twenty-four services a year, is the median requirement for the surveyed congregations. Many synagogues have additional requirements and programs, and a trend toward raising the hurdle for students and families is evident. Fourteen synagogues now demand student involvement in mitzvah or *tzedakah* programs. Others demand project work and attendance at Shabbat retreats and experiences. There is also a new trend toward family education. Five synagogues have introduced a lengthy series of parent-child-rabbi sessions, and ten have adopted the United Synagogues new "*Bonayikh* family education program." These types of programs involve all students, day school as well as supplementary school. As a result of these initiatives, 42 percent of the rabbis report increased teaching and work with children in recent years. The demands on students are in reality also demands on parents for time and involvement, and 42 percent of the parents reported that they "participated more than usual in the activities of the synagogue" during the bar mitzvah year. Most did not seem to resent this enforced involvement, however, and 83 percent of the more involved said they would "continue to be actively involved."

Further good news for Conservative Jewish educators is that the parents of the class of 5755 overwhelmingly (93 percent) reported satisfaction with "the instruction the child received for the bar/bat mitzvah." Moreover, when asked to compare their own knowledge of Judaism at age thirteen with that of their child, 65 percent of parents thought the younger generation knew more. This positive parental attitude was further evident in the fact that 78 percent of the parents wanted their children to continue their Jewish education. This finding is of considerable symbolic value, suggesting that parents value and take pride in their children's Judaic competency. The policy question is whether the Conservative movement can turn this readiness for further education into a reality, since in fact far fewer than 78 percent of teenagers continue their Jewish studies.

All the evidence so far suggests a supportive home environment for Jewish education among this population, and we can predict effective socialization. The positive news on standards has its negative effects on American Jewry, however. The current cohort of students in Conservative congregations is drawn from an increasingly narrow range of Jewish children. The profile of the students shows that they are skewed toward normative traditional Jewish families (83 percent) and that these congregations are attracting neither the intermarried (only 1 percent of couples) nor single-parent families (7 percent), both of which are growing proportions of Jewish families. NJPS showed that half the core Jewish children in this age group live in interfaith families and 13 percent in single-parent families. Even blended families (10 percent) and Jews by choice (8 percent) are relatively rare. Obviously the problematic and non-normative families drop out of the system over the years, and the emphasis on Hebrew language requirements and standards impedes the ability of newcomers to enter the educational system. The positive side is that over two-thirds of the students have been in the Jewish educational system from age six. However, given the educational requirements referred to earlier, we should not be surprised to discover that only 5 percent of the class of 5755 managed to enter this Jewish education system after age ten. The policy issue raised here is the market effects of the need to make early choices in the type of Jewish schooling—whether religious school or, even more clearly, day school. This reality disadvantages and so discourages the involvement of migrants as well as families that are late-blooming religious enthusiasts.

A Comparison of Parent and Child Attitudes

The socialization thesis suggests we should look at the congruence between child and parent attitudes toward their Jewish identities in order to gauge the success of parents in transmitting their beliefs to their offspring. In any assessment, we have to be realistic about the relative power of home background in relation to societal forces. First, not only were the two generational populations born at different historical moments but they also have different backgrounds. All the children were raised in North America, whereas 12 percent of the parents were raised abroad, with Israel and the former USSR the leading sources. This is somewhat higher than the 9 percent of foreign-born adults found by NJPS. All the children were raised as Conservative Jews, while only 60 percent of the parents were. The parents who are new to the Conservative movement are drawn almost equally from the left and the right in terms of their religious backgrounds. Twenty-two percent were raised Orthodox and 10 percent Reform. To these must be added those who have come from outside Judaism: Jews by choice account for 6 percent of the parents, and current non-Jews account for 2 percent.

Among the children, 69 percent reported a desire to continue their Jewish education in Hebrew high school beyond the bar/bat mitzvah, while 78 percent of the parents wanted the child to continue. This is a relatively positive response and shows a high degree of intergenerational consensus. There was also a similar pattern on the negative side, with 25 percent of children wanting to leave the Jewish educational system at this point and 16 percent of the parents wanting to remove their child. An even clearer consensus occurs over an item of informal education, the teenage trip to Israel: 85 percent of the parents are interested in sending the child and 81 percent of the children are keen to go. Again the positive nature of the responses is noteworthy, as is the fact that 54 percent of the parents reported having visited Israel. This is almost twice the proportion among all American Jews in this age group (30–49) found in NJPS. In fact, 25 percent of this sample of teenagers had already visited Israel. Pro-Israel sentiments are obviously a particular feature of this Conservative population, and the intergenerational consensus is striking. When asked if they want their children "to have a strong sense of attachment to Israel," 90 percent of the parents agree (37 percent "strongly"). When asked how important "a sense of attachment to Israel" was for their "own sense of Jewishness," 95 percent of the children said it was important (45 percent "very important").

The positive feelings expressed about Judaism and Jewish peoplehood attachments and the fact that they are continuous across the generations is a very welcome endorsement of the Conservative movement's traditional ideology. The results also suggest that these teenagers are open to more Israel experiences. The children had also internalized parental attitudes toward observance such as fasting on Yom Kippur: 87 percent of parents fast and 90 percent of children intend to undertake this obligation now that they are of age. The almost identical pattern of piety occurs in the distribution of children's intention to attend synagogue services and the current pattern of parental behavior shown in table 5.1.

So where is there dissensus between the generations? It occurs mainly in the area that we categorize as community relations—issues relating to non-Jews. The children are more structurally integrated into North American society. Whereas 78 percent of the parents report most of their friends are Jewish, this applies to only 36 percent of the younger generation. Conversely, only 4 percent

Table 5.1
Frequency of Annual Attendance at Synagogue Services

	Parents		*Children*
Annual *Frequency*	PREVIOUS YEAR %	CURRENT YEAR (BAR/BAT MITZVAH) %	NEXT YEAR (INTENTION) %
Weekly (52x)	18	20	15
Monthly (12x)	50	54	55
Festivals (6x)	17	14	15
High Holidays (3x)	14	11	5
Not sure/Don't know	1	1	10
Total	100%	100%	100%

of the older generation have few or no Jewish friends compared with 19 percent of the children. These patterns obviously affect attitudes toward non-Jews:
88 percent of the parents believe anti-Semitism is a "serious problem" today in
North America, while only 68 percent of the children agree. Conversely, 27 percent of the younger generation deny anti-Semitism is a problem, compared with
only 11 percent of parents. This demonstrates the greater universalism one might
expect among the younger age group. The Americanism of the younger generation, the education they have received, and possibly again their age probably
account for their strong belief in God, with 78 percent reporting that "believing in God" was "very important" and 18 percent that it was "important" to their
personal sense of Jewishness. In contrast the parents gave a more ethnic rather
than religious answer, with 45 percent agreeing that "belief in God is not central to being a good Jew."

    Such differences of opinion possibly suggest that we should posit intermar-
riage and kashrut as ethnic rather than religious behaviors in the eyes of young
Conservative Jews. Only 19 percent of the children thought "living in a kosher
home" was "very important" to their Jewishness, while 30 percent of the parents maintained strict kashrut. Conversely, only 17 percent of the parental homes
abrogated all the laws of kashrut, whereas 33 percent of the children thought it
was "not at all important."

    The issue of intermarriage is an area where concern for Jewish continuity
conflicts with aspirations to universalism. There seems at first glance to be a
considerable generation gap on this issue between parochial parents and universalistic teenagers. Among parents, 86 percent agree with the statement that
"a Jew should marry someone who is also Jewish" (46 percent "strongly agree").
The teenagers were given a similar statement to consider but in reverse, "Do
you think it is OK for Jews to marry people of other religions?" Sixty-five percent said yes and 32 percent replied no. At one level the liberalism of the teen-

agers can be explained in terms of societal norms. Intermarriage is a common reality today; moreover 8 percent of their parents were not Jewish by birth. This translates into a situation, given that parents come in couples, whereby 16 percent of the families have a parent who was not always Jewish and so therefore also have close gentile kin.

The teenagers may also have picked up some of their parents' ambivalence on this issue. Two follow-up questions on interfaith marriage dealing with specific policies received less resolute opposition to intermarriage. There was a split decision, with 49 percent agreeing and 48 percent disagreeing with the statement, "If my son or daughter wished to marry a non-Jew, I would do everything possible to prevent it." Furthermore, once the deed was done this sample of parents of teenagers generally favored outreach to the intermarried couple by their synagogue, with 66 percent agreeing that "rabbis should be more helpful in welcoming non-Jewish partners into the community" and only 29 percent disagreeing.

These findings on intermarriage demonstrate the triumph of American liberal values and universalism among this population. As a result the younger generation of Conservative Jews, those under forty-five years, appears to embrace the outlook of a faith rather than an ethnic community. This argument still leaves the question of how we can reconcile the findings in attitudes about anti-Semitism with those toward intermarriage. The answer again is that these populations perceive very little dissensus or conflict between American and Jewish values. Their liberalism impels them to oppose judgmentalism regarding personal behavior that does not harm others, such as in the choice of life partner. Hence, intermarriage is not a reason to reject an individual. Nonetheless, the contemporary liberal credo accepts that there is indeed prejudice in our society, though of course it should be opposed. Thus, anti-Semitism is acknowledged to be a given in society, but it is not an alienating reality, since most of the non-Jewish friends and family members of both generations of these Jewish respondents are obviously not anti-Semites.

Region and Synagogue Environmental Effects

In keeping with our theme of socialization, we need to examine the extent to which "community" affects the behaviors and opinions of these youngsters and their parents. We looked at two contextual variables: region and size of synagogue. In terms of region, the four census regions of the United States were utilized. The largest number of responses came from the Northeast, with 482 cases, or 34 percent of the sample. The smallest U.S. region was the South, with 267 cases (19 percent). The Canadian subsample was much smaller, with only 61 households (4 percent).

Regional differences were found to be very infrequent on tests of significance. The reasons for this are not clear, but it may well be that controlling for age (of both children and parents) eliminates regional disparities. The exceptions were the Canadians, despite the small size of the subsample. The uniqueness of the Canadian respondents was in the denominational background of the parent generation, since only a minority were raised in Conservative synagogues: 48 percent were raised Orthodox and only 3 percent were raised Reform. By contrast, in the western United States 16 percent were raised in Reform synagogues.

As the aforementioned might suggest, the Canadians are more traditional in a number of behavioral areas. For b'nai mitzvah parties, kosher catering facilities were used by 65 percent of Canadians compared with only 35 percent of American southerners. The Canadians were also much more likely to have a family Shabbat meal on Friday night (85 percent) than were the U.S. respondents (65 percent). However, in terms of public religious behaviors, such as synagogue attendance and social life (such as friendship patterns with non-Jews), the Canadians were very similar to the majority. Surprisingly, given their separate history and different political system, the Canadians showed no differences in attitudes toward anti-Semitism, which as we have noted was regarded as a serious problem by a large majority. In fact, it was Americans resident in the Northeast who had markedly more fears on this issue, which probably also accounts for why they were also significantly more likely to oppose the intermarriage of their children than were Jews in any other region. Thus, from the perspective of socialization of the young we learn that regional cultures are not strong among North American Jews, with the possible exception of more familialism among Canadians and more ethnic consciousness and suspicion of non-Jews among Conservative Jews living in the Northeast. The Canadians and northeasterners were also more stable in their synagogue affiliation because of differences in migration rates;[24] only just over 40 percent of the parents had ever been members of another synagogue since they were married, compared with 57 percent of westerners.

Much effort was made at the outset of this project to control for the size of synagogue. A three-level stratified sampling strategy was devised to represent the continental distribution of the Conservative Jewish population by size of unit. The exigencies of the fieldwork (see methodological appendix) eventually produced a sample of b'nai mitzvah households that was distributed as follows: 32 percent in synagogues of fewer than 400 members, 42 percent in synagogues with 400 to 799 members, and 26 percent in synagogues of 800 or more members. Despite the attention to this issue, the results showed very little variation by size of synagogue, aside from some expected patterns such as size of class or b'nai mitzvah cohort, and the availability of greater variety of educational and social programs for children and parents in the larger institutions, with their greater professional resources. Size was also not statistically significant on "atmospheric" issues, where it might have been thought to result in different degrees of intimacy and impersonality and affect such matters as likelihood of continuing membership after the bar/bat mitzvah year, feeling like a stranger in the synagogue, or exclusion by synagogues of groups such as the poor or singles. Counterintuitively, perhaps, it was parents from small synagogues who were significantly more likely to agree that "the people who run synagogues sometimes make others feel like outsiders."

Egalitarianism Doubling Jewish Participation

The real differences between Conservative synagogues as institutions and agents of socialization is in the area of practice relating to the treatment of women, and this does not run along regional or size lines. A prime issue in the religious socialization of the young is whether there is different treatment of boys and girls and whether there are both male and female adult role models in their community. In practice these issues are interconnected.

It would have been intriguing to investigate the interplay between female clergy and the class of 5755, but there were an insufficient number of synagogues and thus no sample for doing this. Only four of the chosen congregations had female rabbis, three had female assistant rabbis, and five had a female cantor. Whereas women accounted for only 4 percent of the clergy in the synagogues from which the class of 5755 was drawn, they were a majority of the youth directors (53 percent) and educational directors of the supplementary schools (65 percent).

The Conservative movement began to move toward gender equality in Jewish thought and practice after World War II, starting with a decision to allow aliyot for women in 1955. By 1973 women were counted for a minyan, and in 1983 they could be ordained as rabbis. Prior to this period, full Jewish education for women was not considered mandatory and reflected the prevailing opinion that the role of Jewish women was largely limited to the home. However, by the late 1950s, Marshall Sklare's Lakeville study showed what was then thought to be an "unusual situation" in that the "proportion of girls who are exposed to formal Jewish education is comparable with that of boys."[25] This was very much a grassroots parental initiative, though it was reinforced by some elite leadership. The most widely documented symbol was the first bat mitzvah in 1923 of Judith Kaplan Eisenstein (1910–1996), the daughter of Rabbi Mordechai Kaplan, at the Society for the Advancement of Judaism in Manhattan. This was the breakthrough that eventually led to women serving in the rabbinate and as cantors, the direct result of the close association of both Kaplan's father and daughter with the Jewish Theological Seminary of America. The change took time to work its way through the movement. Thus, whereas 87 percent of the fathers of the class of 5755 had had a bar mitzvah, only 31 percent of the mothers, mostly in their forties, had had a bat mitzvah. Nevertheless, by 1995 the trend toward egalitarianism was clear in the synagogues under examination and must affect the attitudes as well as experiences of the rising generation of young Jews.

In 83 percent of the synagogues, women are counted in the minyan, in 79 percent they can lead prayer services, and in 88 percent they can read from the torah. Given these figures, it is not surprising to find that 78 percent of the synagogues reported that they treated bar and bat mitzvah students exactly alike in both training and ritual. The 22 percent of holdout congregations probably accounts for the gender imbalance, whereby 54 percent of the class of 5755 was male and only 46 percent was female.

These figures indicate that though the trend is toward egalitarianism, each synagogue decides on its own pace of change. This is evident from the replies of the students to questions about tefillin and minyan. Although only 28 percent of synagogues admitted any nonegalitarian practices, only 36 percent of the girls reported that they were taught to put on tefillin compared with 76 percent of the boys. Even more compelling evidence of vestiges of the old system is the finding that since their bar/bat mitzvah, 64 percent of those asked to make up a minyan by their synagogue were boys. On the other side of the equation, although 22 percent of congregations reported inegalitarian treatment, the survey results showed only 6 percent of girls affected (see table 5.2).

The survey of synagogue rabbis provides details on the nature of the differences in the treatment of bar and bat mitzvah students. Many synagogues follow a halakhic principle and make what is mandatory for boys voluntary for girls. Tefillin, referred to earlier, is an example of this approach, but others are head coverings and the wearing of tallit. Minor differences occur in the synagogue's gifts of ritual objects—a kiddush cup for boys, a set of candlesticks for the girls.

The nonegalitarian congregations have a variety of practices as regards the bat mitzvah. All of them place the congregation on a continuum between orthopraxis and egalitarianism. However, the overall trend is toward greater liberalism and no cases of retrogression were found. This strongly suggests that the complete egalitarianism for women in Conservative congregations is just a matter of time. The first concession to egalitarianism is usually to allow a Friday night bat mitzvah with the chanting of the haftarah, sometimes with the blessings. The next step is to allow reading from the torah but without recitation of the blessings. Then there is a full service but at the Shabbat afternoon service or, as in one congregation, in a smaller chapel rather than the main sanctuary.

If the inegalitarian congregations are eliminated from the sample, the rest

Table 5.2
Type of B'nai Mitzvah Participation in Leading Prayer Services

Count Row Pct Col Pct Tot Pct		Boys	Girls	Row Total
Musaf, the additional service	1	283 54.4 45.6 24.6	237 45.6 44.9 20.6	520 45.3
Shacharit, the morning service	2	93 56.7 15.0 8.1	71 43.3 13.4 6.2	164 14.3
The Torah service	3	120 63.5 19.3 8.1	69 36.5 13.1 6.0	189 16.4
Ashrei	4	123 51.3 19.8 10.7	117 48.8 22.2 10.2	240 20.9
Girls are not allowed to lead the service	5		36 100.0 6.4 3.2	36 3.1
Column Count Total Pct		614 54.0	530 46.0	1144 100

Number of missing observations: 264
$X^2 p$ = .000 (high statistical significance)

are truly nondiscriminatory, as table 5.3 shows: they have no statistical difference and such close similarity in the distribution of the type of participation in the torah service among boys and girls. However, when all the congregations are included in table 5.2, there is a strong statistical difference between the sexes, because girls are not allowed to participate fully and lead services in the discriminatory congregations. This table also reflects the poor recall of the event (264 missing observations but no gender bias).

For the individual congregation, egalitarianism has a major impact in the level of involvement in religious life, since one obvious outcome is in effect the doubling of the number of Conservative Jews. As we can see among the b'nai mitzvah respondents, this has almost been achieved. But egalitarianism also ventures into unknown territory in terms of outcomes on aggregate behaviors and attitudes. Fortunately, because of the research design of our survey we can measure the intergenerational change in gender patterns. In contrast to some observers' commonly held opinions to the contrary, male-female differences among the generation of parents ages 35–50 years are not stark in the religious sphere.

Table 5.3
Type of Participation in B'nai Mitzvah Torah Service in Egalitarian Synagogues
by Gender

Count Row Pct Col Pct Tot Pct		Boys	Girls	Row Total
The whole sedra entire torah portion	1	193 59.9 26.8 14.8	129 40.1 22.1 9.9	322 24.7
The maftir, other torah portions and *haftarah*	2	356 54.1 49.4 27.3	302 45.9 51.7 23.1	658 50.4
The maftir and *haftarah*	3	119 53.1 16.5 9.1	105 46.9 18.0 8.0	224 17.2
Torah blessing and *haftarah*	4	53 52.5 7.4 4.1	48 47.5 8.2 3.7	101 7.7
Column Count Total Pct		721 55.2	584 44.8	1305 100

$X^2p = .27$ (no statistical significance)

Conservative Jewish women are indeed slightly more likely to attend religious services than are men, and they are more likely to believe that belief in God is central to being Jewish. However, among the parents there were no statistically significant gender differences in the domain of prayer, in terms of belief in its efficacy to overcome personal problems or in the ability to express oneself through prayer. In the communal realm, men and women had almost exactly similar patterns of synagogue office holding (24 percent) and proportions of close friends in their synagogue. There was also no difference in the attitudes toward the intermarriage of their children on the part of fathers and mothers.

The data on parents suggest that egalitarian treatment of the younger generation can be expected to cause little erosion in the religious realm, since there was very little gender difference evident among the parental generation that had been socialized during the 1950s and 1960s. In fact, as might be expected, the trend was to erode the remaining gender differences. The teenagers exhibited no gender differences in their intentions to attend synagogue or in their view of the importance of belief in God. Similarly, among their parents there were no differences based on gender in patterns of personal prayer, friendship patterns, and attitudes toward intermarriage. However, the girls did report more positive attitudes in the civic and educational realms. They expressed a greater willingness to volunteer in the Jewish community and attributed more importance to being Jewish than did the boys. The girls were very slightly more likely to think kashrut in the home was important (p=.06). They were also significantly more likely to have enjoyed their Jewish education and to want to continue in Hebrew high school.

Of course, the more positive female attitudes may well be the result of adolescent development patterns, rather than the effects of more positive Jewish socialization among girls. Certainly we should be cautious about any interpretations that suggest greater Jewish interest and loyalty as a result of the gratitude of newly emancipated females. Nevertheless, we can observe that egalitarianism has been successful among contemporary Conservative Jews. It has almost doubled the numbers of the religiously participating, and more importantly there is no evidence to suggest that it has alienated either generation of males from Judaism or synagogue life. This is as socialization theory would predict, given the overall consensus in the population on this issue. Moreover, the evidence suggests that presently there is little conflict over gender roles between home and synagogue. For most of these teenagers and their parents, both environments are now egalitarian.

The Emergence of a Day School Elite

The emergence of an observant religious elite within contemporary Conservative Judaism and local congregations based upon the influence of the Solomon Schechter day schools is a development that is widely assumed in informal debate on the future of the movement. The Jewish parochial or day school is a relatively recent phenomenon in American Jewry and particularly in Conservative Judaism. It is often asserted that the day school graduate is a much more involved and identifying Jew as a direct result of the type of education s/he receives.[26] However, the reality is that few children choose their own form of education or curriculum. Access to particular types of education varies according to geographical location, financial means, and parental desires. Moreover, the day school student is not purely the product of a formal educational system. As we have noted, children are also socialized through their home environment, their peers, and informal educational and recreational experiences.

This survey provides us with the opportunity to measure the correlation between exposure to certain forms of Jewish education and behavioral and cognitive outcomes for a large sample of young people with controls for age and synagogue affiliation. We also have a relatively homogeneous sample in terms of the number of years of Jewish education (91 percent, with five or more years). For analytical purposes it was decided to create a Jewish educational continuum

based upon the intensity of the form of schooling. The students were distributed across three categories: those who were currently in day school (that is, in
seventh or eighth grade), totaling 9.4 percent of the sample; those who had attended day school in the past, consisting of 33 percent of the student respondents; and those who had never attended a day school and, while educated solely
in the supplementary synagogue religious school, were the majority (57.6 percent). The parents were also distributed into the same three groupings according to the educational experience of their b'nai mitzvah children.

Many people assume that preparation for the bar/bat mitzvah is less of an
imposition on the time and lives of the day school students, since they have
received a more extensive Jewish education. In fact, however, there was no statistical difference between the three groups of students in terms of their need to
give up sports and other leisure-time pursuits in the bar/bat mitzvah year: the
variation in those suffering "deprivation" ranged between 44 and 49 percent,
depending on educational background. The results show, then, that day school
students do not have a free ride as b'nai mitzvah; in fact they spend equal
amounts of time in training and preparation.

We now turn to other domains of the Jewish life of the class of 5755, where
the type of Jewish schooling one has received is of little significance in predicting outcomes. The null hypothesis clearly operates in the voluntary domain,
where willingness to volunteer for the community hardly varies and the range
is only 86–87 percent. This positive trend toward unanimity demonstrates that
all types of Jewish education are equally successful in communicating the importance of this behavior. A similar pattern occurs for the associated behavior,
involvement in "activities in the Jewish community." For the congregations, the
finding that "participating in Jewish religious life at synagogue" yields the same
pattern is probably of some importance on two levels. First, the congregation
should not assume that day school students are more motivated to get involved
than other teenagers. Local leaders should also realize that for this age group,
the community is the congregation. Second, most of these youngster have very
little experience of a wider Jewish world. Just as "all politics is local," so their
Judaism is essentially the local congregation.

The teenagers' attitudes toward the importance of having a good Jewish education also does not vary by education received. Of course, the interpretation
of what constitutes a good education may vary across the groups, but the result
suggests that it is parental rather than student wishes that are reflected in choice
of Jewish schooling. This hypothesis is reinforced by the finding that the level
of interest in Jewish culture, art, music, and literature also has the same undif-
ferentiated pattern.

Much more counterintuitive are the findings linked to theology. The findings in table 5.4 on the students' view of the origin of the torah show that the

Table 5.4
Students' Theological Position by Type of Jewish Schooling

Which of these statements comes closest to describing your feelings about the torah or bible?

	Current Day School n=132 %	Former Day School n=468 %	Supplementary School Only n=817 %	Total n=1417 %
The torah is the actual Word of God	18.2	20.7	19.1	19.5
The torah is the inspired word of God but not everything should be taken literally	62.9	58.3	60.3	59.9
The torah is an ancient book of history and moral precepts recorded by man	18.2	19.9	20.2	19.9
Can't choose/don't know	0.8	1.0	0.4	0.7
	100.0	100.0	100.0	100.0

$X^2P=.51$ (No statistical significance)

distribution of what are in effect Orthodox-Conservative-Reform theological statements are remarkably similar across the three types of school background (care was taken to rotate the order in which the statements were presented during the surveys). This pattern—lack of differentiation by schooling—might be thought an aberration created by the inability of the age group to understand the issue, if it had not also been repeated in a similar question on belief in miracles. Perhaps just as surprisingly, the day school also fails to have an impact on perceptions of anti-Semitism. Given its majoritarian and more embracing Jewish environment, it is remarkable that its students see neither more nor less of a danger in society from anti-Semitism than do those who attend public school and find themselves a small minority. If going to day school does not affect perceptions of the wider society, this suggests that the curriculum and ideology is more religion- and practice-driven and does not result in an enhanced "tribal" identity.

In which areas, then, do young people's Jewish educational experiences seem to make a difference in their outlook and behavior? The domain of rituals seems to be one aspect that is affected, there being a highly significant divergence according to type of education received, in opinions about the overall importance of Jewish customs. This translates into very highly significant differences on the importance of living in a kosher home. This is considered very important by 34 percent of current day school students, by 23 percent of former day school students, and by 15 percent of students who have studied only in the supplementary school. This pattern in turn directly translates into action regarding the laws of kashrut: 57 percent of current and 42 percent of former day school students refrain from eating meat and dairy foods together outside their home, in contrast to only 31 percent of students who never attended a day school.

Intention to attend synagogue in the coming year follows the same pattern along the continuum, as day school education correlates with greater frequency of attendance. This produces a linear-by-linear association of extremely high significance (p=.000). Half of the current day schoolers, 31 percent of the former day schoolers, and 24 percent of the supplementary school students intend to attend synagogue services weekly. The obverse follows the same pattern. Those who intend to be in a synagogue only on the High Holidays (two or three times a year) account for 9 percent of the current day school students, 14 percent of the former day school students, and 20 percent of those who never attended a day school. Another area where there is reinforcement by the day school is in the giving of tzedakah: 90 percent of current day school, 83 percent of former day school, and 77 percent of supplementary school students intend to give from their own pocket money.

The domain of Jewish peoplehood also reflects a similar pattern of progressively more normative Jewish attitudes according to type of education received. The patterns on the importance of Israel and the feeling of closeness to other Jews are significantly different across the groupings. This is probably associated with the attitude toward interfaith marriage, which is opposed by 50 percent of current day school students, 32 percent of former day school students, and 31 percent of supplementary school students. Again the levels of opposition are impressively low. The fact that the figure for former day school students is very similar to the supplementary school students suggests that this issue is in the curriculum of the day school in the later grades and teenage years.

A more staggered pattern by schooling is found when we look at how much these young people enjoyed their Jewish education. It was enjoyed "most of the time" by 68 percent of current day school students and by 47 percent of former day school students, but only by 35 percent of supplementary school students. This could well explain the pattern of receptivity of the former to engaging in Jewish rituals. Further reinforcement of this institutional socialization can be found in the pattern of friendships according to schooling. Ninety-five percent of current day school students stated that "most" of their friends were also Jewish. However, the proportion with mostly Jewish friends in the other two categories was much lower: only 32 percent among former day school students and 29 percent among supplementary school students. To some extent this pattern must reflect the religious composition of the metropolitan areas and neighborhoods in which they reside, since in areas of low Jewish concentration there are few day schools providing education at the seventh- and eighth-grade levels. Nevertheless, the low figure (or falloff) for Jewish friendship networks among the former day school students is noticeable. It also correlates highly with the pattern of attitudes toward intermarriage. Thus, the support current day school students receive from their peer group for behaviors like keeping the laws of kashrut and attending worship services acts to reinforce their attachment to the subculture. By contrast, the much weaker patterns exhibited by former day school students suggest that the lasting impact of intense Jewish education and social-ization in the early years of children's lives may well be questionable without peer-group reinforcement.

These conclusions can be further validated because we can make a direct comparison between the schooling and the home environment of these young people. The parents were grouped into the same three categories according to the schooling they had provided for their children. First, we can investigate whether the parents vary according to the type of education they choose. Then we can ask, do the parents' attitudes and behaviors correlate with the children's within the three educational groupings? Given the overall concordance in intergenerational patterns discussed earlier, we should expect a positive effect to emerge.

On matters relating directly to bar and bat mitzvah, there are few differ-ences by the type of schooling preferred by the parents. Irrespective of the type of schooling involved, they are unanimous as regards their satisfaction with the event and the training and preparation received by their children. Furthermore, in terms of synagogue involvement there is no difference in the proportion of officeholders, which ranges from 24 to 26 percent across the three groupings.

It is in the area of parental aspirations for their children's Jewishness that the groupings diverge. The motivations of the parents are different. Whereas the parents were almost unanimous (95 percent) in wishing their children to be better educated Jewishly than they were, the level of intensity varied along the expected continuum in terms of the investment made in Jewish education. Fifty-seven percent of current day school parents, 47 percent of former day school parents, and 41 percent of supplementary school parents "strongly agreed" that they wanted their children to be better educated that they were. The parents also reported that their hopes, or the return on their investment, were being met in similar fashion. Asked whether their children knew more about Judaism than they themselves did at a similar age, 79 percent of current day school par-ents said they know more and only 8 percent that they know less. This con-trasts with 66 percent who said "more" and 19 percent who said "less" among former day school parents, and 63 percent who said "more" and 21 percent "less" among supplementary school parents.

With regard to parental ambitions for their children "to have a close at-tachment to Israel," the pattern directly correlates with the students' opinions and follows the typology of Jewish schooling. Current day school parents

exhibited the greatest desire: 53 percent strongly agreed with this aspiration, compared with 45 percent of former day school parents and 30 percent of supplementary school parents.

However, as regards aspirations for their children to be "more religiously
observant" than themselves, the usual ordering of the groupings changed. It was
the former day school parents who reported the strongest desire (16 percent),
while the other two groupings had similar lower levels (9 and 8 percent). Interpreting this finding is difficult because it may well be that the other two parent
groupings are relatively satisfied with their children's level of religiosity, but it
is the actual levels they aspire to that are different. Nevertheless, the nature of
the responses of former day school students we have examined and the fact that
the pattern more closely reflects that of supplementary students rather than current day schoolers on some important variables does suggest that there could be
a sense of frustration among some parents in the middle grouping. This frustration could well occur because structured constraints beyond their immediate control prevented them from continuing the day school education of their children.

When we turn to behavior, the expected hierarchy of responses returns. Attendance on an ordinary Shabbat service by a child accompanied by a parent
reveals scores of 90 percent, 83 percent, and 78 percent by type of schooling.
The proportion of parents maintaining strictly kosher homes also ranges in like
manner from 53 percent among current day school parents, to 36 percent among
former day school parents, down to 25 percent among supplementary school parents.

The Jewish peoplehood domain also shows the expected pattern revealed
by the question on Israel. A willingness "to do everything possible to prevent"
the intermarriage of their children is found among 67 percent among day school
parents, 53 percent of former day school parents, and 46 percent of supplementary school parents.

These findings demonstrate that among this sample of Conservative Jews,
the children largely imitate their parents' religious concerns and practices. Moreover, the range of divergence across the three categories of schooling is very similar for both teenagers and parents. On opposition to intermarriage, the range
across the groupings is 18 percentage points for children and 21 points for the
parents. A similar situation exists for behavior. Kashrut in the parental home
has a range of 28 points across the three groupings and children's practice outside the home has a range of 26 points.

Such results, in turn, raise a crucial question, particularly when one real-
izes that some of these students may well be attending more traditional Orthodox day schools rather than Conservative day schools. What exactly is the added
value or real return on the considerable financial investment of parental and
communal funds in day schools?

Despite the benefits of cognitive reinforcement in a controlled educational setting and of peer group support, the students' pattern of religiosity largely reflects their home environment and imitates parental norms. This conclusion is even further buttressed by the finding that in certain domains, particularly in the realm of belief, type of schooling is irrelevant. An alternative argument is that the school influences the parents through the children and that this explains why the ritual index is higher in day school homes and yet beliefs and faith, which are harder to sway, are not differentiated. This position is somewhat undermined by the findings related to the former day school students and their parents, which show stronger parental than student effects. This whole issue of generational conformity is further complicated by the nature of the relationship between Conservative Judaism and patterns of the American environment, which places paramountcy on belief and faith.

Nevertheless, it is correct that an elite of day school families is emerging within Conservative synagogues, but it appears to be more of a self-selecting process rather than the direct result of the day school curriculum or involvement with this educational institution per se. Of course it could be argued that these are early days in the development of this cohort of adolescents and that time is needed for the true cumulative impact to emerge. After the "high" of the bar/bat mitzvah year the non-day school students and their parents may well gradually fade from the synagogue and religious scene because they lack the daily reinforcement that full-time Jewish education provides. Thus, the differences by type of schooling received may grow sharper over the teenage years. But to test this hypothesis, we will need to revisit the class of 5755 and reinterview them in about three years, since only a longitudinal study can test cause and effect in social science.

The Impact of Informal Education

The mixed results on the relative effects of day school education suggest that we should look to other forms of socialization to see if they correlate in any way with levels of Jewish identity and practice. The survey revealed that parents are almost unanimous in wishing their children to have Jewish friends (96 percent), and to this end they strongly encourage them to join a Jewish youth group (83 percent). Parental support and involvement is obviously important, since this age group is dependent on their parents for transportation to meetings. However, only 57 percent of the youngsters actually attend a Jewish youth group. But those who go do not appear to be coerced, as 92 percent of them report that they enjoy going.

The Conservative movement has two vital arms in the area of informal Jewish education. These are the United Synagogue Youth (USY) organization and Camp Ramah, the network of summer residential camps under the sponsorship of the Jewish Theological Seminary. Among this sample of young people, 33 percent (472 cases) belonged to Kadimah, the USY section for sixth through eighth graders. Thus, Kadimah accounts for around 60 percent of all the memberships in Jewish youth groups.

The first question to ask of a recreational Jewish youth movement is whether it has an impact on friendship networks. Surprisingly, the answer for Kadimah members is negative. They are no more likely to have Jewish friends than the rest of our sample. However, the cause may be structural, because Kadimah membership is stronger in areas of low Jewish density, where alternative Jewish youth organizations are lacking. This possibility is further suggested by the fact that whereas Kadimah is underrepresented among current day and supplementary schoolers, it recruits strongly among former day school students.

Tests of significance reveal that Kadimah members are more likely than average to be drawn from the children of synagogue officeholders (29 percent). Presumably as a result of this parental influence, Kadimah members score very significantly higher on the importance of involvement in synagogue life (69 percent, very important) and their intention to attend services (40 percent weekly). They are also more likely to keep kosher out of the home (43 percent) and to place considerably more importance on Jewish culture.

Though no more likely to have visited Israel than other youngsters, they are significantly more likely to value it and to want to speak conversational Hebrew (84 percent). On the local scene Kadimah members are significantly more philanthropic in their sentiments. And when we compare the members of Kadimah with the nonmembers, there were statistically significant differences in the areas of belief in God and miracles, with Kadimah members being more religious. However, there were no differences between the groups as regards opinions on the origin of the torah. Yet they were more likely to oppose intermarriage than the rest of the sample (37 percent versus 30 percent).

Certainly Kadimah members are better and more committed young Conservative Jews than others, but whether this is a cause or an effect cannot be definitively stated. Obviously there is a screening process at work as well as a selection bias. These are the children who agree to go to a religious group at their synagogue and the children of parents who make the effort to take them there. Again, home background is the most likely explanation for the differentiation.

However, we can place the Kadimah findings in a better perspective because we also have the opportunity to analyze those who attend Camp Ramah. Camp Ramah is a Hebrew-speaking environment with a strong Zionist ethos, and it is widely considered the nurturing ground for recruiting the religious and lay leadership of the Conservative movement. The median number of years of attendance for this group is three summers. Camp Ramah members are a much smaller group (165 cases) than the Kadimah members, accounting for only 11 percent of the sample. The small size of this subsample means that it is probably not representative of Camp Ramah continentally. It also means that the statistics it produces would have to be highly skewed in order to produce significant results in any comparative analysis.

The Kadimah and Ramah subsamples overlap. This hardly affects Kadimah (16 percent are Ramah campers), but it does mean that 47 percent of the Ramah campers are also Kadimah members. Nevertheless, the Camp Ramah subsample has a very distinct background profile that distinguishes it from both the total Kadimah membership and the rest of the majority of the sample. Ramah campers are much more likely to be in Jewish friendship networks, with 70 percent reporting that the majority of their friends are Jewish. One reason for this is that they are drawn heavily from the day school population: 31 percent are current and 38 percent are former day schoolers. Their parents are also much more involved in synagogue life, with 38 percent officeholders of some type.

Yet the parents' synagogue involvement appears to make no appreciable difference to this group of youngsters. Unlike the Kadimah group, the campers are no different from the rest of the sample in terms of their views on the importance of synagogue life or their philanthropic intentions. Even more surprisingly, they are not differentiated from the remainder of the sample on items related to belief and faith. They are not even more interested in Jewish culture.

Where the campers are significantly different is in the behavioral areas stressed during the camping experience: religious services, kashrut, and Israel. A majority intend to be weekly service attenders (52 percent) and another 29 percent intend to go monthly. The campers are almost twice as likely to follow kashrut outside the home as the rest of the class of 5755 (63 percent versus 34 percent). Their commitment to Israel is almost unanimous, with 72 percent regarding it as very important to them personally. They also strongly desire to speak Hebrew (85 percent). These Israel-Zionist sentiments must be placed in perspective, for they are buttressed by the fact that 42 percent of these thirteen to fourteen year olds have already visited Israel. This also suggests that they come from affluent homes, since both travel to the Middle East and attendance at Camp Ramah are too costly for the average household. Strong sentiment of Jewish peoplehood also probably accounts for the significantly higher opposition to intermarriage (47 percent) among campers, but once again it is noticeable that even among this select group of teenagers a majority do not hold this opinion.

The importance of these findings on informal education are very relevant to synagogues. Youth groups and to a lesser extent summer camps are areas that require much less financial investment and resources for buildings and personnel than do day schools. They are also more flexible instruments for gearing their programming to fit local conditions. Moreover, the local congregation can have much more influence and control over the group. Perhaps even more importantly, these activities can be offered to a much wider proportion and number of young people in the congregation than can those of a day school.

The Report Card on the Synagogue Religious School

An assessment of the impact of the congregational school is relevant for both this essay and the overall project of which it is part. The synagogue school is still where the majority of young Conservative Jews will receive all of their Jewish education. Because of the close links between the school and the worship and communal activities of the synagogue, the process of religious socialization, which we tend to impute to the school and its teachers, actually reflects a wider institutional environment, including the influence of other adult role models such as the clergy.

The data in table 5.5 should give some satisfaction (and possibly relief) to those involved in the contemporary supplementary school system operated by the Conservative movement. There is no evidence that the bar/bat mitzvah class of 5755 is composed of the ignorant, alienated, self-hating young Jews of the negative stereotype. In fact, the picture is very positive in a number of areas. Somewhat ironically, Conservative Judaism is producing a community of faith where God plays a major role. After commitment to God, these youngsters' strongest commitments are to their Jewish education, personal Jewishness, and their synagogue even before Israel. The local synagogues would also probably be thrilled if the students carried out their intentions regarding regular attendance at services. Public- and civic-mindedness have also been imbibed by these young people.

The disappointing findings, from the perspective of the ideology of the Conservative movement, concern kashrut and intermarriage. Either these students have not been taught the importance of these concerns or they have not been convinced by the arguments they have heard in support of them. Also a candidate for curricular change or development is probably the area of Jewish culture, since for teenagers today music and art are areas of growing interest and importance.

Another positive note is that the synagogue does have the opportunity to reinforce those attributes it wishes to continue, and to compensate for the deficiencies or negative outcomes revealed by this survey. This is because not all the class of 5755 will use the occasion of their bar or bat mitzvah to exit from the Jewish educational system. A majority of both parents and children are committed to continuing their Jewish education into the Hebrew high school, and the vast majority of local congregations now offer this possibility locally or as part of a consortium with other Conservative synagogues.

Table 5.5
Attitudes and Beliefs of Synagogue School Students (n=817)

A. Attitudes/Beliefs of Synagogue School Students

	% Agreeing	% With high intensity score
Being Jewish is important/very important in own life	97	66
Having a good Jewish education important/very important	97	64
Observing Jewish customs in my home important/very important	97	52
Israel somewhat/very important to me	97	51
Believe in all/some of the miracles in torah	97	37
Participating in synagogue life important/very important	96	59
Believing in God is somewhat/very important to my sense of Jewishness	95	76
Feeling of closeness to other Jews important/very important	95	46
Enjoy Jewish education, most/some of the time	94	35
Being active in Jewish community important/very important	93	38
Interest in Jewish culture, art, music, literature important/very important	83	20
Anti-semitism is a major problem in North America	68	—
Living in a kosher home important/very important	62	15
Not O.K. for Jews to marry people of other religions	33	—

B. Behaviors and Intentions of Synagogue School Students

Will volunteer in the community	87	—
Intend to give tzedakah from pocket money	76	—
Most/half friends Jewish	55	29
Intend to attend synagogue monthly or more	51	24
Will not eat meat and dairy foods together outside home	31	—

Perhaps more importantly, the survey results and socialization theory suggest that in the next few years the influence of the peer group will grow in importance in these young people's lives. Therefore the findings about their Jewish friendship networks become relevant. The synagogues should do everything possible to increase their programming for youth, especially in the light of the growing future market for such activities with the current baby boomlet. In today's youth culture, weak behaviors such as kashrut observance cannot be influenced without peer support. If preventing intermarriage remains a goal, then active encouragement of Jewish social relationships can act to counteract the habit of interfaith dating, which inevitably leads to intermarriage.

Conclusions

The survey of the bar/bat mitzvah class of 5755 and their parents is very much an interim report card on Jewish religious socialization and identity formation among contemporary North American Jews. The real story is not in this snapshot but in the movie that is yet to come. However, we have learned that the rite of passage of bar/bat mitzvah is a popular and positive instrument for Jewish continuity and that it has become successfully coeducational. This cohort of young teenagers appears to have been successfully socialized and has a strong Jewish identity.

On the individual level, the bar and bat mitzvah as an event seems to add to the Jewish success story in North America by producing articulate, confident youngsters with self-esteem. Sending their children to religious school for bar/bat mitzvah allows even those parents who know little about Judaism and Jewish history to reinforce the Jewish identification of their children. Parents seem to use the opportunity of their children's bar/bat mitzvah to affirm their own Jewish identity publicly, and, very importantly for a minority group, both parents and children seem comfortable in asserting their religious-ethnic pride in this manner. One final sociopsychological statistic of great relevance to the future is that only 7 percent of the class of 5755 have ever "been embarrassed about being Jewish."

To some extent, during the bar/bat mitzvah period parents try to influence their children's friendship networks to include Jews by sending their children to Jewish institutions that reinforce their children's self-identity as Jews. However, the main focus of both parent and youngster is the actual ceremony, since this is perceived by most Jews in North America as one of the most powerful indicators of Jewish identity. This emotional investment has led to one important finding of the survey, that synagogues are successfully raising the cost of entry for the b'nai mitzvah families by raising the standards for education and insisting on greater synagogue participation. The downside is that in the process, Conservative Judaism is in danger of being transformed, in a fashion similar to what has occurred in Orthodoxy, from a "broad church" to a narrow sect.

Yet the evidence, particularly from the parent questionnaire, does suggest that many Conservative Jews still practice religious rituals not out of a religious belief so much as to affirm a Jewish identity. As a result some Conservative American Jews maintain their Jewish identity by carrying out a few but conspicuous symbolic and episodic behaviors, such as the bar or bat mitzvah of their children, which have little effect on their middle-class lifestyle. However, the student questionnaire suggests that the younger generation's receptiveness to Judaism is less tribal and less ethnic, as their friendship patterns demonstrate. We can expect the "ethnic" style of "1950s Conservative Judaism" eventually to be replaced by a "faith," so that egalitarian religious practice may become the most salient affirmation of what it means to be a Conservative Jew in North American society. This new blueprint for Conservative Judaism even offers the possibility of religious success without fundamentalism. However, until that day arrives the Conservative synagogues would be wise to remember that their success, in the past and at present, is based upon a certain reality: that the Jewish community in American society is so well structured that American Jews are constrained to affirm their family's Jewish identity principally through their local religious institutions. Thus, maintenance of the bar and bat mitzvah monopoly is a sine qua non for any synagogue movement, and rabbis should accept the necessity of running "birthday parties for thirteen year olds." The reality is that these events are the prime reason for formal synagogue membership, as well as the major source of Shabbat worshipers in many synagogues.

If we argue that Conservative Judaism's essentially communitarian norms, structure, values, and lifestyle have been undermined as it has confronted an increasingly individualistic, experiential, and iconographic contemporary world, we have to ask how this ceremony has adapted so well. One possibility is that it is one of the few aspects of Judaism that has managed to create a workable synthesis of individualistic and communitarian values. It is a powerful affirmation of the individual, the family, and the community in time and space. As a strikingly multigenerational context, it may well be the last structured moment of the extended family. Rabbis realize this, often by acknowledging from the bimah those relatives who have traveled the farthest distance to participate in the celebration. Therefore this rite of passage has to be studied, as in this survey, not just as an event for teenagers but as an important part of parenting and family education, as well as a central event in Conservative synagogue life.

Notes

1. Stuart Schoenfeld, "Recent Publications on Bar/Bat Mitzvah: Their Implications for Jewish Education Research and Practice," *Religious Education* 89, no. 4 (1995): 593–604.
2. Barry A. Kosmin, *The Class of 1979: The "Acculturation of Jewish Immigrants from the Soviet Union,"* (New York: North American Jewish Data Bank, Occasional Paper No. 5), 1990.
3. Izumi Sata and Leonard Plotnicov, "Pittsburgh Middle Class Jewish Families: Structural Assimilation Tested through Bar and Bat Mitzvahs," *Contemporary Jewry* 10 (1989): 33–65.
4. William Yancey and Ira Goldstein, *The Jewish Population of the Greater Philadelphia Area* (Philadelphia: Temple University Press, 1984), 120–121.
5. Walter P. Zenner, "Jewishness in America: Ascription and Choice," *Ethnic and Racial Groups* 8 (1985): 123–124.
6. Fredda M. Herz and Elliot F. Rosen, "Jewish Families," in Monica McGoldrick, John K. Pearce, and Joseph Giordano, eds., *Ethnicity and Family Therapy* (New York: Guilford, 1982), 364.
7. Judith Davis, *Whose Bar/Bat Mitzvah Is This, Anyway?* (New York: St. Martin's, 1998), 52–53.
8. E. M. Hetherington and W. N. Morris, "The Family and Primary Groups," in W. H. Holtzman, ed., *Introductory Psychology in Depth: Developmental Topics* (New York: Harper and Row, 1978).
9. D. G. Perry and L. C. Perry, "Social Learning, Causal Attribution and Moral Internalization," in J. Bisanz, G. L. Bisanz, and R. V. Krail, Jr., eds., *Learning in Children: Progress in Cognitive Development Research* (New York: Springer Verlag, 1983).

10. Frederick Elkin and Gerald Handel, *The Child and Society: The Process of Socialization* (New York: Random House, 1984), 102.
11. Ibid., 110.
12. Joseph Erickson, "Adolescent Religious Development and Commitment: A Structural Equation Model of the Role of Family, Peer Group, and Educational Influences," *Journal for the Social Scientific Study of Religion* 31 (1992): 131–152.
13. M. Cornwall, "The Influence of Three Agents of Religious Socialization," in D. L. Thomas, ed., *The Religion and Family Connection* (Provo, Utah: Brigham Young University Press, 1988), 207–231.
14. Erickson, "Adolescent Religious Development," 149.
15. William Martin and Celia Stendler, *Child Behavior and Development* (New York: Harcourt Brace, 1959), 195–196.
16. P. Strain, T. Cooke, and T. Appolari, "The Role of Peers in Modifying Classmate Social Behavior," *Journal of Special Education* 10 (1976): 54–60.
17. Jack Rothman, *Minority Group Identification and Intergroup Relations: An Examination of Kurt Levin's Theory of Jewish Group Identity* (New York: American Jewish Committee, 1965), 12.
18. Charles Leibman, *The Ambivalent American Jew* (Philadelphia: Jewish Publication Society, 1973).
19. Max Zborowsky and Elizabeth Herzog, *Life Is with People* (New York: International University Press, 1952), 51.
20. Joseph Telushkin, *Jewish Literacy* (New York: William Morrow, 1991), 612.
21. Zborowski and Herzog, *Life Is with People*, 351.
22. Stuart Schoenfeld, "Folk Judaism, Elite Judaism and the Role of Bar Mitzvah in the Development of the Synagogue and Jewish School in America," *Contemporary Jewry* 9 (1987–88): 67–85.
23. Board of Jewish Education of Greater New York, *Jewish Supplementary Schooling: An Educational System in Need of Change* (New York: 1988), 63.
24. Sidney Goldstein and Alice Goldstein, *Jews on the Move: Implications for Jewish Identity* (Albany: State University of New York Press, 1996).
25. Marshall Sklare and Joseph Greenblum, *Jewish Identity on the Suburban Frontier: A Study of Group Survival in the Open Society* (New York: Basic Books, 1967), 195.
26. Sylvia B. Fishman and Alice Goldstein, *When They Are Grown They Will Not Depart: Jewish Education and the Jewish Behavior of American Adults* (Waltham, Mass.: Cohen Center for Modern Jewish Studies, Brandeis University, 1993).

Appendix

THE SURVEY OF THE UNITED SYNAGOGUE OF CONSERVATIVE JUDAISM
B'NAI MITZVAH CLASS OF 5755
BARRY A. KOSMIN, DIRECTOR

METHODOLOGY. The present survey was carried out by telephone in the fall of 1995 by Schulman, Ronca, and Bucuvalas (SRBI) of New York. It consisted of two interviews per household, one with a child and the other with a Jewish parent. Both interviews were approximately fifteen minutes in length. In total, 1,412 complete interviews, involving both children and parents, were achieved across the United States and Canada. However, a larger number of children (1,467) were interviewed. There were sixteen sets of twins interviewed and an additional thirty-nine children whose parent could not arrange the interview prior to the cutoff date.

The sampling procedure was multistaged. First a sample of 271 synagogues of three different size categories—over 800 member units, 400 to 799 members, and under 400 members—was drawn, proportionate to their distribution according to current United Synagogue records. The request from the Ratner Center that synagogues participate in the survey was endorsed by the chancellor of the seminary, the executive director of the United Synagogue, and the chair of the Rabbinical Assembly. Nevertheless, each congregation had to go through its own decisionmaking process in order to participate. Each was asked to supply the names, addresses, and telephone numbers of the children and parents of the class of 5755 (September 1994–September 1995). In total, 115 synagogues agreed to participate.

The parents from the cooperating congregations were then mailed a letter from the Ratner Center informing them of the purposes of the survey and inviting them to participate. The procedure for the interview itself was first to obtain parental permission to speak with the child. Among the parents who were successfully contacted, 19 percent refused to cooperate. If the parent agreed, then the child was asked to participate. In only a handful of cases did the child refuse. In every case the child was interviewed prior to the parent; hence the thirty-nine partial surveys mentioned above.

To summarize, to be interviewed, the b'nai mitzvah had to be from a sampled congregation that supplied an accurate list and whose parent agreed to their being interviewed. In the event, students from 112 different congregations were interviewed. The students may or may not be a fully representative group, but their inclusion in the sample is largely the result of a process of random events.

CHARACTERISTICS OF THE SAMPLE. Among the student sample, 45.3 percent were females and 54.7 percent were males. Allowing for the random sampling error rate, this suggests that there is still a very slight bias against female participation in this rite of passage.

The balance of the sexes among the parent sample goes in the opposite direction, with 60.3 percent of mothers and 39.7 percent of fathers. Considerable efforts were made by the fieldwork company to obtain paternal involvement. The problem was largely one of timing, since our desire to interview a child first led us to concentrate on afternoon and early evening calls, when more mothers than fathers were at home. Nevertheless, the size of the sample allows us to fully investigate gender issues including differences in mother-son, mother-daughter, father-son, and father-daughter patterns.

One structural reason for the overrepresentation of mothers is the existence of one-parent families, which constitute 7 percent of the households. Blended families were another 10 percent, but normative first-marriage couples were strongly represented with 82.7 percent. This suggests that nontraditional families are underrepresented among Conservative synagogue members. The data on the religious background of the parents seem to confirm this. Fully 91 percent of the parents were Jews by birth, 7.8 percent Jews by choice, and 1.2 percent non-Jewish. Nevertheless, this means that 18 percent of the families have a parent who was not born Jewish and therefore also have close kin who are non-Jews. Again, if necessary we can use these family type categories to analyze critical variables.

The religious variable overlaps somewhat with cultural variables for analytical purposes. We found that 83.8 percent of the interviewed parents were born in the United States, just over 4 percent in Canada, and the remaining 12 percent in other countries, led by Israel and the former Soviet Union. As regards their Jewish ethnic backgrounds, 51 percent of the students identified as Ashkenazi, 11 percent as Sephardi, with the remainder unsure.

Another form of background difference is denominational origin. It appears that 61 percent of the parents were raised Conservative, 23 percent Orthodox, and 11 percent Reform. Since their marriage, 5 percent had been members of an Orthodox synagogue, 8 percent were ex-Reform members, and 1 percent ex-Reconstructionist or some other Jewish denomination.

As far as regional distribution is concerned, this sample is skewed away from the Northeast and toward the Midwest; the other two regions are correctly balanced in terms of the national Jewish and the Conservative synagogue populations. Among the U.S. households, 36 percent were from the Northeast, 23 percent from the Midwest, 22 percent from the South, and 20 percent from the West. In addition, there are sixty Canadian households from six provinces. They constitute just over 4 percent of the overall sample.

Chapter 6

RIV-ELLEN PRELL

Communities of Choice and Memory

Conservative Synagogues in the Late Twentieth Century

Aᴍᴇʀɪᴄᴀɴ Jᴇᴡɪꜱʜ ʟɪꜰᴇ became a matter of interest to social scientists almost half a century after America's growing number of Jews came to define the landscape of some of the nation's most important urban centers. Following World War II, social scientists, themselves usually Jews, turned their gaze on newly forming suburbs. They found that just as Jews moved to suburbs in impressive numbers, so they built a great many religious institutions, but that comparatively few of them attended the religious services, particularly in contrast to their Christian neighbors.[1]

These sociologists were struck by what they perceived to be a new type of synagogue, one that was a home to children and women far more than to men, who dominated traditional synagogue life. Decorum was subdued, in contrast to the noisy and animated shuls of Europe and the inner cities. Above all, synagogues were oriented to children, seeking to educate them and to instill in them a sense of pride in their Jewishness that their parents felt was crucial to combating anti-Semitism. Many of these parents, often the children of immigrants, felt unprepared to provide any part of that education.[2] Friday night was the important part of Shabbat in those synagogues, attracting families or couples for services, interesting lectures, and socializing.[3] Few men were able to observe Shabbat by refraining from work on Saturday morning, and women brought their children to synagogue for their religious training instead.

Suburban synagogues were usually part of the neighborhood geography as Jews built Conservative or Reform synagogues in their backyards. Sometimes families maintained, in addition, membership in an Orthodox synagogue in an older urban neighborhood. This postwar period, lasting into the mid-1960s, had probably the highest affiliation rate of Jews with synagogues in the twentieth century.[4]

As sociologists saw it, for the descendants of Eastern European immigrants the Conservative suburban synagogues served as a reflection of their new middle-class standing, as an important marker of membership in the American nation for American-born parents and their children. Thus, even as they drew on powerful memories to animate their Jewish lives—of parents and grandparents, of old neighborhoods, of a European world now largely destroyed, of a particular brand of piety—it was not those memories that provided the architecture, interior design, or the conduct of services in suburban synagogues. Those by contrast mirrored the behavior and appearance of the American middle class.

Similarly, synagogues reflected the normative Jewish family of the period. Hence, the family's division of labor was reflected in a synagogue division of labor: men were more engaged by work and growing economic success than by their religious lives. And women, as Marshall Sklare's important study demonstrated, were the foundation of the synagogue:[5] housewives and mothers who attended classes and engaged in philanthropic work and voluntarism in the synagogue. The synagogue, then, was a thoroughly middle-class institution for a middle-class Jewry.

After the flurry of interest in suburban synagogues in the 1960s, only a few social scientists again found it an interesting arena for study, and none has been a study of a Conservative synagogue.[6] Sklare's path-breaking work generated virtually no subsequent research.[7] Perhaps the synagogue's very self-image as the irreducible core of Jewish American life led to a lack of curiosity about it. Indeed, Sklare himself wrote in 1971: "It is hard to find a principled opponent to the American Synagogue."[8] What then became of those Conservative sanctuaries for the children of immigrants, uncomfortable in Orthodoxy or Reform, in search of a halfway house whose aesthetics and decorum spoke to their class, occupation, and suburban location in the late 1950s?

The immediate postwar social scientists used categories that have, to some extent, proved clumsy for more recent studies. "Status anxiety" was a bedrock of analysis. It was linked to acculturation as a new measure of Jews' more recent climb into the middle class. Thirty to forty years later, however, these categories offer little help in understanding the children and grandchildren of that era.[9] Intermarriage and how to problematize that easy contact have come instead to dominate Jewish social science and policy studies. While Sklare and others certainly anticipated waning ritual observance, they operated in a more cautiously optimistic time, believing that the synagogue might continue to support Jewish identity through other means than religious life.[10]

This study demonstrates that the synagogue remains an important site for studying American Jewish life, not because it is the only or most important institution for transmitting Judaism, but because it is a persistent one that power-fully reflects the lives of American Jews and must be responsive to them. Since the breakdown of the "consensus culture" of the 1950s, from the mid-1960s to the present, the American society to which the synagogue responded has dras-tically altered. Therefore, as the synagogue continues to provide idioms for Jewish practice, its relationship to authority, religious meaning, and practice have shifted as well.

Since the 1970s the synagogue has been anything but an uncontested bed-rock of American Jewish life. Affiliation has dropped. The Jewish countercul-ture, with its many alternatives of havurot, spirituality, feminism, healing, and others took the synagogue and suburban families to task for destroying the core of Jewish life.[11] Synagogues in turn have been responsive to cultural and social change and the challenges posed. Rabbis have fought aggressively on all sides of issues to allow their synagogues to reflect passionately held principles about gender equality, the rights of homosexual Jews, access of the intermarried, and the maintenance of halakha. Thus there has been nothing bland about Ameri-can synagogues. To the contrary, they have become important testing grounds, even battlegrounds, for shaping American Judaism in this century and the one to come. The changing forms of American Jewish families have also been re-flected in synagogue policies about membership and programming. In short, one needs to take a closer look at the synagogue to understand the lives of Ameri-can Jews and the practice of their Judaism.

An Ethnography of Conservative Synagogues

Following the lead of an earlier generation of social scientists, I spent a year taking a close look at two Conservative synagogues in suburbs of Minnesota's Twin Cities, Minneapolis and St. Paul. With the permission of the board of di-rectors of each synagogue I became their ethnographer, and they became my subject of study.[12] I set out with the general and modest goal of understanding how these congregants, rabbis, and synagogue professionals went about creating a life together as Conservative Jews in the United States in 1995 and 1996. I conducted my fieldwork as a participant-observer by attending services, classes, meetings, and informal events. I also interviewed men and women of different ages and perspectives from different groups within the synagogues.

What made this study especially interesting was spending a year at two syna-gogues. Comparative research is unusual for an ethnographer, particularly when it is conducted simultaneously. Because I was fortunate enough to spend time in two very different synagogues, both of which were thriving, I learned about the diversity of ways that congregants define their Judaism and their participa-tion in synagogue life.

But this vantage point had its drawbacks as well. Quite simply, I was never able to spend as much time as I wanted in either synagogue or at any one activity. Moreover, the picture I will present of these synagogues is not complete. First, those who spoke to me about their lives as Jews do not represent all Jews or all members of their synagogues. Second, the synagogues I spent a year with are not representative of all Conservative synagogues. And third, neither synagogue believed the year that I spent there was the most representative for that congregation.

This study of Conservative synagogues is anything but disinterested, as I have lived in the Twin Cities for more than twenty years as a faculty member of the University of Minnesota, and have been affiliated with the Conservative movement for half that time. When I began my research, I had been a member of the St. Paul synagogue in this study for three years as a regular Shabbat participant, but not in any leadership role. I live a few blocks from the Minneapolis synagogue under study and knew some of its members. In taking on the role of participant-observer I changed my participation at my own synagogue and became an observer at the other. My goal was to see the synagogues through the eyes of their different constituents and to place their disparate views in the context of late twentieth century American Jewish life. As a member, in some sense, of both communities, my goal has been to treat each respectfully through an ethnographic lens.

The study of a synagogue can be many things. Either of these synagogues would be a wonderful subject of historical study, a rich method for understanding cultural and religious change over the long term. Similarly, a close study of a year in the life of each rabbi would provide a fascinating story of religious leadership and development. The journalistic account *And They Shall Be My People* did just that.[13] Alternatively, simply following several congregants through a single Jewish year might provide a set of life stories that would reveal much about the practice of Judaism for a sample of people.

As an ethnography, however, this study is different in method and intent from any of the above. Mindful of history and interested in the experiences of the synagogues' rabbis and congregants, my goal instead was to examine the meeting points between the synagogue's organizational life, its leadership, and its members. Like ethnographies written about cultures throughout the world, it is based on an examination of key events that illustrate something about congregational life. Of course, because this is an essay rather than a book-length study, much about congregational life necessarily had to be left out. I certainly could not do justice to the complexity of the rabbis' and staffs' work and lives in these two congregations. Only a fraction of the issues that confront the boards of directors can be mentioned.

What I have aimed to do in this account is present two synagogues that share a commitment to Conservative Judaism in different ways, as each builds a religious community for its members.[14] I have learned in the process why Conservative Judaism can be practiced differently, not only by individuals, but by communities as well. In addition, their idioms of religious lives created within synagogues are quite different than ones described by the scholars of Conservative Judaism of the 1950s.

Similarly, I have found powerful evidence of Jewish practice as a developmental process. The Judaism I saw was dynamic, changing constantly, depending on ages, relationships, and location within the developmental cycle of families of the individuals involved. Any attempt to fix Jewish life as a single avenue to Jewish practice misses that very process. Within the context of this dynamic practice of Judaism by individuals, the synagogue helps to shape and articulate their attraction and commitment to Jewish life.

Just as earlier social scientists understood the synagogue in terms of a dramatically new postwar American culture, I look to today's synagogues and their members to understand an American Jewish life that has taken shape in light of the fairly dramatic changes in the lives of middle-class American Jews since the 1970s. I have not found an increased commitment to ritual practice nor greater acceptance of traditional authority in comparison with Sklare's finding of the 1950s. But I have found new idioms for religious life and a different sense of what it means to be an American Jew. No longer driven by anxiety over their non-Jewish neighbors' acceptance or spurred on by memories of European Jewish life, these Conservative Jews search for meaning and continuity in their own and their family's practice of Judaism within a community. They have reshaped the central issue in Conservative Judaism, continuing to ask how to apply halakha within their contemporary culture.

The Synagogues

BETH EL SYNAGOGUE

Beth El Synagogue, located in a suburb of Minneapolis, and Beth Jacob Synagogue, located in a suburb of St. Paul, were the sites of my research. Beth El is the older and larger of the two, and would have been as appropriate a subject of study in 1955 as it was in 1995. This community of about 1,350 "membership units" is nearly seventy-five years old. Founded in the area's first Jewish neighborhood, it moved almost thirty years ago to its present location, Saint Louis Park, a first-ring suburb centrally located among the many suburbs where Jews have moved over the past two to three decades.

Beth El has been from its founding an unusually progressive synagogue. Under the leadership of the late David Aronson, its first rabbi, the members were inspired to create an "American synagogue," liberated from the geography of the

Old World—as he described his dream as a young rabbi when he accepted the position. Beth El was one of the first Conservative synagogues to educate and train girls and boys similarly and to encourage bat mitzvah. Its second rabbi, Kassel Abelson, developed a youth movement that evolved into United Synagogue Youth. These rabbis were regarded by congregants as "intellects," "learned," and "real leaders." Members reflect on their history with great pride.

Beth El continues to have a substantial membership, although some of its leaders note that membership has been fairly flat for at least five years, having experienced its most recent boom in the 1980s. Few members resign from the synagogue. Those who move or die are replaced by a small but steady number of new households. Many congregants describe themselves as "fourth generation Beth El members." The current rabbi, Robert Kahn, estimates that about 80 percent of Beth El's members have been affiliated with the synagogue for several generations. Among the men and women whom I interviewed were a substantial number who were either born into or married into Beth El, in the fashion that one marries into a family. Members ranging from their thirties to their seventies recalled to me parents and grandparents who were synagogue founders, and several couples with college-age children met in the same youth groups that their children had only recently left.

A newer member commented at the kiddush following Shabbat morning services, "It is not unusual for Beth El members to have twenty family members to talk to at kiddush." She was warned as a newcomer to the synagogue some years before that it would be hard "to break in." She said she was patient, and in time found friends. As another newcomer who had been a member for "only a decade" told me, "There are a lot who are fifth generation or whatever. And then there's a chunk of us who aren't, and those who aren't tend to gravitate to one another, so you tend to be one another's family." In point of fact there are probably no more than two families with twenty relatives at a kiddush; nevertheless, the members' perceptions that Beth El includes large numbers of these families is instructive.

Both Beth El's president, Bonnie Heller, and its former rabbi, Haim Herring, described Beth El as a "community of communities" that must meet the needs of many constituencies. Like most synagogues in America, the largest group consists of those who attend only for life-cycle events and the High Holidays. Leadership at Beth El places that number at two-thirds of the congregation. Other groups include young families, families with teenagers and their parents who are active in the youth commission, the observant core of families who live in the neighborhood, those whose families are grown, families of nursery school children at the synagogue, and older members who primarily attend the Men's Club and Women's Club.

Memories of Beth El's first location, the North Side of Minneapolis, remain important to the synagogue and to a great many of its members. The synagogue and its then-rabbi, Kassel Abelson, stayed on the North Side longer than the vast majority of the Jews and their institutions who had occupied the neighborhood. Hence, even Jews now in their forties continued to go there for synagogue services and b'nai mitzvah training. In the 1960s they were bused there from the suburbs. The dense ethnic neighborhood, where Yiddish was the language of the street and the shops and synagogues dotted many corners along with kosher butchers and bakeries, is a remarkably vivid memory, literally inseparable from Beth El for a huge number of its members.

That memory is in part kept strong because of the remarkable fact that Beth El has had only four rabbis in nearly seventy-five years. Two of these—Rabbi Abelson, who became emeritus in 1992, and his predecessor, Rabbi Aronson, who became emeritus in 1959—presided over a North Side Beth El. In 1995, as I began this study, Rabbi Herring, who had served the congregation as senior rabbi for three years and associate rabbi for another seven, resigned his pulpit to work in another capacity in the community. Rabbi Herring had ushered in a new era at Beth El. He and others told me that he introduced "humor from the *bimah*." He encouraged discussions at Shabbat morning services. He changed life-cycle events and restructured the management of the synagogue. In every way he tried to streamline and transform the synagogue and encourage change.

His great successes were for a time overshadowed by his resignation. The unthinkable occurred: a rabbi left the synagogue. Matters were complicated by the inability of the synagogue to find a replacement after a six-month search.[15] More than one congregant described this resignation as "a divorce." One woman who spoke to me remembered board members hearing the news and openly weeping: "How could our rabbi leave us?" Tears were shed at the executive committee as well. The loss was devastating for those most active in the synagogue. Rabbi Herring and his family have remained members of Beth El, however, and attend the synagogue on Shabbat. They have reserved a date for their first child's bar mitzvah, and they anticipate remaining in the community in their new roles as congregants.

Rabbi Robert Kahn, then assistant rabbi, assumed the position of acting senior rabbi for the year of my research, and much of what happened during the year and what people wanted to tell me about was their enthusiasm for Rabbi Kahn and the new presence he brought to Beth El's pulpit. In remarkably short order the perceived trauma of divorce became a smooth transition to a new era. Congregants have spoken consistently about how much they value Rabbi Kahn's informality and innovative sermon topics, his willingness to try new things like a "contemporary" New Year service that focused on discussion and shortened prayers. Both middle-aged and older members describe Rabbi Kahn with the Yiddish word "haimish." He is "homey," informal, warm, and accessible. As one member put it, "Rabbi Kahn takes being a rabbi seriously, but he does not take himself seriously." A widely diverse group of people praised that accessibility as important to them in making Beth El a place they enjoyed being members. Beth El, then, appears to be embracing a new identity at the same time it holds fast to its powerful sense of community history.

Beth El's smooth transition was by no means accomplished solely by its interim senior rabbi. The strength of its leadership and their ability to work effectively with synagogue staff also enabled that success. President Bonnie Heller described the painstaking process of meeting to prioritize every task, and to reassign these tasks in the absence of one rabbi. Lay people were given some of the responsibility. The board leadership learned by hard work how many tasks its clergy undertook on a daily basis.

Beth El, like all large synagogues, needs a number of staff members to run its complex institution. The synagogue devotes huge resources to the education of children and to programs for families and youth. The Conservative synagogues of the Twin Cities do not provide their own synagogue-based Jewish supplementary schools. Instead, each city has a community Talmud Torah that serves as the primary educational institution for the children of Conservative synagogues. The Minneapolis Talmud Torah is over one hundred years old and, like Beth El, moved from the North Side to St. Louis Park. Indeed, those who feel tremendous loyalty to the Beth El of the North Side also link the synagogue to their participation in the Talmud Torah.

The primary educational work of Beth El, then, is a Sunday school and a Shabbat morning program that prepares children to become b'nai mitzvah. In 1995–96, forty-eight children became b'nai mitzvah. Those families who join the synagogue when their children are as old as eleven may find themselves scheduling a bat mitzvah on Christmas or Thanksgiving, the only available dates left on the calendar. Two hundred and fifty children participate in preparation for b'nai mitzvah from grades five to eight. More than half of them will go on to become teachers in the same program, a higher rate than for those who continue with their Jewish educations in the community Talmud Torah. In addition, the synagogue offers a confirmation class, Sunday school for young children, and a pre-school.

This educational work is supervised by the cantor, Neil Newman, an educational director, Mary Baumgarten, and a nursery school director who manages a pre-school that has served as an important entryway into the synagogue for young families. In addition, the rabbi participates in integrating all the parts of the educational process.

Cantor Newman heads up many other adult programs as well, including a variety of adult and youth choirs. High Holiday choirs are magnetic for many adults who otherwise attend very little, and he warmly welcomes college students back to the choir whenever they are home. He also provides instruction for many cantorial skills for adults and encourages their participation as torah readers. He began a program twelve years ago that yearly recognized those congregants who have read seven torah sections during the previous year. In 1995, at their Shabbat service recognition, Beth El's large *bimah* was filled with young adults and men and women who had met this goal, some for as many as ten years.

In addition to education, Beth El's organizational life deals with membership, the daily and yearly liturgical calendar, and the life-cycle events that wed members so firmly to the synagogue. These tasks are managed by an executive director, office staff, and a ritual director who has served the congregation for decades; and this year, because Rabbi Kahn was without an assistant rabbi, he was also assisted by a program director.

Beth El has an active lay leadership as well. During 1995 and 1996, important years of transition, the synagogue was led by a dynamic president, Bonnie Heller, a former president of the synagogue's youth group and the daughter of a former Beth El president. She presided over a large board and added a new vice president for membership, as well as reactivating and expanding a number of committees. Lay members also undertook to solve significant problems in management, ranging from hiring a new rabbi to restructuring dues. The synagogue has many volunteers and an extraordinary roster of very active committees (thirty-seven in 1995), ranging from kashrut to investments to the problems of the intermarried. All committee chairs are board members. There are also numerous ad hoc committees at work to bake and sell hamantashen for Purim, to create special programming for Shabbat, and to engineer new activities. Bonnie Heller, along with Rabbi Kahn, worked hard to encourage members to volunteer and to seek out new opportunities for those who were interested. Under her leadership the synagogue managed the difficult task of adjusting from two rabbis to one; she created an important set of processes that allowed the synagogue to meet congregants' various needs with one fewer rabbi.

Rabbi Kahn surely did not exaggerate when he told me that Beth El's presidents "put in three to five hours a day." The 1996 Ratner Study survey indicates that in the last year, 89 percent of Beth El's respondents had attended a synagogue board meeting and 75 percent had attended a synagogue committee meeting. Undoubtedly, lay leadership is important to congregants. In addition, many capable congregants took on demanding assignments ranging from organizing a process for restructuring dues to volunteer recognition. And parents, particularly those who grew up in the synagogue, compete for the right to serve on the youth commission. If Bonnie Heller hears of a congregant complaining about feeling marginalized, she immediately puts that person in a volunteer position.

This active and complex hub of Jewish life is housed in Beth El's beautiful and impressive synagogue. A sanctuary of warm woods is designed, as official language states, "to lead our attention up toward the heavens and connect us with God and nature." The room's high band of windows suffuses the space with natural light, allowing the worshiper to follow the sun from east to west, to watch birds fly across the sky, and to experience the season's changing quality of light.

Beth El moved to its current suburban location twenty-six years ago. Although leaving the old neighborhood behind was a decision that was not taken without intense deliberation, once the congregation was committed they felt enormous pride in what they accomplished as they dedicated their new building in 1968. As one member told me, "The campaign for the new building was done so joyfully. My husband was gone at least three to four nights a week working on fundraising. And he did it with such a happy heart. I remember the night he called me at midnight on a weeknight to say that they had raised a million dollars."

The aesthetics of the 1990s, however, have left both rabbis and some lay people uncomfortable with those very awe-inspiring vistas of the sanctuary. As Rabbi Herring put it, "The one thing I really would have done to make a statement is to take an ax and cut down the height of the *bimah* (and Beth El is a beautiful sanctuary). Instead of having the lines go like this [pointing upward] to make an *ohel* [a tent] I would have turned them in. That would have been one of my dreams." Both Rabbi Herring and Rabbi Kahn have worked to create a "new" Beth El that values informality. The rabbis of the 1980s and 1990s embraced a different vision of synagogue and Judaism than the one so artfully encoded in the synagogue's commanding architecture.

In the classical terms of the synagogue, Beth El is a house of prayer, study, and assembly. There is a small daily minyan, both morning and evening, which is a mix of mourners and regular attenders. Attendance at Friday night services held at eight o'clock has dwindled over the years to the point that this year they were no longer scheduled each Shabbat. Shabbat morning services are the primary prayer service of the week, regularly filling the large sanctuary, often with a great many guests of the bar or bat mitzvah. The Ratner Center survey found that nearly half of all congregants attend services a few times a year beyond the High Holidays. Somewhat less than a third attend twice a month or more, which is just slightly more than the national average of 29 percent who participated in the Ratner study. And almost 80 percent responded that they were "able to read the prayer book in Hebrew," an astoundingly high level of literacy.[16]

Like the classical 1950s synagogues, Beth El primarily educates children rather than adults. Its building swells with children on the weekend. Adult classes tend to take place in the homes of members who study with the rabbi. Rabbi Kahn leads two study groups that have met for over forty years, and he leads newer ones of men and women in their thirties and forties. Cantor Newman began a two-year-long adult b'nai mitzvah program that drew a surprisingly large number of participants. Finally, as a house of assembly, the synagogue hosts innumerable board and committee meetings every month.

The Ratner Center survey indicates that Beth El's members have long and deep connections to their synagogue and their Judaism. One hundred percent of those surveyed consider being Jewish "very important" or "somewhat important." Almost three-quarters consider Judaism "very important," and 71 percent "agree strongly" or "agree" that a Conservative Jew is "obligated to obey halakha." Sixty-seven percent have been to Israel at least once. More than half the members light Shabbat candles weekly and more than one-quarter keep kosher homes, both percentages just slightly lower than the national average reported in the Ratner Center survey. Finally, the members of this classically suburban synagogue seem to challenge the very definition of child-oriented Judaism in one sense. Sixty-six percent answered that a "very important" motivation for attending services is due to "spiritual reasons." By contrast, only 23 percent find it "very important" to attend to bring their children for bar or bat mitzvah preparation, and 24 percent to set an example for their children. These congregants also have lengthy and deep ties to their synagogue, from between six and nineteen years. Eighty-three percent consider it "very likely" that they will still be members five years from now.

Beth El challenges the assumption of the inevitability of assimilation, which is what persuaded Rabbi Kahn and his wife to come there:

> Beth El has a real core membership of very committed and observant Jews. I think I could count on my hands the number of shuls in the U.S. where I would have twenty families whose observance level matches mine in the Conservative movement, and here at Beth El we have way over that. And they are knowledgeable and young; having our own community here is important to us.

Several years ago the Orthodox Jewish community in Beth El's neighborhood decided, with the support of all the neighborhood rabbis, to construct an *eruv*—a boundary within which one is permitted to carry on Shabbat—to enhance the ease with which families could be observant. When I walked to Beth El on Shabbat morning my path crossed those of men, women, and children criss-crossing the neighborhood on their way to these various synagogues. It appears that the rabbi and the Shabbat-observant community of Beth El share an important sense of neighborhood that in the 1950s marked the Jews' ability to join the middle class and in the 1990s has marked a higher level of observance and separation. Beth El has in some sense, then, moved full circle. With remarkable persistence, the synagogue has, even if not in great numbers, forged powerful links between neighborhood, family, and community.

Beth Jacob

Almost fifteen miles east of Beth El is Beth Jacob Congregation, located in Mendota Heights. It is the first synagogue built in the history of Dakota County.[17] The synagogue has 325 "membership units," and has grown almost threefold in the decade since it was founded.

Beth Jacob was created out of a merger of a newly forming synagogue, the New Conservative Synagogue, and an old and dying one, the Sons of Jacob. The latter had purchased suburban property decades before, and had some cash and a great many Torah scrolls. The congregation, with the small number of remaining members, had to abandon its synagogue because of the building's poor physical condition and was meeting at the Jewish Community Center.

The New Conservative Synagogue was made up of a breakaway group from St. Paul's only large Conservative synagogue, and a majority of its members were nonaffiliated. Teachers and administrators from the St. Paul day school, as well as a local Hillel rabbi, helped found the new synagogue and provided a core of members with a substantial Jewish education.

With the approach of the tenth anniversary of the synagogue, the story of the merger was told regularly. The two groups were rather incompatible. The new Conservative Synagogue was deeply committed to gender equality; Sons of Jacob was totally opposed. They conducted worship differently as well. Any agreement in the abstract about how to conduct their new synagogue was unimaginable. Unable to agree on how to merge, they did agree, as one founding member is fond of putting it, "to daven together." Instead of continuing to pray across the hall from one another in the Jewish Community Center, they joined together in one room and alternated *divrei torah*, Torah reading, and leading services. After about a year and many negotiations, the groups merged and formed a synagogue, raised funds to construct a building, and hired the present rabbi, Morris Allen.

At its founding, many members argued passionately for keeping Beth Jacob a small community by capping membership at two hundred units. In the end all concurred that this was both impossible and undesirable. In 1994 the synagogue built an addition to accommodate the growing membership and the many children in the synagogue, mostly under twelve. In 1996 there were about eight b'nai mitzvah a year. American Jews' baby "boomlet," in combination with the synagogue's attractiveness to young families who were moving into this suburban area, suggest that these numbers will grow dramatically.

The synagogue is weighted toward young families in another striking sense. About seventy children, two-thirds or so of the congregation's school-age children, attend the Talmud Torah of the St. Paul Day School. Two children who live in Minneapolis attend a day school there. There are dense and overlapping ties between families who live in the two worlds of synagogue and day school, to the point where there are expectations that Beth Jacob children will go to day school—an expectation that some members find confining. A woman with a pre-school child explained,

> We're trying to make a decision for ourselves that I consider a very
> private decision about kindergarten, and it's a very public decision in
> Beth Jacob's eyes. It amazed me how many people knew we had been at
> the introduction meeting for Talmud Torah. We're not yet sure what we
> will do. I don't want my children to grow up thinking that Jews are
> better than others. Yet I take wonderful pride in the fact that at five she
> knows the Four Questions and all her holidays.

This mother's concern about the effect of a day school on a child's identity as an American was expressed by others interviewed in both synagogues. It is an ambivalence that weighs heavily on many families.

Other parents, of course, expressed the opposite sentiment; for them the overlap between Beth Jacob and their children's day school represents the realization of the dream of a meaningful Jewish community in which to raise their families.

By any standard of Conservative Judaism, Beth Jacob's members have a high level of observance. According to the Ratner Center Survey, over half the members were raised in Conservative Jewish homes. As adults, 75 percent report that they light candles on Friday evenings (20 percent higher than the national average reported in the study), and 84 percent can read the prayerbook (though not necessarily understand it fully). Forty-three percent have a kosher home (13 percent higher than those responding nationwide to the survey), and of those, 27 percent observe kashrut outside their homes. Sixty-five percent reported attending Shabbat morning services once or twice a month, in contrast with 29 percent of the national respondents who attend about the same amount. When asked how important being Jewish is, 89 percent of Beth Jacob's members answered that they found it very important, and 5 percent said it was somewhat important.[18]

These findings are largely consistent with a survey undertaken by Morton Weinfeld for the Avi Chai Foundation. He found, in a 1991 survey of more than twice the number of Beth Jacob households than in the Ratner Center Study, that 70 percent reported coming to services monthly on Shabbat and 75 percent recited the blessings associated with the Shabbat meal on Friday night.[19]

As a younger synagogue, Beth Jacob's members do not have the deep attachments one is likely to find in an older shul. The Ratner Center survey, however, found that they have chosen membership on other grounds. For example, only 17 percent of Beth Jacob's members, as opposed to nearly 60 percent of Beth El's, joined the same synagogue as their parents. On the other hand, 68 percent of Beth Jacob's members, in contrast to 53 percent of Beth El's members, "liked the community, the congregants." Similarly, 72 percent of Beth Jacob's members, in contrast to 66 percent of Beth El's, joined the synagogue because they "liked the style of worship." Beth Jacob's egalitarian policy on the sexes attracted 63 percent of their members in contrast to 51 percent at Beth El. While 46 percent of Beth El's members wished "the services were more meaningful," only one-third of Beth Jacob's members expressed that concern and 54 percent found the services meaningful. Beth Jacob, then, is an observant community drawn to the synagogue much more for what it does than for ties to family and loyalty to the institution.

While synagogue members have a high level of observance, they do not re-gard themselves as an elite. There is, if anything, a tendency to identify the "learned" members rather than the "observant" ones. And insofar as there is an elite, they are eager to include as many competent Jews as possible in their ranks. Indeed, a great deal of the synagogue's programming is educational, teaching adults about observance of everything from Shabbat to kashrut to reading the Hebrew alphabet. One founder described the ethos as follows:

> Everyone is expected to grow. At Beth Jacob we take our observance
> seriously, and we all do that in different ways. The rabbi communicates
> it from the pulpit and I also see it in the people around me, grappling
> with observance and prayer. It's a davening community, and it is also a
> community that if you don't daven that's OK too; there's room for
> variation there. You can sit quietly and read, you can go in the hallway,
> you can work in the kitchen.

But there is nevertheless consensus that the shul and its membership should be moving in the direction of increasing observance. Virtually every person I in-terviewed thought about his or her Judaism in the categories of the observance of mitzvot, whether practiced or not: "I don't keep kosher"; "I observe Shabbat"; "I know I could do more." Many admitted that they had given more thought to these categories as a result of their membership at Beth Jacob. For example, a man in his early forties, who felt strongly identified with Judaism but partici-pated very little until he joined Beth Jacob, told me,

> I don't think I'll ever be Orthodox and keep kosher or become some-
> thing I'm not, but I can certainly see myself as more observant and, with
> my daughter [six years old] involved and encouraging more participa-
> tion, going to the synagogue more often, doing seders, taking a syna-
> gogue trip to Israel. I feel my Jewishness is getting more affirmed and I'm
> owning it more than ever.

Because the synagogue is still young, its members are quite articulate about Beth Jacob's "values," about traditional categories, whether observed or not. The group defined itself early on as looking "to torah as a blueprint for our community." The synagogue articulates its three commitments to torah, *avodah* (prayer), and *gemilut hasadim* (acts of lovingkindness), and aims to weigh them against all synagogue activities. Early on a rabbi, a faculty member at a local college, visited them as they struggled over how to define themselves in terms of liturgy. "You're worrying about the wrong thing," he reportedly told them. "Define your covenantal relationship, and that will serve as your foundation." They agreed.

One of Beth Jacob's founders explained that blueprint:

> We come together around torah. We use torah as our reason for being together as a congregation. We study together. That is how we grow with one another, and we make decisions about our lives and our communal life with the torah process for making decisions, to reach solutions that are workable.

Many members reported an example of this process to me: a family who held a private luncheon in the synagogue for a bar mitzvah, the only luncheon of its type ever held at Beth Jacob. The board decided to review private lunches as a policy matter and eventually voted to reject future requests, based on a study of traditional sources with the rabbi on the nature of hospitality and community. This is the process, according to board members and others, that makes their synagogue unique and committed to torah.[20]

Congregants see their commitment to egalitarianism as a key feature of that blueprint. Even in the midst of a great many highly educated Jews, Beth Jacob's members never described religious virtuosity as what they most prized. Members and leaders use the word to refer to everything from gender equality to the dues structure, to modesty in celebrating life-cycle events, to the design of their building. One founder, a man in his early fifties, thinks of Beth Jacob as unique because of its "unusual combination of liturgical conservatism and social progressivism." There is a high level of consensus on what this means.

Beth Jacob's daily minyan, which has met for the last six years, provides an interesting example of liturgical egalitarianism. On the window sill of the small chapel where the daily minyan meets sits a lined legal pad. Each day the rabbi or another regular records who leads each portion of the morning service and who reads torah. These responsibilities and honors rotate regularly. One Sunday morning the rabbi was out of town and one member led the entire service, which was the occasion of a celebration in his family. People who heard about it were shocked. "That's not how we do it at Beth Jacob," was a fairly typical response. No single member ever again led the entire service.

Beth Jacob's members also value creating community. Its founders are aware that with the tripling of membership, that goal must inevitably change or be watered down. Several founders attribute the original intensity of community to the smallness of the Jewish Community Center room where they originally met. As one founder said, "Scrunched in together at the JCC at kiddush, you talked to whoever you were scrunched near." "Now," she said, "I don't know the names of people who come every week."

A founding couple of the synagogue remember the creation of community in another sense. They found people, both younger and older, who provided important models of Jewish life. One couple especially impressed them, as the husband recounted:

> The major impact on me has been the relationships. I remember when we were soliciting for the building fund and we solicited a Sons of Jacob member who is about as genuine as they come. He started to tell us about his commitments to other things. I thought, "Here is an example for me, a person who can be a model for me. This is a person who feels deeply and gives generously and is a substantial person who I respect." From there is an entire litany of similar models of people younger than I am and older than I am. A couple, but for the shul we would have never met them. They are fifteen years our senior. They adopted us as friends, generous people who are extremely knowledgeable."

His wife added,

> They live what they believe. They have an understanding of what it is to be Jewish and they live it. They came into a time in our lives when Beth Jacob was forming and the rabbi was being hired. My mother was dying of cancer. It's not that I didn't know these things and hadn't practiced it to some degree, but they were there with food and support. We had minyans in our home. And he was the person who when they said shiva is over, literally came to the chair where I was sitting and helped me out of it. Community meant for these members the opportunity to interact with such people, whom they would otherwise never have known.

Congregants also describe the community created in the context of Shabbat morning prayer. One member, a man in his early fifties who has taken several leadership roles, described what he understands to be unique about the synagogue:

> Beth Jacob's success is the sense of community that it builds. The way in which Sid seeks out the strangers on Shabbat morning for aliyot, the way the rabbi never forgets a name, is remarkable. So [there is] that sense of being welcomed and instantly included, even though I think it has changed in comparison to where it was three, four, or five years ago. People who came from other synagogues still remark that they have never experienced anything like this. They are instantly made to feel at home.

The community is also unusual, according to members, because it is an intergenerational synagogue. The Sons of Jacob's elderly members, fewer now because of the passage of time, are very present in the congregation and on the *bimah*, both on Shabbat and at the daily minyan. Other elderly men and women have joined as new members as well. A small group of women well into their seventies have taken on increased ritual roles. A Russian immigrant in her late sixties read a *haftarah* for the first time in 1995. Another became a bat mitzvah and learned to read torah. A third woman learned from a younger woman in the congregation to daven *Kabbalat Shabbat* services. These "connections," as people describe the links between people at Beth Jacob, fundamentally define their vision of community. As one founder put it, "Beth Jacob is about community, community, community."

Beth Jacob incorporates the more informal and intimate aesthetics of the past few decades in its building, which is an important manifestation of its key commitments. One of the chairs of the building committee told me:

> It was very rewarding to me to have a role in creating a building that functions well for us as a community, but that reflects our values as well in its modesty and unpretentiousness. It is a building that has beauty, but there is nothing extra in the building. I'm always proud to have people enter the building and see that.

The sanctuary benches form a semi-circle which is, as the former committee chair explained, "designed to cause us to look at one another and to be involved with one another." The *bimah* is a mere two steps from the rest of the sanctuary. It is a warm room built from golden-tone wood. Natural light filters through three walls of windows and a high skylight. The room is comfortable and beautiful, but not grand or pretentious.

The synagogue has a small staff, including a much respected manager, as well as a bookkeeper and a few assistants. Wendy Schwartz, the director of education, runs holiday and family programming. She oversees a huge range of responsibilities. Her most important job is running a Shabbat enrichment program for about 120 children. The synagogue attaches its education to Shabbat morning worship to encourage and link the participation of families and children. Children and their parents all tend to go to synagogue on Shabbat morning. Other Twin Cities synagogues do not follow that pattern.

Beth Jacob educates children within the context of Shabbat observance. It does not do the work of either a supplementary school or a day school, and it must educate children who receive both kinds of educations. Training for b'nai mitzvah takes place primarily through weekly instruction with the rabbi and a skills-training Shabbat morning program; students occasionally supplement their study with tutors. Like Beth El, Beth Jacob recruits its own b'nai mitzvah to teach in the Shabbat program, but most often as assistants rather than as full teachers. The year after their b'nai mitzvah, students study in a special program preparing them for teaching. In any given year between 80 to 100 percent of the b'nai mitzvah continue their Talmud Torah studies. A smaller number have continued on in the teacher training program, but in the past many of those who did not teach instead came to synagogue nearly every Shabbat.

Unquestionably, Rabbi Morris Allen is at the center of the synagogue. Many spoke publicly about his importance to them at a recent synagogue anniversary celebration. In a meeting with the current adult b'nai mitzvah class of seven people—several converts among five women and two men—virtually all spoke of him as a model of the type of Jew they wanted to be.

One of the congregation's long-time members and leaders described Rabbi Allen's role:

> I see the rabbi as the lead shaper of the personality of the synagogue. It's his leadership that says which paths and ways of being are open and encouraged and closed off and frowned upon. He clearly values learning, fun, kids, and rigorous analysis of text, and [he] sets the tone. The rabbi is not solely responsible for the shul, and it would continue without him, but he is the driving force of the shul.

This view is echoed by Wendy Schwartz, who at the time had been at the synagogue three years. When I asked her how torah serves as Beth Jacob's "blueprint," she responded as a staff member:

> It's clear that the rabbi is the leading voice from my perspective. He is the visionary. [He] has a very clear set of principles and ideas and standards. He doesn't waver from them. Because he keeps pushing at it, I think this congregation is the way it is. It is a Shabbat congregation because he has made it so clear that that's important. Everything he does is around that, and focusing and pushing that. He has created a group of people who follow through on what he considers the most important values and principles. Now he is beginning to do that with kashrut. He follows through consistently. He is very strongly principled and sticks by that, and some of that is what has created Beth Jacob and the ritual nature of Beth Jacob. Other rabbis might have been flexible and been into the reality of where their congregants are. But he exudes his principles, and it attracts people who want that, and then people begin to try it and like it.

Another long-standing member, a man in his fifties, underlined to me that Beth Jacob could not be understood apart from the rabbi.

> To talk about the congregation and the success of the congregation without talking about the rabbi would be a mistake. If God forbid

anything ever happened to him, I would really be hard-pressed to know how the community would continue. He has the genuine outreach to people that somehow communicates, "You're really important to me," even if it's only a look in the eyes and a quick handshake as he is trying to cover as much territory as he can in the social hall. It's incredible, it's just incredible. He's personal, not stand-offish, and to balance it with an intellectual rigor so that it's not just warm fuzzy stuff, and he is this combination of social worker, community activist, and scholar all rolled into one.

Rabbi Allen teaches a weekly Talmud class in English, offers sessions on mitzvot and other subjects, teaches a weekly adult b'nai mitzvah class, prepares a weekly study sheet that usually includes sources from the Mishnah as well as the torah, prepares daily study for a *daf yomi* program (a page a day of Talmud), gives a weekly *d'var torah* and sermon, and has responsibility for all other rabbinic duties. In 1995, he led the congregation's first trip to Israel. Perhaps most remarkably, Rabbi Allen studies individually with each convert and each bar or bat mitzvah. Rather than providing a standardized curriculum for b'nai mitzvah, he shapes each child's preparations according to his or her Jewish education, background, ability, and interests. He believes that the personal relationship of rabbi and congregant, of teacher and student, is critical to the experience of Judaism.

As the shul's only rabbi, he has done much to define the ethos of Beth Jacob. The Ratner Center survey reports that 90 percent of Beth Jacob's respondents said that "liking the rabbi" was a "very important" or "somewhat important" reason for joining the synagogue, and 92 percent list "teacher" as the rabbi's ideal role. The many testimonies to Rabbi Allen's importance—the lives of the members and his focus on education—mesh well with the synagogue. But congregants also worry. They fear about the possibility of burnout on the part of the rabbi after ten years, because of his tremendous commitment to the synagogue and its members.

Beth Jacob does not employ a cantor and has no plans to do so in the future. A member organizes the torah readings; the ritual committee assigns cantors for the High Holidays; and the rabbi appears to randomly ask various members to lead different portions of the service on Shabbat. The synagogue's ritual committee chair, a member from the original Sons of Jacob congregation, assigns the ritual honors on Shabbat. The rabbi may tell him who needs or wants an honor, but he makes all other decisions. Few people were mentioned as consistently for his contribution to Beth Jacob as Sid Goldfarb. His quick offer of an *aliya* to any person who enters the sanctuary for the first time is often remembered by members years after they joined. He invites children up to the *bimah* to carry Torah crowns in the Torah procession, and distributes all other honors to the adults as well. He keeps a close eye on fair distribution.

Beth Jacob's founders have provided an important core of lay leadership over the past decade, to raise funds to build and expand the building and to make the synagogue viable. Congregants are proud of the fact that board members are regular Shabbat attenders and that participation, rather than wealth (of which there is very little at Beth Jacob), is an important criteria for participation.

Nevertheless, the professional staff feels some frustration that in this deeply committed and engaged shul, there is relatively little volunteer effort. The board is sometimes characterized as "passive." At the October 1995 board meeting, the rabbi chastised the board for not taking bolder initiatives and not trying new things. The professional staff has various explanations for this absence of widespread effort. There are many dual-career families in the synagogue and many families with young children. The rabbi has consistently noted that one of the critical features of Beth Jacob is its close association with the St. Paul day school. Over half of the children in the day school are associated with the synagogue. Rabbi Allen has repeatedly pointed to that relationship as very good for the school and the synagogue. But at the same time that means that parents' labor and dollars must be divided between school and synagogue, and the synagogue often comes up short.

Moreover, some of the newer members I interviewed commented that they found it difficult to participate and to have their suggestions heard. One person who joined within the past year told me, "I volunteered to be on two committees, but I never got called to participate in any of the meetings." His remarks would certainly surprise the beleaguered staff and leaders. But the comments might not surprise those founding members who are aware that the third generation of Beth Jacob's members, those who are the majority, are simply not well known to those who founded the synagogue. Unless newer members are extremely assertive about their interest in becoming involved, they are far less likely to be called or solicited than those who have been members for the past decade. In an interview on this subject of leadership and responsibility, Rabbi Allen wondered aloud if he should practice more "*tsimtsum*—contraction—so that expansion is possible." He was clearly self-reflexive about whether his strong leadership stood in the way of a more aggressive and active board. One of Beth Jacob's members, whose profession involves working with nonprofit organization boards, was asked to work on board development several years ago with the synagogue. He was struck by the fact that "the rabbi was only supportive of this process. He has done an excellent job of laying out 'this is what the board is for.' He doesn't dominate the board."

Beth Jacob, then, inverts the almost classic pattern of American Judaism. Its members are more likely to come to a Shabbat service than to a committee meeting. And it is possible that with the election of a new president in 1996, a board that continually adds newer members, and the synagogue's realization that it is moving into its second decade, Beth Jacob may be creating a more self-conscious vision for its future, not as a new synagogue but as an established one.

Organizational Life

As Conservative synagogues, Beth El and Beth Jacob share many features in common. Some members I interviewed are "uncomfortable" in Reform synagogues, reacting to the absence of Hebrew, the uncovered heads of men, and the extensive liturgical innovation. Over 60 percent of both synagogues' members surveyed in the Ratner Center survey agreed or agreed strongly with the statement, "I don't think I could be a Reform Jew." Between 70 and 87 percent agreed or agreed strongly with the statement, "I don't think I could be an Orthodox Jew."

Furthermore, Rabbi Allen told me that on a Shabbat in 1995 quite a few Beth El members attended his synagogue to celebrate the bat mitzvah of the granddaughter of one of their friends. The child's grandmother told him: "Rabbi, your synagogue reminds me so much of Beth El when we were young and starting out. It has that same sense of spirit and excitement." She clearly recalled the synagogue in the 1950s and early 1960s, when Beth El was becoming a major suburban shul.

What is perhaps more interesting, however, is how the two synagogues differ. They go about the business of creating Jewish community and religious life with some shared but many different goals. They envision different types of communities, and to some extent they serve different types of Jews. Judaism is not practiced or organized according to a single model. Beth El and Beth Jacob have remained vital because each has its own vision and mission. Further, they epitomize another basic organizational principle that change is essential. Each community must grapple with how to continue to grow and change.

Beth El and Beth Jacob reflect two contrasting foundations for creating a Conservative Jewish life. Beth El continues to draw in powerful ways on memory and historic traditions that have shaped the institution, to address new challenges. The synagogue increasingly understands its need to replace what neighborhood once made possible. The old neighborhoods that nurtured a powerful and unshakable sense of a shared and homogeneous Jewish community identity cannot be replicated. The anti-Semitism that persisted in Minneapolis through the 1960s finally lost its grip over community life, opening in turn many doors to Jews in business, education, and social clubs. As a result, Jews have become less dependent on the synagogue for their social lives and friends. The synagogue today focuses on transmission of memories, commitment, and shared experience. Thus, Beth El has defined itself as "the Jewish point of contact for family, for loss, school, community," and many other aspects of life with the "point of contact" being the necessary replacement for the Jewish neighborhoods, which used to serve as one of the strongest expressions of American Jewish culture for those aged forty-five to eighty.

New members join Beth El because they are attracted to understanding their Jewishness in multigenerational terms and because they understand Judaism's core to be its transmission to younger generations, which is central to the synagogue's vision of nurturing Jewish community and mutual support. A congregant in her late forties characterized her experience of the synagogue in relationship to ties of family and neighborhood. Married to a high school boyfriend who also grew up at Beth El, she told me,

> It's very nice because my husband's family and my family get along and we all sit together and that is very nice. It's four generations. When I grew up we felt the web of connectedness. You would look around and you were related to people in the choir. Your family all came from the same roots and you're celebrating your ties to the culture. And I think also having grown up on the North Side we knew everybody in shul. It still amazes me when I go to shul and look around and know very few people. There's a sense of sadness because you can't go back. There really was a web of connectedness and it was like an extended family. I think the web was there for my children when my children were young by virtue of geographic proximity. My family lived on the north side and that whole northside community knew each other. It seemed that they all went to Beth El. When people moved to St. Louis Park then some went to Beth El and some went to another shul, and we were geographically spread out too, and then we didn't have that generational connectedness to the same extent.

Several members I interviewed talked about both missing the synagogues of their own youths, and knowing that they would never share the multigenerational families' feeling of belonging. As one woman put it, "This isn't a place I grew up and I will always be an outsider. Where I grew up my synagogue was founded by my grandparents and great grandparents. I had ten cousins there. Even my dreams often take place in the halls of that synagogue." She hastened to add, however, "It won't be like that for my kids." Like many other members, she looked forward to the fact that her children would call Beth El "home" as so many multigenerational Beth El families do today.

That very sense of home is crucial to the memories that nourish Beth El as a Jewish community, where "continuity" and "family" were inevitably at the core of how most members described their Jewishness and the synagogue. I was struck by the fact that Beth El's members were far more likely to describe their synagogue as a "home" than a "community," the most common term used by Beth Jacob's members. A widow in her mid-eighties told me, "I call Beth El my second home because I spend a lot of time there. I've been in the choir for 14 years.

I go when I can go to committee meetings for the nursery school. I like listening to the young mommies. I'm active in Women's League. I come every Saturday morning and I feel very spiritual." A woman in her seventies explained, "All of our friends are from Beth El and our life revolved around it. I don't know any other way to live." Another woman in her seventies thought "friendship" might be a more apt description: "It's like a friendship in the good times and the bad. When there's a *simcha*, you're at the synagogue; unfortunately when you lose someone, you're at the synagogue. When there's a wedding, you're at the synagogue. It becomes a part of you. That's where you go. It's a friendship."

These sentiments did not come only from those who grew up and grew old in Beth El. New members also idealized Beth El as home. Others who told me that their children, but not they themselves, would see Beth El as a home reminded me of their immigrant ancestors who looked forward to their own alien status dying with them as their children became Americans. The evocation of home is a powerful source of identity and community that shapes the experience of being Jewish.

Women were far more likely to use the word "home" for Beth El than men, though age seemed to make a less significant difference. Men and women alike talked about the comfort and ease that they and their children found at Beth El. One woman, a longtime member, recalled that her children's friendship with Rabbi Abelson's children brought her family into the synagogue. She called Beth El's rabbis "warm, family-minded people who made all of us feel at home." With some important complexities to be discussed below, Beth El provides for its members and represents to them a Judaism that reflects and enforces the generative relations of neighborhood and family, relations that promise continuity. That continuity is represented as much by the memory of Rabbi Aronson, for many, as familiar music, prayer, and Shabbat observance. Perhaps it is no accident that congregants' great pleasure in Rabbi Kahn's leadership was expressed by the Yiddish word haimish, "homey." He made them feel at home, even as they admired his sermons, his innovations, and his ideas.

When Beth El's leadership addressed problems about its dues structure in 1995, leaders took the occasion to define the synagogue's vision as the replacement for neighborhood and as the source of support for changing forms of Jewish family. Beth Jacob, by contrast, draws on a different set of values, in part because it is merely a decade old. Its founders' vision was shaped by a powerful 1980s perspective on the importance of participation and equality. Jewish life was to be about community and access.

Although congregants do not self-consciously use the term, I have come to understand the synagogue as a "community of choice," in contrast to Beth El's central premise as a community built on "memory."[21] Neither foundation reflects nostalgia or backward glances. But they do rest on different visions of Jewish life.

One of Beth Jacob's founders, a man in his early forties, noted that "one of the strengths from the very beginning has been the cross-generational nature of Beth Jacob. Beth Jacob has had a history of pretty strong unlikely contact between people who are more often than not separated in other social settings." What is striking about these multiple generations is that many of them are not related to one another. Some older members are unmarried, some childless, and some alone. Similarly, a significant minority of the middle aged and young adults are also not in traditional family units. Some are single and some are gay; some live separated from their families geographically. Beth Jacob has a large proportion of converts whose religious practice does not tie them to immediate memories of family. The "strong connections" described by many members are therefore neither bonds of kinship nor bonds of neighborhood.

The ritual committee chair noted at a board meeting: "Members are not here because of their parents or grandparents. I meet people at shul who searched for several years before finding a synagogue. They made a judgment and joined. They are here by choice, and not by default, and the result is a wonderful group."

Beth Jacob models the power of a community of choice. It is embodied in self-conscious decisions about applying an articulate ideology, as well as in a consciously constructed community. That sense of choice is linked to a rabbinic leadership that focuses its congregants on mitzvot and increased observance. One congregant described the rabbi as "having a way of putting you in the middle of whatever he is talking about," by which she meant making her feel that Jewish history and observance is about her—as, I might add, the "choosing Jew" who assumes increasing Jewish commitments.

The founder who reflected on the importance of an intergenerational community told me, "Beth Jacob is the second or third tier after my family and some work relationships where I expect to find the most lasting and profound responsibilities. There will be people there whose living and dying will make a claim on me in a more than casual way. And it's different to the extent that I have chosen that place unlike my family."

Beth El, too, certainly has members who have chosen to join, have been unhappy elsewhere, and, surveying their possibilities, found a "warmth" and "friendliness" that was unmatched. But the ethos of this synagogue continues to inspire a strong relationship between memory, neighborhood, and community.

What I have called the "organizing principles" of synagogue life serve as what other scholars have called congregational "idioms," the metaphors, symbols, and images that create a unique congregational "culture." These two synagogues provide different approaches to Conservative Judaism, for each one has implications for the congregation's relationship to halakha, not in formal practice in the synagogue but in the way Judaism is communicated to their congregants. Each idiom plays on different meanings of the relationship between the

obligations of halakha and the choices made by these Jews to accept its requirements. Attention to idiom suggests that the synagogue is a significant site for
working out that all-important relationship.[22]

Beth El and Beth Jacob are not reducible to these two organizing principles
or idioms, of course. Nor is it appropriate to exaggerate their differences. They
do offer, however, important insights into each congregation.

Memory and choice are powerful poles in the experience of most Americans. As Jewish assimilation becomes increasingly possible in the United States,
Jews' decisions to maintain their identities are often explained in terms of
memory as continuity with the past and the choice to affirm a unique identity.
At the core of the postwar synagogue was memory, Americanization, and a child-
centered Judaism. Each of these terms has registered enormous shifts over the
past thirty years, and these two synagogues continue to respond to their challenges. Confronted now with dual-career families and a wide variety of family
forms, with limited time and high demands on family incomes, Beth El and Beth
Jacob must shape the demands and meanings of Conservative Judaism to the
real lives of their congregants.

The next section of the essay examines the types of events and processes
that ethnographers turn to in order to highlight key features of communities,
that make evident with special acuity how a group goes about being who and
what it is. The opportunity to compare two synagogues allows me to contrast
such key events in the lives of both synagogues.

Rabbis' Initiatives: "Celebrate Shabbat" and "The Ladder Of Kashrut"

During the High Holidays, both Rabbi Kahn and Rabbi Allen undertook an important initiative in their synagogue to encourage members to increase observance of a specific mitzvah. My interviews with a sample of each congregation
suggested that people heard, thought about, and, surprisingly, often responded
to these challenges to observe the religious commandment more fully. Each rabbi
followed the Yom Kippur sermon that announced the initiative with education,
programming, and written materials that kept the issue before the congregants.
Both Rabbi Kahn and Rabbi Allen showed their religious and organizational
leadership in areas that asked their congregants to change, and, in Rabbi Kahn's
case, to relinquish the long-standing institution of late Friday night services.

These initiatives were particularly interesting because they linked the synagogue as a religious institution to the private lives of members. Beth El's "Celebrate Shabbat" focused on the family, and Beth Jacob's "Chew by Choice" on
the individual and then on the household and family.

"Chew by Choice"

Rabbi Allen once referred to Kol Nidre (the service on the eve of Yom Kippur) as Beth Jacob's real "annual meeting." It is the occasion when the largest number of Beth Jacob's members gather to fill its expanded sanctuary. From the rabbi's point of view, it is the moment to impart his most important message of the year.

How to define a significant sermon topic was clearly on Rabbi Allen's mind when he chose to begin his Kol Nidre address in the voice of a doubting congregant who asks, "Of all the things to speak about tonight, why, Rabbi are you choosing to speak to me about food?" The skeptical voices continue to reflect not only on his discussion of food on a fast day, but on the "real big issues out there: Serbs and the Croats, Arabs and Jews, Jewish continuity." The rabbi answered these voices by recapitulating the messages of his sermons on Rosh Hashanah:

> The case for awe is central to our lives. The need to hear the voices of
> women and men within the narratives of our tradition is necessary if we
> truly believe that the tradition is vibrant and vital, ever able to include
> those who seriously want to be included as members of a covenantal
> people, willing to hear the voice of a commanding God. And yes, food is
> part of that story.

Each congregant found on his or her seat that evening a pink card shaped exactly like a pledge card with fold-down tabs, a model created because of the prohibition of writing on the holidays. The card included an advertisement for the new Jerusalem McDonald's restaurant, with the thick black symbol of negation superimposed over it. It was the arrival of McDonald's in Jerusalem that served Rabbi Allen as a segue into his discussion:

> On the 3000th year of Jerusalem, is our legacy to the next generation of
> Jews a cheeseburger in Jerusalem, only steps from where the *kohanim*
> once reminded the Jews, *lo t'vashel g'di b'chalev imo*—don't boil a kid in
> his mother's milk? There is something wrong with us as a people when
> that incongruity is not repulsive.

Rabbi Allen was careful not to paint a picture of gloom about Jewish life at the synagogue and in the community, but he added:

> The process of a holistic approach to Jewish life which defines us as an
> *am kadosh* [holy nation] is quickly disappearing. Without a sense of
> distinctiveness about who we are and what we are all about, all the
> buildings and all the programs and all the love and wonder and awe we
> generate here in the shul will one day simply disappear. . . . The act of

eating can become a means for holiness, for sanctifying the world in which we live. . . .

Each of us—that means me, too—can move one step further up the rung of holiness by increasing our level of kashrut. That is all we need to do tonight—start the process in motion. OK, before you tune me out and say, "No way—I'm willing to hear about great causes, to give to make the shul vibrant, but I'm not willing to give up my pepperoni pizza," hear me out. While all the world's problems will not be solved by your increased observance of kashrut, you at least can become increasingly sensitized to what it means to be a feeling person, a passionate Jew, and a member of a covenantal people extending back through history. And that maybe it's not liberalism or conservatism we're looking to for answers, but Judaism which holds the keys.

Paraphrasing Rabbi Daniel Gordis, he characterized the dietary laws as "rungs on the ladder of holiness," leading to a "life of pure thought and deed, characteristic of the nature of God." He asserted the importance of kashrut because of its "constancy," as an opportunity to make Judaism "a regular part of our life. . . . These brief moments when we have to stop and think about what we are doing to create connections to God, to the Jewish people, create brief but important moments when it becomes likely that we may experience a sense of God's presence."

Rabbi Allen asked his congregants to take their pink cards home, to think seriously about their next step, and to discuss it with family members and partners. The cleverly designed pledge card provided a place for a signature and nine fold-down tabs that represented the "ladder of kashrut." The lowest rung, "No pork," led up to other prohibited foods, followed by separation of milk and meat, the transformation to a kosher home, and finally eating "only hechshered products outside of the home."

This sermon initiated a year of regular programming about kashrut. Rabbi Allen convened two discussions to allow members to talk about keeping kosher, the conflicts it might create with family members, and their concerns or desire for information. One discussion was sparsely attended, and the other was canceled because of severe weather. A congregant taught a cooking class about vegetarianism and kashrut. Every household at Beth Jacob received a kashrut package that included *A Guide to the Jewish Dietary Laws*, by Rabbi Samuel Dresner and Rabbi Seymour Siegel, on the philosophy and methods of kashrut. The package contained a second kashrut pledge card urging members again to "take seriously the climb toward greater holiness and observance." Finally, Rabbi Allen was at his whimsical best in printing the title of the kashrut campaign on a refrigerator magnet: "Chew by Choice."

"Chew by Choice" reveals much about how Beth Jacob goes about the business of being a synagogue. Rabbi Allen stands firmly at the center of this process. He chose the theme not just for his sermon but as an important focus for the year. In the letter that accompanied the packet, Rabbi Allen reiterated what he had said at Yom Kippur:

> Not every one of us can daven everyday or even every Shabbat. But the reality is that each of us eats daily. Even when we remind ourselves of God's presence by knowing which drawer or which food items go together, we bring the Divine presence into this world. In an increasingly homogenized world, uniqueness is hard to come by. For us, uniqueness is found on our kitchen table. It was Heschel who said that in doing the finite we can perceive the infinite. In eating a slice of bread, we can discover God.

He closed his letter with an exhortation: "Make your move, Chew by Choice."

Rabbi Allen is well aware that his focus on mitzvot is hardly the daily fare of most of his rabbinical colleagues in the Conservative movement. A colleague told him: "I never could have gotten away with giving a sermon like that. My congregants would have thought that I was on another planet." But Rabbi Allen's approach to what he calls "my rabbinate" is such that he believed he would have continued to seek a congregation in which the topic was appropriate, had Beth Jacob not been receptive. "Chew by Choice" represents two of his fundamental perspectives about the life of a synagogue: it places Jewish values at the center of shul life, and it allows his congregants to move at their own pace in increasing their Jewish observance.

Long before Rabbi Allen wrote the first paragraph of his sermon in the voice of the doubting congregant, he had struggled with the relative balance of world and Jewish events and the daily nature of kashrut. He once thought that his sermons should be the rabbinical version of the politically progressive *I.F. Stone Weekly*. But he came eventually to understand the purpose of his sermons quite differently:

> On one hand, this year it's hard not to want to speak about Bosnia and racism, the obvious racism that society still has and that we want to believe is the aberration. And yet there's a part of me that says, "That's the easy sermon to give." That used to be how I thought of my rabbinate. People can get better political analysis than I can offer and can read the *New York Times* as effectively as I do. My job is to understand the implications of what is taking place and the larger implications of the religious life of a person. My personal transformation came about when a professor of mine in class said, "You know, I used to think that I was supposed to try to present Judaism in its multifaceted dimensions. Then I realized that if people want a concert they're going to the Brooklyn Conservatory of Music. If they want to hear an analysis of an event they

can go to the New School for Social Research more easily. What I can do is what I know." That's how I look at *yontef.*

Rabbi Allen envisions a synagogue that, like his sermons, can do only some things and not all things. He explained that Beth Jacob never set out to provide "a whole range of things that I'm not sure that shuls need to be providing." Thus, the synagogue never had a sisterhood or a men's club. Rabbi Allen explained further:

> People clearly know that it's not going to be a shul that is just another kind of social service agency in the Jewish community. It is clearly setting out a program that not everyone is going to be or remain attracted to it. By and large people know that what we stand for is clearly commitment to Jewish learning, a developing commitment to religious sensitivity and sensibility, and an openness to the world that is both a challenge to it and provides us an opportunity. The eclectic nature of our synagogue population is amazing. Here is a guy who had a fight with Lubavitch and is really *frum,* sitting in the same shul with people who at the ritual committee he tells, "Your lifestyle is totally against torah," and they don't care.

Rabbi Allen asserted that the synagogue must respond to "an entire human being's package," and that the shul has never defined "being a Jew as simply davening from the *omud* on Shabbos morning." Nevertheless, at the end of the twentieth century, he argues vigorously that facing diminishing resources and people's busy lives, American synagogues will have to define seriously "the central core of synagogue life." Beth Jacob might need "to do a little better at bringing people together," but its "core programs" will, it appears, remain tied to mitzvot.

These core activities involve congregants in opportunities to grow as Jews. In reflecting on "Chew by Choice," Rabbi Allen believed it would afford congregants the opportunities to see even small steps as profound ones:

> Kashrut is one of those things that, given the highly individualistic world that we live in, and even though we give lots of credit to the community, a lot of people don't study and don't come to shul. Everyone eats. I think for many people it is the crucial element of how they define themselves as human beings and as Jews. Kashrut is one of those areas that is a challenge. It clearly demands some sort of observance of boundaries and creating separation from the world. If separation is defined as *kedusha* [holiness], that is what's supposed to happen. If by elevating the decision-making process around food, we invite people to see themselves as engaged in this enterprise called Judaism. People need to learn that this is theirs. Kashrut cannot simply be defined by the

labels on a product. I really believe that if someone gives up pork products they have entered into the discussion. If you can get people to make a conscious stance that the symbol of kashrut is "no pig," if you can get them to that point, then suddenly they feel connected to something that certainly is a central, defining element of Judaism classically. I don't think everyone is going to read torah, study torah, or be a great *shaliach tsibur* [leader of services], but we need to demonstrate that Judaism is part of your everyday consciousness and I think the easiest way to do it is kashrut.

Through the kashrut campaign, Rabbi Allen put his congregants "in the middle of what he was talking about," as a congregant put it. He did not ask his congregation of overwhelmingly young families to *kasher* their homes for the sake of their children, or for that matter for the sake of the memories of their families. He sidestepped the hygienic and sociological explanations that one man remembered from his own Pennsylvania childhood in the early 1950s. Rather, Rabbi Allen asked his congregants to put themselves into a conversation with "classical Judaism," by understanding how to make ordinary life holy and set apart.

Although "Chew by Choice" was "rabbi driven," it did affect many congregants. Months following the sermon, many people brought up the issue with me and talked about it in light of not only the religious requirement but also of the rabbi's decision to focus on kashrut.

From Rabbi Allen's point of view the response was small. About 50 members returned the pledge cards from the synagogue's 325 households, though it was unclear if congregants were supposed to literally mail in the card. He recalled that two people folded down the tab at the "ladder's" first rung, "No pork." The remainder moved up from some level of commitment to a greater level, for example from not eating milk and meat together to keeping a kosher home, or from keeping a kosher home to observing kashrut outside of the home. In addition, Rabbi Allen had offered to assist families with the cost of creating a kosher kitchen from the synagogue's Avi Chai grant, and two households requested that support.

Pledge cards were not the only response. Congregants who were disappointed and even angered by the sermon called the rabbi directly: some felt judged and found wanting about something they believed did not matter. They told the rabbi, "How can you be concerned with something so trivial?" Another said, "Don't you know, Rabbi, that what is in the torah related to kashrut is not what matters?" One congregant who was raised as a committed Reform Jew expressed her feelings on the topic:

> This past year I've given a lot of thought moving in the direction that the rabbi wants congregants to move. I've given a lot of thought to his Kol Nidre sermon. I was angry wondering, "Is this going to become an

expectation?" Am I going to feel that I'm not meeting the expectation of a good congregant and a good Jew? How can I participate comfortably with it?

Unquestionably, the topic might have alienated some congregants. But the rabbi also heard from appreciative congregants. One wrote to him:

> I never expected, at least quite the way it occurred, to be so moved by your words as I was this Yom Kippur. I thought how easy it was to please people at other synagogues with a simple sermon or a cantor's beautiful voice, and how you chose so deliberately to do the opposite by asking more of us, by asking us to observe the laws. People respect you because you made a statement and you weren't going to ignore it.

And many congregants responded quite simply by thinking about kashrut. For example, a member in his late thirties told me:

> I'm exactly one of these people who is very comfortable with where I am in terms of what I do, what I eat, what I don't eat, what I do in my home and outside my home, but I haven't looked at it for a long time, and I haven't been challenged to think about whether there is another higher level of observance that I might be attracted to if I were pushed a little bit. There was a challenge there.

A newly married couple in their thirties spoke to me about the great transformation each of them experienced at Beth Jacob, where they met one another. The husband came to Beth Jacob after dropping out of Orthodox Judaism, to which he had converted. His wife joined from a local Reform synagogue that was not offering her what she wanted. The husband, whose paternal grandfather was a rabbi, explained:

> Since I joined Beth Jacob I keep a kosher home and I try to think of keeping more commandments. One of the things I like also about the Conservative approach is the notion of the ladder of mitzvot. . . . You can strive for an ideal, but you're not going to get there overnight. You take one step for now and think about the next step later.

His wife echoed those sentiments by asserting that too many rules make her want to rebel. "Tell me all the rules and I'll say 'no.' If I feel that if I have room to do what I want, I'll go further as long as I have the space to do what I want to do." They have found that the right to choose observance has been more effective in their lives. Their substantial commitment to observe Judaism as they do today was not something either of them would have assumed a decade before.

Another member, a man in his early fifties who joined Beth Jacob about five years ago, is a Shabbat morning regular, does not yet keep kosher, but understands himself to be involved in a process, standing on a lower rung of the ladder. That climb was marked for him by a new understanding of the torah service offered by Rabbi Allen one Shabbat. He explained,

> Not long after that I took a torah reading class and relearned the trop (the musical notes for chanting) that at that point I had not used for thirty-five years. And I have since read torah in shul many times. It also enhanced my desire to do other kinds of things . . . to learn the haftarah trop . . . to be a *shaliach tsibur*. I've increasingly been making a mental commitment to a resumption of kashrut (but that's all it is). That began when I began reading torah, because the more I read torah the greater became the incongruity between what I was doing on the *bimah* and what I was doing in my personal life.

I asked him if "Chew by Choice" affected his practice.

> It has begun to affect my practice anyway. . . . We're only talking about it. We are redesigning our kitchen and we are talking about doing it so that it can easily serve as a kosher kitchen. It has begun to affect my eating patterns. There are certain things that I just don't eat anymore. It's not because I willfully cut them out, but because the incongruity makes me uncomfortable.

His wife has not yet made the commitment, but they are actively discussing it. He observes that he now has an understanding of kashrut entirely different from the one with which he was raised:

> For the last few days I've been reading the book that the rabbi sent us on kashrut. I grew up in a strictly kosher home. . . . I very clearly understood kashrut as I was growing up in the context of identity, but never in all those years . . . did I understand kashrut as . . . the concept of hallowing God and hallowing one's relationship to God through sanctifying even my most mundane activities. Why is that a new concept for me? What did that generation think it was accomplishing, that kashrut would continue to be passed on when the single richest justification was completely omitted from our educations formally and informally? It stunned me to read this thing. I wonder how I would have felt giving up kashrut as a young adult had I seen it in this light.

Another couple in their forties, who come monthly to the synagogue, had opposite responses to the rabbi's sermon. The husband was interested, his wife adamantly opposed. The separation that the rabbi explained as *kedusha* she saw as an attack on the most democratic principles of American society. She found the practice repugnant: "The purpose of these laws is to separate Jews from others, to make it difficult for us to eat with them. I could never practice something that is such a basic attack on the pluralism of American society, which is so thoroughly under attack at this moment." Her husband understood her perspective, but he was, after the Jewish New Year, planning to experiment by giving up pork.

Beth Jacob congregants are unusually committed to the practice of the Jewish dietary laws. As noted above, 43 percent of Beth Jacob's congregants separate milk and meat dishes and 27 percent refrain from eating meat in nonkosher restaurants. About 50 percent of both Beth El and Beth Jacob's congregants recalled that when they were adolescents their parents had separate dishes. Beth Jacob congregants have decreased their observance of kashrut far less precipitously than most Conservative Jews, but even their falling numbers suggest that observance of halakha is hardly the norm of Conservative Jewish life.

These numbers do not indicate, as they are not intended to indicate, how gradual this process has been. No one that I interviewed, including the rabbi, had observed kashrut continuously throughout his or her life. Nor did Beth Jacob's congregants consider their observance of kashrut as a single, unchanging package of decisions, activities, and attitudes. People used words like "experiment" or "try" as they described their relationship to kashrut.

What was equally interesting was the degree to which a Kol Nidre sermon topic affected the congregants to whom I spoke, including ones who do not attend Beth Jacob regularly. One congregant in his thirties told me, "I will never keep kosher," but the rabbi appears to have gotten him to consider other Jewish practices that he once rejected as thoroughly.

Eight months after the sermon, Rabbi Allen told me that he never judges his effectiveness over a single year, because that is far too short a period for gauging change. Rather, he is committed to continue to link his focus on kashrut, Shabbat observance, and study so that they will reinforce one another. Two incidents of the year came to mind as we discussed "Chew by Choice." Rabbi Allen was recently at a celebration for a congregant's promotion. One of the gifts the guest of honor received was a gift certificate to a restaurant whose symbol is a a a lobster. The congregant was obviously embarrassed, and during the party told Rabbi Allen, "A year ago I would never have imagined feeling embarrassed about this gift." Another congregant had lunch with the rabbi and told him as he ordered his turkey on a bagel sandwich, "I don't have it with cheese any longer." Rabbi Allen noted, "That was true, by the way. He used to always order cheese on his meat sandwiches when we had lunch together."

Clearly the congregant had folded down that tab on the ladder of kashrut, even if he hadn't sent it back in. Rabbi Allen mused that some might see these examples as a complete "trivialization of kashrut," whereas others might see it as "victory." For him they were important first steps, and he planned to keep the issue before the congregation.

Wendy Schwartz, the synagogue's education director, explained that what made Rabbi Allen particularly effective was his ability to keep issues alive for the congregation. She told me, for example, that family education is currently one of the reigning ideas in Jewish education, but that Rabbi Allen interprets its meaning somewhat differently:

> He wants to give families the materials and knowledge to do things in their homes and not in the synagogue, where it becomes a substitute for the home. Some synagogues, like the public schools, are becoming the sole educators, taking over what families do. He is focusing on not taking that away. That's all the packets we're always sending about how to do Shabbat in your home, tapes for home. The Passover issue of the bulletin is always about how to do this and that. Call the rabbi. He will do it for you; he will show you how.

Rabbi Allen's educational model allowed him to teach and offer materials for home use, emphasizing mitzvot that could not be compartmentalized into the shul.

Beth Jacob was clearly a congregation with unusual expectations for the practice of Judaism. Individuals were asked by their rabbi to commit themselves to self-consciously Jewish practice, even as they practiced in different ways and at different rungs on the ladder of observance. Paradoxically, by selecting a mitzvah that another rabbi commented would sound like outer space to his congregants, Rabbi Allen in fact moved toward the middle rather than to the extreme of expectations. He asked his members to choose what was in some ways most accessible, to choose some aspect of a Jewish practice that drew a boundary, that included them in a "Jewish conversation." He told them that they lived in a culture and time that created a crushing homogeneity and that kashrut was a source of both holiness and cultural uniqueness. In sum, the kashrut campaign nicely pointed up the complexity of the idiom of choice at Beth Jacob. While members chose to create an egalitarian synagogue, "choice" on the ladder of mitzvot has a rather different meaning. Congregants do describe choosing to be commanded, and Rabbi Allen places the sense of obligation at the center of his vision, acknowledging that people come to that obligation in different ways and at different paces. Choice, that is, exists in tension with commandment in the life of the synagogue.

"Celebrate Shabbat"

Yom Kippur, for the nearly fourteen hundred households of Beth El, is an organizational wonder. Early and late services, as well as the more traditional "Hebraic" service, a "contemporary service," and a family service accommodate thousands of people, as the choir, rabbi, and cantors re-create powerful religious experiences—sometimes three times. The rabbi delivers his sermon to each service, and by the holiday's end the vast majority of the congregation has shared one of the few events they ever experience in common.

Rabbi Kahn took full advantage of this opportunity to announce a change that was by turns small and dramatic. During the months preceding the holiday, the rabbi and the rest of the staff had begun rethinking the weekly Friday night services and their long history. During the fifties, sixties, and early seventies, Friday night services were the centerpiece of Beth El's week. One congregant in her sixties remembered hiring a babysitter each week so she and her husband could attend. They often heard lively speakers, and the rabbi talked about the pressing issues of the day. Following the socializing after the service, they typically went to the home of a neighborhood congregant and continued the conversation for several more hours. The synagogue was the center of their religious and social lives.

Attendance at Friday night services began to dwindle in the eighties, and by the nineties it was quite small. Cantor Newman remembered services of 200 to 250 people in the early eighties on Friday night. By the early nineties, unless there was a special event, there would be twenty people for a late Friday night service, usually only older congregants.

Rabbi Kahn and his staff decided to confront this change and use it as the occasion to encourage families to celebrate Shabbat in their homes. Though 57 percent of congregants surveyed in the Ratner Center survey said that their household usually lights Shabbat candles (in contrast to 82 percent of their families when they were eleven or twelve years of age), the rabbi and cantor believed that a smaller percentage of congregants currently observed Shabbat regularly in their homes on Friday night over a shared meal. They were anxious to help Beth El's members, particularly those with young children, to enhance their home observance. Their strategy was to hold late Friday night services only once a month and to offer educational opportunities throughout the year for congregants to learn the hows and whys of observance.

Their summer work involved conversations with many groups in the synagogue about these changes, starting with those who most regularly attended Friday night services. The staff held discussions with the board officers, the executive committee, the Women's League, which made the Oneg Shabbat following services, and finally the board approved the change.[23] The rabbi, cantor, lay people, and other staff had done a great deal of work prior to this sermon to reach a consensus about the need for change regarding Friday nights at Beth El, and how to use it as an opportunity for "new programming." On Yom Kippur congregants found a bright pink sheet with the schedule of services for 1995–96, and an announcement of the three workshop/dinners "where we'll experience together the beauty of 'Celebrating Shabbat'":

We'll discover how to bring Shabbat into your home if you've never done so before, or how to enhance the rituals you are already practicing today. We'll provide suggestions for helping families learn how to fit Shabbat into their hectic lifestyles. We'll experience how celebrating Shabbat can make the family more cohesive and provide the welcome respite from the busy work week.

These same themes were prominent in Rabbi Kahn's much appreciated and discussed sermon. Rabbi Kahn began not by discussing Shabbat, but by referring to the Conservative movement's position papers on "various aspects of sexuality." He read a single sentence from the report that he said "struck me as very insightful": "Overzealous commitment to work does have a deleterious effect on one's sexual and family relationships." He said the sentence was "almost an understatement, because I believe overzealous commitment to work is the number one danger we face as a community":

> Look at our American Jewish community. When our parents, grandparents, or great-grandparents came to America, they had two goals. One was to become an American. To be accepted not as an immigrant, or as a Jew, but to be considered an American. The other goal was to make a lot of money. Given those goals, American Jews may be the most successful Jewish community ever, for those goals have been achieved probably way beyond those immigrants' wildest dreams.
>
> But what has happened in the meantime? In the meantime, we've become *kotzer ruach*. We are "short on spirit," and to be honest, our Yiddishkeit, our Jewishness, has, in too many cases, become almost nonexistent.

Rabbi Kahn then cast himself in the role of a "late night infomercial" salesman offering a piece of exercise equipment. His product was "Celebrate Shabbat," which "can change your life." He warned his congregants that a recent Federation survey showed that only 26 percent of Twin Cities Jewish families celebrate Shabbat, "just doing something special like lighting candles, not [even] fully observing." Then Rabbi Kahn asked his congregation to close their eyes and to "picture a Shabbat dinner, maybe even a particular Shabbat dinner in your memory, maybe with family at the table." Along with the choir, the cantor hummed the melody "Sabbath Prayer" from *Fiddler on the Roof*.

Rabbi Kahn wondered if the song led people to remember Tevye and his family around the Shabbat table:

> That image bothers me. . . . For Tevye and his family, Shabbat was an escape from poverty, the hard work and the dirt of the *shtetl*. On Friday night, Jews in Anatevka felt like they had been catapulted into a whole new world, different from the world they experienced during the week. So for us, when we celebrate our Minneapolis or suburban Shabbat, we must catapult ourselves into a whole new world, different from the world

we experienced during the week. Our Shabbat must emphasize relaxation, self-reflection. It must emphasize family; it must serve as a break
from busy-ness, technology, consumerism, and modernity.

Then Rabbi Kahn delivered the most memorable lines of his sermon:

I have found that one of the biggest barriers to celebrating Shabbat is
what I call the "*bubbe* syndrome." Everyone feels that the Shabbat they
make must be just like bubbe's (Grandmother's) was. With homemade
challah, chopped liver, chicken soup, kugel, everything. But this image
of the traditional meal, while wonderful, represents further enslavement
for the person who literally has to slave away to prepare it. So I say, "Buy
frozen." Or make pasta. We need Shabbat not for its potential fat
content, but because it allows us to relax and to be with family. Let me
share with you how Camille, Avinoam, and I have celebrated an
occasional Shabbat. Every once in a while, maybe once or twice a year,
we have a week where we are just swamped, but by the end of the week,
we are in desperate need of Shabbat. Yet neither of us has the energy to
make it. On those occasions we have gone to Green Mill, and picked up
a pizza, and made Shabbat over wine and pizza. Why not? We didn't
need the chicken or the kugel. We needed Shabbat.

At these words, a large number of the normally staid congregants of Beth
El broke into applause on this solemn occasion. Rabbi Kahn then described the
other barrier he sees that keeps people from celebrating Shabbat—the "all or
nothing" attitude in regard to the laws of Shabbat.

Today I have purposefully spoken only about Friday nights, and I have
purposely used the word celebrate, not observe Shabbat. I do not want
people to get hung up on questions like: Does that mean I can't work?
Do I have to go to the synagogue? Do I have to say all the blessings?
    I feel very strongly that if a family or an individual intentionally
sets aside time on Friday evening to give attention to those things which
are important to us, and which our spirits crave, those things that during
the week we neglect, then that is the beginning of Shabbat. And so
tonight I am not just talking about Shabbat. I'm also introducing
Shabbat as our programming theme for the year. Our staff and hard-
working members of the congregation have put together programs this
year which will enable you, the entire congregation, to taste and
celebrate Shabbat here at Beth El. . . . I look at all of you now. It's
amazing that you are here. It is a work day today, as you know. Yet you
have chosen to be in the synagogue with your family, because you also
know that your spirit, your soul, your religion, your people, your
conscience would not allow you to be at work today. Yom Kippur is
known as the Shabbat of Shabbatot. Make the very important decision
you have made today a weekly decision. "Celebrate Shabbat."

Rabbi Kahn's decision to emphasize the "celebration" of Shabbat marked his own evolution as a congregational rabbi, as he explained to me later:

When I came out of rabbinical school I thought of Judaism having four pillars: Jews have to come to shul a lot and pray. Jews have to keep kosher. Jews have to celebrate Shabbat. I used to say, "observe Shabbat," but that's changed. Jews have to do *gemilut hasadim*. So when I came here that was my goal, to convince all Jews to do that. That's changed because I have encountered so many people who don't do that. I don't want to try to force them to change. I definitely have recognized that being Jewish means having very strong ties to a Jewish heritage, being a good person, having the sense that when you do something good it's because you are Jewish. I am amazed [that] when I go to a *shiva* minyan here, there are 100–200 people in the house. People have a sense of it as an obligation. That's how they express their Jewishness. I don't feel I need to tell people that in order to be Jewish you have to do this and this. They really do feel Jewish and they are transmitting a tradition to their children. There are a ton of people here who light candles and have a Friday night dinner. I started seeing that observing Shabbat doesn't only mean this—it can also mean that. That's how I'm changing in my views. I never thought that would happen. I always thought that my colleagues would do that, but not me. I think I'm slowly, slowly, slowly saying not only is that not the answer for everyone, it's almost an impossible task; so why make yourself do that? I haven't given up on it on some level—which is the "Celebrate Shabbat" Program. I don't have a goal for the entire synagogue. I want people to feel more identified and I want people to be more observant, but I'm not willing to look upon people negatively who aren't willing to. I also think that there are a lot of people who just need to be made aware of the beautiful things of Judaism because they don't really know that they are available.

Rabbi Kahn's transformation from a rabbinical student to congregational rabbi was powerfully expressed in his differentiation between the "observance" and "celebration" of Shabbat. His goal was to maximize his congregants' experience of Shabbat by focusing on their ability to observe it more selectively—that is, to "celebrate" it.

Both Shabbat initiatives—the change in Beth El's Shabbat rhythm from "late" to "early" Friday night services, and Shabbat as a programming theme—were bold moves. Congregants were feeling vulnerable after the loss of their senior rabbi, but Rabbi Kahn quickly made the transition from a young associate to a solo senior rabbi. The New Year services were a testing ground for him.

The responses seemed to be unqualified enthusiasm and excitement. Beth El congregants appeared to have fallen in love with their rabbi again. Rabbi Kahn created a small committee of congregants to provide ongoing feedback about services and to offer suggestions about scholars-in-residence and other guests for his solo year. Congregants seemed especially pleased with the message of the sermons, which had involved both "theology" and "action." Others found them to be "inviting, telling us the things we can do, not should do." The rabbi and cantor had also added a new, more participatory service, involving more study and less praying, and the response to that, too, was enthusiastic. No one heard any complaints.

Beth El had signs of "Celebrate Shabbat" throughout the building. The five-person volunteer committee put many of the rabbi's ideas into place. They came up with the title, discussed the programs, and developed a creative format for materials for members to use at home. And they designed a logo of the Shabbat symbols encircled with the words "Celebrate Shabbat," "Beth El," and "5756," the Hebrew year. The logo appeared on a button that the rabbi wore to every committee meeting and event. Flyers were sent out announcing the how-to workshops. And a beautiful large banner with the logo was hung in the social hall.

Programming was at the heart of "Celebrate Shabbat," and the staff had tailored the new plans to Beth El's constituencies. The choir sang at the monthly late Friday night services. The choir also performed at monthly services at a large Jewish senior facility in the community. Some Shabbat dinners and services were directed to particular groups—singles, preschool and religious school families, college-age youths and their families, the Women's League. The rabbi, his committee, and staff were particularly interested in introducing younger congregant families to this observance. The synagogue's preschool had Shabbat dinners for their children and families in addition to the "Celebrate Shabbat" events, because these young families were seen as a group who needed this information and support. There was also an "Informal Shabbat" that encouraged people to dress casually and included a dinner and Israeli dancing. "Artsy Shabbat" was a weeknight crafts program designed to allow people to create beautiful "heirloom" objects for Shabbat. Its planners were startled when it attracted all ages, not only families with young children. It was so popular that it was held again in the spring.

The core programs of the initiative, to which the entire congregation was invited, were three Shabbat workshop/congregational dinners that followed an early evening (5:45) service in December, February, and April. The programs promised to help congregants learn about making Shabbat in the nineties' home and progressed from the most basic information to one focused on "Shabbat insights and enhancements."

The first Shabbat program had a solid showing, with 120 people attending, 20 from the family of the bar mitzvah. Following the event the Beth El newsletter carried a letter from a congregant commending the event as the most intergenerational he had attended.

The second program in February attracted almost two hundred congregants of all ages. The chapel was completely full for the 5:45 service, and most stayed for the program and dinner that followed. The social hall was divided into two halves. One half of the room was set for the dinner. Placecards had table numbers with assigned seats in an attempt to connect members to others they might not know. There were families with young children and grandparents. One *havurah* of newly marrieds came as a group and sat together. Some seniors were seated with those of other generations.

The other half of the social hall was used twice during the evening for teaching. Rabbi Kahn devoted the learning session to the blessings, asking congregants questions and answering any they had. Food was available; the vast majority of the congregants appeared to know the appropriate blessings, but they had many questions about their meaning and the meaning of the Shabbat symbols. "Why do we pull the light toward us? Why do we use two loaves?" The rabbi instructed congregants in how to bless their children, and asked children to say something special to their parents. The blessings were exchanged with very young children as well as adult children. Sometimes families were seated together, and other young adults walked sheepishly across the room to receive their blessings. The rabbi was quite successful in getting people to participate. The questions and answers were not perfunctory, and people were actively engaged for more than a half hour.

When Rabbi Kahn discussed lighting candles, he was careful to state that different families practice different customs with regard to the time that candles are lit. Rabbi Kahn described his mother's custom of lighting candles when the family was gathered. He did not describe his own halakhic observance, in which candles are lit before sundown. He left room for families to "celebrate" Shabbat, even if they did so outside halakhic requirements.

The dinner tables were brightly decorated and set up for a Chinese dinner with chopsticks and fortune cookies. One of the event's planners explained that the committee wanted the event to be "fun," "to show Shabbat can be different, to surprise people." Each table had several recipe boxes filled with materials to create Shabbat at home, put together by a committee of congregants and staff "to serve as a one-stop resource to make Shabbat accessible for today's busy families."

The materials on the index cards were divided into several categories. "Preparations" offered suggestions about what was needed for the table, how to ensure fire safety with candles, and for making Shabbat special. The "Blessings" section provided all the required blessings and explained them. "Meals" suggested and provided an array of simple and complex meals, including suggestions for purchasing cold foods and ordering Shabbat dinners from the Jewish Community Center. Recipe cards were also included. There were two different "Study" sections, one with a weekly summary of the *parsha* and the other with suggestions for reading. The "Crafts" section was directed to families with young children and included songs, a tape, and the United Synagogue songster. Participants received boxes at the first dinner and continued to add cards and other resources at subsequent events. The synagogue gave away 140 of these boxes. Others asked to purchase them as gifts for family and for a bar mitzvah. Nearly two hundred households received the boxes.

At my table men and women in their thirties and late forties were in families in which, with one exception, both spouses worked. They talked about the business of their lives and their anxieties about money. One man worried about his sixty-hour-a-week job not producing enough to allow him to send his preschooler to the Minneapolis Jewish Day School. Another man at the table retorted, "I wish I worked only sixty hours a week." These concerns were mixed in conversation with concerns about Patrick Buchanan's power as a presidential candidate and where to camp for family vacations in northern Minnesota. The people at the table seemed to be just those whom Rabbi Kahn had in mind when he described Shabbat as a respite from his congregants' busy lives.

Participants were asked to bring their dessert back to the other side of the social hall for a second session. By contrast with the near universal knowledge of the Shabbat blessings, the Grace after the Meal seemed to be alien to more than half the people in the room. The remainder of the evening was devoted to a game invented by the rabbi, "Jewpardy." The host, in this case Rabbi Kahn, gave an answer from one of several categories chosen by the contestant, who must answer in the form of a question. Beth El contestants had several categories to select from: "Shabbat Table," "Laws and Customs," "Kugel and Knishes," "Hamantashen and Grogers" (Purim was upcoming), and "Our Beth El." Many of the questions reinforced information given earlier in the evening. The teams were usually intergenerational and the crowd was enthusiastic, with much applause, hooting, and excitement. The rabbi was funny, teasing people from time to time, and was warm and congratulatory with every victory. He kept things moving, as the event went on for more than an hour. The winners were elated and loudly supported by their teams.

A few older men and women told me of their excitement about the rabbi trying new things, and of their pleasure in how intergenerational these events were. One woman who has observed Shabbat her entire life told me that she had learned things at each dinner. Others told me that they enjoyed the food and liked the fact that the synagogue was trying different things. They all wished there would be more events like this one.

On Shabbat morning following one of the three workshops, I often heard congregants talking about the event. People joked about the Chinese or Mexican food upsetting their stomachs. They also remarked on the large turnouts and how pleasant the evenings were. The growing popularity of the workshops led to "Casual Shabbat," which encouraged people to come to a 5:45 Shabbat evening service dressed informally, followed by dinner and Israeli dancing. Both "Casual Shabbat" and the final workshop were sold out in advance with 200 reservations, and each had a waiting list.

What startled both participants and the synagogue staff was how multigenerational the evenings turned out to be, and how much this appealed to the participants. There were younger families but also empty-nesters. What the staff learned from these events was that hundreds of Beth El's members hungered for Jewish community within the synagogue. They loved the Shabbat programs; they liked being with one another; they liked dancing and eating together and learning together as well. From "Artsy Shabbat" to dinners to "Casual Shabbat," congregants wanted to spend time together. As one congregant in his late twenties said,

> The thing that's been most inviting to me lately has been these programs about Shabbat. I think [it's] because you go and you meet people and you learn something about Shabbat. It just seems that if you go on Saturday morning it's not very inviting. You go and there's a million people there. They're not as personal as these "Celebrate Shabbat" programs.

The synagogue's program coordinator, Audrey Abrams, received a few financial contributions for the programs and several letters congratulating and thanking those who organized the events, again focusing at least partially on an educational and religious opportunity that was "fun," "innovative," and "meaningful."

Congregants also responded to the educational aspects of "Celebrate Shabbat." A congregant in her early thirties told me:

> We've found a different connection at "Celebrate Shabbat" than I have for quite a few years. I feel like there's something more symbolic. I can identify with the symbols and there are explanations of things that I really yearn for that aren't in the *Jewish Catalogue*, or I don't really want to ask someone. I want to form my own understanding. How do we want to celebrate Shabbat? We are pretty good about lighting candles; the hard part is summer because it gets dark so late. I'm sure that when we have kids we will be doing more. I think it's important that we find our own renewed observance or kindling of observance in shul.

This congregant used "Celebrate Shabbat" to learn more, to begin to think with her husband of nearly three years about the type of Jewish home they were creating for themselves and the children they would eventually have. As an adult, it was clear that she did not find it easy to ask those questions—some too basic, some in search of more profound information. "Celebrate Shabbat" created space for her to do all these things.

A very active member who had observed Shabbat his entire life also found these programs helpful. Initially, he thought the programs would be of little interest to him. His wife explained:

> We didn't go to the first dinner because we didn't feel we needed it. But then at synagogue everyone was giving it rave reviews, and even people who had the background really enjoyed it and it wasn't talking down to them. So we tried the second one and really enjoyed it. We felt we learned something.

Her husband continued:

> It was reinvigorating because it had been quite some time since we had done that. It was like, "Oh yeah, I know about that. I haven't done that in a while." We haven't been out to dinner on a Friday night, unless we're out of town, in two years now. Yes, after Friday night dinner we'll go for a walk around the lake and maybe go get ice cream; we're not Shomer Shabbat, but there's a strong Friday night presence. But in the last year we've had friends over who are Shomer Shabbat and live in the neighborhood. Since going to this, it's given us a greater confidence.

Another congregant in her late thirties found one program especially helpful: the final class with the rabbi that reviewed all the information previously discussed. Seated around a table they created a "mock" Shabbat:

> What I learned at the wrap-up was wonderful. There were about twenty of us. . . . I was concerned that it might be too simplistic, but it wasn't at all. I ended up motivated to find something more than we do. . . . I wish I had time to learn Hebrew again. For example, he was talking about what do you do here in Minnesota when candle lighting is supposed to be eighteen minutes before sunset; how do you deal with that fact? Someone said she doesn't light them if she gets home after 6:00 in the winter because that would be after sunset. But more of us were talking about doing it as a family and doing it at dinnertime. I know what she was talking about was more legally correct. He told a little bit about what he does at home. He's very nonjudgmental; he's very diplomatic. He told about how he grew up even though he has gone on to do more.

This congregant's husband had told me with both pride and affection that his wife had created Shabbat in their home since their first child was six months old. He described the special set of dishes that she purchased and the tablecloths they use only for Shabbat. And the Beth El Nursery School allowed their children to create special candles and other objects that they took turns using as well. Although this woman was motivated to want to learn more, she also was

very relieved by the flexibility of the rabbi's approach to Shabbat, which dif-
fered from her memories of other rabbis. She liked learning about his family's
observance, the home in which he grew up, and the approaches of other
congregants who attended the class. Many other Beth El members expressed a
similar appreciation of the rabbi. One woman commented that his "joy, creativity,
and spontaneity" were qualities she had never before seen in a rabbi. She recalled his Kol Nidre sermon:

> I loved what he said about Shabbat. It was the first time I ever heard a
> rabbi say that. He said you don't have to do it like your grandmother.
> You don't have to do it right. Just do it. That was just wonderful. I never
> heard that permission from a rabbi before. Always, it's never enough. I'll
> never do enough because I'm not organized. I'll always have someone in
> my family doing more than me. He was the first person that said it's nice
> that you do it, and we do always do it. I relaxed about it and I feel what I
> do is fine. The kids relaxed too.

An architect in his late forties, raised as an Orthodox Jew in Chicago, had
a similar reaction:

> Something is happening here. I have to single out Rabbi Kahn for giving
> me more freedom as a Jew than I thought I was allowed. Growing up in
> a very traditional environment and going to a very Orthodox school, [I
> found that] rabbis could be scary people. The laws and traditions were so
> demanding; they were rules to be followed instead of a door to experi-
> ences that could be enjoyed. Rabbi Kahn is changing that experience for
> me. You could come casual on a Friday night. Something as simple as
> that just makes me stop and think. You mean these laws aren't things to
> be afraid of breaking? It lets me take a step back and take a relaxed view.
> And this quite frankly might be one of the reasons that I moved away
> from Judaism. These were very narrow paths to follow and if you went
> off the path it had severe consequences, whatever that might be.

His wife is in her mid-forties and runs a preschool. She was raised in a family
that did not belong to a synagogue or observe Jewish holidays. As a teenager
she sought out Jewish experiences and asked her parents to join a synagogue so
that she could be confirmed. She, too, was impressed by the sermon:

> Rabbi Kahn once said about Shabbat dinner, "You don't have to slave in
> the kitchen all day because it was another pressure when you're working
> all week." We have found that given all of our schedules Friday night is
> our focal point; it is our dinner, and we really do make a conscious effort
> for all of us to be together. We always thought it had to be this formal
> dinner with soup and everything. Now I can relax and enjoy Friday
> night. . . . More and more families [are] coming to these programs. More

families are saying, Gee, I can do that. I really see this in the nursery school. It used to be that unless it was a nursery school program they would not come. Now they come because they're family oriented.

If the rabbi's intention with "Celebrate Shabbat" was to be as "user friendly, as open, as inviting as possible," he certainly succeeded.

Rabbi Kahn told me that the majority of responses he received to the program were "informal," offered at other synagogue occasions. Again and again, congregants expressed appreciation for the permission to create a different kind of Shabbat than what they took to be the ideal associated with mothers and grandmothers. Rabbi Kahn also said that Beth El congregants had never heard that they might combine Shabbat "celebration" with going out on the weekends. That was a new message for them. Instead of simply ignoring or disregarding Shabbat, he believed he moved them toward integrating Shabbat into their lives.

Many congregants seemed to feel that Rabbi Kahn's sermon marked a more accepting attitude than one found at Beth El in the past, not only about Shabbat observance, but also in not demanding that busy families expend a tremendous amount of hard work.[24]

The volunteer committee, participants, and the coordinator for the events often focused on the fact that the programs were "fun," a word used quite consistently about food, the learning exercises, the attractive recipe box full of serious Shabbat materials, and of course "Jewpardy." And the fun that worked for families seemed also to appeal to the empty nesters or multigenerational Beth El families who like sharing these experiences with the larger community. The program brought in about twenty families who were not currently marking Shabbat in any way in their homes.

And for a very diverse group the program tended to strengthen and deepen the Friday night celebration that was already marked in some way. The program was, however, unlikely to bring families to synagogue at 5:45 for an early service. Rabbi Kahn explained how the thinking on this evolved:

> The change in the Friday night service structure was definitely designed with young families in mind, and that has worked to some extent. [At our monthly service] we're now saying kiddush on the *bimah* and we invite anyone under the age of bar and bat mitzvah to share some of the kiddush and a sweet. We've had a lot more young people than we have ever had at a service because we used to have none. The 8:00 time doesn't make sense anymore. A family can't come out with young kids that late at night. But the early service doesn't make sense for young families either. And I'm just starting to learn that congregants don't want to come to the synagogue with just one parent. If a family is planning on Friday night dinner at home they can't leave the house

from 5:45 to 6:35 if they're planning on eating dinner at 7:00. That
wasn't a problem in the traditional form of Judaism where only the man
went to shul and the woman stayed at home. We're not very supportive
of that model. So, I'm almost reconciled to saying, "Let's be a Shabbat
morning synagogue." There are lots of synagogues in the U.S. that are
Shabbat morning synagogues, and we'll continue to have our minyan on
Friday night and it will be thirty to forty-five people. Maybe Friday night
services just don't fit today's world. I think that having a Friday night
dinner at home is much more important than coming to synagogue.

Ironically, then, Beth El set out to change a communal event Friday night
into a familial one by urging families to stay at home with one another.

Like Beth Jacob's "Chew by Choice," Beth El's "Celebrate Shabbat" provided a regular and consistent reminder to congregants through programming,
mailings, and events that Judaism could on the one hand sacralize eating and
on the other transform time and space. But whereas services would not draw
people together, early services, combined with a meal the family could share at
the synagogue, did. The all-women members of the volunteer committee could
now attend services, because they didn't have to prepare dinner at home. Indeed, the whole language of celebration became an ingrained part of the daily
vocabulary of many congregants. Over the year many congregants consistently
described their own activities to me as "celebrating Shabbat." "We celebrate
Shabbat every other week." "We don't celebrate Shabbat as often as we would
like." I came to realize how widespread the awareness of the programs was.

"Celebrate Shabbat" had two effects. Some congregants were "reinvigorated"
in their observance, and some began to create a Shabbat experience for their
family. At the same time, however, the programs suggested that congregants were
hungry to make the synagogue more homelike, a more intimate environment.
They liked the communal aspects of synagogue life, including meeting new
people.

"Casual Shabbat" occurred the same year that one of Minnesota's outstanding orchestras featured a concert series emphasizing causal attire for both the
orchestra and the audience. It followed on the policy of many large corpora-
tions to make Friday "dress-down day." Beth El sought to acknowledge how much
people appreciated a more "comfortable" way of doing things. The simple fact
of not wearing a tie signaled this change.

Many of Beth Jacob's congregants responded powerfully to the opportunity
to move at their own pace in developing their observance of Judaism. Beth El
congregants responded to an approach to ritual that acknowledged the complexity of their lives and allowed them to feel that they were doing things right.
Rabbi Kahn changed the traditional mix. He urged his congregants to focus on
the meaning of "relaxation and self-reflection. It must emphasize family; it must

serve as a break from busy-ness, technology, consumerism, and modernity." Like Rabbi Allen, he urged his congregants to break with the dominant culture's values through their celebration of the weekly day of rest.

In a community of memory, Rabbi Kahn asserted a new way of understanding observance. Shabbat did not have to be a family event that assumed certain food, a family member devoting her day to cooking, or even a vision of a type of family. In addition, the synagogue came to serve as a desirable site for Shabbat dinner and observance, introducing grandparents whose children lived elsewhere to families living apart from other members. The Shabbat he envisioned was about rest from stress and strain of a two-career family, an evening spent in a way the following day might not be, a flexible sacredness that was better than no marking of Shabbat at all. In short, "Celebrate Shabbat" reinforced family and community within a model of celebration that focused far less on obligation and more on living a Jewish life. The rabbi put his vision of Shabbat in opposition to a Judaism that asserted, "If you can't do it right, don't bother." He asked congregants not to sacrifice Judaism from the lives of their families just because it was not the ideal form of Shabbat, Judaism, or observance.

Over the course of the year I heard only two criticisms of the sermon. One congregant suggested, "Rabbi Aronson would turn over in his grave if he heard a rabbi say that you could have pizza for Shabbat." It was unclear to me if he thought the sermon suggested actually going to a restaurant. The second comment, which was reported to me, came from a woman in her forties who was outraged because she and her mother had always set "a beautiful table for Shabbat and that is how it should be." When asked by her friend who told me the story if she could see any value in more people celebrating if the preparations were less demanding, she dismissed the idea as unambiguously wrong. "We recognize Shabbat by special food and a beautiful table and I'm offended at the suggestion that there is another way to do that."

Synagogue Initiatives as a Reflection of Late Twentieth Century Conservative Judaism

Both congregations initiated change with the New Year. Rabbi Allen's more observant congregation was challenged to increase personal observance within the context of the home. Rabbi Kahn's exceptionally diverse synagogue was challenged to acknowledge the end of the era of Friday night services. Both rabbis raised the threshold for observance. Rabbi Allen clearly indicated that the dietary laws were a ladder to ascend. Rabbi Kahn urged his congregants to see that Shabbat was a time to be at home nurturing the soul in the context of family, or at least to structure it into Friday evening. Both rabbis' initiatives asserted that the demands of work and family necessitate a serious consideration of mitzvot that allowed their congregants to separate themselves from the demands of a secular culture through food and rest.

These two synagogue initiatives, which bear the stamp of rabbinic leadership, locate the practice of Conservative Judaism in the late twentieth century. Rabbi Kahn once pondered the difference between Beth El of the 1950s and the 1990s. He wondered, "How could the rabbis of that generation not have the foresight to ask, 'If I help them achieve the goal of wealth and Americanization, what is the next generation going to look like?' So many sacrifices were made in order for people to reach their goals of success."

The Ratner Center survey demonstrates that members at both synagogues are less observant than their parents, although more than half of Beth Jacobs' members and more than three-quarters of Beth El's were raised as Conservative Jews. Beth El members are significantly less observant than their childhood memories of their parents; Beth Jacob members are somewhat less observant. With regard to observance of home rituals such as lighting Shabbat candles and separating dishes for meat and dairy, Beth El members were about a third to a half less likely to perform these commandments. Beth Jacob members were about as likely as their parents to light candles and one-third less likely to keep a kosher home. At the same time congregants interviewed in both synagogues tended to see their practice of Judaism as of a different quality from that of their parents. For example, many congregants explained that they perform mitzvot with feeling and thought, and not simply in response to social coercion. Congregants, then, in both synagogues are looking for new ways to practice and understand their Judaism.

Each rabbi's campaign provided a complex idiom for Jewish life and observance. Each asked his congregants to alter their lifestyles. If the idiom of the postwar synagogue was the parallel between suburban church and synagogue, Rabbis Allen and Kahn asked congregants to consider disjunction and transformation to break with the dominant culture through personal action, and thereby build the foundation of a Jewish life.

At the same time, both initiatives emphasized the different aspect of a process: each rejected a totalizing approach to any aspect of observance; each held that any step in and of itself could constitute a transformation; and each rejected the notion that negotiating observance is rejecting it. As Bonnie Heller, Beth El's president, described it, "Less can be more." The "permission" Beth El members felt and wanted was to move away from a style of observing Friday night that placed a woman in the kitchen devoted to the meal. Rabbi Kahn thought they also wanted permission to integrate Shabbat into a secular weekend. Clearly, authority shifted more to individuals and families, but what was authorized was to move toward partial observance rather than dismissing it.

Communities within Synagogues

As a "community of communities," Beth El, the paradigmatic large suburban synagogue, has a substantial number of constituencies whose needs often collide and have to be balanced. But even small and young synagogues like Beth Jacob must also deal with the problem of how to balance the various expectations and needs of its congregants.

Whereas the first set of case studies focused on rabbinical initiatives that defined a vision of a Judaism that was possible for their congregants, the second set of case studies examines how the two synagogues respond to conflicting demands of congregants. The organization of each synagogue—how its committees and rabbis respond to challenges—also reveals the issues raised by late twentieth century Judaism.

BETH JACOB: A DECOROUS COMMUNITY

The summer months moved at a different pace at Beth Jacob. The number of adult education courses increases as the days grow longer and warmer. As early as July, various teachers offer minicourses related to the upcoming Days of Awe on the meaning of repentance, ethical wills, and paths to Judaism. Shabbat classes for children are replaced by storytelling and other programs. By the last half hour of services congregants often look out the sanctuary's window onto its verdant lawn, where hordes of children are running and playing under the watchful eye of parents. Out of the icy grip of Minnesota winter everyone seems to relax.

By late summer, however, it became clear that a number of congregants questioned the message that Beth Jacob was sending to its congregants, with its high degree of informality. One board member was deeply offended, various congregants learned over several weeks, when a family arrived at synagogue late into the torah service, their children dressed in shorts and sandals. They slumped into their place on the pew seemingly unmindful that they were, according to those who were concerned, in a holy space. "What," this Beth Jacob regular asked, "is going on in the minds of these families?" This concern was not about the invasion of Beth Jacob by callous and insensitive outsiders but about the behavior and lack of good judgment of those who came regularly, davened frequently, but just did not seem to understand, according to some, what it meant to be in a synagogue.

The conversation continued informally for weeks. Beth Jacob members from the original Sons of Jacob had found the informality of many congregants scandalous from the start and had complained that it was "irreligious" to read from the torah wearing tennis shoes or jeans or for women to be in slacks and men to be without ties. But something about the shorts and late arrival at the service seemed to be the last straw.

At the October board meeting some members officially raised the "decorum problem." One of the vice presidents and most of the committed volunteers expressed serious concerns about the children's programming over the High Holidays, which matches nearly a hundred volunteer parents with the management of over a hundred children. This lay leader was troubled about what occurred:

> I saw a complete lack of respect on the part of the students for the
> volunteers. But I was equally concerned about the role of the volunteers
> in the synagogue. When they saw children throw food or misbehave,
> they seemed to shrug their shoulders and say, "But I'm just a volunteer."
> How do we get the message across that we're in it together?

Various congregants described children ranging in age from five to twelve as "mouthy" and "disrespectful of synagogue rules." Many parent volunteers dismissed the problem as "day school kids," suggesting that those kids who spend most time at the shul and know one another best are the most difficult. But others were not sure it was that easy to explain. Another board member with responsibilities for the kitchen complained that the teenagers were equally difficult, showing "no respect for the people who worked in the kitchen, taking food at will."

Perhaps most distressing was learning from a board member with cerebral palsy, which affects her gait, that as she walked to the bathroom on Kol Nidre, children she did not know imitated her walk. She asked, "What's going on with the kids; what are they thinking and feeling? I'm more curious about why they act this way."

At this point Rabbi Allen raised his hand to speak. His comment widened the conversation to the synagogue as a whole.

> People assume it all comes from on high. It would be worth our while to
> open up a discussion about this with the whole shul. We need to
> understand why there seems to be an inverse relationship between
> decorum and participation.
>
> The sanctuary is a place to daven, not to chitchat or catch up on
> news. There are people who sit in shul chewing gum. There's a whole
> layer of decorum that we've resisted at Beth Jacob and it might be time
> to discuss it.

Board members continued for some time to try to identify the locus of responsibility for this problem. The ritual committee, too, had concerns, and some congregants suggested that they be asked to draw up a dress code. Others felt that it was the education committee that needed to confront the problem of children's behavior during Shabbat Enrichment classes. But Rabbi Allen and others continued to direct the problem back to Beth Jacob itself. Rabbi Allen asked, "Are we going to kick out people who look wrong? As long as kids be-have, I don't care what they wear." Others disagreed. Both rabbi and congregants worried about "the parental lapse." Why did they seem unwilling to take respon-sibility? "What is magical," Rabbi Allen asked, "about the two steps up to the bimah that convinces parents I can get a child to open the siddur?"

The decorum conversation, framed by Rabbi Allen as the inverse relation-ship between participation and controlled behavior, mirrors a second inversion. Beth Jacob, according to its education director, Wendy Schwartz, is "an unusu-ally participatory synagogue. People have a tremendous range of skills here." But, she sighed, "only two people volunteer to do everything. It's very hard to get volunteers, and we're not a check-writing shul. We need volunteers." Highly skilled congregants do not want to teach in the Shabbat Enrichment program. They want to have Shabbat as Shabbat. Given their busy lives, many seem to understand their participation in terms of a religious life and less in terms of fundraising, communal meals, and clean up. They want to pray rather than join committees. They want their children to find a degree of comfort in the syna-gogue so that they can be less watchful.

As the synagogue expanded and the number of children grew, that relaxed atmosphere was beginning to present problems. As Wendy Schwartz noted,

> No matter how many ways we deal with it, the decorum issue doesn't go away. . . . What was acceptable when we were 200 families is different when we are 300 or 330. There are more and more kids and there's going to be more kids. Parents still think "Oh, it's Beth Jacob." One of the great things about Beth Jacob is that parents think their kids are safe and welcome here. I've seen parents walk in the building and say, "OK, see you. You know where to find me." Two hours later they see them at kiddush.
>
> They abdicate any responsibility about supervising their kids. I talk to the high school kids about it. One of them said, "The beauty of Beth Jacob is that you do have this level of comfort and freedom in the building. Everyone should take upon themselves the role that when they see something inappropriate to do something. We should be communal parents of our communal children." [But] it isn't the consensus.[25]

The decorum problem and the conversations it generated allowed Beth Jacob to try to reassert its central values and ideas about communal life. It pointed up a very real and inevitable cleavage between synagogue as community and syna-gogue as sacred place. Rabbi Allen, in reflecting on "the problem," described it as the direct result of the larger culture. "We live in such a boundaryless world that people are freaked out that it has now entered into the sanctuary. That should be the last bastion. We should have realized that sooner or later that would affect us in shul." The source of the shul's community life was also the

source of tension. Parents and children constituted different communities at Beth
Jacob. Kiddush was often the occasion for each generation to spend time in its
own community. Other adults were distressed that children, and even adults,
lacked respect. They sometimes rushed at the tables for food before the blessings over wine and bread were completed. They seemed to be indifferent to the
needs of older adults. Children were operating, according to many, too autono-
mously. They lacked boundaries.

The decorum issues of 1995–96 crystallized the extent to which Beth Jacob
can be understood as a community firmly grounded in its members' choices. It
became clear that different congregants brought inevitably different expectations
and sensibilities; indeed, Beth Jacob as a community was predicated on the fact
that a variety of behaviors were acceptable. As the synagogue grew, consensus
could be reached on many things, but clearly not on matters of clothing, gum
chewing, and setting limits on children's behavior. Beth Jacob's congregants
wanted to make their own choices in creating a different type of synagogue, and
they collided in ways that left congregants surprised and even shocked.

Rabbi Allen continued to use these discussions to urge the congregants to
find a process for dealing with these concerns, to see that Beth Jacob's own values and principles could aid in responding to these diverse issues. He told me
that an important role that he had to play was "encouraging people to talk to
one another":

> Part of it is to appreciate the highly eclectic nature of the synagogue.
> There is a row's worth of people who have been in the rabbinate longer
> than me. There are PhDs in areas of expertise in Jewish Studies. And at
> the same time [there] are people who have had no background in
> Judaism at all. If you elevate the discussion in such a way that you
> assume people are intelligent, you'll succeed. People who have passion-
> ate feelings on what is appropriate can talk to one another. . . . Our
> challenge is to figure out how to remain committed. The decorum issue
> then was the problem of both eclectic membership unified by an
> approach to prayer and synagogue life and the inevitable changes of a
> growing organization. A burgeoning population of children and a
> community that has tripled in size cannot depend on informal sanctions
> and "communal parenting." Precisely what scandalized one
> congregant—informal dress of children—is what attracts others, who
> want to be liberated from the conventions of postwar synagogues. Thus,
> the symbolic value of blue jeans on young parents.

Both Rabbi Allen and the leadership of the ritual committee took up the
decorum issue as a way to reassert synagogue "values and principles." They engaged in what Rabbi Allen had called the "operationalization" of Beth Jacob's
dream and vision. The ritual committee's discussions were no less difficult than

those of the board, however. Members' calls for dress codes and rules were inevitably countered by statements by others. One committee member said, "Isn't the point to learn to appreciate the *kedusha* [holiness], regardless of how they're dressed?" Another member commented, "We know what respecting the *kedusha* is about, but we haven't a clue about what respectful clothing is for everyone."

The committee did not abdicate responsibility. Its members simply acknowledged that it was virtually impossible to fix decorum as a matter in and of itself, let alone to imagine consequences for those who would not consent to it. They settled instead on a language that would place decorum within their own vision of Judaism and community. In its final form, their work appeared on a single page of the synagogue bulletin under the heading, "Decorum at Shul." The article translated the decorum issue into one concerning "community and the presence of God within our midst." A set of behaviors in the sanctuary, including affection between spouses, talking, and sweets for children, were all put into the article. Interestingly, neither unruly children nor a dress code bore mention. Instead, the decorum of the sanctuary was the focus of the article. Pragmatically, though, a series of steps were taken to address issues of children and parental responsibility. Every single Shabbat the congregation is reminded what is considered appropriate behavior at kiddush and that parents are responsible for the control of their children. Plans for the upcoming holidays include far more attention to supervising children and training volunteers to take more responsibility.

Like so much of the symbolic life of groups, powerful interpersonal matters like decorum create grave concerns but cannot be resolved. Consensus is rare. As the year went on, however, people appeared to be talking and worrying less about decorum. At the same time, no one believes that this issue will be or could be solved. The synagogue's rabbinic, professional, and lay leadership all chose to address it, but different people and groups understood the problem differently. It was no accident, however, that the issue emerged a decade into the community's life as its numbers, particularly of children, have expanded dramatically. It provides the occasion to ask, "Who are we?"

Thus, in the life of this congregation, there are issues such as "Chew by Choice," an important occasion for underlining the voluntary, private nature of Jewish life; and there are issues such as decorum questions, which proceeded in the opposite direction, raising highly public concerns driven by community standards rather than specific religious requirements. Those most engaged by the conflict sought something resembling halakhic principles; they wanted rules, lists, norms, and certainties. After many discussions, they reluctantly realized that these were not forthcoming. The aesthetic that demanded only two steps between the bimah and congregants guaranteed that neither neckties nor long pants for boys would ever be the sine qua non of community life.

The decorum fights created considerable heat but did not ignite the sorts of fires that can destroy communities. They simply underlined the diversity of Beth Jacob as a community and pointed up the difficulties in organizational life that are the product of respecting that diversity. A commitment to talking and reflecting did not ensure a particular standard as much as acknowledge that some type of standards needed to be reiterated.

BETH EL'S PLURALIST ORGANIZATION

Once a month a sign stands in the entry hall of Beth El synagogue in front of the small chapel. It says, "Minyan Hadash meets today." The minyan's meetings are announced in the bulletin and from the bimah by the rabbi. Guest speakers during 1995 often delivered a d'var torah in both the large sanctuary and the small chapel. In years past torah readers moved from the large sanctuary to the small one, reading their sections twice. This extraordinarily cooperative process allows many of Beth El's most traditional members to daven together apart from the larger congregation.

The "New" minyan has had several lives at Beth El. Its members describe it as entering its third generation. The group met for a few years in the late 1980s, then in 1989 stopped meeting for lack of interest. It started up again in 1991 with the same leadership, who passed it on to younger members in 1994. Now three highly competent coordinators have taken over, bringing with them a group of men and women in their late twenties and early thirties.

Minyan Hadash is not a radical alternative to Beth El's Shabbat morning service. Rather, its liturgy, torah reading, and often its d'var torah are essentially the same. Perhaps the greatest difference is simply the fact that there is no bar or bat mitzvah at Minyan Hadash and therefore the associated speeches, prayers, and presentations are absent. Minyan members seem to enjoy sleeping in, so the minyan meets much later than the regular synagogue service and ends considerably later.

Minyan Hadash does not want to provide an alternative service as much as an alternative experience, by offering an environment for prayer that is "intimate," a term that one of the new coordinators, a man in his late twenties, said is "key for our generation." The large and imposing sanctuary, along with the formalities of events surrounding b'nai mitzvah, are the exact opposite of intimacy for these participants, who want to create their own experience. At Minyan Hadash people can take an active role in a non-threatening setting. Thus, for example, two of the day's torah readers had not read for the past ten years. One of the coordinator's commented: "In a smaller minyan they can have the confidence to do that."

For others, the minyan's intimacy is experienced as liberation from the routines of the weekly bar or bat mitzvah, a sanctuary filled with one-time guests.

At Minyan Hadash everyone knows one another and there is a fairly high level of knowledge and observance.

The greatest challenge for the minyan is, nevertheless, finding enough people to assume the roles required for the service, and that challenge is taken on by the coordinators.[26] Finding members to lead the services is not a problem. But finding torah readers and those willing to comment upon the torah portion is more difficult. One woman was disappointed that the synagogue was not more helpful in allowing them to recruit people for these positions. She said, "We wanted the rabbis to give us more support. They started coming to give a *d'var torah*; or sometimes they would give a different version when there were two [rabbis]. We would time [our service] to them. Finding someone to give the *d'var torah* is hard. The torah reading is hard because we have a full reading [as in the main sanctuary]." But many torah readers taught in the synagogue's education program on Shabbat morning and also read in the main sanctuary and therefore were not available to read in the minyan. Contributing to the problem was the fact that there was no second rabbi at the time, and so Rabbi Kahn could not offer an additional *d'var torah* for the minyan. The former coordinator explained why it is often difficult to find someone to comment on the portion:

> It takes a lot of preparation. I've done it several times. Very high caliber people would come, and it was very learned. I prepared for twenty-five hours for Vayikra and it didn't go very well. I don't know nearly as much as the people in the room. People started to ask me questions, but somebody asked a question and I just had no idea how to answer. They asked me a question related to the historical timeline. If you do a d'var torah really right, it takes tons of preparation. I never volunteered since that time. I'd rather read two aliyot [from the torah]. My husband was asked, and he said to Rabbi Kahn, "Are you nuts? I wouldn't do that."

Minyan Hadash is an interesting representation of Beth El's committed core. On the one hand, the group's davening varies greatly. They are very tolerant of variation in the quality of davening. Certainly on several occasions I heard people leading the service who were quite unsure of how to do so. On the other hand, because members are very learned, delivering a comment on the torah is an intimidating task. The minyan is therefore participatory but also committed to especially high standards of learning.

Finally, more than any other factor, congregants who attend Minyan Hadash are in search of an alternative experience of community and an ethos of participation. Young children sit with their parents and talk and play. Congregants know one another quite well and know one another's children. Whoever serves as gabbai walks throughout the chapel recruiting participants for a variety of honors at the torah. The pace is slow. Many different people participate. "Casual," "participatory," "comfortable," and "informal" are all words people have used to describe the minyan.

Beth El's great tolerance for and celebration of an alternative minyan suggests an open acknowledgment of the synagogue as a "community of communities." Minyan Hadash is in many ways an exceptionally homogeneous group. The Shabbat-observant families who have moved to St. Louis Park are an important core of the group. Younger, rather observant families and congregants, even if they travel on Shabbat, also attend. One family in the neighborhood comes to Beth El only when Minyan Hadash meets and for the holidays. The husband, a man in his mid-thirties, though an exceptionally competent, well-educated Jew, does not observe Shabbat regularly. His ideal religious observance is participatory and communal. Many of the minyan's participants are regular and highly accomplished torah readers. Though the approximately thirty-five people who attend are only a tiny percentage of Beth El (nor are they all of the observant core), they have a very powerful presence. A few of them have served on committees and the board. They are seen as a constituency in matters of ritual, education, and hiring a senior rabbi. They clearly set a standard of observance for the synagogue that is not represented by the rabbi alone.

Some congregants are uncomfortable with the presence of an alternative minyan. A minyan coordinator told me that she is routinely accosted by a member who tells her, "'I think maybe we'll have a people-with-brown-shoes minyan, and a people-with-yellow-hair minyan.' He thinks we're separating and fracturing into little groups. He's concerned about the community."

Remarkably, this opinion is simply not representative of the clergy or those congregants who attend services. Dating from the time of Rabbi Abelson, Beth El always tried to keep its various groups feeling like part of the synagogue. Rabbi Abelson's view was to "keep them in the building and then they won't have to leave the synagogue." It was just that philosophy that encouraged the board to accept Minyan Hadash and make it one more of Beth El's many constituencies. President Bonnie Heller remembers an alternative minyan of older men davening at Beth El's North Side synagogue from when she was a child. The synagogue has clearly always included diversity.

Minyan Hadash raises the powerful question of how a large, pluralist Conservative synagogue can integrate its many constituencies. While Beth El cannot provide all the services that Minyan Hadash would like, the synagogue does consider the minyan to be very much part of its regular liturgical life. The rabbi's wife and young son, for example, are regulars at Minyan Hadash. But many of the members of Minyan Hadash have a more complex relationship to Beth El and reflect some of the shifts in Jewish identification of Conservative Jews in the mid-1990s. Most of these minyan members were born and socialized in the Conservative movement, but all of them are far more observant than the families in which they were raised. As one man said, "Who was Shomer Shabbat in the 1960s?" The answer for young, professional families in Minneapolis would have been virtually no one.

Thus, growing traditionalism has led roughly seven families to hold dual memberships in Beth El and in the Modern Orthodox synagogue a few blocks away. The husbands and fathers of these families attend the Shabbat evening minyan at the Orthodox synagogue, where the experience of prayer and celebration is closer to their own ideal of Judaism. The observant core goes to their daily minyan as well. They are not looking for family-oriented programs. One member complained that the evening of Purim at Beth El is a "Halloween-type event," directed to nursery school families, although the smaller service in the morning was "wonderful" because the synagogue's regulars attend. Nevertheless, Shabbat morning at Beth El continues to attract them, for reasons that may not be entirely apparent. Shabbat morning baby-sitting, for example, is a great draw at Beth El. Another draw is that daughters are able to become bnot mitzvah, something all of them want—there are, in fact, families who primarily attend the Orthodox synagogue but also belong to Beth El for just this reason.

A member of Minyan Hadash, who is the granddaughter of Beth El founders and a very active congregant, reflected on why her family remains at Beth El, despite their growing tie to the Orthodox synagogue: "If Knesset [the Orthodox synagogue] was not such an unattractive place, and if they had moved the mechitza, which they tried to do, a lot of these people would be there. I might be there except for the bat mitzvah." She later added that she would never leave Beth El as long as her elderly grandmother is still alive.

The Orthodox synagogue had voted against moving its mechitza to stand between two side-by-side sections, thus retaining separate front (men's) and back (women's) sections. That vote sent some of its members to Beth El and contributed to some Beth El members staying put. Nevertheless, there have continued to be a number of joint members. Rabbi Kahn considers this a "recent phenomenon," but also something very positive:

> Sometimes I think [joint members] are not committed to our principles, mostly around gender equality. I'm always trying to be supportive of people who are further right than me. But recently, a family requested an all-woman's minyan for their daughter's bat mitzvah. She attends Torah Academy [the Orthodox day school]. She was embarrassed to invite her friends here, and she now believes that men and women should be separated. I said no to that. I wouldn't do it for an all-male minyan, so I couldn't do it for an all-woman minyan.

The types of boundaries that used to firmly separate Orthodox and Conservative Jews are remarkably blurred in this community, and Beth El and its congregants are working hard to continue to define and create a pluralist community.

Rabbi Kahn also noted that Beth El families whose children attend the Orthodox day school feel particularly caught between worlds. The majority of the children there do not attend the Modern Orthodox synagogue, but a far more right-wing breakaway congregation. Beth El children at that school began to feel that their Judaism was second-rate, that girls should not have a bat mitzvah, and that they wanted to be like those around them. One family resolved the problem by having their son's bar mitzvah in Israel so they would not have to choose between communities. The school and the peer group that it creates have the potential to pull children and their parents out of the right-wing of Conservative Judaism into Orthodoxy.

The members of this particular group whom I interviewed rarely called Beth El home, even though they are deeply connected to the synagogue, and its other observant members constitute their most important community. They virtually never discussed continuity. They talked about their observance, their children's needs to have the synagogue recognize their greater level of education and commitment, and the importance of study and always seeking "knowing more." One former coordinator of Minyan Hadash reflected on why Beth El shortens certain readings of texts or adds additional readings on some holidays:

> I think for most of them—and I hate to use the word "them" because it sounds so condescending—their Jewish educations are so weak and they don't have the sense of what prayer is all about, what the siddur is all about, what Jewish text is all about. It's all pretty boring because they don't have the tools to interpret what it is they are doing. So what they're looking for is pizzazz, for a sermon that will grab them—aren't we all—or a reading that will be fresh and stimulate their thinking. But the rhythm of Judaism, the regularity that comes with Judaism, they don't have the tools to make meaning for themselves. For them the less is better, so they don't have to suffer through the siddur, the long torah reading, the megilla. The rabbis see their job as balancing diverse needs. I think they succeed reasonably well at it. They do try to allow diversity. They are aware of the needs of "the remnant."

This man contrasts his experience of Judaism with what he understands to be the practice of the majority of congregants at the synagogue. He believes the synagogue finds it difficult to serve both of their needs, although he recognizes the efforts. To this end, he found Rabbi Kahn particularly helpful. He consistently described him as "flexible," rather than "haimish," whereas in general the committed core continually expressed frustration over a lack of flexibility at the synagogue. They resented the inability of the synagogue to meet their children's needs, for example, requiring them to attend for several years to prepare for their b'nai mitzvah, when their educations were such that several months was all that was necessary. They were frustrated that if they were required to come, they could not be given a more meaningful opportunity to learn. This congregant, however, had noticed significant changes under Rabbi Kahn's leadership.

The other former coordinator, a woman of forty, expressed her sense of bewilderment at the insensitivity of Beth El congregants to Shabbat itself:

> I was very saddened when Tarbut [the Shabbat educational program] had its first session. Not only did parents drop off their kids—I accept the way that [it] is—but what really upset me is that all the parents came into the lobby with their jeans on. They didn't even know it was Shabbat. Shabbat is such a big part of my life now that to see people who don't even recognize it—maybe they lit candles the night before and they would say that they celebrated Shabbat but it's such a chasm; it's such a huge life difference. To them, coming into the building on Shabbat morning is no different than dropping off their kids at Hebrew school. They invaded my space. I told my husband, and he said, "That would have been us. There but for the grace of God go I." We're so grateful for being where we are, and so aware of what an enriching lifestyle it is. But other people think we're nuts.

The challenge for the synagogue's pluralism, then, is to try to accommodate both sets of needs and attitudes.

Many of the congregants who hold Minyan Hadash dear have created a Judaism of the type that is often evoked in memories of the North Side: it is located in a neighborhood, among other Jews who practice their Judaism similarly and who adhere to a vision of the world that is shaped by Judaism. That vision, however, is much more loosely tied to Beth El as an institution and more strongly linked to like-minded members of the community and the other observant Jews in the area.

Beth El has responded to many cultural changes over the decades. Rabbi Aronson's early evocation of Beth El as an American synagogue promised that such compromises would occur. In the 1970s Beth El changed policies regarding women receiving aliyot. Rabbi Herring convened a task force on the intermarried that generated a wide range of policies to make in-marrying spouses feel comfortable and welcome within the dictates of halakha. The synagogue responded to the realities of blended and divorced families in its structuring of life-cycle events for the children of these marriages, because these concerns presented important challenges about Jewish life in America, and because, as Rabbi Abelson believed, it was important to keep members "in the building."

The challenge of Minyan Hadash is the simple fact that they are attached to more than one building. Ironically, what keeps them in the Conservative movement—commitment to their daughters' right to a bat mitzvah—does not seem to trouble them about the Orthodox one. Several of these members consider themselves ideologically Conservative Jews, committed to applying Judaism actively to modern life. Some of the women are outstanding torah readers and serve as leaders of services, obviously supportive of gender equality in Judaism. But they are nevertheless disappointed that the Conservative movement is less responsive to them and frustrated at how few of Beth El's members live their lives at the level of observance to which the Conservative movement is committed.

The synagogue's longtime commitment to pluralism is challenged by a group that regularly leaves the synagogue, acknowledging that Beth El cannot meet all its needs. This powerful core of observant Jews is largely atypical of Beth El but exceptionally important to its longtime commitment to halakha and tradition. It must also remain a constituency, like the many others who demand a place at Beth El emphasizing youth, the men's club, or young families. Beth El's ability to manage that pluralism continues to depend heavily on both its lay and its professional leadership. As they continue to see Beth El as a "home" when so many Jews are spiritually "homeless," in the words of one lay leader, or as the replacement for Jewish neighborhoods, they must constantly balance the needs of increasingly diverse groups who will probably never again share the vocabulary and norms of the previous generation.

Thus, Minyan Hadash gave voice to the needs of its observant core. At the same time, during 1995 and 1996 the synagogue created opportunities for other constituencies to meet and articulate their concerns about what they wanted of Beth El. The occasion for these parlor meetings was a budget deficit. President Bonnie Heller assembled a talented committee to look at the problem. Rather than going to the same core of big givers, the committee charged with looking at the problem decided to take a new, more egalitarian route: they would turn to all congregants to rethink their dues to the synagogue. Over the course of a year, this group of planners, with advice from a local Federation professional, devised a sophisticated process to allow congregants to learn about the problem and to let the synagogue's leadership know what they wanted and needed.

Beth El's observant core chose not to be involved in this process. Those most likely to attend were congregants in their fifties and older. Many of those who came, including the chairs of the committee, were concerned with their own children's future as Jews. The three meetings that I attended all devoted time to the theme of unmarried adult children in their twenties, and the synagogue's responsibilities came up repeatedly.

The president was struck by the diversity of the congregants' needs: at virtually every meeting congregants wanted nearly opposite things of their synagogue. Some loved the presence of small children and others were frustrated by their noise and lack of decorum. Some complained about ending Friday night services and others were thrilled about the changes in the synagogue. A few congregants were angered at the management of the synagogue and the fiscal problems, and others praised the responsible stance and hard work of those changing the dues structure.

What congregants did agree on was the desire that Beth El serve as a destination for teenagers, young adults, and older members. Most who spoke evoked the Beth El of the North Side or of the newly growing Jewish sections of St. Louis Park in the 1950s. They recalled dances at every North Side synagogue that virtually all Jewish teenagers attended. They wished for neighborhoods that were primarily Jewish.

More than one congregant worried that moving out of "the Park" (the neighborhood of St. Louis Park) had created problems for their teenage children, had taken them away from other Jews, and had alienated them from synagogue life. They wanted the synagogue once again to serve their families as it had done in the 1950s. Even as they knew that they would never return to the Jewish community of the past, they did look to the synagogue to help provide a space and resources that could provide meaning for their adult children as they sought what one member called "a spiritual home."

The challenge of pluralism for large and successful synagogues like Beth El that have counted on their ability to serve the needs of diverse groups is to understand how to speak to traditionalists who do not as easily separate themselves from movements to the right of Conservative Judaism, and to respond to congregants who find secularism appealing and for whom intermarriage is far easier than it would have been for their parents. The breadth of these needs is certainly wider than ones faced by Beth El of the 1940s and 1950s, when congregants were wedded to one another's lives in part by the simple lack of choice created by anti-Semitism. At the same time, a more pluralistic society has also made religious observance more acceptable and available. Not surprisingly, Beth El now counted among its numbers both the more religious and the more assimilated and secular.

The challenges at both ends of the spectrum have undermined Beth El as a second home, an identity that to some extent was built on the homogeneity of the past. At the same time, by continually creating subcommunities and opportunities for congregants to articulate and meet diverse needs, Beth El asserts its capacity to remain a community of communities, if not a home for all of its members.[27]

Developmental Judaism

Those who have joined Beth El and Beth Jacob are distinguished by their aesthetic and organizational commitments, as well as by neighborhoods and ideas about Judaism. Their Jewish lives are made, of course, outside of the synagogue as well, and are brought into the synagogue by those experiences. In this sense, congregants of both synagogues share a great deal in common. The majority of men and women I interviewed ranged in age from their early thirties to their mid-fifties. Their practice of Judaism is most likely descriptive of men and women born close to but primarily following World War II to the newly suburban Jewish families, about which the early sociology of Jewish life was written. They have been shaped by a series of culturally and historically specific events, with the feminist revolution probably the most significant change for those who now operate in a Jewish world that assumes gender equality.[28] They were also affected, however, by a dramatic attack on the nature of authority in American culture that has had important implications for the practice of religion in general, and for Judaism in particular, as well as by the changing role of religion in American culture over the last thirty years.[29] Earlier versions of these foundational changes were at the core of the founding of Conservative Judaism in the United States in the 1920s and 1930s. They allowed women and men to be seated together in synagogues and to liberalize Jewish practice. The post-1960s transformations of gender roles and cultural authority have only intensified these processes, creating debates over the conduct of the synagogue and more active participation of as many members as possible.

Understanding these Jews, mostly of the baby boom era, is the other face of any study of the public life of the synagogue. That question of understanding asks what the processes are that affect Jews' practice of their Judaism. In addition, what is it that links them to synagogues and to ritual, and what deters them? How do they articulate the meaning of Judaism and how to they go about living it? The "liberalized" Conservative synagogue has an analogue in the lives of individual Jews. How do these Jews understand their Judaism apart from the synagogue? What does the synagogue do to respond to those lives?

In hearing the narratives of their Jewish lives, I was struck by how dynamic the process of being a Jew is for these men and women.[30] The dramas of conversion or for those who "return" to Judaism are often recorded in scholarly works, popular articles, and in the Jewish press. However, the practice of Judaism for people who all their lives have "felt" Jewish or are "proud of being Jews" contains its own dramas, revelations, transformations, spiritual experiences, and disappointments.

Jews practice Judaism within their life cycles. Their pathways into, out of, and back into Judaism had striking parallels and interesting differences. None with whom I spoke practiced Judaism in 1996 as they had as children or, for the vast majority who attended college, as they did as college students. Nor did these Jews, men and women, imagine that in a decade they would practice Judaism precisely as they currently did. Clearly, Jewish practice can be understood in terms of developmental processes. However, the very stages in the life cycle that seem to welcome or deter Jewish life are a backdrop for, rather than an explanation of, the meaning and significance that Jews place on their religious practice. How Jews experience their Judaism is not identical to their practice of it. These men and women speak of "feeling" Jewish, of Judaism being "in here"—as they point to their hearts—of "pride" in their Judaism, which is not equivalent to the practice of mitzvot. Similarly, as was evident from synagogue initiatives around mitzvot, some Jews understand themselves to be in a process moving toward observance, even when they are not yet practicing it, or moving away from practice even when they are still doing it. It is the fact of engagement that seems to be central. Understanding how Jews came to that engagement to define it, and live with it, is what is worth pursuing.

The developmental cycle of the individual practice of Judaism is obviously paralleled in the life cycle of the synagogue. Beth Jacob is too young a synagogue for it to be apparent what the life cycle of its membership will be, and Beth El may be exceptional in that it does not appear to lose its members after their children become b'nai mitzvah. Nevertheless, the birth of children remains the critical portal to synagogue life for Beth El. In addition, the synagogue has a special appeal to young families, and children tether parents to synagogue life.

Entry Points to Jewish Life

As the vast majority of congregants look back over their lives, their children's early years motivated them to join a synagogue and to begin to consider how they would practice Judaism.[31] I was surprised by that simple fact on two counts. I had assumed that as Jews married and bore children they would not put off their Jewish lives for so long. At the same time, I was equally surprised that people in the congregations who were observant and committed Jews began those commitments as adults only after they had children. For example, one of Beth El's most active torah readers who teaches other adults is a physician in his mid-forties. He was raised at Beth El, but only went to synagogue on the High Holidays during college and medical school. He and his wife, who also grew up at Beth El, returned to the Twin Cities when he began to practice medicine. He told me,

> My family came to services on all the major holidays, but not necessarily
> Shabbat when I was a child. My wife and I became more observant
> when the kids were growing up. We came back with a one year old. We
> started getting involved in the nursery school and that was an entry
> place where we started saying, "What are we doing; what do we want to
> do as far as practice?" We did a lot of little things one at a time. I think
> we're fairly observant [now], keeping kosher in the home and observing

holidays, but we didn't do all of that before we were married or in our early married years. We started doing things one at a time. We started keeping kosher a little at a time. It was a gradual process, and we kind of would try things. . . . We added things over the years to the point that I think it would be fair to say we're pretty observant. We do lots and we like it and our kids are pretty comfortable with it.

This man's story is reflected in the lives of a Beth Jacob couple of about forty who contacted Rabbi Allen when they were adopting a baby, in order to discuss a baby-naming ceremony. They joined the synagogue after they met the rabbi and their baby arrived. The husband, a psychologist, explained,

When you have a child you really have to put your values into practice and convey them to someone else. It's not as though we didn't know what we valued before. We became more observant. We go to synagogue more often, though Beth Jacob is a synagogue where people go with children. Before we had a child we would sometimes go to Jewish friends or have friends here on Shabbat, but it wasn't a huge part of our experience.

A group of couples without children who belong to Beth El shared the same perspective, that children are an essential part of creating a Jewish life. Without children, they found observance difficult and sometimes pointless. I spoke to them at the home of one member of their *havurah*.[32] These men and women, in their late twenties and early thirties, are the only organized group of young marrieds in the synagogue. In general, this is an age group that is particularly inactive in synagogue life at Beth El and that is underrepresented at Beth Jacob. Although they are an unusually synagogue-committed group, they found it difficult to observe with regularity the religious practices that they valued in the abstract. A pharmacist in her late twenties was fairly representative of their sentiments:

My Shabbat candles from my bat mitzvah are sitting on the counter just begging to have candles put in them on some Friday night. We tried that for a while and did well, and then it was summer and it got dark so much later. I thought we'd do better this winter, but we haven't. I have a consciousness about doing more Jewish things in preparation for having children. I'm somewhat obsessed about making them Jewish kids.

Echoing her frustrations, another woman of her age, who is completing a graduate degree in social work, told me,

Sometimes we've lit candles, just the two of us, and it almost feels silly. . . . The second we have children things will be different. We won't just push the bread to the back of the cabinet [on Passover], we will actually remove it from the house. We'll go that extra step. I remember that my mom changed the dishes and it was a pain in the butt. I don't think she did it because she believed it halakhically, but it was a matter of making us Jewish and making it a Jewish home. We don't do a lot of things now, but we plan to. We have plans for more of a Jewish home.

I asked the group what difference children would make for them; why, when they would be under even more time and work pressure, would they be able to "go the extra step"? One couple in their early thirties found that question quite easy to answer. The woman, an attorney and convert to Judaism, explained:

Maybe it's easier to teach when you have something to teach, than simply to do. It's more difficult to do the action for its own sake. We always feel like something is missing. We know that if we don't give our children a viewpoint about Judaism, they won't get it. I want them to be a practicing Jew, not just in name only.

Another member commented with confidence, "I know it won't even be a hard transition. . . . Going to the synagogue for Purim or to celebrate Shabbat would feel different if I had kids here. I just felt like a lot of things center around the kids."

The birth of children, or wanting to put them in a Jewish setting for their first preschool experience, may evoke a powerful desire to resume or increase Jewish practice because these men and women are committed fundamentally to the transmission of Judaism. These dilemmas had also faced their parents and grandparents, who developed the child-oriented synagogue of the suburbs. Nevertheless, the men and women with whom I spoke often wanted a more engaged relationship with their children around Judaism than they remembered from their own childhood. A psychologist who is forty described the difference:

I want my children to have Judaism, plus I feel so obliged to give it to them. I want them to love it. My parents gave Judaism to me, but they basically sent me somewhere else to get it. I didn't quite get it from them, but they provided the opportunities. They wanted to assimilate themselves, but they wanted to do the right thing by giving us a good Jewish education. I want it to be much more for my kids. I want them to love it and appreciate it, and to be sure that they are proud of their identity.

By contrast, this woman remembers her Russian grandmother as a strong Jewish presence in her life. She wants to emulate her grandmother's ability to make Judaism "immediate": "Her frequent comments were about appreciating the U.S. because you were allowed to be Jewish here. Her whole attitude toward family was bringing us all together on a constant basis." This Beth El congregant has tried to re-create that immediacy for her children by focusing

on the Jewish calendar and making each event important in their lives. Her child
attends a day school in Minneapolis,

> so through the school calendar I make more preparations for the
> holidays. Just about every holiday I felt prepared. We make decorations,
> talk about the stories. At Purim my [preschool-age] daughter knew every
> song; we made hamantashen. As a psychologist I see it as multiple
> associations—what you cook, what you read, what you do. That's what
> I'd like to do for them.

For herself, this articulate woman believes that Judaism provides the guiding principles of her life and her foundation for understanding the future and death itself.

> Judaism solves the existentialist dilemma because of continuity. The
> reason for my being is to pass on certain cultural knowledge and
> inheritance to my children, so they can pass it on to their children. Also
> tikkun olam, that you try to make the world a better place. It's a very
> strong response, not quite strong enough to avert all of my midlife crises,
> but it's definitely a pretty strong response.

The vast majority of men and women whom I interviewed offered variations on the stories I have retold. They became reacquainted with Judaism
through the lives of their children. Synagogues, either through their nursery
schools, or through providing services for the brit mila (circumcision) or baby
naming, conversion, or as the logical place to answer the question, "How do I
make my child a Jew?" are crucial agents cooperating with families in the socialization of Jewish children. They are magnets that are far more likely to attract families with children than singles, couples without children, or those whose
children are grown. Parents discussed at length the process of making their children Jews and their concerns about the future of Jews. Thus, the Ratner Center
survey found that fewer than a quarter of Beth El's members and slightly more
than a quarter of Beth Jacob's respondents even listed preparing children to become b'nai mitzvah as a reason for joining. By contrast, 45 percent of Beth Jacob
and Beth El respondents joined their congregations to make their children Jewish and set an example.

Neither was the synagogue the sole Jewish institution to which they turned
for this partnership in transmitting a deeply felt identity and set of values. Parents frequently mentioned day schools, and they often thought camps, particularly Camp Ramah, gave children experiences that stayed with them into college
or beyond. These more intensive experiences often gave children skills that the
parents lacked and might not have wanted, but respected and admired in their
own children. A fifty-year-old lawyer, raised in a smaller Minnesota town where
his access to education was limited, spoke of his children's experience: "Clearly
to me, their becoming as observant as they are, the number one thing would be

Ramah. They learned pride in services where I never learned to daven in my life. Ramah was a primary influence on them." Beth El's families were especially proud of the synagogue program that gave their children camp scholarship money in exchange for their working in the Shabbat morning program that educated younger children. Several families liked the idea of this obligation and the message it sent their children about the importance of camp to Jewish life and the teenagers' importance to the synagogue.

Scholars and professionals alike have long recognized that children are perhaps the most important component of a family's decision to join a synagogue. These interviews suggest that the transmission of Judaism is a personally felt obligation of parents, even those who drop their children off on Shabbat and spend their time in pursuit of secular life. One of the most powerful expressions of feeling Jewish is the desire to give children what parents believe is necessary for them to become Jews. That the synagogue is crucial for this endeavor suggests both continuity with the Conservative synagogues of the 1950s as well as changes. The child-oriented synagogue of the postwar period was driven by parents' desire to give their children a Jewish education and fight their own fear of the fragility of Judaism for the younger generation. Those same concerns clearly operate for the parents and couples I interviewed, regardless of where they fell on the continuum of observance.

At the same time, today's synagogues are not synagogue "centers." They do not constitute the total social and recreational focus of either the parents or their pre- and post-b'nai mitzvah children. That realization intensifies parents' anxieties and commitments and directs their concerns to making their children share those concerns. They continue to see the synagogue as a crucial partner in that work. In contrast to the 1950s, the more observant also turn to day schools, with the result that there are subgroups of "more" and "less" committed families. That differentiation is also a newer feature of synagogue life, reflecting greater levels of observance among Conservative Jewish families.

Having children is by no means the only entryway into Jewish life for adult congregants. Many come out of their own interests. For those raised as Jews, the passage to adulthood is itself a time to renew interest in Judaism and Jewish community, often following a time of inactivity during the college years.

A woman in her mid-thirties who married recently had belonged to a Reform congregation before joining Beth Jacob. When she moved to the Twin Cities, she wanted to rejoin the Jewish community as an adult. As a single woman she often felt marginalized in synagogues. She explained her initial reaction to Beth Jacob: "When I went into the sanctuary it was very warm. The physical space and the feeling that I could test and experiment with things and that I could learn and grow in that environment were important to me. I felt immediately invited." That sense of being invited was so significant to her precisely because she fell out of the norm of typical synagogue membership. She was willing to work at finding a place for herself at Beth Jacob and she succeeded. She also eventually married another congregant.

What led her to persist in finding the right place for her Judaism was a sense of her Jewishness that she connects to her family, her upbringing, and inspiring experiences as a Jewish teenager at a leadership camp. Her Jewish identity is deeply rooted in her development, but she created one first as a single adult, and then with a husband and his son, with whom she has formed a new family.

Another Beth Jacob congregant, a man in his early thirties who is completing a graduate degree in public policy, came to the Jewish community through a different route. He was raised in a Reform household and came to dislike the Judaism of that synagogue. After college, "being Jewish was important to me, but not in terms of personal observance." He explained that in his twenties his younger brother "returned" to Judaism and studied in Israel:

> Seeing his personal transformation and character development, I had this conviction that I wanted to be part of a synagogue and community. In my mind the first step was finding a Jewish woman. It was always important to me, especially since the time of my brother's transformation, that my life partner be Jewish.

He described the woman that he married, a Beth Jacob congregant, as "my first Jewish girlfriend." She brought him to Beth Jacob. His wife had converted to Judaism three years before they met. Her deep conviction about Judaism and her knowledge about Jewish prayer and practice were all important to him. During their courtship, as he described it, he too joined the synagogue. He was attracted by

> a sense of warmth and intellectuality and rootedness to the tradition, along with the character and personality of the rabbi. . . . The critical experience is moving from being single to being partnered. I was unwilling to shop around as a single person. My relationship to conservative Judaism is bound up with my partnership with my wife. My friends who are single are not institutionally related to the Jewish people.

Indeed, family relationships repeatedly emerged as an important foundation of synagogue membership.

Others are brought to Judaism out of personal conviction, a life transformation, or a new way of seeing the world. As is consistent with Judaism as a behaviorally oriented religion focused on practice, virtually no one told me a story of a belief that changed their lives. Some did speak, however, of growing convictions and new directions that forever transformed them. A Beth El congregant's story is a particularly powerful illustration of that very experience.

A forty-year-old granddaughter of Beth El founders, she came from a family deeply engaged with Jewish communal life. She has a graduate degree in Jewish social services and, in contrast to most people I interviewed, she was very active in Jewish campus life both as an undergraduate and as a graduate student. She never regularly attended synagogue on Shabbat until she was thirty, and her husband, a high school sweetheart, did not grow up in an observant Jewish home. However, both were, almost inexplicably, profoundly moved by a friend who was also at Hebrew Union College to study for a master's degree in social work. As the woman tells it,

> We didn't even keep kosher or anything when we were students living in LA. She talked to us one day and told us why she keeps kosher. . . . It was literally a flash. We decided that day that we were going to keep kosher, which we did when we moved into an apartment. She is this wonderful down-to-earth person and came from a more right-wing Conservative home. She grew up keeping kosher. She said, "It's just so beautiful. I remember that I am Jewish with every meal that I eat." We trace everything that we've done to that moment. We really feel that once you start keeping kosher that sets you on a definite path.
>
> Then we started going to synagogue [when they returned to the Twin Cities], but I don't really know why. When my son was born and he was a baby we started coming to shul. In fact, the first time we came to shul with my daughter was when my son was six months old and my daughter was eighteen months. She screamed her head off and I felt so guilty. My daughter has never been to a synagogue and she thinks this is a horrible place. This is telling me something. We began to be friendly with the people we met going every week. We started having our kids at the Orthodox day school. All the people whose kids were at Beth El and the day school were going every week. We formed a *havurah* four years ago, which led to us moving into the neighborhood. It was the biggest step we made. We lost a lot of money on our house. We occasionally walked four and a half miles if we attended a bar mitzvah and it would offend the family if we drove. We became Shomer Shabbat and live near our friends.

The growing involvement for this family, slow and awkward at first, steadily evolved into their present-day commitment to traditional Judaism.

Conversion is also a powerful entryway into Jewish life and practice. Indeed one convert of decades ago who teaches Hebrew in a variety of synagogues told me that the majority of people she teaches are converts. She finds their level of commitment, like hers, very high. At Beth Jacob, she explained, "Converts take the lead in Hebrew and b'nai mitzvah classes." People's reasons for converting to Judaism certainly vary. Men and women who I interviewed converted because of marriage, an uncanny sense that they were always drawn to

Jewish people and things, a growing alienation from their own tradition because of attitudes toward women, or many other reasons. Jews who come to Judaism by choice tend to be active Jews and synagogue participants.

These life stories suggest that there is considerable variation in what brings men and women to Jewish observance and identification, usually after some years away from a synagogue or the practices of one's family. Children, particularly young children, remain a significant motivation for increasing one's practice of Judaism in order to transmit it, with the synagogue being a crucial setting to facilitate that transmission. Many Jewish families were willing to "try" or to "experiment" with Jewish practices, as they undertook to make their children and often themselves Jews on their own terms.

Claiming Judaism

Synagogue members are typically thought to be Jews who attend synagogue two or three times a year on the High Holidays. At Beth El, in addition, affiliation is more powerfully tied to life-cycle events: weddings, deaths, coming of age, and to a lesser extent births. These events bind synagogue members to their institution and their rabbi. Congregants in their sixties and seventies recalled to me their rabbi visiting them in the hospital, helping them to plan a funeral for a family member, or being by the bedside of a dying spouse or relative. The prominence of passage, rather than the High Holidays, suggests that the compelling experience of Judaism are those translated into one's private life. Committed Jews, I found, were those who found ways to define and claim Judaism on their own terms, and life passages created their readiness for making those claims.

A Beth Jacob couple in their late thirties described how this process had worked in their own family. Both grew up in the Twin Cities, attending different synagogues. The husband's parents were completely alienated from Jewish practice. The wife's parents were more communally involved but attended synagogue only infrequently. She and her husband had positive memories of the synagogues they had grown up in. With their daughter's adoption and their subsequent decision to enroll her in kindergarten at the day school, they have thought a great deal about creating a Jewish family life. In describing their experiences of Passover, the husband recounted the various ways they have tried to celebrate a seder:

> Her parents . . . whip through a service in an unorganized way; . . . [at] my parents . . . we have to bring over the kippahs ourselves, and force some basic blessings, and then we went to the rabbi's this year. We were there for what felt like eight and a half hours, and I'm not quite ready for this, though it was a very nice experience, a learning experience. So this year we decided that every year we're going to do our own and

invite others, Jewish and non-Jewish, and make it what our ideas are about what it's supposed to be. Much as we're trying to push for it, our daughter pulls us along. Whether I like it or not I want to do it for her and make sure she has good experiences, so that it's fun for her.

Consequently, in adulthood these parents are working to formulate their own Judaism.

A Beth El member found in her increased skills of chanting a variety of Jewish texts the path into a powerful experience of Jewish life:

When the ritual director saw during our son's bar mitzvah that I had Hebrew and singing skills, he asked me one day if I would be willing to learn how to do the *haftarah* for Rosh Hashanah. I was reluctant. Well, I thought I'll try it, and if it doesn't seem to be going well I'll just tell them I won't do it. The cantor gave me a tape of the Rosh Hashanah *haftarah* and then the trop. I found out that I loved practicing. The idea wasn't so much the occasion on which you did it as the practicing, which became something I looked forward to doing every day. Chanting something that was ancient, chanting itself, a system that has been around for hundreds and hundreds of years, it just gave me a sense of real bonds with the past, with Jewish people everywhere all over the world. . . . It helped me find ways to forge connections that have become increasingly important over the years. And since being Jewish was a central part of my childhood, especially Camp Ramah, I think that sense of connectedness had a lot to do with connecting me back to my childhood, and that was very important. And it's musically beautiful and I was discovering that I love to sing. I did not even know that I had a voice that was exceptional in any way. And it's strange, but I have no interest in singing other things.

This woman, a painter and art historian in her late forties, went on to have an adult bat mitzvah, in part inspired by a friend.

After I learned *haftarah* it didn't occur to me to try torah because it seemed so much more difficult. The cantor encouraged me because he said that we need torah readers. I thought I might as well do it. Then I thought if I am going to do all of this I might as well be bat mitzvahed. . . . A very dear friend of ours who was a convert to Judaism, and four of her women friends, had a group bat mitzvah. She has a terrible voice; she couldn't keep a tune. She had weak Hebrew skills, and it was such a moving experience. They did the whole service. . . . I thought if she could do this, it is outrageous that I should still be afraid or reluctant to put in the time. I called the cantor and asked him to make me a tape with the torah trop, and I have never looked back. The process has been so very, very rewarding and meaningful to me.

Indeed, this gifted torah reader told me at synagogue that she now felt "empty" when she was not preparing a torah reading. She had come to define her Judaism most profoundly through her "ownership" of important skills that connected her to her own childhood, as well as to the Jewish people, to Jewish history, and to weekly Shabbat prayer at the synagogue. She literally found her Jewish voice.

Many of the congregants with whom I spoke experienced their Jewish competence and power within their families and in home rituals. Like the Beth Jacob family who learned to express their Jewishness by creating their own seder, many families find that Shabbat rituals play that role. A Beth El couple in their late forties, like so many others, never joined a synagogue until their first child was nursery school age. The husband began, "We became more observant just to make sure that our children had a Jewish identity." His wife continued, "We started observing Shabbat." And her husband explained further:

> To me it's perpetuating a culture and a religion. I already had an indoctrination for a ten-year period. I didn't need to be connected. But after I had kids it became important and I've seen that importance grow as they've gotten older. I think it's more of a life-cycle thing. I take more of a generational, historical perspective. I feel that Judaism is more a cultural phenomenon than religious. I'm not a very religious person in that sense.

His wife responded, "I'm more religious. Shabbat was equally for the kids and myself. I do enjoy lighting candles and saying the blessings."

In discussing their sons' *b'nai mitzvah* they again expressed their different ways of constructing their Judaism. The wife learned to read torah for her oldest son's bar mitzvah and read a few more lines for her younger son's rite of passage. She added, "My husband passed his bar mitzvah tallit down to our older son at his bar mitzvah, and then at my younger son's bar mitzvah it got passed down to him. Our older son got the tallit he had bought in Israel the summer before. Our youngest son's job is to pass it on to the next generation." This transmission of identity remains a powerful medium for many families.

In addition, though, this couple found another meaningful Jewish experience with a study group of ten couples, led by Rabbi Herring. When Rabbi Herring left the pulpit, the group did not continue and they "miss it very much." They also thought that with more time they would enjoy studying more intensely.

When I asked them how they imagined their lives in ten years, their immediate response was their concern for intermarriage. The wife responded, "I hope I will be showing you photographs of my Jewish grandchildren." The husband added, "I don't see us going back to where we were [before our children were born]." They anticipate continuing their observance of the Shabbat and about the same level of involvement in synagogue life. They are prouder of their sons' greater competence and commitment to their Judaism than their own, and equally secure in their own development into a Jewish family.

This family appears at one level to be the very embodiment of a child-oriented Judaism. At the same time, they continue to pursue their own limited avenues of Jewish practice that feel significant enough to convince them that they have evolved as Jews who often celebrate Friday night as a family. Their younger son's desire to have regular, rather than occasional, Friday night celebrations mattered a great deal to them. After studying with Rabbi Herring, they began to put aside money for *tzedaka* before lighting Shabbat candles. Like so many other congregants, their subjective experience of their Jewish practice is committed within their own terms.

Parenthood, marriage, and personal faith have all served as important motivations for congregants to change and develop their Judaism. Another important feature of identity in religious development was gender. Both Marshall Sklare's and Jack Wertheimer's studies of the Conservative synagogue found women's growing involvement a significant feature of a changing Judaism. They noted their presence after World War II and their growing religious involvement after the 1970s as well. The meaning of that involvement has not yet been fully analyzed, since it is still unfolding. At a minimum, women's presence has quite simply doubled the pool of available Jews to recruit for congregational life and leadership. Women reflected on their Jewish practice in a self-conscious way that men did not.

No man in this study mentioned wearing a tallit as a choice or decision, for example. Adult male Jews wear them as part of prayer. It is a given. The particular tallit might have sentimental value or was chosen for other reasons. But wearing it is not an issue. For women, by contrast, whether to wear a tallit was a question. When a woman chose to wear a tallit, it became a personal statement and a ritual act that more consciously linked her to Jewish practice.

Similarly, many women I interviewed were torah readers. Each told me about the importance of other women's torah reading in her own decision to learn this skill. They felt encouraged and supported by the presence of other torah readers who were women. It was a simultaneous experience of continuity with Jewish history and of innovation.

The sense of self-conscious choice that I heard from these women was not unlike what I heard from Jews who considered themselves newcomers to observance and Jewish knowledge. Their choices in Jewish practice seemed to personalize their Judaism and create a strong sense of conviction.

Creating Jewish practice does not always move from less to more, or smoothly from childhood commitment to young adult autonomy to mature involvement. One Beth Jacob member, an attorney in her late thirties, came from a family that was minimally attached to a synagogue. Her interest in Judaism grew out of her work as an attorney with virtually all non-Jews. She was struck by some of their stereotypes about what Jews believed and did, and as a result she began her own remarkable journey of education and discovery. She organized others like herself to hire teachers, attend a learners' minyan, and generally act as an important force in Beth Jacob's early years. Now that she is married and a mother of a young child, her Judaism has shifted. She told me,

> I think that Beth Jacob exists as a place to build community. Since I've had the kid I can't concentrate in the way that I used to. . . . Half the time I'm in the crying room. Just to be there with other Jewish couples and their kids and to have our baby get to know their babies is important. I have a whole different relationship with it now with the baby. It's still wonderful, just in a very different way. I stopped wearing a tallis because I was getting spit up on it every week. . . . I imagine it will swing back once she is in the nursery and you can sit in shul again.

Another Beth Jacob congregant stands at the other end of the family cycle, age sixty and with grown children. Her evolution as a Jew was atypical:

> We moved into the Jewish community when our daughter was four and started nursery school and that brought us to the big Conservative synagogue. I had this [urge] to be involved in the community. I must have chaired every bake sale. I was a member of every Jewish board in the community. There was always something missing. As my kids moved through Talmud Torah, when my youngest moved up the grades a new rabbi came to head the school. I can't tell you what a difference that made. We've always lit shabbos candles and made motzi every Friday night since we were married, and that's thirty-six years. We have a thoroughly kosher home. Our youngest started working with real Jewish texts. He would come home with such dinner table conversations that it was the impetus for me to go over to the university. I suddenly looked around and thought I am driving myself so frantic with all these committee meetings and all the things I'm doing, but I'm not really learning anything. It's a shame our whole Jewish community needs to acquire tools to study. I studied Hebrew, then Jewish history, then Talmud. I have found enormous satisfaction in my Judaism from getting back in touch with our texts. This is what Judaism has been for 3,000 years. Everything comes with different stages in life. I have to be out of town or on my deathbed to miss the rabbi's Talmud class. It's the high point of my week. . . . Now I've taken three Talmud classes at the university, but it was a university look at the Talmud—that is very different than what he is doing. He's introducing us to the way that for two thousand years Jews have studied text. It's so exciting I can't believe how fast the time flies by. My husband is in a different place than I

am. . . . No one goes in lockstep in their trip through life. I feel happy to come to services by myself. When he feels like coming to services, he comes with me. I read Hebrew texts with three different groups every week and that's my Judaism. We say motzi when we sit down to eat every night, and that's my Judaism. I feel that my Judaism is a little more widely disbursed over my life. It isn't so focused on Shabbat morning.

These examples suggest that congregants' subjective experience of their Jewishness connects feelings of identity and meaning to specific practices of varying commitment and intensity that change over time, whether with the practice of kashrut, Shabbat observance, torah reading, attending services, or study.

A Beth Jacob congregant in his thirties saw the synagogue as a place that allowed him to grow:

Joining Beth Jacob has been a really empowering experience for me as a Jew because there is so much emphasis on adult education. I had an adult bar mitzvah. I learned how to *layn* [chant] torah. . . . The message that is very clear is that every individual can do anything within the tradition that can be done and should do it.

What sets Jews on this type of path varies, of course. But the very act of asking people to participate is a critical role for Jewish professionals in this process. At Beth El the synagogue's ritual director asked two of the synagogue's finest torah readers to consider learning to read the *haftarah*, something that at the time seemed unlikely. The Beth El member who now teaches the skill vividly remembered the moment he was first asked:

I think as far as involvement in the synagogue, our ritual director personally was monumental in getting me more involved in participation in services. One day I was sitting in Saturday services and he asked me to read the *haftarah* for the upcoming holidays. I said, "You know I haven't read since my bar mitzvah." . . . He opened to my *haftarah* from my bar mitzvah. It made the hairs on the back of my neck stand up. It was twenty-five years before. I don't think he looked it up. It kind of got to me that I was intended to read again. . . . Now I teach torah reading and Hebrew to adult bar and bat mitzvah students.

This congregant was unsure if the ritual director remembered his *haftarah* or if finding it was a coincidence. In either case this uncanny confrontation with a skill he once possessed certainly moved him to relearn it.

As I discovered in my many conversations, this story was fairly typical. None of the men and women to whom I spoke recounted being asked to participate and refusing, although certainly people must have for many reasons. At Beth Jacob one couple, both Jewish professionals, said that they did not consider themselves "daveners" and had not planned to attend synagogue regularly. But, the husband commented, "Beth Jacob is part of the weekly circuit because of our involvement in Jewish communal life. We didn't intend it that way at all. . . . But we have a rabbi who notices when you're gone and it gradually changes over time. He would ask, where were you when you were gone?" I asked the man if he found the question intrusive. He replied, "No, because ultimately I would rather be remembered when I'm gone."

In addition to inviting Jews to participate Jewishly in synagogue life, rabbis often have a great effect on their congregants. This was particularly the case with Rabbi Allen, who was completing his ninth year at Beth Jacob, of which he was the first rabbi. Because the year I spent at Beth El was a transitional one for a young rabbi, I had fewer opportunities to learn about the rabbi's place in the lives of congregants, though in a brief time it was apparent that he had touched many members. Anecdotally, congregants mentioned Rabbi Herring's importance to their children or the Abelson family's role in lives of individuals.

What Beth Jacob's members particularly value about Rabbi Allen is their unshakable sense that he will be there for them at times of loss, personal crisis, spiritual searching, or uncertainty. What congregants have described is a rabbi who is there with a strong Jewish presence. One congregant, a forty-year-old woman who has had both a chronic illness and major heart surgery, had many experiences with rabbis' visits in hospitals, where she was offered platitudes. By contrast, she described an occasion created by Rabbi Allen for her to address her illness through ritual:

> In terms of my illness, Rabbi Allen has been right there. Last year I had open-heart surgery and he was there every day. . . . He was just there as a friend, and as a rabbi. He gave me a book of Psalms about healing that was really beautiful and he would say a *mi sheberakh*. That aspect was there, but I always feel that he respected who we are and where we're at. He'd come over just to talk to me. Recently he suggested that I go to the mikvah to do a renewal around a difficult time with my health. I had never been to the mikvah except for my child's conversion. This was about a month ago. It was really one of the most incredible spiritual experiences. . . . I was very ambivalent about going; I canceled a few times. I finally decided to go because I felt I owed it to him. . . . I was telling my mom I was going, and I was ambivalent because I didn't know what it would be like, and she wanted to come. We went. . . . He asked me if I wanted to read any Psalms so I brought this book of Psalms. I read one; he read a few; my mom read one. It was right before Passover, so we started talking about the waters of transition, the Red Sea, then relating to what I've been through. He makes everything so accessible and meaningful and whole. Then I went into the mikvah. My mom was there and I said the prayers. He said the prayers from the outside. . . . I just had this feeling afterward that I was so sorry that I had not brought

people who were close to me because it was so meaningful. . . . It's
something I would like to incorporate into my life. I've never done it
and I'm forty years old.

Another congregant described seeking out the rabbi while he worked out
his feelings of anger at his ex-wife. An attorney in his mid-forties, he had an
excellent Jewish education and had taken Jewish studies courses at the university level as well. He told me that he turned to his rabbi, not for technical advice or psychotherapy but for understanding:

> I am sure that some of this thinking about that relationship was jarred
> loose by my father's impending death and feeling as though something
> was changing in my life. I wanted to find some way of letting go of the
> anger and the past. I had a conversation with Morris. I told him, "I
> know what the tradition says about forgiveness, but I'm not sure I know
> how to do it." And at some point in the course of the conversation he
> said, "You know, it might be helpful to think about this in terms of the
> category of the tradition, of sins that are punishable by a human court
> and sins that are punishable only by God." I knew about the category, of
> course, but I had never thought about it. "There may be some sense in
> which you can think about saying this is out of your hands. You no
> longer have to hold this against her. This is now between her and God."
> And things clicked. . . . I think I can let go of feelings and not continu-
> ally hold onto my anger and hurt at what she did to me. It's about her
> life and her relationship with a higher power, even though I don't
> believe in a traditional notion of God.

Rabbi Allen is self-conscious about his role in his congregants' lives and in
the lives of other Jews who seek him out. He explained:

> As a rabbi I have some understanding and a real sense of responsibility
> that people feel the shul is there for them. I'm not sure that we can meet
> everyone's needs, but the shul is a presence for them. In times of people's
> crises I demonstrate that Judaism can and should speak to
> them. . . . Over these ten years I could not have imagined that people
> would have shared with me the kinds of honesty that I'm dealing with
> now. . . . There's a lot more pain out there and disarray about how to
> organize one's life. . . . It's not so easy to offer a prescription. On the
> other hand I really believe that there is something eternal about the
> message of Judaism that can't get lost in the wishes of the moment. The
> traditional understanding of service of God is so under attack. We want
> to be users of God. The real question is how to serve God.

Rabbi Allen's presence to his congregants, calling them during times of difficulty, seeking them out if they stop coming to shul, praying with them, and
using ritual moments to respond to their crises, have been immensely important

to his congregants. As a rabbi he serves God and moves his congregants to serve God through their very private life experiences. He places his congregants inside Jewish experience and history. He links their stories to that story.

These narratives of development and change are not necessarily stories of faith or belief in a personal God. Rather, these men and women, in their various ways, assume a personal relationship to Jewish practice, Jewish categories, and Jewish community. They are moved by very private experiences, by feelings of belonging, and by others asking them to learn skills or participate more actively in Jewish life.

I have learned from these Jews not only how varied those paths are, but how important it is to them to be shown that they have a place within Jewish practice and beliefs. Many of Beth El's members told me how pleased they were that their practice, however imperfect, was acknowledged as legitimate, that doing less might lead them to do more. Similarly, I was told by Beth Jacob's members that being asked to do more, being asked where they were last Shabbat, mattered and allowed them to feel counted in their community. These multiple portals link private and synagogue life to one another. They suggest that Judaism is a partnership between congregant, rabbi, and congregation.

Challenges to Development

And then, sometimes not. I have also spoken to synagogue members who cannot participate as they might like or their community would like them to. They find prayer in particular a virtually impossible medium for Jewish identity and observance. But they do not follow the obvious route of becoming secular Jews and disappearing from the synagogue. They remain for their children, their spouses, and because they want to support synagogues. Nevertheless, any picture of a "developmental Judaism," or of synagogue life that overlooks the great struggle of some Jews with prayer would be partial at best.

The majority of both congregations does not attend Shabbat services regularly, but Shabbat morning nevertheless remains a central focus of synagogue life. Its constancy, its source of community for synagogue regulars, and its setting for marking a variety of life passages, including b'nai mitzvah, weddings, anniversaries, and anniversaries of deaths, draws congregants in.

Within the developmental Judaism of a variety of congregants, Jewish identity may be high, even when tolerance, understanding, or the significance of prayer is low. Several people I met felt that they simply could not pray and hence could not attend synagogue regularly. One of these congregants declined the presidency of his synagogue board because he knew it would require his regular attendance, something he felt he could not do.

Several of the men—and it was overwhelmingly men who held this position—were products of the Conservative movement's most elite institutions. They had attended Camp Ramah. One had participated in Beth El's leadership training program with Rabbi Kassel and Shirley Abelson and subsequently taught at the local Talmud Torah. The other had taken courses at the Jewish Theological Seminary while a student at another institution. Each continued to do secular and sacred Jewish study and sent their children to day schools. In one case, the family rarely went to synagogue on the Shabbat. In the other case the mother took the children to synagogue.

Neither of these Beth El congregants described a personal crisis of faith that led to these choices. A physician in his late forties said,

> Unlike a lot of Conservative practice, there has not been a lot of evolution in the prayer. A lot of it is still taken from texts written a thousand years ago [and] a lot of it is based on a supernatural conception of God that I don't share. I don't mind the torah reading and interpreting the texts, but the repetitious aspect bores me very quickly and it's not a good use of my time. Given my schedule and how limited my free time is, I just don't want to spend it in synagogue.

This congregant's family has a special and elaborate Friday night celebration each week. Their teenage children are always home for their shared meal and time together. He draws an important distinction between home and synagogue practice. On the High Holidays, when four generations of his family are seated together in the synagogue, he brings a work of Jewish history or philosophy to read instead of the prayer book.

A younger congregant, in his early forties and a lawyer, looked at the problem of prayer in a different way:

> What I don't like about any big synagogue that I've been involved with is that the whole thing focuses on services and prayer and that's not my favorite part. . . . I'm trying to teach myself Yiddish . . . to read Yiddish literature. I think there's a lot of richness in the Jewish tradition. As it was originally practiced, prayer was only a piece of what you were doing. For a lot of people you would study a lot and prayer would be woven into that. In its proper place it would be more meaningful. But if all you do is go to synagogue and do a set service it's not going to be meaningful.

Beth Jacob members often openly discuss the fact that the community draws individuals who come to shul but do not pray. One of the synagogue's founders, a man of sixty, explained:

> There's a real power to coming there Shabbos morning, and for me it's not the essence of the prayers because I still haven't learned how to pray. . . . I don't know what the prayers mean except for a few. I have trouble concentrating on the prayers. I'll sometimes just bring some-

thing else to read. It's a prayer service, but I don't pray. It doesn't trouble
me so much.

These three men have taken different routes to integrating synagogue and
Jewish practice into their lives. They remain connected to the synagogue
and Jewish practice while largely giving up on prayer. Realities of American
Conservative Jewish life have defined observance in terms of prayer in the synagogue. But my study revealed that across the spectrum of education and knowledge, committed Jews find prayer a difficult and even confounding aspect of
Jewish life.

This closer look at the development of individual Jewish practice suggests
a voluntary and dynamic process. Age, background, gender, an openness to religion, and many other factors shape the practice of Judaism. These men and
women look to their Judaism as a way to locate themselves in households and
communities, in history and in family. They expect the synagogue and its rabbis and other professionals to help them and in some cases not to hinder them
in that process.

Conclusions

I began this essay with a comparative question. If the Conservative synagogue
of the 1950s reflected the American Jewish culture of its time, what does the
Conservative synagogue tell us about contemporary life? The answer lies in great
part in understanding what the attraction of Conservative Judaism was after
World War II and even as early as the 1920s and 1930s. Social scientists of suburban Jewish life argue that children of immigrants turned to Conservative Judaism to meet two needs. On the one hand, this new form of Judaism was to
provide the appropriate setting in which to articulate the immigrants' children's
class mobility and their embrace of American suburban life. On the other, Conservative Judaism's maintenance of tradition through liturgy, Hebrew, torah reading, and the goals of observance linked its participants to a Judaism they
understood as authentic. Synagogues also focused on educating suburban children in a contemporary fashion so that they would understand and continue to
practice Judaism.

Social class and traditionalism were especially powerful in a movement that
was thought to be dominated by its laity. Sklare noted that new suburbanites
created Conservative synagogues and then hired rabbis. Although the rabbi provided leadership and thus set out certain expectations, he rarely was a founder
of these synagogues.[33] Despite the towering presence of some pulpit rabbis such
as David Aronson at Beth El, the movement has been distinguished by the power
of the laity and its own definition of Conservative Judaism.

There is remarkable continuity between the synagogues that Marshall Sklare studied and the ones where I spent a year. Both the Ratner Center survey and my interviews indicate that many members define themselves against a Reform Judaism in which men do not cover their heads and English is the language of liturgy. Congregants look to the synagogue to facilitate innovation, but within a context of a traditional style of worship. Women's equality is very important to both synagogues and a source of differentiation from Orthodox Judaism. By the second edition of *Conservative Judaism*, Sklare noted that women were interacting in the religious sphere and not just in the organizational life of the congregation. The education of children remains a crucial role of the Conservative synagogue and, given increasing demands for what children should learn and be competent to do and know as Jews, the function is all the greater. It is not difficult to find the core of suburban Conservative Judaism still alive and well fifty years later at Beth El and Beth Jacob.

But in another, less apparent sense, these synagogues differ dramatically from the Conservative synagogues of the 1950s. In these four decades it is simply a fact that Jews are not joining a Conservative rather than a Reform or Orthodox synagogue as a matter of their class or as a statement of their mobility. Beauty and civility are no longer primary points of differentiation among synagogues.[34] The very uniformity of Jews' social class position in the United States has removed the once powerful links between denomination and social class.[35] Indeed, in the final decade of the twentieth century, Beth Jacob has an ideology of modesty and egalitarianism that is a direct reaction against synagogues of a former time.

These synagogues are different from an earlier period for a second and related reason. Their congregants do not conceive of their lives as centered in the synagogue. Indeed, a considerable range of the synagogues' members are committed to a number of Jewish institutions, religious and secular. Day schools in particular attract the time, interest, and funds of many congregants. Communities overlap. In general, Jews' far greater access to the dominant culture diminished their need to socialize exclusively in the synagogue. American pluralism, for all its limitations, cuts in both directions. It intensifies and diffuses Jewish involvement by making Jewishness more acceptable and by lowering the barriers to access to the larger society for Jews who want it.

Therefore, the synagogue no longer symbolizes American Jewish life as it did for the period that stretched from the late 1940s to the late 1960s. I suggest instead that what these two synagogues do is locate congregants far more specifically within the practice of Judaism. The synagogues increasingly articulate what they do and what they want congregants to do within a "religious idiom," in terms of competence, active participation, and observance. These rabbis and synagogues have created a more demanding curriculum for what children must learn in order to become b'nai mitzvah. Adults learn a variety of skills, and whether in a synagogue with or without a cantor, increased emphasis is placed on members' own skills at reading and chanting sacred texts and prayers.

This "religiously competent" idiom does not mean that congregants are in fact more observant, particularly at the larger synagogue, nor that the majority does not remain in some sense passive participants in religious life. I simply suggest that what embodies a synagogue culture is less likely to be a social program than a religious one, due to the obvious fact that the synagogue does not serve a primarily social function. Both congregations must create community, but the methods used by the synagogue-center simply are no longer relevant to these late twentieth century Jews. Thus, Beth El's Men's Club is still an active and important part of the synagogue, but it serves only the senior population rather than all male congregants as it once did. The child-rearing generation is more likely to come to family programs like "Artsy Shabbat" or "Tot Shabbat," or to a study group or Shabbat morning services. Family participation as a unit and Jewish observance are now important orienting points.

Ironically, therefore, what is left to Conservative synagogues is to serve as a key site for creating a Jewish life. Beth Jacob and Beth El go about this quite differently, as this essay illustrates, despite the fact that they are clearly both Conservative synagogues committed to egalitarianism. And Congregants within each synagogue also practice and understand their Judaism quite differently from one another as well. Those differences are instructive about Conservative Judaism.

Both synagogues used idioms of observance, albeit differently, to focus their congregants' lives for the year. The highly observant core and the rarely attending members, in their interviews, both made strong claims for the importance and significance of their Judaism. The synagogue is a powerful emblem of Jewish life for all these Jews. In these claims, subjective identification and objective activity are far from identical, though paradoxically that is not apparent to those who rarely attend.

Particularly at Beth El, but at Beth Jacob to some extent as well, those who participate less often understand their Judaism in highly personal ways. They link their Jewish practice and synagogue participation to "continuity," to the importance of family, home, and the transmission of Judaism to other generations. These issues are not irrelevant to more observant Jews, but they are not the sole focus. Given these powerful associations, it is not a surprise that children are a very important entry point for congregants into renewed Jewish practice.

For the more observant members, choice, participation, and active involvement are at the heart of Jewish practice. Members discussed the importance of the tradition, their pleasure in their competence, their decision to take on mitzvot, and a general sense of the importance of involvement. They also talked about choosing to send children to day school and their "pride" in making a choice different than the generations that preceded them.

In contrast to another generation, more and less observant congregants are not differentiated by age or class. The observant members of each synagogue are not older and are not immigrants and do not possess many of the features associated with traditionalism following World War II. It is not the intention of this ethnographic study to explain what differentiates more and less observant Conservative Jews from one another. These congregants' biographies do not readily reveal why the adult son of a cantor loves the continuity of the Jewish people but cannot tolerate praying, or why the daughter of thoroughly ethnically committed but secular Jews today is among the Shabbat-observant community of one of these synagogues. Nevertheless, the vast majority of the Jews whom I interviewed did come from families who belonged to synagogues, and a synagogue member is far more likely to produce another synagogue member. As a social fact of the late twentieth century, however, observant and committed Jews might be younger than they were fifty years ago and are likely to still be in families of their own with children.

Jews who are inclined to seek out a Jewish life in the Conservative synagogues where I spent a year are more likely to become torah readers, to undertake an adult bat mitzvah, and to learn to read Hebrew.[36] Certainly at Beth El there are still congregants whose lives may well focus around synagogue voluntarism, but the idiom of congregational life is shifting. Under Rabbi Herring there was considerable discussion of whether board members should be expected to be more Jewishly active, and board presidents now feel that they should be present at Shabbat morning services. For a year, Rabbi Kahn's very full and well-spoken charge to the bar or bat mitzvah consistently had one theme in common. He asked the adolescent how he or she would make Jewish practice an important part of life, and to what new mitzvot he or she was committed the day after the event. Rabbi Kahn was unabashed in praising more observant families and especially commending children who continued their Jewish educations. There was no ambiguity from the *bimah* on these public occasions.

In the 1950s Marshall Sklare did not anticipate that the idiom of observance and Jewish practice would lead to Jewish identification. Rather, he believed that the ability of the synagogue to attract Jews for social and cultural reasons would facilitate a high level of identification even in the face of decreased religious observance. This is not the path of these synagogues, which embody a vision for the future that is committed to community, but not through a "center" model. These synagogues address observance directly, but not in the language of right-wing Judaism. Thus, by encouraging "celebration," Rabbi Kahn believed he was forging a new path at Beth El that urged Shabbat observance, even if it was partial and imperfect. Rabbi Allen regularly challenged his congregants to move in a single halakhic direction, but to do so slowly or gradually if necessary.

These approaches to Jewish practice were not inventions of the liberal Judaism of the 1990s, but they are nevertheless striking in light of the Jewish lives of congregants. The Judaism envisioned at Beth El and Beth Jacob is not rationalized solely through memory, responsibility to children, or because it fits well into American society—bedrocks of an earlier time. In both synagogues Jewish practice is acknowledged to exist by necessity within the realities of congregants' limited time and the multiple demands placed on them. The Judaism of these congregations focuses on active participation in a relatively private dimension of life, home, and eating, as well as in increased public participation in Shabbat and holiday services. In different ways, the rabbis taught Jews how to build their Judaism into a different type of life and family than existed four decades ago.

Beth El and Beth Jacob are differentiated by age and size, by history and founding principles. Beth El's members are deeply tied to family, to neighborhood memories, and to a Judaism that evokes them both. Beth Jacob, through its own founding vision and expectations about observance, evokes the power to choose community and observance. Both of these powerful themes shape the Judaism of the professional middle class so widely represented in these communities. Along several dimensions, among rather different experiences of Judaism, choice and personal meaning seem very important to these Conservative Jews. The depth of feeling that ties many Jews to synagogue and limited Jewish practice is frankly a world apart from Shabbat-observant Jews who pray daily and frequently study the classical texts of Judaism. I would not presume to find a single set of symbols and meanings that tie all these Conservative Jews to their synagogues. Yet beyond self-definition as Conservative Jews, the men and women who spoke to me seem to share an intense desire to participate actively in their Jewish lives, whatever form they take. They talk often about that process of self-definition, the choices they make for themselves and their children, and their desire to make their Judaism meaningful.

This need to make Judaism meaningful through personal activism, albeit along many dimensions, certainly created the need met by Minyan Hadash and other such alternative groups. That fact has been well documented in the study of religion in the United States. But less apparent perhaps is how such a need strengthens the relationship of rabbi and congregants. Rabbis Morris Allen and Robert Kahn were always part of the conversations I had with congregants, and not because I brought them up. Very little surprised me as much in my year of research as the role of the rabbi. Because I am a product of the 1960s, when authority was so much under attack, and did not join a synagogue until I was in my thirties, I had become accustomed to thinking about religious community in fairly voluntaristic and egalitarian terms.

While lay leadership was quite powerful in both synagogues, the importance of the rabbi to congregants was neither trivial nor minimal. What the rabbis said was important to congregants. They looked to the rabbi for guidance. Kol Nidre sermons mattered to hundreds, if not thousands of people. Challenging sermons about practice and expectations were taken seriously by congregants. Words spoken at a sickbed, at times of mourning, in celebration, and at life passages wedded congregants to their synagogues and their rabbis.

I learned from these two synagogues what it means to have a rabbi who has a vision, despite the fact that their two visions were rather different from one another. Nor does one need to minimize that a vision may well be worked out between the rabbi and congregants, to acknowledge that when articulated by the rabbi that vision has a force it would otherwise lack. To describe the Conservative movement as "lay-led" should never obscure the meaning of rabbinical, and for that matter cantorial, leadership. I was surprised to learn repeatedly that the simple offer of an aliya or the offer to teach a new skill was often the source of a congregant's feeling invited into their Judaism, not just their community. These clergy are exceptionally powerful figures in personalizing Jewish life for congregants.

Rabbis may and should have organizational skills. If, therefore, Conservative movement synagogues are indeed moving toward an increasingly "religious" definition of their roles, rabbis will surely need not only a vision but also a way to communicate it. Like these rabbis, they will have to express that vision not just from the bimah, but in the life passage, the classroom, and the boardroom.

At their most cynical some experts in American Judaism described the role of the rabbi to me as that of a mezuza: "You display him at all important events." But it is clear from these two congregations that the rabbi did not serve as a passive symbol. In both the Shabbat and kashrut campaigns the rabbis defined and shaped the meaning of observance. Congregants described the important things that rabbis did for them as Jewish interventions that helped them understand situations differently. In this sense the rabbis served to make that critical link between personal life and Jewish practice.

Many of these synagogues' religious activists were in some sense newcomers. Adult women became active participants as adults because they did not have the option of equal participation in their younger years. Many highly observant Jews were raised in minimally observant Conservative homes. Some were converts to Judaism. Active participation mattered to all these categories of Jews. Women and converts typically remarked that their newly acquired religious competence allowed them to do what Jews had always done. Active participation seemed to be the rule for regulars, and offers to learn and to teach were important to them.

I have presented a picture of late twentieth century Conservative Jewish life that paradoxically puts Judaism at the center, without suggesting that Jews are more likely to be observant than previous generations. While synagogue members are more observant than nonmembers, the Ratner Center survey revealed that even members seem to observe fewer commandments than they recall their parents observing. They live in more diverse communities than their families did, and they lack the sanction of a more homogeneous Jewish community that enforced, to some extent, kashrut and Shabbat observance. Their levels of education are higher than their families, and they are more likely to be professionals than their fathers, let alone their mothers. Their time is more limited and their options for how to spend it far greater. Their families continue to anchor them to their Judaism.

Synagogue life appears to communicate a Jewish idiom for the lives of Jews. The social action of the 1960s (an American concept) has been replaced with *tikkun olam* (a Jewish-inflected concept) and mitzvot in the 1990s. Kashrut and the Shabbat, always important to the Conservative movement, are mitzvot, and have become a somewhat different set of issues in the lives of American Jews who must confront the demands of two-career families and the homogenizing forces of contemporary society. Even among the minimally observant whom I interviewed, Judaism provides an idiom of Jewish identification through occasional, if not regular, observance of the Shabbat. They invest a range of resources into the family as a Jewish unit—camp, day school, and family time spent in rituals, synagogue attendance, and study. From the most observant often to the least, a continuum was apparent to me of Jews locating themselves within Jewish life. The nature of that participation varied dramatically. For some it was filling a pew at Beth El with twenty family members praying together at Rosh Hashanah. For others it was observing an increasing number of mitzvot. For those who participate, engagement with Judaism increasingly defines their membership. That participation takes a variety of forms. Active and inactive members look to the synagogue as a defining point of their Jewishness, and it is Judaism that the Conservative synagogue must shape, define, and teach in the twenty-first century, not as a center of ethnic life, but as a diffuse arena for a diverse community.

Notes

I wish to acknowledge the helpful comments I received on drafts of this chapter and the responses to my research throughout the year. I was fortunate to present this material at an early stage to a seminar at Hebrew Union College, Los Angeles. My colleague Isa Aron has offered insightful and thoughtful responses on both a draft of this essay and on the research. I appreciate the feedback of Steven Foldes on both the research and the draft. It was a particular pleasure to share and debate these ideas with the members of the research team for this study: Nancy Ammerman, Steven M. Cohen, Sidney Goldstein, Alice Goldstein, Samuel Heilman, Barry Kosmin, Paul

Ritterband, and Jack Wertheimer. I appreciate Steven M. Cohen's willingness to isolate and analyze the data from the Ratner survey specific to the two synagogues studied for this research. This work went beyond the call of duty for his own research.

1. This portrait of American Jewish life is derived from the major works of the period: Albert I. Gordon, *Jews in Suburbia* (Boston: Beacon Press, 1959); Judith R. Kramer and Seymour Leventman, *Children of the Gilded Ghetto: Conflict Resolutions of Three Generations of American Jews* (New Haven: Yale University Press, 1961); Herbert J. Gans, "The Origin and Growth of a Jewish Community in the Suburbs: A Study of the Jews of Park Forest," in Marshall Sklare, ed., *The Jews: Social Patterns of an American Group* (New York: Free Press, 1958); and Marshall Sklare and Joseph Greenblum, *Jewish Identity on the Suburban Frontier: A Study of Group Survival in the Open Society,* 2d ed. (Chicago: University of Chicago Press). Deborah Dash Moore examines the processes of Jews' suburbanization in *To the Golden Cities: Pursuing the American Jewish Dream in Miami and LA* (New York: Free Press, 1994).

2. On the suburban synagogue, see Marshall Sklare, *Conservative Judaism: An American Religious Movement* (New York: Schocken, 1972); Will Herberg, "The Postwar Revival of the Synagogue," *Commentary* 9 (1950): 315–325; Samuel Heilman, *Portrait of American Jews: The Last Half of the Twentieth Century* (Seattle: University of Washington Press, 1996); and Gans, "Origin and Growth of a Jewish Community." Jack Wertheimer's first chapter in *A People Divided: Judaism in Contemporary America* (New York: Basic Books, 1993) summarizes postwar synagogue and religious developments. His chapter "The Conservative Synagogue," in Jack Wertheimer, ed., *The American Synagogue: A Sanctuary Transformed* (Cambridge: Cambridge University Press, 1987), 111–152, also contains a helpful historical overview.

3. A United Synagogue survey revealed that the Friday night service was the main service for all synagogues consisting of fewer than five hundred families. Larger congregations listed Friday night and Saturday morning services as equally important. Marshall Sklare included this survey in his 1955 study but gave no date for it (*Conservative Judaism*, 104). Wertheimer also discusses attendance and frequency of services in "Conservative Synagogue," *American Synagogue*, 130.

4. Arthur Hertzberg, "The American Jew and His Religion," in Jacob Neusner, ed., *Understanding American Judaism*, vol. 1 (New York: Ktav, 1975), 15. The 1990 National Jewish Population Study reports that only about one-third of its "core group" surveyed belonged to synagogues or temples. Sidney Goldstein, *Profile of American Jewry: Insights from the 1990 National Jewish Population Survey*, North American Jewish Data Bank, Occasional Papers No. 6, 138–139.

5. Sklare, *Conservative Judaism*, 86–90.

6. See Samuel Heilman, *Synagogue Life: A Study in Symbolic Interaction* (Chicago: University of Chicago Press, 1976); Frida Furman, *Beyond Yiddishkeit: The Construction of American Jewish Identity* (Albany: State University of New York Press, 1987); and Moshe Shokeid, *A Gay Synagogue in New York* (New York: Columbia University Press, 1985). For a more recent historical study of the synagogue, see Wertheimer, *American Synagogue.*

7. A parallel gap exists in the study of American Christianity as well. The congregation has not served as an important source of scholarly study. This issue has been addressed in James F. Hopewell, *Congregation: Stories and Structures* (Philadelphia: Fortress Press, 1987), and James P. Wind and James H. Lewis, eds. *American Congregations* (Chicago: University of Chicago Press, 1994).

8. Marshall Sklare, *America's Jews* (New York: Random House, 1971), 24.

9. The social science of American Jewish life has also flourished in this period, but its practitioners have become increasingly interested in Jewish behavior and attitudes, rather than in synagogue life. With increasingly sophisticated statistical methods,

American Jews have been counted and their ideas and practices have been measured and compared, but their synagogues as sites for the reproduction and transmission of these ideas has frankly been overlooked.

10. Sklare, *Conservative Judaism*, 39.

11. See Riv-Ellen Prell, *Prayer and Community: The Havurah in American Judaism* (Detroit: Wayne State University Press, 1989).

12. At the time that I spoke with each board, I told the synagogues that they would have the right to read my essay before it was published. I would not give them the right of censorship, but if there were disagreements I would write that into the essay. Drafts of this essay have been read by Rabbi Robert Kahn, Rabbi Morris Allen, and Bonnie Heller, president of Beth El; they corrected mistakes of fact. In each conversation I learned many things about their perspectives and continued to learn about the communities. Their feedback was an exceptionally important part of the research. While this essay is not a collaboration, it has been affected by those conversations. Where there is disagreement, it is noted in a footnote.

13. Paul Wilkes, *And They Shall Be My People: An American Rabbi and His Congregation* (New York: Atlantic Monthly Press, 1994).

14. I believe that this narrower focus is in keeping with anthropology's more modest claims for the nature of ethnography as a form of representing human experience. Anthropologists George Marcus and Michael Fischer crystallized these changes in ethnographic research in their important book, *Anthropology as Cultural Critique* (Chicago: University of Chicago Press, 1986). They suggest that a generalized attack on knowledge that developed in the 1960s and flowered in the 1970s seriously undercut the ability of anthropologists to make totalizing claims about the nature of other cultures and societies. In this same period anthropologists were increasingly interested in both the United States and other Western cultures, in which their work was even more open to scrutiny by those it purported to understand. This generalized "crisis in representation" has limited anthropologists' claims that they speak for a whole group or beyond the narrow confines of the time and place in which they worked.

15. Beth El did hire a new senior rabbi in June 1996, just after I had completed my research.

16. Rabbi Kahn said that on the basis of what he observes, that number seems exceptionally high.

17. The synagogue is virtually on the same site where numerous negotiations took place between the Dakota peoples and the U.S. military that eventually seized nearly all their land.

18. The national sample reports that 80 percent of those surveyed considered it very important to be Jewish.

19. The Avi Chai Foundation is a private Jewish foundation that supports a variety of initiatives supporting increased Jewish observance in the United States and Israel. Beth Jacob was an early recipient of an Avi Chai grant to create a program to encourage the observance of the Shabbat at home and to extend the hours of observance. The study cited was an evaluation of that program. As an acknowledgment of the synagogue's success, Avi Chai continues to support programming at Beth Jacob through an outright grant.

20. Another such occasion that combined policy and study was related to the construction of the new synagogue. Members discussed whether plaques should be placed on individual items in the building to spur fund-raising. They used the values and principles of the torah as blueprint models to decide that no item in the sanctuary would carry a donor's name. On at least two occasions they turned down substantial gifts because they refused to put the donor's name in the sanctuary.

21. Robert N. Bellah et al. use this term in *Habits of the Heart: Individualism and Commitment in American Life* (Berkeley: University of California Press, 1985).
22. Hopewell, *Congregation*, 5–9.
23. Bonnie Heller explained to me that the board had for some time been concerned about the quality of life of the rabbis in regard to Friday night. They supported having only one rabbi at services on Friday night, giving the other the opportunity to stay home with his family on alternating weeks. Their support for this program was in keeping with that earlier commitment.
24. Several congregants did not recall previous Beth El rabbis as being rigid as some seemed to paint them, in contrast to the "Celebrate Shabbat" initiative. Several women recalled getting advice not from the rabbi in the past, but from his wife. Shirley Abelson was much beloved to both adult and teenage congregants who worked with and learned from her. One woman recalled that when she was a young mother and wife, Shirley Abelson had advised her to "try one thing at a time" when they talked about the Shabbat. Others found her a person with practical advice about matters ranging from kashrut to children. As one congregant recalled, "She never said, 'Don't,' but 'Why not try this?'"
25. I learned at a Beth El parlor meeting in 1995 that the synagogue had also faced a problem with disruptive children on the Shabbat. The behavior became so problematic that they formed a committee of educators, parents, and a psychologist to discuss how to handle these issues. I learned that another large Conservative synagogue in Minneapolis was also at a loss that year as to how to deal with inappropriate behavior on the part of preadolescents. In all cases the staff expressed concern about parents exercising virtually no control over their children's behavior and lacking awareness of what was appropriate synagogue behavior, including such elementary issues as keeping children quiet when a program or service was under way.
26. Rabbi Kahn noted, "Minyan Hadash isn't thriving to a great extent because it doesn't offer too much that our main sanctuary doesn't." He then laid out his own vision of an alternative minyan that would allow for more study and discussion.
27. Beth El members who read this essay found the discussion of Minyan Hadash difficult. Rabbi Kahn and Bonnie Heller were concerned because, although the group of people described are important, they are nonetheless a very small part of the synagogue. One member of Minyan Hadash suggested that my own level of observance, which he assumed was higher than the norm at Beth El, might have made me more sensitive to this particular group. There was less consensus in the synagogue about this section than any other in the essay. I have kept it in the essay because of my interest in the meaning of pluralism at Beth El, and because, as the demographic research suggests, Conservative Jews today are much less likely to have been raised in Orthodox homes than was the case in previous generations. Thus this section addresses the question, What is the relationship between mainstream Conservative Judaism and its observant wing?
28. For a sociological study of the impact of feminism on the lives of American Jewish women, see Sylvia Barack Fishman, *A Breath of Life: Feminism in the American Jewish Community* (New York: Free Press, 1993).
29. For a discussion of the role of authority in the development of American Judaism, see Prell, *Prayer and Community*. See also Robert Wuthnow, *The Restructuring of American Religion: Society and Faith Since World War II* (Princeton, N.J.: Princeton University Press, 1988). Wuthnow is particularly effective at laying out the material and structural conditions that dramatically changed the nature of American religion, particularly Christianity, bifurcating it dramatically between liberal and fundamentalist religion.
30. Roof and Gesch argue that the old "life cycle" theory of religious involvement that

locates high religious activity in youth and then following marriage deserves reconsideration in light of their empirical research. They contrasted those in the baby-boom generation by whether they thought families should worship together or not. Those high in "personal" autonomy, they argue, are less likely to be drawn back around the life cycle. See Wade Clark Roof and Lyn Gesch, "Boomers and the Culture of Choice: Changing Patterns of Work, Family and Religion," in Nancy Ammerman and Wade Clark Roof, *Work, Family, and Religion in Contemporary Society* (New York: Routledge, 1995), 70. An important discussion of "moderately affiliated" Jews' religious identities and its change over the life cycle may be found in Steven M. Cohen and Arnold Eisen, *The Jew Within: Self, Community, and Commitment among the Variety of Moderately Affiliated* (New York: The Wilstein Institute of Jewish Policy Studies, 1998).

31. Goldstein and Goldstein (this volume) have found this to be the case nationwide for Conservative Jews. Conservative Jews unaffiliated with synagogues are more likely to be couple-only or single-person units. They argue that the presence of children in the household is a key factor in whether a family joins.

32. A *havurah* (fellowship) began as an alternative to the synagogue. By the late 1970s most Conservative synagogues, following Rabbi Harold Schulweiss's innovations at a large Southern California synagogue, created havurot within their synagogues as a way to promote community. Beth Jacob had one active havurah during the course of my study, and Beth El had several. They tended to work best when they consisted of families with children roughly of the same ages. See Prell, *Prayer and Community*; and Bernard Reisman, "The Havurah: A Jewish Support Network," *American Behavioral Scientist* 23 (1980): 559–573.

33. Sklare, *Conservative Judaism*, 114.

34. The year that I began my study of Beth El, the other large Conservative synagogue in the area moved into a beautiful new building, not far from Beth El. There was some anxiety that such an attractive and impressive new building might draw away members, but it simply did not occur. Obviously, those old ideas about synagogues as statements of class and mobility remain alive.

35. Robert Wuthnow argues that this is the case for the waning significance of denominationalism in general in the United States. See Wuthnow, *Restructuring of American Religion*, 83–84.

36. This assertion is not easy to demonstrate statistically. A relatively small number of respondents to the Ratner Center survey stated that they had chanted torah or haftarah in the past year: at Beth Jacob less than 10 percent, and at Beth El less than 4 percent. Lacking that quantification, it is more accurate to state that the idiom of congregational life is more likely to be religious.

Conservative Jews within the Landscape of American Religion

Conclusion

NANCY T. AMMERMAN

T HE STORY SOCIOLOGISTS have often told about religion in this century, especially in the North Atlantic world, is a story also familiar in the popular imagination. It is a story peopled with religious heroes of the past, nostalgic visions of village greens and white steeples (or perhaps the shul and the shtetl), and a steady erosion of faith as the saints and rabbis have been eclipsed by captains of industry and science, and the steeples have been dwarfed by skyscrapers. This is the story of Enlightenment and "progress." Blind faith is replaced by reasoned investigation, eventually putting the magicians and holy men out of business.

This is a way of narrating history that rings at once both true and false. In this chapter, I want to propose that the story of religion's encounter with "modernity" is only a starting point for understanding the Conservative Judaism that has been revealed in these pages. To bring the story up to date will require that we go considerably beyond the questions and modes of explanation that sociologists have used for much of this century. Indeed, I will argue that this study of Conservative Judaism can help sociology to continue its task of elaborating a new paradigm for understanding religion, especially in the most "developed" sector of the global system. Religion clearly has not gone away. Jews (and others) have not utterly assimilated. Even the people who are most deeply entrenched in the world of modernity have often failed to accede to its secularizing demands. An assessment of those demands and of the religious resources being brought to bear in dialogue with them will tell us a good deal both about Conservative Judaism and about the larger cultural world in which we live.

Modernity and Its Challenges

Much of social science has been preoccupied with the great transition that has transformed western culture from "traditional" to modern. In some places that transition has been underway for several hundred years. In other places it is a transition accomplished in living memory. William McNeill (1993) has noted that just in the period since World War II we have moved from a world in which the vast majority of people live in villages into a world in which cities are more likely to be our home. We are, he says, a world of peasants and ex-peasants. Alongside that literal transition from countryside to city have come changes in epistemology, culture, and social structure. We think and act differently for having to exist in this modern urban world. I want to point to three major components of that change, examining the very real challenges they have posed for religion. The story of encounter with modernization, accommodation, and decline is not a story to be ignored. It is the prologue with which we begin.

The most fundamental cognitive challenge of the modern era is the move to a dependence on science and reason as primary modes of knowing. In earlier times, people often turned to their religions to explain the unexplainable in life: Where do babies come from? Why does the moon pass through phases? What makes the crops grow and the rains come? What happens to us when we die? In the earliest days, priests and shamans offered solutions and cures, rituals and explanations for things people had no other way of understanding. But beginning at least with the Enlightenment, experts located in and trained by universities began to displace the priests as dispensers of approved knowledge about life's mysteries. If we want to know why we are sick, we go to a doctor. If we want to know about the moon, we ask an astronomer or even an astronaut. If we want to know about crops, we consult an agricultural scientist or perhaps an economist. If we want to understand the mysteries of the human mind, we go to the biology and psychology departments.

Although the range of questions that people took to their religious leaders narrowed, another shift was more important: the way we expect knowledge to work. For the most part, we do not expect knowledge to be revealed to us or even handed down to us. We are taught not to accept information just because everyone has always believed it to be true. Rather, we expect to discover knowledge through systematic, rational methods. This epistemological move is described by Max Weber as a shift from traditional and charismatic bases of authority to authority based on "rational-legal" forms of legitimacy.[1] There are rules to be followed, ways of defending one's evidence, and recognized credentials that allow one to claim expertise. In this "modern" way of thinking, it is not sufficient to say that "the torah commands it" or that "the rabbi advises it." Rather, the torah itself is to be subjected to historical, critical, archaeological, and anthropological investigation. And the rabbi must gain advanced training in psychology and management before his or her advice will be taken seriously. This, as we have understood it, is the modern dilemma. We have pitted science against religion, and religion has lost.[2]

This reading of the evidence is bolstered by the consistent finding that people with higher levels of education are less likely to hold traditional religious tenets or to have high levels of religious participation. This is sometimes complicated by social class effects: people who are better educated also tend to be better off, and those who are better off tend to be joiners of all types of community organizations, including religious ones (Demerath 1965). In spite of this, the finding has endured; education is one of the strongest predictors of a person's relationship to traditional religious patterns. When analysts went looking for reasons for the most recent declines in religious affiliation, rising levels of education were often found to be associated with lower levels of attendance and "orthodoxy."[3] Modern modes of thought, represented especially by higher education, erode the power of traditional religion to define the contours of the world we know.

In addition to these cognitive dilemmas posed by the Enlightenment, our modern urban world has also presented us with an unprecedented range of social and behavioral differences with which to contend. Certainly there has been pluralism in the human past; nothing was ever as homogeneous as it appears to distant, later observers. But changes in transportation, communication, and the density of urban life have made that pluralism an everyday reality for increasing proportions of the world's population. Throughout much of human history, being religious and being a citizen were the same thing. One might be more or less religious, more or less observant of the rituals, but you simply could not avoid being a part of the religious tradition of your community. Today there are fewer and fewer places where such consensus exists. Most people live in the midst of real differences. People believe in different gods or no god at all; they worship on Saturday and Sunday and five times a day. Some fast during Lent, others on Yom Kippur, and still others between sunrise and sundown during Ramadan. Some ordain women to lead their religious communities, and others cover the bodies of women from the forehead to the toes and/or command them to be silent. The range of practice and belief is enormous, and it is no longer in distant lands, but all around us.

Such pluralism has, according to many observers, undermined the plausibility of any single religious tradition.[4] Because no religious tradition can define a taken-for-granted world, all religious traditions suffer. Because we are surrounded by people of faith whose god is not our god, we must confront the reality of our own god's contingency. Combined with the claims of science, these pluralist religious claims erode our ability to see any single truth as "the truth" about the world. Everything must be chosen and partial. All relationships must

be couched in humility; one's own ways can be justified only as personal preference and never imposed on another. In this modern, pluralist situation proxely-
tization seems impossible, impolite, even dangerous. The safest form of religious
belief is that chosen and discreetly held by an individual.

Such a pluralism in religious experience has been part of the American situation from the beginning. Even where official and unofficial religious establish-
ments existed, they have long since declined. Jay Demerath and Rhys Williams
tell the story of the long-term erosion of Protestant power in Springfield, Mas-
sachusetts, for instance, as that city has become increasingly plural in its religious populations (Demerath and Williams 1992). Similarly, David Hackett
documents the transformation of Albany, New York. As it became increasingly
religiously plural, it was held together not by a single religious establishment,
but because everyone agreed "that economic growth, democracy, education, and
individual rights were important values" (Hackett 1991: 157). Religious experiences and ideologies helped to make sense of these new values, but the values
themselves came largely from the economic and political world. Kevin Christiano
asks the question differently, but he too tells the story of an increasingly diverse
religious ecology over the last century (Christiano 1988). Immigration has, in
distinct spurts, added new kinds of religiosity to the mix, while urbanization and
the U.S. "free market" in religion have created a climate for a bewildering array
of religious alternatives. Historian Jon Butler has noted that already by 1760,
the degree of religious pluralism in the American colonies probably exceeded
that in any single European society and equalled the pluralism found on the European continent as a whole (Butler 1990: 174).

One of the results of this American pluralism is a tendency toward individualism in matters religious. The same forces of mobility and education and
commerce that have brought diverse people together have also dislodged those
people from traditional communities in the process. And in the dislodging from
ascribed loyalties, the modern individual has been created.[5] We are not first identified by our family and town and ancestral occupation. Rather, we are identified by occupations and places and even names that we have chosen for ourselves.
Faith, in this individualist mode, is an internalized meaning system that may
combine elements from a variety of traditions.[6] At its extreme, individualized
faith ceases to be recognizable beyond the psyche of its holder. In their explorations of the ills individualism has wrought, Bellah and his associates recount the
story of the now-infamous "Sheila." She describes her religion as her own private beliefs, as "Sheilaism." It demands of her only that she love herself and try
to take care of others (Bellah et al. 1985: 221). The authors seem not so much
offended by the content of her beliefs as by the fact that she claims them as her
own individual creation. They worry that we may be headed for a day when
there are 200 million different religions, none of them grounded in a community or a tradition.

Somewhat more measured assessments of the individualism of U.S. society are found in two recent studies of "baby boomers." Both emphasize the degree to which religion involves change over a lifetime. Wade Clark Roof documents the way the particular events of the 1960s helped to shape a "generation of seekers." Coming of age in the midst of a "question authority" era, little about religion has been taken for granted. That generation has sought out their own paths, borrowing from eclectic religious sources, sometimes inside organized religion and sometimes not. In fact, they insist on a distinction between their own individual spirituality and the institutionalized religion of the churches and synagogues (Roof 1993). Dean Hoge and his associates selected a sample of baby boomers who began the 1960s inside organized religion as Presbyterian confirmands. Interviewing them thirty years later, these researchers discovered that only about a quarter were still in Presbyterian churches. Many had left religious involvement for at least a time, and many others were in other religious traditions or outside the faith entirely.[7] Both of these studies give flesh to the patterns of individualism and choice that are sketched dimly in answers to pollsters' questions. When 78 percent say that a person can be a good Christian or Jew without attending church or synagogue,[8] they are often speaking from the experience of their own institutional disaffection and spiritual seeking.

Taking up the question of religious autonomy directly, Philip Hammond shows that those least embedded in traditional local community and familial networks are also least committed to involvement in a parish (Hammond 1992). He, too, sees the 1960s as a watershed period in which choice became the norm in religion, and existing religious communities failed to create structures for encouraging and sustaining meaningful choices. Autonomy has therefore taken individuals increasingly outside traditional religious communities and into a vast religious (and secular) marketplace of ideas.[9]

If science has limited the cognitive range of modern religion, and pluralism has limited its behavioral range, the very diversified character of the world in which each individual must live has also limited religion's authority. As our base of knowledge has expanded and as the size of our communities has grown, we have moved more and more to "specialization" to dividing up the tasks that once went together under one roof.[10] Such specialization is perhaps most dramatically apparent in the proliferation of academic departments, of medical specialities, and of business enterprises. But just as dramatic (although further from our awareness) is the basic differentiation of labor that has created separate domains for scholarship, business, or medicine in the first place.[11] Not so long ago, none of those enterprises existed as an activity separate from the household. Business was what one did when one needed to trade crops for tools, and medicine was what one practiced with the remedies kept in a corner of the kitchen. Scholarship was the collected wisdom of the tribe.

Today, however, we have experts to build our means of transportation, experts to make our clothes, experts to take care of our children when they are young, and experts to educate them when they get a bit older. We have experts to take care of our money, and experts to package and advertise goods we do not need to buy. We have experts to grow our food and experts to get it to market and experts to put it on the shelves. We have experts to invent and maintain the devices that let us communicate with people around the world who can now be considered our neighbors. We have experts at politics and even experts at religion. Whatever we need can be found in the Yellow Pages.

The result of all this specialization, then, is that each person comes to occupy a growing number of increasingly limited domains. No one person understands enough about the world to get through life without the help of others. And no one person lives consistently with a single set of significant others. The social world is complex and multilayered.[12] We are at the same time, perhaps, members of families, teachers in college, shoppers at the mall, Democratic voters, fans of ER, members of a synagogue, residents of a neighborhood, and avid bird watchers. Each of these roles has its own demands and different sets of people with whom we cooperate. Even if we are devout believers and faithful shul members, the rest of this modern world of experts conspires to compartmentalize those roles. Law and custom tell us that religion does not belong in the marketplace, the school, the court, or the public square. If we take them there, it must be at our own private initiative.

Disappearing mysteries, compartmentalization, and pluralism: these are the cards the modern world has dealt us. While this is neither the whole story nor the end of the story (as I will argue in the remainder of this essay), this is the place where the story begins. For much of this century, people inside and outside religious traditions have understood the religious world as one dominated by these modern challenges. We have heard that for religion to survive it would have to become believable to rational, scientifically attuned minds—a set of moral precepts, perhaps, but certainly no claims for mystery or miracle or transcendence. We have also heard that for religion to survive it would have to accommodate to individualism, offering a smorgasbord of options and being content with whatever individuals might choose to consume. Likewise, modern religion would have to accommodate to pluralism by being modest in its claims, dropping "mission" in favor of ecumenism. The liberal project, at least for the last century, has sought uniquely modern forms for religious faith and practice, updating old doctrine and ritual and eschewing any claims to timeless truth.

Standing opposite this liberal project has been an equally adamant conservative one. Theorists and practitioners alike have claimed that for religion to survive the modern challenge, it would have to form relatively isolated, "sectarian" communities with strict rules, firm beliefs, and a strong collective identity. Dean Kelley advised Protestant churches a generation ago that growth would depend on "strictness." People wanted to have a clear sense of identity, he claimed, and that identity would come from unwavering beliefs, clear guidelines for behavior, and no doubts about the presence of God in the world (Kelley 1977). His practical advice echoed the theoretical words articulated by Peter Berger. In the face of a pluralistic world, religion could construct small sheltering social worlds. Various religious countercultures and sectarian groups could give up the illusion of dominating society and instead undertake the formidable social engineering task required for the "erection and maintenance of barriers strong enough to keep out the forces that undermine certainty—a difficult feat in the context of modern urban life, mobility, and mass communication" (Berger 1982: 20).

More recently, this "strictness thesis" has been given mathematical precision by economists who claim that people have no incentive to invest in religious products that offer them no unique advantage and that can be gotten for a minimal price anyway.[13] These "free riders" decrease the perceived value of the goods others may be investing in and diminish the ability of any group to generate real rewards for its participants. Since religion is a collectively produced good, it needs strong "collectives" to produce it. Both belief and practice, so these theories go, can be produced and sustained in spite of modern challenges; but they require intentional work at creating religious enclaves in which those ideas and practices make sense.[14]

The challenges of the modern world, then, have appeared to present two radically different alternatives to those who would continue to be religious: a creative synthesis that merges faith with modern sensibilities or a strategic retreat into intentionally antimodern communities.[15] Such posing of polarities has been a habit of modern sociological theorizing (indeed of the modern mind itself). Equally common has been the assumption of human progress, progress that was often assumed to imply the eventual withering away of religion. In the mid-1980s, Wade Clark Roof and William McKinney reported that "nones" (people with no religious preference) were the fastest growing segment in the U.S. religious market (Roof and McKinney 1987: 236). Those three alternatives—accommodation, withdrawal, and demise—have described much of the western religious world in this century. Researchers have found evidence for all three and until recently saw little reason to look for other alternatives or new explanatory models.

The Search for New Models

If we call the old paradigm for explaining religion a modernist one, then the emerging new paradigm might be called postmodernist. It is not postmodernist in the sense of the radical deconstructionism one might find in art and literature or the hyper-pluralism that insists that no rules can be imposed beyond the immediate community that invents them. Rather, the postmodernism I mean is one that has a "yes, but" character. It begins with the realities of modern reason, individualism, and pluralism and looks for the ways in which those modes of explanation are no longer sufficient. To invoke a postmodernist paradigm is to suggest that the realities of the modern situation are still with us, but their limits are recognized and overcome. Reason, specialization, and pluralism are not likely to go away, but we are beginning to recognize that what looked solidly modern has all sorts of cracks and crevices in which new forms of life are emerging, and old, unnoticed ones have been thriving all along.

We have been seeing the limits of reasoned solutions to human problems, for instance, at least since 1945. In the horrors of nuclear war and genocidal holocaust, we have seen what science can do and that it may only deepen our basic dilemmas. We are also recognizing that we have always depended on other ways of knowing, alongside our reasoned inquiry. We have always trusted tradition more than we ever admitted. Vast areas of our lives are still governed by rules that come to us through habit and advice that have never been tested in any scientist's laboratory. We also know that sometimes our knowledge and insight comes from sources we have a hard time explaining. Sometimes we call it a "gut feeling" or "intuition" or a "vision" or "wisdom," but we still know it is true. Science is not about to disappear, but its domain has shrunk.

It is worth noting here that these other sources of knowledge—art, wisdom, intuition, sooth-saying, the spirit—are much more likely to be found among and practiced by people who have been outside the dominant culture of the modern, western world. These are sources of knowledge more likely to be found among women than among men, among peoples of color than among Euro-Americans, in the "third world" more than in the "first." The claim that the modern world is characterized by rationality is primarily a claim about a very particular slice of that world.

Not only are we seeing the limits of old forms of knowledge, we are also seeing the limits of our drive toward specialization. One of the great insights of the women's movement is that human beings do not thrive on such calculated separation of one part of their lives from another.[16] While we cannot soon expect to see the modern western world giving up its propensity to create specialists, those specialists are increasingly located in networks and consortiums that re-create connectedness. Compartmentalized organizational boundaries are blurred by flextime and outsourcing; hierarchies are flattened to include workplace democracy.[17] Modern skyscrapers remain, but they are filled with phone and cable lines connecting them to workers and buyers and advisors around the world, few of whom are exclusively connected to any one company. Such work may seem even more specialized, but it is increasingly lodged at the center of networks, rather than in isolated compartments. These new forms of integration and connection, building out of and going beyond old modernist forms, signal another of the postmodern realities to be explained.

If persons are less defined by discrete roles and functions, the pluralist society we live in is less defined by the universalist melting pot either as metaphor for the reality we observe or as model for the society we wish for. Neither an intolerant fundamentalism nor an accommodated and tolerant liberalism seems to promise a way forward. More promising are proposals that postmodernity will be inhabited by people who are (at least culturally) bilingual, speaking a native, parochial language while also speaking a common language shared with people they do not know.[18] We live in a world where people can be both rooted in particularistic ethnic and religious communities and more aware of the larger world and the choices that have brought them to their current practices. They are, to use Stephen Warner's extremely helpful term, "elective parochials" (Warner 1988).

To be a parochial, of course, is to have a community, to go beyond one's presumed autonomy as an individual. The presumption of autonomy is neither so unquestioned today nor so welcomed as it once was. While choice and voluntarism are still celebrated as the hallmark of democracy and a key source of religious vitality, both the constraints on choice and the commitments implied by choice are entering the vocabulary of social observers.[19] The picture that is slowly emerging emphasizes the complexities of the relationship between individual and community over time, space, and function. We are neither as free and disconnected as the modernist paradigm would have had it nor as utterly embedded in ascribed communities as our traditionalist forebears. In the nexus of choice and community new understandings of person and commitment are emerging.[20]

Understanding religious phenomena today requires both the lenses that came to us from modernist paradigms and new lenses that will let us see the realities that are challenging those paradigms. It is especially in looking at what statisticians call deviant cases or outliers that we may learn more about where we are headed. These cases that do not fit old patterns, that lie outside the predicted model, may signal the beginnings of new directions.

Surely Conservative Judaism is one of those useful cases. The three alternatives posed by modernity fit nicely the realities of the Reform movement, Orthodoxy, and the growing number of "secular" Jews. Reform set out to lower the boundaries between Jewish practice and the modern world. Rituals, beliefs, and practices were made amenable to individualism, rationalism, and the limits of modern pluralism. Orthodoxy, on the other hand, created strong synagogue communities in which the whole law could be honored and practiced in a highly bounded society of co-religionists. Secular Jews shed the religious trappings entirely, keeping only a sense of ethnic identity. The fact that Conservatism has never fit this model suggests that its struggle to find a viable religious path is an especially useful case to examine. If the larger western religious scene demands new models of explanation, perhaps we will begin to find them here.

The evidence that has emerged from the multiple efforts of this study has offered a consistent "yes, but" answer to modernity's questions. Here is a movement shaped by the modern western situation in which it was born, but now acting back on that situation to create new religious institutional spaces, new religious identities, and new religious sensibilities.

Choice and Loyalty in the Formation of Religious Identity

Unlike Orthodoxy, Conservative Judaism has been shaped in a modern, North American context. Its identity has always been an attempt to draw together the long traditions of Jewish practice with the contemporary realities of a cosmopolitan world. While many of today's older Conservative generation are the children and grandchildren of European immigrants, the practices of Conservative Jewry are rooted in being Jewish on this side of the Atlantic. And one of the most distinctive aspects of religion in the United States is its voluntarism.[21] Some have interpreted that voluntarism as a detriment to religious loyalty, while others see it as a key to institutional vitality. In the story of Conservative Judaism, we may have evidence for both points of view.

The patterns of choice in and out of Conservatism certainly present us with such a mixed view. It is clear that Jews in this country can choose how they will be Jewish, and over 40 percent of today's Conservatives have exercised that freedom by moving from one form of Judaism to another. This movement among Jewish denominations is happening at roughly the same rate as movement among denominations within Protestantism.[22] Americans switch far more within religious "families" than between them—liberal Protestants to other liberal Protestant denominations more than across Protestant-Catholic lines, for instance. But within the religious families that are recognized as similar, the norm in the United States is for membership at any given time to be dictated as much by the immediately available options and the person's current needs as by loyalty to any specific tradition. The group that suits the thirty-year-old single person living in a large metropolitan area may not be the group that suits the forty-year-old married person with children or the sixty-year-old empty-nester in Florida. People switch when they marry and switch when they move (Wuthnow 1988). We will return later to the ways in which Conservative Judaism is shoring up its sense of distinct identity. At this point we simply need to note that the history that has shaped this Jewish denomination has been a history of considerable movement across denominational lines.

In earlier decades of this century, social scientists hypothesized that the more liberal denominations (which were also more attractive to those of higher social status) would gain at the expense of the more conservative (lower class) ones (Demerath 1965). This also fit nicely with notions of secularization that predicted the gradual demise of religions that demanded strict behavioral codes and propagated supernatural beliefs. By the late 1970s, however, the growth of conservative religious groups was too great to ignore. People seem to switch both to strict, conservative religious groups and to liberal, low-commitment ones.[23] In a diverse religious marketplace, with diverse populations seeking out religious alternatives, both kinds of groups will experience the gains and losses associated with switching across time, space, and personal needs.

In this case, about 40 percent of people raised Conservative have moved to Reform and other more liberal alternatives, and most of those who have joined the Conservative movement have moved from Orthodoxy. But nearly 10 percent have entered the ranks of Conservative Judaism from Reform, secular, and non-Jewish backgrounds. While the switchers from Orthodoxy (and the Conservatives who become Reform or secular) might be seen as fitting an accommodationist model, moving from the stricter alternative to a less strict one, these others are less easy to categorize within a framework that expects increasing compromise with the modern world. At least some of Conservatism's new adherents have chosen a stricter alternative. Perhaps, like the returnees to Orthodoxy described by Lynn Davidman and by Debra Kaufmann, these are modern seekers for whom a Conservative way of life provides meaning, structure, community, and a new sense of self-esteem (Davidman 1991; Kaufmann 1991).

The datum that most forcefully illustrates the impact of religious voluntarism on Jewish life, of course, is today's high intermarriage rates. Among people who identified themselves as Conservative, 23 percent were in mixed marriages and only 28 percent said they would oppose such a marriage (as reported in chapter 4, this volume). Indeed, among the most recent marriage cohort (those married since 1980), the rate of intermarriage among all American Jews is 53 percent. Even within a religious tradition that has claimed strong tribal identity, adherents in this country are exercising a remarkable degree of choice. Those choices, unfortunately for their native religious tradition, seem to have the consequence of creating and/or exacerbating distance from the Jewish community. Those who are in mixed marriages experience conflicting institutional and religious loyalties. As both Cohen (chapter 1) and the Goldsteins report, very few of these intermarried couples—only 15 percent—are synagogue members. Such a small percentage suggests considerable distance between these intermarried couples and organized synagogue life. Which came first—disaffection from the synagogue or the intermarriage—we cannot tell.

Yet even here there are signs that choice may not be the death knell of religious community. While intermarried couples are very unlikely to be involved in Jewish synagogue life, many Conservative Jews, especially in the younger generation, do not think that should be the case. Kosmin (chapter 5) reports that both parents and youth in the bar/bat mitzvah class of 5755 agree that synagogues should be more welcoming of non-Jewish partners. While Conservative Jews are ambivalent about whether their rabbis should perform these marriages, they are insistent that intermarriage should not isolate Jews from the religious community. Those inside the community are ready to embrace even the choice to intermarry as a communally based alternative, not as an utterly individual decision.

These decisions about whether to participate—switching, defection, conversion and so on—give us a mixed picture about the balance between individual and community in Conservative Judaism. Community is being both built and destroyed by the choices being made. Robert Wuthnow's research on small groups makes clear that our mobile, urban, well-educated society is one where both joining and leaving are a reality (Wuthnow 1994). On the one hand, small groups that meet for activities such as self-help and Bible study often appear very introspective and self-oriented. On the other hand, they also have real impacts on their members, who make substantial commitments to participation. People are rarely members for a lifetime (about five years is the average), but such relatively short-term commitments are well-suited to a mobile society. Likewise the balance of intimacy and distance is well-suited to the formation of supportive, nonfamily relationships. Pessimists look at this sort of commitment as too easy. Others see it as a basic building block of community. In this view, our society is neither a sea of autonomous individuals nor a roster of lifelong memberships. It is, rather, a web of constantly shifting, somewhat contingent, affiliations.[24] As a place where commitment is both real and voluntary, Conservative Judaism is a part of this web of affiliations.

Choice and Loyalty: The Journey of Commitment

Inside the community, choice is no less a reality. Perhaps Conservative Judaism's most distinctive feature is the way in which adherents relate to observance of the law. Conservative Jewry is a genuine mix of those who are observant and those who are not, of people observing one part of the law and others observing another, of active participation during one part of life and inactivity at another. For instance, only 29 percent of bar and bat mitzvah parents keep kashrut completely, but 83 percent keep it selectively, and 50 percent threw kosher parties for their children (see chapter 5). Observing dietary laws was clearly something many of them recognized as part of their tradition and honored in part, but complete observance was an ideal reached by very few.

This is a story echoed over and over again in Conservative Jewish life. The ideal of complete observance is clearly honored, but imperfection and individual variation are taken as the norm. Strong majorities agree that Conservative Jews are obligated to be observant, but equally strong majorities claim that they are able to choose how to be so and that they can be "religious" without being observant (see chapter 1). On the surface, these appear to be contradictory or hypocritical statements. Surely one must either obey the law or simply bargain it away. Those are the alternatives posed by the modernist frame. But Conservative Jews appear to be doing something different, neither obeying in full nor absolving themselves of that obligation. Conservative Judaism joins Orthodoxy in declaring that there are no unimportant laws, but departs from Orthodoxy in allowing for, indeed encouraging, a different mode of commitment to the law. In chapter 3, Samuel Heilman describes Central Synagogue as providing people "with a strong sense of being held to something concrete [as well as] a great deal of freedom to move away and broadly interpret the nature of their attachments and commitments." It is a place, said one member, that "wrestles with tradition."

Observance is not, then, an either/or matter, but a journey of faithfulness, a "ladder of mitzvot" to be climbed, something one grows and strives toward. One can begin at a given level and gradually work toward greater faithfulness. Likewise, there is recognition that observance and synagogue involvement change over a lifetime, often growing as children arrive and grow up, perhaps waning when they leave home. Samuel Heilman quotes one very wise rabbi as advising, "There are 613 commandments; find one and begin." Notice that the choice is not which commandment to obey, but where to begin. The invitation is to enter the journey and keep going. Prell quotes a member of Beth Jacob: "Everyone is expected to grow. At Beth Jacob we take our observance seriously, and we all do that in different ways." The obligation is still total, but the expectations recognize the variations that will exist among persons, within the community, and over time. The expectation is not that one will have arrived, but that one will be on the journey. This is neither the unchosen tradition of an earlier era, nor the sectarian insistence on total commitment. But neither is it the sort of individualism that mixes and matches beliefs and practices, with the person as the final and sole arbiter of goodness.

Interestingly, my colleague Adair Lummis and I have found a very similar phenomenon in a group of Episcopal parishes we studied. Each was identified by its peers as especially "spiritually vital." These are places where people take religious practices seriously, where spiritual realities intrude in all sorts of ways. But they are certainly not sectarian in any usual sense of that word. There is tremendous room for individual variation in practice and style and an expectation that people's lives are full of institutional entanglements beyond the parish. Yet there is also an expectation that one's spiritual life should be a growing commitment. They express it in many different ways, but they expect their members to be seeking God, to be actively working at religious fidelity and growth.[25] Perhaps they could say, "There are 613 prayers in the Book of Common Prayer; find one and begin."

One of the secrets of maintaining this blend of expectation and grace is the ability to maintain congregations in which there are models of observance and an ethos that supports the journey. Rabbis may be especially important as models. In each of the synagogues Heilman and Prell studied, committed and innovative rabbis found ways to meet their members where they were, while challenging them to move forward. Prell describes how Rabbi Morris Allen invited his congregants to make a gradually escalating commitment to "Chew by Choice," while Rabbi Robert Kahn invited his members to a year of learning how to "celebrate Shabbat." His confession that his own Sabbath dinner was sometimes wine and pizza provided the sort of graceful encouragement his busy congregants needed to see that observance does not have to begin with the culinary perfection they may remember from childhood.

Alongside the rabbi, however, is the community itself. Conservative Jews are not uniformly observant, as we have seen, but neither are they uniformly nonobservant (see chapter 1). No one would have to look very far to find models of kashrut and Sabbath observance even if they are a minority, and these models offer members a living reminder of Conservative Jewish ideals toward which they can strive. The relationships formed in the synagogue establish the ethos for religious commitment and growth. It becomes a kind of second family, a haven, a place to which to return in celebration and mourning—themes we heard again and again from the people Prell and Heilman interviewed. Even if they were not fully observant, many were willing to make real sacrifices for the sake of the community, to choose where they will move, for instance, based on the presence of a Conservative synagogue. As Heilman says of a woman who grew up largely outside Jewish practice, "In part because she was becoming involved with other Kehillath Achim couples, Ella began the journey from a marginal religious existence to being a committed Jew whose life was filled with Jewish content and observance." When those relationships also include commitment to a day school, as was the case for many of the Beth Jacob families Prell observed, the result is "dense and overlapping ties between families who live in [these] two worlds" and extensive community involvement in what might otherwise be private family decisions.

That balancing of individuality and community has perhaps reached its peak in the tremendous success of the bar and bat mitzvah ritual. It has become a near universal rite of passage for Conservative Jewish youth—both boys and girls. While observers have worried about the excesses of the celebrations, the diversion of energy into parties and gifts more than torah and worship, those worries seem not to be borne out in this study. On the one hand, it is a celebration of the individual youth coming of age and a time for individual families to take center stage. But, on the other hand, it stands at the center of years of hard work and sacrifice, years of investment in becoming a competent member of the community.

Kosmin's study shows that the vast majority of youths who are anticipating bar or bat mitzvah spend large amounts of time preparing. They attend classes for years in advance and add extra study time in the months immediately preceding their big day. All this preparation interrupts their regular routines of sports and leisure, so there is real sacrifice involved. Yet overwhelmingly they say it was worthwhile and that they would like to continue their Jewish education even after the bar/bat mitzvah. Their parents are certainly not unaffected observers of all this activity. They have helped their children prepare, organized and paid for a party, and become more involved in synagogue themselves. In some synagogues they are required to take classes as well. Now that it is over, they report that their children know more about Judaism than they themselves did at that age, and they too are glad for the religious investment the family has made.

This coming-of-age ritual is a process of education and investment that seems to be tying a new generation (and their parents) to synagogue life. Kosmin notes that the bar/bat mitzvah is a major ritual declaration of Jewish identity for both parents and teens. The entire family declares to the synagogue community and beyond that they are invested in the work of being Jewish. The result of all that hard work is "articulate, confident youngsters with self-esteem." But, he notes, it is also a "synthesis of individualistic and communitarian values. It is a powerful affirmation of the individual, the family, and the community in time and space."

As we see in Prell's case studies of Beth Jacob and Beth El, youth are not the only ones investing in becoming more competent and observant Jews. Adults who never learned Hebrew in their own formative years are now making that investment. Women, especially, who did not have the opportunity for a bat mitzvah in their teens are working to catch up with their daughters. Now that they are allowed to participate fully in synagogue life, they want to have the necessary skills to do so and they are willing to make the investment of time and energy to gain them. The opening of full participation to women—a liberalizing move—has had the side effect of increasing overall levels of knowledge and observance in every synagogue community. As Kosmin points out, the number of potential participants in synagogue worship life has doubled. Such an increase in overall participation has the effect of raising the norms for everyone.

That norms of observance and participation are increasing rather than decreasing is seen in the comparisons between today's youngest cohorts and those in their middle years. Not only have levels of Jewish education steadily increased, but among Conservative Jews between thirty-five and sixty-five, the younger the person, the more observant and active in synagogue life they are. Increasing willingness to make and keep commitments to the community is also seen in the fact that younger cohorts are more likely to have been raised Conservative and to have chosen to stay. There is at least some evidence here that exercising individual freedom can result in higher levels of religious commitment, not just lower ones.

Like other American religionists, Conservative Jews expect to be able to choose their ways of being religious. They choose where and when to belong and how to be observant. On the one hand, these choices can be seen as a symptom of modern individualism and they are certainly that. But every choice also signals a commitment. The individual self, ironically, is largely accounted for by its accumulation of choices and attachments. The mixture of kinds of choices we have seen makes clear that individualism and mobility are a fact of American Jewish life, but they are also a resource out of which strong communities can be constructed.

Creating Institutions for a Distinctive Way of Life

One of the most striking findings of this study is the increasing strength and clarity of Conservative Judaism's "denominational" identity. It has always been a middle way between the strictness of Orthodoxy and the accommodation of Reform, and it is still the case that average levels of belief and practice consistently place Conservative Jews between the other two major groups. But increasingly that position in the middle is more a choice than a "default," more a distinct way of being Jewish than a compromise between more seemingly coherent alternatives. As we have seen, part of this distinctness is in the mixture of observance and choice that characterizes Conservatism. It is a journey with full observance as its goal, but with the complexities of everyday life as its partner. In chapter 1, Cohen found that Conservative Jews are clear that they could be neither Reform nor Orthodox, but they refuse to think of themselves as less authentically Jewish for having made that choice. They reject negative stereotypes of themselves as wishy-washy for not being Orthodox or irrelevant for not being Reform. While this is a middle way, it is one that is both/and in people's minds—both relevant and observant.

Perhaps this is most clearly seen in the inclusion of women in Conservative worship and synagogue leadership. Egalitarianism has become a key part of Conservatism's sharpened denominational identity, and with good reason. The inclusion of women is clearly a decision in the direction of "relevance," but the way they have been included has increased the community's overall attention to its observance. What women are doing, after all, is praying, reading the Torah, and engaging in all the other practices that remind the community of its connection to God and to its traditions. While some male-only practices are changing only slowly, Kosmin finds that there is a logical and inexorable movement to this process. Once the first steps for inclusion are taken, there is no going back. Today, as Kosmin notes, men and women in the younger cohorts are nearly identical in their patterns of Jewish education and synagogue participation.

This pattern among younger adults is echoed in other aspects of distinctly Conservative beliefs and practice. Cohen's measure of "Conservative militancy" includes a variety of questions that tap ideas that uniquely set one denomination apart from the others. When all are put together, he finds that Conservatism's denominational identity is growing stronger with each new cohort. Rather than melting into a more universalist, compromised middle, the differences among Jews are setting them apart into increasingly cohesive communities. They are building the "elective parochialism" of which Warner speaks, creating a distinct community that nevertheless has permeable boundaries and ample contact with others across those boundaries.

In part this distinct identity has been enhanced by the patterns of denominational switching that have characterized Jewish life over the last generation or more. In earlier years, Conservatism gained adherents from Orthodoxy (probably often the children of immigrants). They brought in high levels of Jewish education and a history of ritual observance. Those raised Orthodox are today more likely to be regular synagogue attenders than are those who were raised either as Reform or Conservative Jews. Today's higher overall levels of observance have in part been enhanced by an earlier infusion of persons shaped by Orthodox upbringing (see chapter 2). Current patterns, by contrast, show Conservatism gaining small numbers from Reform. These recruits are relatively young and well educated in Jewish schools, perhaps reflecting the willingness of a younger generation to engage religious tradition more seriously. And they are more likely to be synagogue members than those who have remained Conservative throughout their lives. As is usually the case for new recruits, they exhibit a higher level of conformity to their new tradition than do those who have always been members.[26] Again, Conservatism benefits from this infusion of new blood.

Those who switched out of Conservatism, on the other hand, were (or at least became) less observant than those who stayed or switched in. The vast majority have switched to Reform or to being "Just Jews," exercising their choice to live a less rigorously religious life than Conservatism called them toward. While losing adherents is never good news, it has had a kind of winnowing effect, shedding those least involved in belief and practice and leaving the more devoted core. The picture is an ironic one—fewer adherents today, but more loyal and observant ones. Overall levels of observance seem to be rising, which changes the normative ethos of the group. Examples of observance are somewhat easier to find, while examples of non-observance—still widespread—may be losing ground.

Finally, a rising proportion of today's Conservative Jews are Conservative from birth, as Cohen notes. This means that they have had the opportunity to be exposed to Conservative institutions and culture for a lifetime, increasing the overall level of denominational cultural knowledge.

But Conservative Judaism's distinct denominational identity has not been created solely out of the last generation's patterns of switching in and out. Far more important to the creation and nurture of this "elective parochialism" has been the spread of Conservative institutions for Jewish education. In a context in which Conservative Jews do not live in insular communities, intentional institution-building is essential. When Jewish customs cannot be learned in taken-for-granted and insular interchanges of family and village, synagogues and schools and youth camps have been invented to fill the breach. These studies make clear that such education has a major impact on Jewish observance and identification. Those who attend day schools and youth camps are simply immersed in Conservative Jewish culture in ways that can be sustained over a lifetime.

The relative absence of these institutions in earlier years is evident in the differences we see between older and younger cohorts. While older Conservative Jews were relatively unlikely to have high levels of Jewish education, those in the youngest cohort were more than twice as likely to have remained in training beyond the bar/bat mitzvah years (see chapter 2). The under-45 cohort are dramatically more likely to have participated in Camp Ramah, United Synagogue Youth, and Israel programs, to have taken Jewish Studies courses in college, and to have had opportunities for other forms of Jewish education (see chapter 1). The number of Conservative adults who have participated in such programs is growing as the number and availability of day schools, camping programs, and other educational opportunities spreads. A significant number are still unreached by educational programs, and relatively few are in day schools, but this generational movement toward increased Jewish education portends long-term health for Conservative Jewish institutions and identity.

The growth of this denominational system of education and youth programming is striking for having occurred in an era in which other religious groups in the United States were scaling back their educational efforts. The proportion of Catholic youth enrolled in Catholic schools declined from 44 percent to 29 percent just over the period from 1964 to 1974.[27] Lutherans, as well, mourned the decline of their elementary and secondary school system (Lueking 1995). As these groups lost their distinct ethnic identities and moved toward the religious "mainstream," they increasingly found public schools palatable.[28] They no longer thought they needed separate schools as a way of preserving a religious-ethnic enclave. At the same time, of course, conservative Christian schools have been multiplying rapidly, as has home schooling by conservative Christian parents.[29] As these more conservative Christians recognize the growing gap between their values and those of the larger culture, they have turned to schools as key instruments in preserving their religious culture.[30] Similarly, Conservative Jews have recognized that their distinctive religious culture may not easily be preserved without significant cohorts of youth who experience full immersion in Jewish schooling.

These younger, Jewish-educated cohorts are, as a result, simply more skilled in the practices of Jewish life and able to participate in home and synagogue rituals with more competence (see chapter 4). The youngest cohort, for instance, on some measures is as observant as the oldest, and both are much more so than those in the middle. Indeed, Cohen finds that within the middle adult group (35–64), younger cohorts are consistently more involved and observant than older ones, even controlling for family life-cycle stage. The fact that younger cohorts describe their own observance as at least equal to that of their (usually Conservative or Reform) parents compared to older cohorts who were considerably less observant than their (often Orthodox) parents indicates that among those who are involved at all, observance is holding steady or increasing with the younger generation (see chapter 1).

These increasing levels of observance, again, run directly counter to the predictions of secularization and modernization theorists. Youth should be less observant, not more. By giving attention to the educational institutions necessary for inculcating a Jewish way of life, youth have increasingly been given the skills and the sense of community out of which to construct a more observant way of life. Jewish education increases the likelihood that one will participate in a synagogue and keep kosher. It also insures that more of one's friends will be Jewish (see chapter 5). But these youths have clearly not abandoned the modern world in the process. They have become, if anything, more open and tolerant of other ways of life (about which more below). They have simply been offered a context in which a distinctive Conservative Jewish identity could be worked out in the midst of a frankly pluralistic existence.

The complexity of this negotiation between distinctive identity and assimilation is illustrated by Ritterband's exploration of the effects of college education on synagogue attendance. Those who went to college and did not get involved in Jewish activities—Jewish studies or Hillel, for instance—showed a linear decline in adult synagogue attendance: the more education, the less attendance, precisely what the secularization theorists would predict. But for those who connected with Jewish institutions while they were in college, adult synagogue attendance was more likely. These college-level educational opportunities extend the Jewish educational milieu even beyond the day schools, supplemental synagogue programs, Camp Ramah, and trips to Israel.

As important as this Jewish educational system is, it of course stands alongside the most basic of Jewish institutions, the synagogue. Indeed, there are strong links between higher levels of Jewish education and higher levels of synagogue membership. Both, in turn, make observance much more likely. From their earliest experience of diaspora, Jews created houses of prayer and learning, and it is to these voluntary gathering places that Jews return today. Roughly half of Conservative Jews reported in 1990 that they or someone in their household held membership in a synagogue, and these synagogue members were significantly more observant than nonmembers. They are far more likely to keep kosher, light Sabbath candles, and fast on Yom Kippur, for instance (see chapter 2). They are also more likely to be members of other Jewish community organizations and to have visited Israel. While much of Jewish observance can be accomplished without attending a synagogue, nonmembers participate no more in the private and family duties than in the public and communal ones. They have decided, at least for a time in their lives, to disconnect nearly entirely from Jewish religious life.

To find half of those who identify with Conservative Judaism outside of active membership and participation is surely a worrisome thing for the movement's leaders. Still, such numbers are not entirely unusual. Penny Marler and Kirk Hadaway found that one quarter of those in the U.S. population who identify as Protestant are neither church members nor church attenders. They are "mental affiliates" (Marler and Hadaway 1993). Added to a slightly lower percentage of "marginal members" (people who do belong, but who participate only minimally), the number of Protestants who are effectively participating in church life is not much more than half. Given that membership in Protestant churches costs no more than a declaration of intentions (with few mechanisms for removing inactive members who have ceased participating), comparing church members with synagogue members is not really equivalent. In both cases, however, it appears that roughly half of those who claim a religious identity support that claim with active membership and participation in a religious community.

One of the primary attributes that separates members from nonmembers is family status. Synagogue membership is closely tied to family formation (see especially chapter 1). Those who are married and have children are far more likely to belong than are single, divorced, childless, and mixed-married individuals (see chapter 2). This is a pattern that echoes the patterns of American Protestantism.[31] Affiliation with a local congregation seems strongly tied in the cultural consciousness with the task of child-rearing. U.S. culture simply expects parents to get involved in congregational life and does not send similar pro-religious messages to singles and those without children. Beyond those cultural messages, congregations themselves are often perceived as inhospitable to divorced people and couples in unconventional partnerships. The result in many instances is a congregational culture dominated by families with children, which in turn reinforces that pattern as the normative one for membership.

This tie to child-rearing is most dramatically seen in the involvement of synagogues in a continual round of bar and bat mitzvah ceremonies (see chapter 5). Not only are weekly services constantly shaped by the performances of the latest youth to reach this moment of recognition, but there are classes for youth and parents in preparation, and attendance is swelled by the presence of families there by force or by choice who are anticipating their own offspring's rite of passage. There is, in fact, a good deal of worry that families are simply joining and participating for the requisite time, giving their son or daughter a proper ritual event, and then dropping out of sight. That such a pattern of behavior would have little long-term impact on those involved is clear. Ritterband's study demonstrates that parents who are involved solely for the sake of their children are probably not very good either as members or as exemplars. In addition, adults who as children attended synagogue with both parents are today more active and more observant than those who attended with one parent or with neither.

Nevertheless, childhood attendance has lifelong effects. The habits, skills, and values instilled in the early years have evidently carried over into adult predispositions. Having attended regularly as a child makes adult attendance more likely, and that pattern is even stronger, as we noted, if one's parents attended as well. In addition, synagogues are often gateways to involvement in other aspects of Jewish life. Childhood synagogue attendance makes one more likely to get involved in Jewish activities while in college, for instance. And in the event of intermarriage, persons with a history of involvement in synagogue life are more likely to persuade their non-Jewish spouse to convert (see chapter 4).

Similarly, Dean Hoge and associates found that a variety of childhood patterns of experience and practice had an impact on current church involvement among the Presbyterian baby boomers they studied. For that sample, belief was much more central than it is for the Conservative Jews in this series of studies, but the effects of childhood attendance are still present (Hoge et al. 1994: 172). They venture the opinion that both their interviews and past studies support the notion that precollege religious experiences are decisive in shaping adult predispositions to religious participation.

Synagogues seem to be increasingly diligent about enhancing the effects of childhood and parental involvement. Kosmin notes that most children anticipating their bar or bat mitzvah must be involved in classes that usually approach six hours per week for at least the year prior to their ceremony, and the actual preparation for chanting the torah and haftarah must take place on top of that.

Many synagogues are also requiring that parents not only attend services regularly during the year before their child's ceremony but that they participate in classes as well. Given that today's generation of parents sometimes lacked the opportunities for Jewish education that are now available, these classes are often welcome as a chance to catch up. Indeed, rising expectations for Jewish participation and competency are apparent in the reports of parents that their children know more today than they themselves knew at the same age. Educating both children and parents is a task with immediate and long-term consequences for synagogues and for the Jewish community as a whole.

Why are synagogues so important? In part they train the young (and sometimes their parents) in the skills necessary for being a full participant in the community's life. But they also impart ideas that are at the heart of being Jewish and surround their participants with a company of sympathetic others. As Ritterband has shown, synagogues have both communal and ideological functions. They sustain beliefs about God and about living a good Jewish life, but they also provide friendships and community. Ritterband found that people may attend out of either motivation, but when the two are combined, attachment to synagogue life is strong indeed.

Students of religion have long looked to this twin "believing" and "belonging" function of local religious congregations. Wade Clark Roof found that those who were most oriented toward local life and most attached to the local congregation through relationships were also most likely to subscribe to orthodox beliefs (Roof 1978). Participation in such traditional communities can have powerful conservative effects, holding the status quo in place through both habit and divine sanction. But even in less conservative social circumstances, the tie between religious belonging and religious believing remains (Hammond 1992). Even though orthodoxy of belief has been less central to Judaism than to the Protestants that Roof studied, we see in the research reported here that both observant practice and orthodox belief are supported by synagogue participation.

Indeed, synagogue participation is intimately tied to a whole complex of indicators of Jewish identity and practice. As Cohen shows, several different indicators of involvement in Jewish life are all tied to each other. On the one hand, synagogue participation and leadership are important. People who lead in the community's liturgical life are also involved in its governance. In addition, it is important to have Jewish friends and neighbors, to have immediately visible models of Jewish life. And finally, it is important to include home rituals in one's routine of religious life. The more one is involved in one aspect of Jewish life, Cohen found, the more likely are the other involvements. The synagogue is, then, but the most visible institution in a complex of relationships extending outward from the home and together creating a supportive Jewish milieu.

The result of attention to home, neighborhood, synagogue, Jewish community organizations, the Jewish educational system, and all the rest is an institutional system sufficient for supporting a distinctive denominational group. The growth of this infrastructure and of the increasing sense of denominational identity that has gone with it is striking for having taken place in an era in which Protestant denominations have become increasingly indistinct. With their modern message of ecumenism, liberal Protestants effectively convinced their parishioners that denominational differences were unimportant. At the same time that a message of universalism and tolerance was altering attitudes, denominational structures for sustaining distinct identities were also being dismantled. Denominational colleges became less identifiable with their parent traditions; youth camps and youth programs concentrated more on social action than on doctrine; and even preaching lost its theological edge (Witten 1992). Meanwhile, on the evangelical Protestant side, a similar blurring was taking place. New "evangelical" institutions (schools, media, and the like) began to transcend old doctrinal differences among premillennialists, inerrantists, Pentecostals, and others (Wagner 1997).

All these structural changes were taking place alongside demographic changes that made denominational differences harder to perpetuate. While the "melting pot" may not have melted away ethnic differences in this country, it did blur many of the boundaries among religious groups. In *American Mainline Religion*, Wade Clark Roof and William McKinney document the ways in which the old "ascriptive" ties, bonds that had helped to hold American denominations together, have diminished significantly over the last two generations (Roof and McKinney 1987: 63–71). Conservative Jews are affected by these forces of education and mobility no less than others. There is every reason to expect less distinct religious identities among younger and more mobile cohorts. We have seen, in fact, that high levels of general education, unaccompanied by immersion in Jewish activities, can erode participation and observance among Conservative Jews. In addition, the Goldsteins found that those who have recently moved are less likely to be affiliated with a synagogue than are those who have maintained the same residence for at least five years. Increasing numbers of those who move are journeying to the South and West, where Jews have historically been only sparsely settled, Jewish institutions relatively less available, and levels of observance significantly lower. That levels of Conservative identification and allegiance, even levels of observance, are increasing among this younger, better educated, more mobile generation is remarkable indeed.

The picture that emerges, then, is of a religious community that has created ways of gathering together, educating its youth and adults, and holding out models of observance that are helping to sustain that community in spite of the "acids of modernity" that might erode belief and practice. This is a community in which individual choice is honored, but in which the norms of the group itself are increasingly clear and strong. Conservative Judaism exemplifies well the elective parochialism of which Warner writes. It is a chosen alternative, but it is an alternative with consequences. It is also "parochial"—in the sense of intentionally constructing a community in which a religious way of life can be sustained.

Of Enclaves, Sects, and Tribes: Conservative Jews and American Culture

In their 1985 bestseller, *Habits of the Heart*, Robert Bellah and his coauthors spoke of the groups being formed by self-oriented Americans as "lifestyle enclaves." They were merely gatherings of convenience, the authors said, assemblies of the like-minded and unlikely to have any real effect on their members or to aid in the establishment of real community. Robert Wuthnow (1994) comes close to a similar gloomy assessment of the small groups he studied (although there is a good deal of evidence to the contrary in his book). We have already seen that the sorts of commitments Conservative Jews are making do not neatly fit this picture. While there is a great deal of individual variation and choice, there are also commitments that entail real change and sacrifice.

In addition, there is an increasing sense of distinctive denominational identity, bolstered by a thriving set of denominational institutions. What we have here may be an enclave, but it is not the casually affiliated "lifestyle enclave" of which Bellah and associates wrote. Just what sort of group is it, then? In many ways, of course, Judaism remains a "tribe." It is a group whose membership is defined primarily by birth, indeed not just any birth, but matrilineal descent. It is also a group with a homeland—Israel. That tie to land has been instrumental in shaping Jewish identity, especially since mid-century. A common way of life, a common "family," and a common homeland have kept the "tribal" character of Jewish identity alive. While there is ample movement across denominational lines within Judaism, there has historically been little movement between Judaism and other faiths. Blood and land are not as easily adopted or abandoned as are mere doctrine and practice.

But all of that may be changing. With intermarriage rates approaching 50 percent, the Jewish tribal sense of identity will either change or disappear. The fact that intermarried people are less likely to join synagogues and less likely to be observant makes the specter of complete assimilation loom large. Still, there are contrary signs as well. Not all intermarried people have left synagogue and observant life. As we have seen, many people think their synagogues should, in fact, be more aggressive in welcoming such folk. More striking still, they say that what matters most to Jewish identity is whether the child is raised Jewish, not just whether he or she is born Jewish. The requirement of a Jewish mother is seen by 69 percent of Conservative Jews as optional. Again, ties of blood are being replaced by ties of practice.

Only support for the State of Israel may remain as the foundation for a Jewish sense of peoplehood. Kosmin found that 90 percent of parents say that they want their children to have a strong sense of attachment to Israel, and 95 percent of the bar/bat mitzvah class of 5755 said that attachment to Israel is important for their own sense of Jewishness. Eighty-five percent of the parents want their children to go to Israel, and 81 percent of the youths say they want to go. At least for Jews who are synagogue members and committed enough to be preparing for bar/bat mitzvahs, Israel is a real presence. To that extent, then, the sense of peoplehood linked to land remains.

Beyond that, if the importance of marriage and blood ties within the faith continue to decline, one alternative for group survival is to become "sectarian." As we saw, many analysts of religion have seen this as the only viable alternative for traditional religions wishing to survive the onslaught of modernity. Are Conservative Jews becoming more sectarian? Have they heightened the organizational and ritual barriers between themselves and a hostile world? Have they established the sorts of strict membership standards that establish a recognizable way of life for their members in contrast to others? Have they adopted a highly voluntaristic insistence that each adult member choose to belong?[32] In some ways, the answer to all these questions is yes. The institutional infrastructure that has made a heightened sense of denominational identity possible can also be seen as a sectarian shield. Parents bring their children to the synagogue to protect them from the world's pressures toward assimilation. In addition, the goal of being fully observant establishes a distinctive way of life as the ideal. Rabbis in both Minneapolis-area congregations Prell studied place a great deal of emphasis on being different from the rest of the world, of living a holy (that is, set apart) life. And finally, the acceptance of intermarried and non-Jewish-born members of the community indicates the degree to which choice more than birth establishes a person's membership and identity.

However, at the same time, Conservative Jews are also joining the American mainstream. As Kosmin notes, bar and bat mitzvah celebrations are now sufficiently accepted by the larger culture to warrant their own Hallmark greeting cards. Members who miss work and fast on Yom Kippur are increasingly likely to find that their co-workers understand and accept what they are doing. With distinctive religious dress and customs more and more common in U.S. society, religious differences no longer necessitate withdrawal.

Indeed, withdrawal and insularity are less and less the situation in which Conservative Jews find themselves. Younger people are increasingly likely to live in a mixed context, not solely surrounded by Jews (see chapter 2). Today's younger generation is much less segregated from the mainstream, less likely to have only Jewish friends, and less likely to believe that anti-Semitism is a serious problem (see chapter 5). Whether that belief is merely naive, we do not know, although it does seem likely that more virulent strains of anti-Semitism may have receded to the radical fringes of U.S. society, emerging occasionally in tragic, widely condemned attacks. Younger Conservative Jews seem to be saying that their experience has made it difficult for them to believe that the non-Jewish world is an inherently threatening place.

Nevertheless, the nature of that world does make a difference. We know that observance is easier when one is more thoroughly surrounded by others who are acting in the same manner. We also know that more mobile Jews who move into nontraditionally Jewish regions are less observant (see chapter 2). But what all this points to is the increasing permeability of Conservative Jewish boundaries, not their increasing solidity. Outsiders are apparently less hostile, and Jews are more likely to be moving about among those outsiders.

Even within the community there is permeability. The behavioral standards are, as we have seen, a commonly held ideal more than a uniformly practiced reality. The "journey" motif we have noted is far from sectarian in its ability to accommodate widely varying paths with many different starting points. But neither are these communities fostering the laissez-faire individualism of a thoroughly modernized religion. They are sectarian in their enumeration of clear ideals for living a set-apart life.

Can, then, Conservative Judaism be both more mainstream and more distinctive? Yes. The realities of post-modernity are that the both/and character of life is being recognized. Distinctive communities with their own customs, language, and points of view are not only inevitable, but essential. They provide us all with places to call home in the midst of a complex, urban society. They provide the moral grounding that can only come from particular stories and "tribal" heroes and heroines. Sectarian communities that are only sectarian can, of course, be a danger to the larger world's need for communication and cooperation. But sectarian communities that nurture both their distinctiveness and the ability to work with the larger society are a positive contribution to a postmodern order.[33] Even a small religious minority like Conservative Jews can carve out a respected and thriving niche in a religious ecology populated by dozens, even hundreds, of other religious minorities.

Conservative Judaism and Transcendence

At the beginning of this essay, we noted that the first hallmark of the modern worldview was its dependence on reason and science. Certainly Conservative Judaism's high education levels indicate that it is not a religious tradition seeking to avoid this modern predilection for Enlightenment discourse. In addition, the movement of younger generations into secular Jewish identities confirms the pull of rationalism on the religious traditions of the group. Similarly, both mobility and intermarriage, as we have seen, are increased by exposure to higher education and decrease the likelihood of Jewish observance. In sum, there is ample evidence here for the power of modernity's reasoned, secularizing influence.

However, there are also evidences to the contrary. For a very long time Jews have insisted that living an observant Jewish life does not require belief in God. We hear this repeatedly in the stories of those Heilman and Prell interviewed. Adults who have returned to more active practice or who have been observant all their lives nevertheless have grave doubts about the existence of God. But younger generations of Conservative Jews are more likely to say they believe in God and to see that as central to their sense of Jewishness (see chapter 5). Their rising levels of Jewish education have not necessarily made them more "orthodox" in their beliefs about God and torah, but they are more willing to add a transcendent dimension to their practice. When we look at the youth in the synagogues Heilman describes, we see this transcendence being experienced. As they are invited to touch the torah scrolls, they do so with awe. They speak of their "own unique relationship with God," with one youth speaker noting that if people's "prayers are from the heart, Hashem will hear." Such an awareness of God's personal presence and care would seem odd to many in an older generation, but among younger adults and teens the notion that religious practice can and should have a spiritual dimension seems to be growing. Perhaps these younger Conservative Jews have simply absorbed the American notion that religion is supposed to be about belief in God. But more likely, they have found space for such beliefs and experiences in a postmodern world that no longer insists that rationality and belief are incompatible.

Conclusion

Conservative Judaism at the end of the twentieth century provides a window on emerging patterns of religion in a postmodern society. The incorporation of transcendence alongside high levels of education and obvious respect for reason exemplifies the postmodern acceptance of multiple modes of knowing. The construction of a distinctive Conservative Jewish denominational culture alongside increasing levels of intercourse with the larger culture bespeaks the both/and nature of communal identities situated in cosmopolitan lives. Increasing levels of belief and observance among younger members of the community evidence the strength of communal commitments made out of modern choice more than premodern necessity. And the willingness of those same members to accept intermarried couples and children of non-Jewish mothers as community members further illustrates the primacy of choice over birth. Choice has indeed become a postmodern virtue. Rather than signaling corrosive individual autonomy, choice increasingly signals communal commitments. By embarking on a journey toward observance, Conservative Jews are using the freedoms gained through modern life to assert a postmodern effort at honoring and maintaining the traditions of their past.

Notes

1. See Weber (1947) for this classic treatment of the contrasts between the traditional and the modern world. He also includes attention to "charisma," a form of authority that can occur at any time as a challenge to the world as organized.
2. Malinowski (1948) makes this most clear, but it is the underlying premise of the historical accounts given by Freud about the human psyche, and by Marx and Weber of human history.
3. Among the recent studies to give attention to education's effects are Roof and McKinney (1987) and Wuthnow (1988).
4. See especially Berger (1969, 1982).
5. Among the theorists who have made the links between modernity and individuality, see Coser (1991), Giddens (1991), and Simmel (1971 [1908]).
6. Among those who have argued that modern religion is characterized by individualism, see Bellah (1963), Hammond (1992), Berger and Luckmann (1967), and Parsons (1964).
7. See especially Chapter 3 in Hoge et al. (1994).
8. Reported in Roof and McKinney (1987: 57).
9. See also Marler and Roozen (1993).
10. The division of labor is at the heart of the modernizing process, as Durkheim (1984 [1893]) saw it.
11. This same process has separated "church from state," thereby both limiting the power of the church to use coercion and enabling the church to act as an independent critical voice on public issues. On this see Casanova (1994). This separation of powers is, at heart, what is meant by secularization, but, as Casanova argues, separation need not mean loss of influence. See also my review of Demerath and Williams on the cultural power of religion (Ammerman 1993).
12. Among those who have written about the complexity of the modern self are Shotter (1984) and Fischer (1975). On the geographic and spatial dimensions of modern identity, see Eiesland (2000).
13. Most prominent among recent theorists who have worked out this argument is Iannaccone (1994).
14. This, in effect, is the thesis behind Ammerman (1987). It also informs work by Davidman (1990) on Orthodox Jewish women.
15. Hunter (1983) argues that even evangelicalism has fallen prey to the wiles of modernity, accommodating in subtle ways to the pressures of reason, pluralism, and privatization.
16. In addition to arguments for the integration of work and family life in more humane patterns, feminist theorists have argued for the blurring of lines between "public" and "private" as a way of breaking down neat gender barriers. On the insufficiency of defining the "public" as universal, see Fraser (1990).
17. On postmodern organizational trends, see Clegg (1990).
18. This metaphor is borrowed from Brueggemann (1989).

19. Wuthnow (1994) is an example of the quandary experienced by an old paradigm thinker trying to explain the commitment found in small groups of all sorts. See Sherkat and Wilson (1995) on the way choices are shaped by the membership and value constraints within which they are made.
20. Bender (1978) provides an excellent historical argument for the "both/and" character of modern community. It is both alien and impersonal and laced with dense webs of affiliation. Documenting the shape of those webs has been the work of Fischer (1982, 1975).
21. On voluntarism in U.S. religion, see Warner (1993), Finke and Stark (1992), and de Tocqueville (1835).
22. Roof and McKinney (1987: 165) report that 40 percent is a good estimate of the number of Protestants who have switched denominational affiliations at least once. Among the Presbyterian baby boomers Hoge, Johnson, and Luidens studied, 41 percent had switched at least once (1994: 49).
23. This argument is worked out in dialogue with the rational choice theorists in Ammerman (1997).
24. This argument is elaborated in Ammerman (1996) and depends heavily on the work of Claude Fischer (1991) and Thomas Bender (1978).
25. This language of journey is common in the small groups Wuthnow (1994) studied and among the baby boomers of Roof's "Generation of Seekers."
26. Roof and McKinney (1987: 177) suggest that those who switch to a new religious group are likely to be better members (stronger believers and more frequent attenders) than those who have stayed.
27. Greeley et al. (1976) document declines in the proportion of Catholics who are enrolled in parochial school, despite continued high regard for the schools and clear evidence of their positive effects on Catholic adult participation.
28. For a general overview of the situation for parochial schools, see Carper and Hunt (1984).
29. Peshkin (1986) reported that in the mid-1970s Christian school enrollment was approaching half a million and apparently climbing fast.
30. In addition to Peshkin, on Christian schools see Rose (1988), Wagner (1990), and Ammerman (1987).
31. On the link between family formation and church attendance, see Marler (1995) and Hertel (1995).
32. A classic statement of the definition of sectarianism is found in Niebuhr (1929).
33. Here I again borrow from an argument made by Brueggemann and elaborated further in Ammerman (1996).

Bibliography

Ammerman, Nancy T. 1987. *Bible Believers: Fundamentalists in the Modern World*. New Brunswick: Rutgers University Press.
———. 1993. Review of "A Bridging of Faiths," by N. J. Demerath and Rhys H. Williams. *Society* 31 (November-December): 91–93.
———. 1996. "'Bowling Together': Congregations and the American Civic Order." The Arizona State University Lecture in Religion.
———. 1997. "Golden Rule Christianity: Lived Religion in the American Mainstream." In David Hall (ed.), *Lived Religion in America*, 196–216. Princeton: Princeton University Press.
Bellah, Robert N. 1963. "Religious Evolution." In Bellah, *Beyond Belief*, 20–50. Boston: Beacon.
Bellah, Robert N., Richard Madsen, William M. Sullivan, Ann Swidler, and Steven M. Tipton. 1985. *Habits of the Heart*. Berkeley: University of California Press.

Bender, Thomas. 1978. *Community and Social Change in America.* New Brunswick: Rutgers University Press.

Berger, Peter L. 1969. *The Sacred Canopy.* Garden City, N.Y.: Anchor Doubleday.

———. 1982. "From the Crisis of Religion to the Crisis of Secularity." In Mary Douglas and Steven Tipton (eds.), *Religion and America,* 14–24. Boston: Beacon.

Berger, Peter L., and Thomas Luckmann. 1967. *The Social Construction of Reality.* Garden City, N.Y.: Anchor Doubleday.

Brueggemann, Walter. 1989. "The Legitimacy of a Sectarian Hermeneutic: 2 Kings 18–19." In Mary C. Boys, *Education for Citizenship and Discipleship,* 3–34. New York: Pilgrim.

Butler, Jon. 1990. *Awash in a Sea of Faith.* Cambridge: Harvard University Press.

Carper, James C. and Thomas C. Hunt, eds. 1984. *Religious Schooling in America.* Birmingham: Religious Education Press.

Casanova, José. 1994. *Public Religions in the Modern World.* Chicago: University of Chicago Press.

Christiano, Kevin. 1988. *Religious Diversity and Social Change: American Cities, 1890–1906.* Cambridge: Cambridge University Press.

Clegg, Stewart. 1990. *Modern Organizations: Organizational Studies in the Postmodern World.* London: Sage.

Coser, Rose Laub. 1991. *In Defense of Modernity: Role Complexity and Individual Autonomy.* Stanford: Stanford University Press.

Davidman, Lynn. 1990. "Accommodation and Resistance: A Comparison of Two Contemporary Orthodox Jewish Groups." *Sociological Analysis* 51, no. 1 (spring): 35–51.

———. 1991. *Tradition in a Rootless World.* Berkeley: University of California Press.

Demerath, N. J., III. 1965. *Social Class in American Protestantism.* Chicago: Rand-McNally.

Demerath, N. J., III, and Rhys H. Williams. 1992. *A Bridging of Faiths: Religion and Politics in a New England City.* Princeton: Princeton University Press.

Durkheim, Emile. 1984 [1893]. *The Division of Labor in Society.* New York: Free Press.

Eiesland, Nancy. 2000. *A Particular Place.* New Brunswick: Rutgers University Press.

Finke, Roger, and Rodney Stark. 1992. *The Churching of America.* New Brunswick: Rutgers University Press.

Fischer, Claude S. 1975. "The Study of Urban Community and Personality." In Alex Inkeles (ed.), *Annual Review of Sociology,* 67–89. Palo Alto: Annual Reviews, Inc.

———. 1982. *To Dwell Among Friends: Personal Networks in Town and City.* Chicago: University of Chicago Press.

———. 1991. "Ambivalent Communities: How Americans Understand Their Localities." In Alan Wolfe (ed.), *America at Century's End,* 79–90. Berkeley: University of California Press.

Fraser, Nancy. 1990. "Rethinking the Public Sphere: A Contribution to the Critique of Actually Existing Democracy." *Social Text* 25/26: 56–80.

Giddens, Anthony. 1991. *Modernity and Self-Identity: Self and Society in the Late Modern Age.* Stanford: Stanford University Press.

Greeley, Andrew M., William C. McCready, and Kathleen McCourt. 1976. *Catholic Schools in a Declining Church.* Kansas City: Sheed and Ward.

Hackett, David. 1991. *The Rude Hand of Innovation: Religion and Social Order in Albany, New York, 1652–1836.* New York: Oxford University Press.

Hammond, Phillip E. 1992. *Religion and Personal Autonomy: The Third Disestablishment in America.* Columbia: University of South Carolina Press.

Hertel, Bradley. 1995. "Work, Family, and Faith: Recent Trends." In Nancy T. Ammerman and Wade Clark Roof (eds.), *Work, Family, and Religion in Contemporary Society,* 81–122. New York: Routledge.

Hoge, Dean R., Benton Johnson, and Donald A. Luidens. 1994. *Vanishing Boundaries:*

The Religion of Mainline Protestant Baby Boomers. Louisville: Westminster/John Knox.

Hunter, James Davison. 1983. *American Evangelicalism: Conservative Religion and the Quandary of Modernity*. New Brunswick: Rutgers University Press.

Iannaccone, Laurence R. 1994. "Why Strict Churches Are Strong." *American Journal of Sociology* 99 (March): 1180–1211.

Kaufmann, Debra. 1991. *Rachel's Daughters*. New Brunswick: Rutgers University Press.

Kelley, Dean M. 1977. *Why Conservative Churches Are Growing*. Second edition. San Francisco: Harper and Row.

Lueking, F. Dean. 1995. "Parochial Education: For the Sake of the Children." *Word and World* 15: 99–101.

Malinowski, Bronislaw. 1948 [1925]. *Magic, Science, and Religion*. New York: Free Press.

Marler, Penny Long. 1995. "Lost in the Fifties." In Nancy T. Ammerman and Wade Clark Roof (eds.), *Work, Family and Religion in Contemporary Society*, 23–60. New York: Routledge.

Marler, Penny Long, and C. Kirk Hadaway. 1993. "Toward a Typology of Protestant 'Marginal Members.'" *Review of Religious Research* 35, no. 1: 34–54.

Marler, Penny Long, and David A. Roozen. 1993. "From Church Tradition to Consumer Choice: The Gallup Surveys of the Unchurched American," in *Church and Denominational Growth*, 253–277, edited by David A. Roozen and C. Kirk Hadaway. Nashville: Abingdon.

McNeill, William H. 1993. "Fundamentalism and the World of the 1990s." In Martin E. Marty and R. Scott Appleby (eds.), *Fundamentalism and Society*, 558–573. Chicago: University of Chicago Press.

Niebuhr, H. Richard. 1929. *The Social Sources of Denominationalism*. New York: World Publishing.

Parsons, Talcott. 1964. "Religion and Modern Industrial Society." In Louis Schneider (ed.), *Religion, Culture, and Society*, 273–298. New York: Wiley.

Peshkin, Alan. 1986. *God's Choice: The Total World of a Fundamentalist Christian School*. Chicago: University of Chicago Press.

Roof, Wade Clark. 1978. *Community and Commitment*. New York: Elsevier.

———. 1993. *A Generation of Seekers*. San Francisco: Harper and Row.

Roof, Wade Clark, and William McKinney. 1987. *American Mainline Religion*. New Brunswick: Rutgers University Press.

Rose, Susan D. 1988. *Keeping Them Out of the Hands of Satan: Evangelical Schooling in America*. New York: Routledge.

Sherkat, Darren E. and John Wilson. 1995. "Preferences, Constraints, and Choice in Religious Markets: An Examination of Religious Switching and Apostasy." *Social Forces* 73, no. 3: 993–1026.

Shotter, John. 1984. *Social Accountability and Selfhood*. New York: Basil Blackwell.

Simmel, Georg. 1971 [1908]. "Group Expansion and the Development of Individuality." In Donald N. Levine (ed.), *Georg Simmel on Individuality and Social Forms*, 251–293. Chicago: University of Chicago Press.

Tocqueville, Alexis de. 1969 [1835]. *Democracy in America*. Garden City, N.Y.: Doubleday.

Wagner, Melinda Bollar. 1990. *God's Schools: Choice and Compromise in American Society*. New Brunswick: Rutgers University Press.

———. 1997. "Generic Conservative Christianity: The Demise of Denominationalism in Christian Schools." *Journal for the Scientific Study of Religion* 36, no. 1: 13–24.

Warner, R. Stephen. 1988. *New Wine in Old Wineskins*. Berkeley: University of California Press.

———. 1993. "Work in Progress Toward a New Paradigm for the Sociological Study of Religion in the United States." *American Journal of Sociology* 98, no. 5 (March): 1044–1093.

Weber, Max. 1947. *The Theory of Social and Economic Organization*. New York: Free Press.

Witten, Marsha. 1992. "The Restriction of Meaning in Religious Discourse: Centripetal Devices in a Fundamentalist Christian Sermon." In Robert Wuthnow (ed.), *Vocabularies of Public Life*, 19–38. London: Routledge.

Wuthnow, Robert. 1988. *The Restructuring of American Religion*. Princeton: Princeton University Press.

———. 1994. *Sharing the Journey*. New York: Free Press.

The Study Design

ΤHE NORTH AMERICAN Study of Conservative Synagogues and Their Members 1995–96 is based upon three new surveys, the reanalysis of the 1990 National Jewish Population Survey, as well as ethnographic and comparative research. The three new surveys utilized mailing lists provided by the United Synagogue of Conservative Judaism, the congregational arm of the Conservative movement. Not every Conservative synagogue is currently a member of the United Synagogue, but the preponderant majority are. Those that are not are difficult to trace. The sampling procedure throughout the project was multistaged. First, congregations were stratified according to their distribution in the following size categories: congregations with 800 or more membership units; congregations with 400–799 units; and synagogues with fewer than 400 memberships. Samples were then constructed and sampled as follows:

The 1995–96 Conservative Congregational Survey

The 762 affiliates of the United Synagogue of Conservative Judaism in the United States and Canada were stratified into the three size groups. One hundred and twenty rabbis (or other synagogue representatives) were interviewed over the telephone, representing a proportionate sample from each of these three groups. The interviews were conducted from July until December 1995. The second stage of the study involved mailing 300 revised questionnaires in February 1996 to an additional sample of synagogues. The third stage consisted of mailing 169 questionnaires in July 1996, aimed particularly at the small synagogues, in order to ensure their proportional representation. Ultimately, the telephone interviews and mailings yielded 378 completed questionnaires from U.S. and Canadian congregations, with each size category roughly proportional to their distribution within the United Synagogue. Jack Wertheimer and Ariela Keysar designed the questionnaire, supervised the gathering of data, and analyzed the findings.

The 1995 Conservative Membership Survey

The Membership Survey was designed to ensure that any member of a Conservative congregation would have the same chance of inclusion in the random sample. Twenty-two congregations in the United States and five in Canada were randomly selected solely on the basis of their proportional membership size. A sample of one hundred congregants was then randomly drawn from each congregation. These members were sent a questionnaire in the fall of 1995. In all, 2,200 questionnaires were mailed to U.S. members and 500 to Canadian members. A total of 1,187 were completed and returned by members in the United States and 230 from Canadians. In order to increase the response rate, 200 telephone interviews were conducted with members of the original random sample who had not responded to the mailed questionnaire. Overall 1,617 Conservative synagogue members participated in the survey. Steven M. Cohen and Paul Ritterband designed the questionnaire, supervised the gathering of data, and analyzed the findings for this survey.

The 1995 Bar/Bat Mitzvah Survey

A telephone survey was carried out in the fall of 1995 with a bar/bat mitzvah child and his/her parent. Overall, 115 synagogues of varying sizes cooperated by supplying names, addresses, and telephone numbers of children and parents of the bar/bat mitzvah class of 5755 (September 1994–September 1995). In total 1,467 families from throughout the United States and Canada participated in this survey. The parents of b'nai mitzvah were first informed of the survey by mail. Telephone interviewers then called to obtain permission to interview children. After obtaining parental consent, an interview was scheduled with the bar/bat mitzvah child. Following this, an interview was conducted with a parent as well. This procedure minimized bias and the potential influence of the parent on the child's responses. Barry A. Kosmin designed the questionnaire, supervised the gathering of data, and analyzed the findings for this survey.

All telephone interviews and mailings for the Membership and Bar/Bat Mitzvah Surveys were conducted by Schulman, Ronca, and Bucuvalas, Inc., a market and opinion research firm. The Congregational Surveys employed staff members of the Ratner Center for telephone interviews.

The 1990 National Jewish Population Survey

In order to contextualize findings about Conservative synagogue members, Sidney and Alice Goldstein engaged in a major project to reanalyze the 1990 National Jewish Population Survey (NJPS), as well as a dozen local surveys conducted in the past decade. Their entire report has been published by the Ratner

Center, entitled *Conservative Jewry in the United States: A Socio-Demographic Survey*.

The 1990 NJPS was a telephone survey based on random digit dialing (RDD) of a representative national sample of 125,813 U.S. households. Following a screening process, 2,444 qualified Jewish households were interviewed. Data was collected on demographic characteristics as well as on the Jewish content of the household and its members. NJPS provides rich data on the Jewish population across all religious denominations and on unaffiliated Jews.

Ethnographic Research and Contextual Commentary

Two ethnographers, Samuel C. Heilman and Riv-Ellen Prell, each engaged in first-hand observation of Conservative synagogue life. Their direct encounter with Conservative synagogues informed the thinking of the entire research team and, in turn, was informed by the survey research. Each ethnographer spent nine months closely studying two congregations, the former in the Northeast and the latter in the Midwest of the United States. Their complete reports appear in this volume. To situate findings about Conservative synagogues in the broader context of American congregational life, Nancy T. Ammerman analyzed the way in which this project connects to broader trends in American congregational life. As a member of the research team, she actively shaped the team's thinking about critical questions at every stage of the project.

About the Contributors

NANCY T. AMMERMAN is professor of sociology of religion at Hartford Seminary's Center for Social and Religious Research. She has written extensively on congregational life in the United States, including *Congregation and Community* (Rutgers University Press, 1997) and has taken up issues of religious commitment in late-twentieth-century society in her presidential address to the Association for the Sociology of Religion, "Organized Religion in a Voluntaristic Society." Earlier, she examined congregational life in a conservative Christian congregation in *Bible Believers: Fundamentalists in the Modern World* (Rutgers University Press, 1987) and contributed essays to "The Fundamentalism Project."

STEVEN M. COHEN teaches at the Melton Center for Jewish Education of the Hebrew University in Jerusalem. His books include *The Jew Within* (with Arnold Eisen), *Two Worlds of Judaism* (with Charles Liebman), *Cosmopolitans and Parochials: Orthodox Jews in the United States* (with Samuel Heilman), *American Assimilation or Jewish Revival*, and *American Modernity and Jewish Identity*.

ALICE GOLDSTEIN is research associate in population studies at Brown University. Her research interests include the demographic situation in several countries of Asia and Africa, as well as the study of the Jewish American population. Using both local and national data, she has been concerned particularly with women's roles, philanthropy, and Jewish education and their relation to strength of Jewish identity. She serves on the National Technical Advisory Committee of the United Jewish Communities as it plans for the National Jewish Population Survey of 2000, with special responsibilities for the sections on Jewish identity and Jewish education. Her publications (coauthored with Sidney Goldstein) include *Jews on the Move* and *Conservative Jewry in the United States: A Sociodemographic Profile*.

Sidney Goldstein is George Hazard Crooker Professor Emeritus and professor of population studies at Brown University. He served as director of the university's Population Studies and Training Center for twenty-five years, and is a former president of the Population Association of America. His research has focused both on nations in Asia and Africa and on the Jewish population of the United States and Lithuania. Considered the dean of Jewish population studies, he has played a key role in the development of the field on both the national and local levels. He chaired the National Technical Advisory Committee of the Council of Jewish Federations during the period when the National Jewish Population Survey of 1990 was undertaken, and continues to serve on that committee as it plans the survey for 2000. Among his many publications (coauthored with Alice Goldstein) are *Jews on the Move* and *Conservative Jewry in the United States: A Sociodemographic Profile*.

Samuel C. Heilman holds the Harold Proshansky Professorship in Jewish Studies and Sociology at the City University of New York. He has also been Scheinbrun Visiting Professor of Sociology at the Hebrew University in Jerusalem, visiting professor of social anthropology at Tel Aviv University, and a Fulbright visiting professor at the Universities of New South Wales and Melbourne. He is the author of seven books, including: *Synagogue Life*, *The People of the Book*, *Cosmopolitans and Parochials: Modern Orthodox Jews in America* (with Steven M. Cohen), and *Defenders of the Faith: Inside Ultra-Orthodox Jewry*. Most recently his Stroum Lectures at the University of Washington appeared as *Portrait of American Jewry: The Last Half of the Twentieth Century*.

Barry A. Kosmin is director of research at the London-based Institute for Jewish Policy Research. He was founding director of the North American Jewish Data Bank at the City University of New York Graduate Center and Research Director of the Council of Jewish Federations. He has directed a large number of studies of Jewish populations worldwide, including the U.S. 1990 National Jewish Population Survey and the 1998 National Survey of South African Jews. He is coauthor of *One Nation Under God: Religion in Contemporary American Society*.

Riv-Ellen Prell, an anthropologist, is professor of American studies and adjunct professor of Jewish studies and women's studies at the University of Minnesota. She is the author of *Fighting to Become Americans: Jews, Gender, and the Anxiety of Assimilation* and *Prayer and Community: The Havurah in American Judaism*, and coeditor of *Interpreting Women's Lives: Personal Narratives and Feminist Theories*. She writes and teaches about twentieth-century American Jewish culture and is currently at work on a book on American Jewish youth culture from 1945 to 1970.

Paul Ritterband is professor emeritus of sociology and Jewish studies at the City

College and Graduate Center of the City University of New York. He has served as director of the Center for Jewish Studies at the Graduate Center, where he participated in the establishment of the first computer-readable data archive of the North American Jewish community. He is author or editor of a number of books, including studies of Israeli migration to the United States, Jewish learning in American universities, Jewish philanthropy, Jewish fertility, and contemporary Russian Jewish migration. He is now a visiting professor at the University of Haifa.

JACK WERTHEIMER is provost and the Joseph and Martha Mendelson Professor of American Jewish History at the Jewish Theological Seminary. He is also the founding director of the Joseph and Miriam Ratner Center for the Study of Conservative Judaism at JTS. Among his books are *A People Divided: Judaism in Contemporary America* and a two-volume edited history of the Jewish Theological Seminary, entitled *Tradition Renewed*.

Index